general editor John M. MacKenzie

When the 'Studies in Imperialism' series was founded more than twenty-five years ago, emphasis was laid upon the conviction that 'imperialism as a cultural phenomenon had as significant an effect on the dominant as on the subordinate societies'. With more than ninety books published, this remains the prime concern of the series. Cross-disciplinary work has indeed appeared covering the full spectrum of cultural phenomena, as well as examining aspects of gender and sex, frontiers and law, science and the environment, language and literature, migration and patriotic societies, and much else. Moreover, the series has always wished to present comparative work on European and American imperialism, and particularly welcomes the submission of books in these areas. The fascination with imperialism, in all its aspects, shows no sign of abating, and this series will continue to lead the way in encouraging the widest possible range of studies in the field. 'Studies in Imperialism' is fully organic in its development, always seeking to be at the cutting edge, responding to the latest interests of scholars and the needs of this ever-expanding area of scholarship.

The colonisation of time

SELECTED TITLES AVAILABLE IN THE SERIES

MATERIALS AND MEDICINE
Trade, conquest and therapeutics in the eighteenth century
Pratik Chakrabarti

EUROPEAN EMPIRES AND THE PEOPLE
Popular responses to imperialism in France, Britain, the Netherlands, Belgium, Germany and Italy
Edited by John M. MacKenzie

MUSEUMS AND EMPIRE
Natural history, human cultures and colonial identities
John M. MacKenzie

REPRESENTING AFRICA
Landscape, exploration and empire in southern Africa, 1780–1870
John McAleer

CHILD, NATION, RACE AND EMPIRE
Child rescue discourse, England, Canada and Australia, 1850–1915
Shurlee Swain & Margot Hillel

The colonisation of time

RITUAL, ROUTINE AND RESISTANCE IN THE
BRITISH EMPIRE

Giordano Nanni

MANCHESTER UNIVERSITY PRESS
Manchester and New York

distributed in the United States exclusively by
Palgrave Macmillan

Copyright © Giordano Nanni 2012

The right of Giordano Nanni to be identified as the author of this work has been asserted by him in accordance with the Copyright, Designs and Patents Act 1988.

Published by Manchester University Press
Oxford Road, Manchester M13 9NR, UK
and Room 400, 175 Fifth Avenue, New York, NY 10010, USA
www.manchesteruniversitypress.co.uk

Distributed in the United States exclusively by
Palgrave Macmillan, 175 Fifth Avenue,
New York, NY 10010, USA

Distributed in Canada exclusively by
UBC Press, University of British Columbia, 2029 West Mall,
Vancouver, BC, Canada V6T 1Z2

British Library Cataloguing-in-Publication Data is available

Library of Congress Cataloging-in-Publication Data is available

ISBN 978 0 7190 9129 2 paperback

First published by Manchester University Press in hardback 2012

This paperback edition first published 2013

The publisher has no responsibility for the persistence or accuracy of URLs for any external or third-party internet websites referred to in this book, and does not guarantee that any content on such websites is, or will remain, accurate or appropriate.

Printed by Lightning Source

For Margaret, Paula and Lucy
who have given so much of their time

Time is life itself, and life resides in the human heart.

— Michael Ende, *Momo*

He put this Engine to our Ears, which made an incessant Noise like that of a Water-Mill. And we conjecture it is either some unknown Animal, or the God that he worships: But we are more inclined to the latter Opinion, because he assured us (if we understood him right, for he expressed himself very imperfectly) that he seldom did anything without consulting it. He called it his Oracle, and said it pointed out the Time for every Action of his Life.

— Jonathan Swift, *Gulliver's Travels* (1726),
1/II, 'A Voyage to Lilliput'
(in which the Lilliputians scrutinise
the contents of Gulliver's pockets)

CONTENTS

List of figures and maps—viii
List of abbreviations—x
General editor's introduction—xi
Acknowledgments—xiii
Note on terminology—xvi

	Introduction	1
1	Clocks, Sabbaths and seven-day weeks: the forging of European temporal identities	25
2	*Terra sine tempore*: colonial constructions of 'Aboriginal time'	59
3	Cultural curfews: the contestation of time in settler-colonial Victoria	85
4	'The moons are always out of order': colonial constructions of 'African time'	122
5	Empire of the seventh day: time and the Sabbath beyond the Cape frontiers	148
6	Lovedale: missionary schools and the reform of 'African time'	185
7	Conclusion: from colonisation to globalisation	217

Select bibliography—237
Index—247

LIST OF FIGURES AND MAPS

1.1 Military technology: the 'K1' Larcum Kendall chronometer (1764)   *page* 28
©National Maritime Museum, London, Ministry of Defence Art Collection. Reproduced with permission.

1.2 Robinson Crusoe's calendar, by N. C. Wyeth   32
Daniel Defoe, *Robinson Crusoe* (New York: Cosmopolitan Book Corporation, 1920).

1.3 'Family Prayers', by Samuel Butler (1864)   44

1.4 Working-class family prayers (1849)   45
J. A. Quinton, *Heaven's Antidote to the Curse of Labour; or, The temporal Advantages of the Sabbath, Considered in relation to the working classes* (London: Partridge & Oakley, 1849).

2.1 Map of Victoria, showing approximate territories of Kulin nations and other Aboriginal peoples mentioned, at time of British invasion   62

2.2 Phrenological report by P. Sohier, submitted as evidence to the Victorian Select Committee of 1858–59   68
Victorian Aborigines 1835–1901: A Resource Guide to the Holdings of the Public Record Office of Victoria (PROV), p. 33. Reproduced with permission.

3.1 Map of Victoria, showing European pastoral expansion from 1834   88
Joseph M. Powell, *The Public Lands of Australia Felix* (Oxford University Press, 1970). Reproduced and modified with the author's permission.

3.2 Account of 'Sabbath Flour' by Assistant Protector of Aborigines, William Thomas (1842)   90
PROV, VPRS 11, mf 8, unit 2, item 463; reproduced with permission of the Keeper of Public Records, PROV, Australia.

3.3 Time-ball tower in Williamstown, Melbourne (*ca* 1900)   92
Pictures Collection, State Library of Victoria Collection, State Library of Victoria, H81.61/3. Reproduced with permission.

3.4 Map of Victoria, showing locations of mission stations and Government reserves   94

3.5 'Group of Aborigines at Coranderrk mission', with manager's house and bell-post in background (*ca* 1903)   98
Pictures Collection, State Library of Victoria, H141215. Reproduced with permission.

3.6 Coranderrk: 'Going to morning prayer', with bell in action (1904)   99
Photograph by N. J. Claire, 1904. Pictures Collection, State Library of Victoria, H141275. Reproduced with permission.

3.7 A vision of order: Warrangesda mission (New South Wales), showing bell and flag   104
J. B. Gribble, *Black But Comely, or Glimpses of Aboriginal Life in Australia* (London: Morgan & Scott, 1884). Special Collections, Information Division, The University of Melbourne.

LIST OF FIGURES AND MAPS

3.8 *'Dolce far niente*: an Aboriginal interpretation' (*ca* 1900)   114
Melbourne: David Syme & Co. (Pictures Collection, State
Library of Victoria, IAN01/10/95/1). Reproduced with permission.

4.1 Columbus predicts lunar eclipse of 1509 in Jamaica   123
Camille Flammarion, *Astronomie Populaire* (Paris: Marpon
et Flammarion, 1880).

5.1 Map of Cape Colony: advancement of settler frontier, 1799–1835   151
Following A. S. MacKinnon, *The Making of South Africa*
(Upper Saddle River, N.J.: Prentice Hall, 2003).

5.2 Moravian mission of Genadendal, Cape Colony, showing   152
belfry at heart of village
C. I. La Trobe, *Journal of a visit to South Africa*
(London: Seeley, 1821), p. 585.

5.3 Map of Cape Colony, showing approximate locations of   154
missions and schools

5.4 Wesleyan mission of Clarkebury, showing bell-post   166
National Library of South Africa (NLSA), Cape Town, MF558: WMMS,
Wesleyan Missionary Notices, 104, 1846. Reproduced with permission.

5.5 Lily Fountain mission: sketch by Reverend Barnabas Shaw   168
NLSA, Cape Town, MF558: WMMS, *Wesleyan Missionary
Notices*, 49, 1819. Reproduced with permission.

5.6 Lily Fountain mission grounds (*ca* 1900)   169
NLSA, Cape Town, Album 178, INIL 9519. Reproduced with permission.

5.7 Lily Fountain chapel, showing bell-post (*ca* 1900)   169
NLSA, Cape Town, Album 178, INIL 9520. Reproduced with permission.

6.1 Lovedale: interior of technical building   189
James Stewart, *Lovedale: South Africa: Illustrated by Fifty
Views from Photographs* (Edinburgh: Andrew Elliot, 1894).

6.2 Lovedale: '9 A.M. Waiting for the bell'   Stewart, *Lovedale*.   193

6.3 Lovedale: mustering of afternoon work parties   Stewart, *Lovedale*.   196

6.4 Lovedale: inside the printer's shop   Stewart, *Lovedale*.   199

6.5 Clock-tower at Lovedale (*ca* 1940)   213
R. H. W. Shepherd, *Lovedale, South Africa: The Story of a Century:
1841–1941* (Lovedale: Lovedale Press, 1940).

7.1 Firing of noon gun in Cape Town (*ca* 1911)   218
NLSA, Cape Town, PHA Collection. Reproduced with permission.

7.2 Noon gun (*ca* 1934), showing Cape Town and Table Bay   218
in background
NLSA, Cape Town, PHA Collection. Reproduced with permission.

7.3 The GMT matrix of time and space   220

7.4 Aerial view of Greenwich Observatory, showing Prime Meridian   220
and time-ball
P. Hood, *How Time is Measured* (London: Oxford University Press, 1955).
Photograph taken especially for the above title by Photoflight Ltd (1955).

LIST OF ABBREVIATIONS

AAV	Australian Archives, Victoria
BPA	Central Board for the Protection of Aborigines (1869–1957)
CBPA	Central Board Appointed to Watch Over the Interests of the Aborigines (1860–69)
CCP	Cape Colony Papers
Cory	Cory Library for Historical Research, Grahamstown
GMT	Greenwich Mean Time
KAB	Cape Town Archives Repository, Western Cape Archives and Records
LMS	London Missionary Society
NLSA	National Library of South Africa, Cape Town
PPV	Parliamentary Papers, Victoria
PROV	Public Records Office of Victoria
SANAC	South African Native Affairs Commission (1903–5)
SLV	State Library of Victoria
UCT	University of Cape Town Archives
VPRS	Victorian Public Record Series (PROV)
WMMS	Wesleyan Methodist Missionary Society

GENERAL EDITOR'S INTRODUCTION

This thought-provoking book leads us to think of the ways we are all socialised into Western concepts of time. As babies, we establish our own timetables for feeding and sleeping, yet very early in our lives the position is reversed and we become slaves to the clock. Primary school does this to us from the age of five (in Britain, though perhaps later in other countries); we have to be there for a certain time. All through the day, bells signal the periods of study, the time in the playground, the lunch break and the welcome release to go home. When I was a boy, I lived in a city where the day was punctuated by sirens, which summoned workers to the shipyards of the Clyde, or to the iron foundries and other heavy industries of the city of Glasgow. I was well aware that the evening sirens led to the formation of great rivers of workers rushing through the streets and on to the ferries or the trams to get as much free time as possible before the summons on the next day. While these noises have largely vanished from our cities and towns, we still hear the bells of the local church and we see public clocks everywhere. There have traditionally been clocks on the roofs of the stable blocks of great estates, often combined with bells. Every town had its clock steeple as a symbol of its status and its modernity. Clocks were set into the faces of town halls, the towers of churches, and above all railway station buildings. Unless we are determined on non-conformity, time-watching and time-keeping enter into the very fabric of our lives. Time even blinks at us from the screens of our computers.

Giordano Nanni applies this concept to the social and cultural revolution wrought by imperialism throughout the world. Indigenous peoples had different notions of time, based on the positions of the sun, moon or stars, ideas that demarcated days, divisions of the year and seasons in largely different ways. This book charts the manner in which Europeans saw the introduction of Western concepts of time (including weeks and months, as well as hours) as part of their necessary reformation of the world, a reformation that was indeed moral as well as practical in its import. Yet, as he shows, different peoples were handled in different ways, depending on their own indigenous economies and where they were placed on the sliding scale of cultures and their supposed relative 'value'. The ways in which Europeans set out to impose forms of 'time discipline' on the Aborigines of Victoria or the various African peoples of southern Africa can be distinguished according to the manner in which such people were valued for their potential for contribution to the colonial economy.

Missionaries constituted the shock troops of such colonial conversions, in the widest possible sense. Protestant missions, particularly those with a Calvinist theology, were more or less obsessed with the significance of the Sabbath and with the essential character-forming value of time disciplines. Extraordinarily, they indulged in the wholly atavistic practice of returning to the disciplines of medieval monasticism, marking out the day's devotions and work through the ringing of bells, the sounding of bugles or other noises designed to mark out the day. In analysing this, Nanni makes an important contribution to the debate about the role of missionaries in the crucial socialisation processes of imperialism. But, significantly, he goes further. He recognises that not all Aborigines or Africans accepted such disciplines, often to the despair of their mentors. As in the whole business of offering labour itself, indigenous peoples found ways of resisting, sometimes overtly, often subtly and in a variety of covert fashions.

In other words, Nanni offers a fresh and highly important dimension to the social, economic, religious and cultural aspects of imperialism. In doing so, he demonstrates the ways in which metropole interacted with periphery. He also addresses the kind of issue which too many histories, obsessed with strictly outward-looking forms of political, military and economic issues, have missed. He offers modes of analysis that are of universal application and in doing so he has driven significant approaches to imperial history in fresh and stimulating directions. This book will prove highly illuminating to other scholars, to students at all levels and to those general readers who are simply intrigued by the manner in which imperialism created so many of the characteristics of our modern world. The concept of globalisation has, perhaps, become over-used (and sometimes misused) in modern times, but this book reveals an area of genuine globalisation, the worldwide adoption (if not always acceptance) of one set of concepts of time, one that supremely symbolises the dominance of the imperial powers.

John M. MacKenzie

ACKNOWLEDGMENTS

My gratitude goes out to all those who have been involved – whether willingly or not – in the creation of this book over the past few years. It all started somewhat fortuitously, in 1998, towards the end of my undergraduate studies at the University of Western Australia, when I decided to formulate a personal question for my final research essay: how did Indigenous cultures around the world measure and relate to the concept of time? (I was secretly questioning whether I wanted to be a historian or an anthropologist.) The paper ended up being marked by Julian Cobbing, a visiting professor from Rhodes University in Grahamstown, South Africa. Whilst the mark he gave me did not suggest that he was overly impressed with my take on the subject, the feedback I received and the subsequent conversations we had during this period inspired me to continue with my history studies; thus, in effect, sowing some of the seeds which have led to the writing of this book. If one day he were to read it, it is my hope that he will find some improvement on that original essay. I am also grateful to Norman Etherington, who supervised the Honours dissertation that emerged from that essay, providing ideas and suggestions for its future development; and to Iain Brash, who offered valuable counsel. Gratitude also goes out to my friend and fellow student at the time, Vaarunika Dharmapala, for her sharp and humorous critiques – then and over the following years. For generous and fruitful conversations about clocks, calendars and all things temporal during this period, I wish to thank Maureen Perkins, whose own work on time has been a significant influence on the writing of this book.

In 2002, after living and working as a tour-guide in Namibia for some time, I resolved to move back to Australia to undertake a Ph.D. at the University of Melbourne. My sincere thanks go out to David Philips (who is sadly no longer with us) and Julie Evans who jointly supervised me in this endeavour. Pointing me in many of the right directions, David's guidance and humour, and Julie's insights into settler-colonialism, have been absolutely invaluable. For useful comments, feedback and vital encouragement during this time I am also grateful to Elizabeth Elbourne, Patricia Grimshaw, David Goodman, Zoë Laidlaw, Paul Maylam, Shurlee Swain, Andrekos Varnava and Patrick Wolfe.

During the months of research in South Africa and Australia in

ACKNOWLEDGMENTS

2002–3, I was assisted by several generous people, including the late Michael Berning, and Jackson Zweliyanyikima Vena, who helped me to navigate the valuable records at the Cory Library in Grahamstown; Sandy Shell (African Studies Library, University of Cape Town) for assistance with the James Stewart papers; Jaco van der Merwe, principal archivist (who knows his way around the repository like no other) at the Cape Town Archives Repository; and the staff who assisted me at the South African National Library in Cape Town, at the Australian National Archives and at the Public Records Office of Victoria.

I respectfully thank Aunty Joy Murphy Wandin, Uncle Colin Walker and Uncle Albert Mullett for giving their permission to quote excerpts from their interviews in the 'Mission Voices' project; and the Koorie Heritage Trust for assisting with the permission process. Jeffrey Peires and Sally Schramm at the Cory Library assisted me with image permissions, as did Larry Manuel at the Wilmington Institute Library and the staff at the Pictures Collection of the State Library of Victoria. I have endeavoured without success to trace copyright-owners for permission to reproduce figure 6.5 (the Lovedale clock-tower) and figure 7.4 (Greenwich Observatory). Whilst I have acknowledged sources in the List of illustrations, I invite the owners of these two photographs to contact me should they wish to claim copyright. Much gratitude also goes out to Zoe Tame for generously helping with the laborious creation of all of the maps and figure 7.3.

A great part of the research for this book was undertaken thanks to the support of a Melbourne University International Research Scholarship, as well as to financial support to undertake overseas research from the Arts Faculty and the University. A Publication Subsidy Grant from the Arts Faculty and the School of Social and Political Sciences at the University of Melbourne provided funds to cover expenses related to image permissions. Sections of an earlier version of Chapter 3 have appeared in *Time and Society*, 20:1 (2011), and are reproduced by kind permission of Sage Publications. I am particularly grateful to John MacKenzie and the whole production team at Manchester University Press for their helpfulness, kindness and patience in preparing this publication over the course of the past two years; to Corinne Orde for copy-editing and proofing the typescript; and to Leonie Twentyman-Jones for creating the index.

On a more personal note, my gratitude goes to family and friends who have expressed interest, shown patience and curiosity and shared conversations with me about the subject of the book – which has often been of greater comfort than they might realise. Beth Dickerson offered her warm hospitality in Grahamstown during my research there; and Sheila Meintjies and her lovely family welcomed me during my sojourn

ACKNOWLEDGMENTS

in Johannesburg. Those who read chapters and drafts of the manuscript provided invaluable comments, criticisms and suggestions: I am grateful to Paula Geldenhuys, Margaret Geldenhuys, David McGinnis, Julie Evans, Adam Ferguson and Lucy Cahill. Our benevolent landlady, Ann Brown, also deserves my thanks for keeping our rent down to reasonable levels (despite current trends in Melbourne), thus enabling me to dedicate that extra bit of time to writing. (Time is money, as they say.) Lastly, I am deeply appreciative of the comments by the anonymous reviewers of the manuscript, who provided valuable suggestions for its improvement. Any errors or omissions are, of course, my own.

But above all, I want to express my most profound gratitude to the people who actually made this book possible: to my dear partner, Lucy Cahill, whose patience and moral support has been saintly and who has put up with the book (and me) for a surprisingly long time; to my parents, Paula Geldenhuys and Carlo Nanni, for making all this possible in the first place – and to my mother in particular, for constant encouragement over the years. And finally, to my wise grandmother, Margaret Geldenhuys, whose love, patience and support has been boundless ever since I can remember. Thank you.

Giordano Nanni

NOTE ON TERMINOLOGY

The principal object of analysis of this book is colonial discourse. Accordingly, terms such as 'native', 'black', 'blackfellow', etc. are reproduced here to reflect their usage in colonial discourse and in the primary source material. I am mindful, however, that many of the structures of colonial discourse also endure in contemporary discourse. For this reason, I would like to outline my own choice of terminology.

In recent years, Australian society has witnessed the gradual adoption of the official term 'Indigenous people' to refer collectively to Australia's first peoples, rather than 'Aborigine' or 'Aboriginal people'. However, whilst this gesture of political correctness is usually employed with good intentions, the term 'Indigenous' can also be problematic. As I have learnt during various conversations with people of Indigenous/Aboriginal descent, the adjective 'Indigenous' (commonly used to describe all First Nation peoples around the world) deprives the Indigenous people of Australia of their separate identity on the world-stage – an unwelcome reminder of past colonial policies which sought to deny the existence of a distinct Aboriginal identity. It is with this thought in mind that I have opted for the use of 'Aboriginal' instead of 'Indigenous' people. However, where I intend reference to Indigenous people generally, and where I intend to emphasise the fundamental, structural distinction between the latter and settler-colonists, I use the adjective 'Indigenous'.

In any case, it is worth noting that neither 'Indigenous' nor 'Aboriginal' fully reflects the fact that many Aboriginal people across the Australian continent self-identify as distinct peoples, each with their own language, law and kinship system. The original inhabitants of the land now known as Victoria, for example, comprise numerous groups, such as the Kulin, Yorta Yorta, Gunai/Kurnai peoples, etc. Each of these in turn includes different 'clans' which share language and kinship ties. For example: the five Kulin nations whose people inhabit the area of central Victoria – and whose ancestors were the objects of the colonial observations examined in this book – comprise the Woi Wurrung, Wathaurong, Boon Wurrung, Daung Wurrung and Dja Dja Wurrung peoples (see figure 2.1). Whenever possible, I have used the most specific term possible. At other times, I have opted for the collective term, 'Kulin' or (when dealing with broader populations) 'Aboriginal people'.

In the South African context, the question of the identities and

NOTE ON TERMINOLOGY

naming of the Cape's earliest inhabitants represents an ongoing subject of debate among scholars. Given that we remain ignorant of the names which many groups adopted for themselves, historians have been left to make difficult decisions about which terms to employ. Without wishing to weigh-in on the nomenclature debate, my choice of terminology is as follows. To refer to southern Africa's nomadic hunter-gatherer population, instead of 'San', I have opted for the term 'Bushman', which is now generally regarded as acceptable. 'Hottentot' (the name popularised by Dutch settlers in reference to the Khoikhoi peoples, who practised a semi-nomadic pastoralist economy) has long been considered derogatory; accordingly, I have used the term sparingly, only to signal contemporary usage. Whenever possible, I have used more specific names of individual Khoikhoi groups (e.g. the 'Namaqua'). It is worth noting, however, that the identity-boundaries between these two peoples (Bushmen and Khoikhoi) had already become highly blurred by the nineteenth century; in effect, they were anything but evident or distinct. For this reason I have occasionally adopted the term 'Khoisan', a portmanteau term which has been applied in more recent times to refer to both the Khoikhoi and Bushmen. It is necessary to remember, however, that this term was not used during the nineteenth century.[*]

The term 'Kaffir' or 'Kafir' (also sometimes spelled 'Caffre', deriving from the Islamic religious term 'kafir' and rendered in English as 'infidel') was generally used by settlers to refer to the Xhosa-speaking peoples of southern Africa in the eighteenth and early nineteenth centuries. It was extended by whites to include all African speakers of Bantu languages during the twentieth century and under apartheid. Today this appellation is considered extremely insulting. Accordingly, its use in this book is limited to primary-source quotation, except for the expression 'Kaffir time', in quotation marks, following use of the term by Keletso E. Atkins.[†] Like other populations, the Xhosa-speaking people comprised various subgroups (including the Ngqika, Gcaleka, Ndlambe, Thembu, Mpondo and later, other immigrant groups such as the Mfengu). To avoid confusion arising from too many different names, however, I have opted for the term 'Xhosa', unless the context requires more specificity.

[*]For more on the San/Bushman/Khoikhoi nomenclature debate, see: Shula Marks, 'Khoisan Resistance to the Dutch in the Seventeenth and Eighteenth Centuries', *Journal of African History*, 13:1 (1972), pp. 55–60; Susan Newton-King, *Masters and Servants on the Cape Eastern Frontier, 1760–1803* (Cambridge: Cambridge University Press, 1999), pp. 25–8, 59–62; Elizabeth Elbourne, *Blood Ground: Colonialism, Missions, and the Contest for Christianity in the Cape Colony and Britain, 1799–1853* (Montreal: McGill-Queen's University Press, 2002), pp. 72–5.
[†]Keletso E. Atkins, '"Kafir Time": Preindustrial Temporal Concepts and Labour Discipline in Nineteenth-century Colonial Natal', *Journal of African History*, 29 (1988), 229–44.

NOTE ON TERMINOLOGY

A certain level of generalisation applies, by necessity, not only to the terms which I have adopted to refer to African and Aboriginal populations, but also to European agents. Thus, whilst this study is primarily about British colonialism and focuses on two British settler-colonies, I have often used the term 'European', to convey the sense that many of the events and trends documented in this history were not exclusive to Britain and its Empire. At certain times this appellation also seemed more accurate, given that a number of the individuals mentioned in the following pages were not necessarily British, but came from elsewhere in western Europe (eg. Germany, France, the Netherlands, etc.). The even-more generic term, 'Western', also appears occasionally – again, when geographic descriptors such as 'European' seemed to be too limited. It may well be that some readers of this book may find it necessary to question my use of terminology in certain sections. Notwithstanding this, I hope that its underlying argument will still hold true.

Introduction

Much of the world today is governed by the clock. Its presence is so often taken for granted and its internationally spoken language of hours, minutes and seconds has become so familiar that an alternative consciousness of time seems scarcely conceivable. And yet, not so long ago, clock-time represented but one of the countless vernaculars devised by humans as a means of expressing the concept of time. Clocks, it is often forgotten, do not keep *the* time, but *a* time.

The phenomenon has not gone unnoticed. Since the mid-twentieth century scholars have investigated in ever greater detail the various factors – from the monastery to the railway – which have shaped the distinctive, dominant perception of time in Western society and the rituals and routines it now performs, quite literally, around the clock. But the manner in which 'the *rest*' of the world came to share the 'West's' dominant view of time has received much less attention. Who were the first emissaries of the culture of the clock to clock-less societies? What inspired their visions of a world marching to the beat of a single drum? And, most importantly, by what means did they gain a following? Whilst we have attained some measure of knowledge regarding the role of time as the location of power and struggle within western European societies, we have not benefited as much from an understanding of its extension to other parts of the world.

Such a path of enquiry leads us back to the period of nineteenth-century European colonial expansion, during which projects to eliminate, subsume and reform – and thus in effect 'colonise' – alternative cultures of time were first deployed by European societies as a means of establishing control over other lands and peoples. From a practical perspective, there is little doubt that the globally interconnected society to which colonialism gave rise by the end of the nineteenth century necessitated a common discourse of time – a temporal *lingua franca*. 'If time is to be shared as an intersubjective social reality', claims sociologist Eviatar Zerubavel, 'it ought to be standardized'.[1] For if people 'had no homogeneous concept of time, space, causality, number, and so on', as Émile Durkheim commented at the start of the twentieth century, 'then any agreement between minds, and therefore all common life, would become impossible'.[2] If this is so, then any nascent global society must inevitably ask itself the following question: whose definition of time should provide the standard whereby all others can share in this 'intersubjective social reality'?

The most unequivocal answer to this question, from an occidocentric perspective, came in 1884 with the official deployment of Greenwich Mean Time (GMT) – the corollary of Western, temporal imperialism – which at the height of the colonial era effectively sought to replace the miscellany of 'local times' around the world with a single, centralised and standardised notion of – rather aptly named – 'mean time'.[3] Computed and calculated at the geographic heart of imperial London where the world's most accurate clocks ticked-off the hours, GMT is a clear sign, and a daily reminder, that European global expansion in commerce, transport and communication was paralleled by, and premised upon, control over the manner in which societies abroad related to time. The project to incorporate the globe within a matrix of hours, minutes and seconds demands recognition as one of the most significant manifestations of Europe's universalising will.

As the imagery suggests, the conquests of space and time are intimately connected. European territorial expansion has always been closely linked to, and frequently propelled by, the geographic extension of its clocks and calendars. From as early as the fifteenth century, through the search for an exact spatio-temporal method for calculating longitudinal positions at sea, the science of horology was instrumental in the exploration and charting of oceans and in the 'discovery' of the so-called New World. The invention of the mechanical clock towards the end of the Middle Ages, historian David Landes maintains, was one of the technological advances that 'turned Europe from a weak, peripheral, and highly vulnerable outpost of Mediterranean civilization into a hegemonic aggressor'; and which 'made possible, for better or for worse, a civilisation attentive to the passage of time, hence to productivity and performance'.[4]

But the story of Europe's rise to global temporal dominance is not exclusively – as many traditional histories of Western time have implied – about the technological advances of indefatigable clock-makers. Deep ideological currents were also at play: the widespread belief that non-European societies were somehow 'not attentive enough' to the passage of time, for instance, functioned as a powerful legitimising discourse for colonial and missionary projects and therefore European hegemony. Indeed, whilst societies the world over were just as attentive to time (to the notions of time and productivity that mattered to them), it was partly by *imagining* itself as a time-conscious civilisation in opposition to a time-less Other, that western Europe staked its claim to universal definitions of time, regularity, order; hence also to definitions of knowledge, religion, science, etc. In a very real sense, this temporal hubris, together with the mathematically abstracted idea of time which was distilled into the mechanical clock, created the necessary culture of time for building empires.

On the other hand, the path towards global temporal standardisation was not paved solely through global events and grandiloquent gestures of imperialism, such as the proclamation of GMT. The process also entailed a series of world-wide, localised assaults on alternative cultures of time, whose perceived 'irregularity' threatened the colonisers' dominant notions of order with conflicting attitudes towards life, time, work, order and productivity. Frederick Cooper and Ann Laura Stoler note that 'social transformations are a product of both global patterns and local struggles' – while Jean Comaroff and John Comaroff describe 'the colonial encounter' as being 'first and foremost an epic of the ordinary'.[5] It is with these local, everyday struggles that this book is primarily concerned; for here – particularly during the course of the evangelisation, education and employment of colonised peoples – Christianising and 'civilising' entailed imposing the temporal rituals and routines of the dominant society, whilst disempowering, subsuming and reforming competing modes of temporal practice and perception.

As we will see, it was partly by interrupting the cycles of Indigenous and local seasons and calendars, and replacing them with the colonisers' rituals and routines, along with a new calendar for counting the days, months and years, that heathens were visibly Christianised, and that idle hands were put to productive work. Missionaries, settlers and colonial officials adopted different means, while also pursuing different ends in their attempt to reform the world and its inhabitants. But whether it was a case of securing regular and disciplined labourers for farms, mines and plantations, legitimating the dispossession and displacement of nomadic populations, or advancing 'savages' along the scale of civilisation or securing souls for the kingdom of heaven, all such projects relied on forms of temporal conversion and the establishment of a specific language and consciousness of time. In assuming the authority to determine when other societies could work, rest and play, the emissaries of the clock worked daily, and hourly, in their quests to bring about a sense of world-wide 'order', by exporting their ways of structuring the flow of time to distant lands, and by preaching to their inhabitants new ways of thinking about what time itself is. Such efforts were driven by significant cultural, as well as concrete economic, imperatives. Without a shared sense of time, there could be only a limited degree of communication and exchange of commodities in the rapidly-expanding networks of capitalism and Christianity – no synchronisation of labour rhythms and meshing of industrial timetables; no sense of uniting all the world's peoples under one God. At the most fundamental level, therefore, time was both a tool and a channel for the incorporation of human subjects within the colonisers' master narrative; for conscripting human subjects within the matrix of the capitalist economy, and ushering 'savages' and superstitious 'heathens' into an age of modernity.

For colonised societies, the overall process entailed nothing less than a series of cultural curfews and a collective reorientation in the understanding of what constituted the permissible time for each and every activity, even including movement across the land. Despite all this, however, we will see that the colonisation of time did not go uncontested on the ground. Even though imperial fictions such as GMT could be imposed, with the stroke of a pen from the top-down, attempts to institute a new rhythm of life and a new consciousness of time among colonised societies were consistently challenged – or appropriated, and often repeatedly thwarted – before the clock succeeded in attaining a measure of dominance. And even then, colonial timetables, rituals, clocks and bells always remained prone to their observers' tardiness, sluggishness, dissent, defiance, resistance and procrastinations. From the outset, the 'colonised' shaped the new tempo of colonial society – whether by flouting the missionaries' Sabbath, by negotiating compromises between new and old rituals or by exploiting the temporal discourses of their self-styled reformers to their own advantage. The history which is recounted in this book is not about the imposition of one culture's temporality over another, therefore, but about the everyday struggles and negotiations which occurred during the colonial encounter as regards the dominant perception of time in society.

Just as the history of colonialism is often written without much reference to time, the history of time is frequently narrated without due reference to colonialism. By bringing the two subjects together, therefore, this book aims at a twofold objective. In the first place, it seeks to add new depth to our understanding of imperial power and of the ways in which such power was exercised and limited. Given that colonialism is generally conceived of primarily, and sometimes solely, as a spatial project, recovering its temporal facet provides an additional dimension through which to better understand this phenomenon and its ongoing cultural legacies. Acknowledging and extending the invaluable work of various scholars which has preceded it,[6] this book seeks to revitalise and refine the enquiry into time and colonisation. Rather than focusing on a single location, moreover, it explores the relationship between temporal discourse, power and resistance across two British settler-colonies – Victoria (Australia) and the Cape Colony (South Africa) – in order to illustrate how 'the colonisation of time', whilst tending towards global centralisation and uniformity, unfolded in ways which varied in response to localised objectives, challenges and circumstances.

On a secondary level, this book emphasises the centrality of empire within the history of Western time. All too often, as noted, the history of Western time has been narrated without reference to European colonialism, seemingly oblivious to the extent to which these two subjects are imbricated.[7] And yet, from 1492, these narratives should be regarded as virtually inseparable; for the global expansion of western Europe's clocks was often explicitly contingent, as we will see, on the interruption, elimination and reform of 'other' cultures of time. This represents a central, oft-forgotten chapter in the making of the global temporal order which today we find in full bloom.

Time, culture and identity

'What is time?'

In contrast to investigations which seek to understand what time *is*, this study is concerned primarily with the manner in which time has been constructed and understood, with the meanings and values that have been attached to it, and with the ways in which these have operated as a means of crafting identities and civilities. St Augustine's ancient question – 'what is time?' – need not worry us excessively therefore. For, after all, the ways in which time is imagined, from the idea of a flowing river to concepts of its loss and redemption, may well be the only way in which time exists at all. 'Time is nothing', Immanuel Kant wrote in his *Critique of Pure Reason*, 'but the form of inner sense, that is, of the intuition of ourselves and of our inner state.'[8] The same might be said of the temporal artefacts – from sundials to digital wristwatches – which humans have devised and adopted over the ages to express and communicate the idea of time. Often perceived as time *per se*, these too are merely avatars of 'time' – material embodiments of the time-consciousness of the societies that created them. ('Because our inner intuition yields no shape', Kant suggests, 'we endeavour to make up for this want by analogies.')

One of the most recognised 'analogies' of time today is, of course, the clock. Designed and corresponding to the laws of classical mechanics, its internal cogs, levers and springs are a fitting incarnation of Isaac Newton's theoretical projection of an 'absolute, true and mathematical time [which] flows equably without regard to anything external'.[9] ('A clock' as Norman Mailer proposed, 'is a philosophical fiction among men'.[10]) But not all embodiments of time are of the material and mechanical sort. Rituals, whether sacred or mundane, are another manifestation of a collective time sense, and are particularly relevant to this study given that their function is to reaffirm and renew the shared sentiments of 'order' upon which all human societies depend.[11] Consider the example of the seven-day week, a ritual which silently affirms and reactualises the underlying master narrative of Judeo-Christian mythology ('And God blessed the seventh day, and sanctified it: because that in it he had rested from all his work which God created and made' Genesis 2:3), whilst synchronising the rhythms of capital and labour. As the word itself implies, rituals (from the Proto-Indo-European base *re(i)* – 'to count, number') rely on a common understanding of time and regularity. This is why temporal exactitude is an important dimension of life, not just in Western, industrial-capitalist culture, but in all cultures; for punctuality effectively embodies the site of authority that ensures a collective sense of social regularity and wellbeing.

This book is accordingly based on two key premises; firstly: that time, being above all an idea, is embodied in the various rituals, routines, calendars, discourses and devices which provide a sense of regularity and rhythm and which orientate human collectives towards an accepted source of temporal authority, whether they be the celestial motions of the stars or the mechanical ticking of clocks. Secondly, that the experience of time is a human universal – one that all societies share in common – but the ways in which that experience is measured, perceived and conceptualised can vary widely from culture to culture.[12] ('Times are not the same; only clock times are all the same'.[13]) This explains why the meanings of notions such as 'punctuality', 'regularity' and 'order' can differ considerably from culture to culture; and in fact, also within cultures, since every society contains values and standards of time that differ from dominant understandings.[14]

Despite the chimerical nature of time itself, notions about how it should be kept, counted, patterned, measured and communicated have long had a very real and concrete impact on humanity. Rituals and calendars, for example, have helped to define and separate entire nations and religions. Consider the example of the seven-day week and how the early Christians sought to distinguish themselves from the Jews by celebrating the Sabbath on Sunday rather than Saturday; how Muslims chose Friday as their gathering day to differentiate themselves from both; and how French revolutionaries attempted to secularise time altogether by abolishing the seven-day week and the Sabbath, *tout court*. Time, clearly, is both cultural *and* political.

As this suggests, the ways in which time is embodied and ritualised in society are a powerful determining factor in the construction of collective identities. In Zerubavel's words: 'a temporal pattern that is unique to a group contributes to the establishment of social boundaries that distinguish as well as actually separate group members from "outsiders"'.[15] Of course, the opposite also holds true: rituals can operate as mechanisms of inclusion and assimilation when used to absorb 'outsiders' within the temporal culture of the dominant society. An apt illustration of this phenomenon, and one that will be examined closely throughout this book, is the case of the zealous missionaries who traversed the British Empire preaching the gospel of the seven-day week – a ritual that was unique to Europeans in the colonies, where, as we will see, the act of Christianising and civilising 'heathens' entailed, as a first step, the conscripting of 'outsiders' within a group that distinguished itself by its practice of ordering the days in groups of seven. But we will return to missionaries later on.

Given that time is a key marker of identity it is not surprising that humans have shown a keen interest in how other cultures 'keep' theirs. Such concern stems from the fact that time is often treated – like other universal categories of perception – as a mirror wherein we presume to see reflected key aspects of another culture's values and beliefs. ('Time', as anthropologist Johannes Fabian observes, 'is a carrier of significance, a form through which we define the content of relations between the Self and the Other'.[16]) Time's mirrored image, however, is often lost in translation given that its meaning is interpreted according to a different set of values and beliefs about what makes time 'temporal'. Under such conditions, time can easily become a node of conflict and misunderstanding, particularly when a perceived absence of 'punctuality' and 'regularity' is associated with a lack of knowledge, respect and entitlement – as was often the case during colonial encounters.

Throughout this book we will in fact see how the rhythms and rituals which provided local populations around the world with a sense of social order and regularity were interpreted by Europeans through the culturally convex lenses of colonial discourse in altogether opposite terms – as irregularity, capriciousness, aimlessness and superstition. 'The relative absence of specialised timekeeping technology', as Carol Greenhouse points out, 'does not in itself mean that time is of no interest or concern.'[17] Yet it was on this very count that colonial discourse portrayed non-European temporalities as primitive, irrational and heathen – a perception which was exacerbated by the apparent absence of an abstract language of time (years, weeks, hours, minutes) which, to the exclusion of all other units, constituted *the* time. 'The Hottentot has a constitutional inability to compute time', a popular natural-history book – *The Uncivilized Races of Men in All Countries of the World* – informed British readers in 1878. 'A traveller can never discover the age of a Hottentot,' the book claimed, 'partly because the man himself has not the least notion of his age, or indeed of annual computation at all, and partly because a Hottentot looks as old at thirty-five as at sixty-five.'[18] By way of a similar line of reasoning, British missionaries in the colonies interpreted the absence of the seven-day week and a sacred day of rest among Indigenous populations as evidence of their state of sin and superstition, and their ignorance of true religion.

Thus, in order to understand the temporal standards by which nineteenth-century Europeans came to measure and judge the validity of 'other' cultures, we will require an understanding of the colonisers' own temporal culture. With this in mind, Chapter 1 sets out to provide a broad historical introduction to the socially dominant time-consciousness of nineteenth-century Britain. Whilst covering familiar ground for the reader who might already be acquainted with the existing historiography on this topic, this chapter emphasises the extent to which British identities and civilities came to be defined to a significant extent by certain rituals, routines and attitudes towards time. In the British metropolis, as we will see, obedience to the clock, a strict respect for the Sabbath ritual and the principles of time-thrift came to be correlated with dominant ideas of morality, foresight and discipline – in short, with middle-class, Protestant notions of 'civilisation' – whilst deviations from the dominant understandings of 'regularity' and thus 'normality' came to be associated with symptoms of sin, vice and degeneracy. Since representations of societies as lacking in an adequate degree of reverence for time came to function as a means of expressing their inferiority, discourse of temporal *absence* and *lack* permeated bourgeois perceptions of working-class temporalities in much the same way as they featured in colonial portrayals of African and Aboriginal attitudes towards time. As this suggests, the correlation between civilisation and correct notions of time was also a product of the colonial encounter, which brought Europeans into contact with different temporal cultures against which they could define their own identities and civilities. Reverberating between colony and metropole, therefore, discourses of time were central to the process of defining and maintaining nineteenth-century British notions of identity, religion, class and – ultimately – civilisation.

INTRODUCTION

Time and the irregular Other

Accusations of 'irregularity', abundant in colonial representations of Indigenous societies, suggest that conceptualisations of the Other were often framed within discourses of temporal aberrance. Of course, 'irregularity' only makes sense in relation to its opposite ('regularity', 'uniformity', 'order'), of which the exemplars in nineteenth-century colonial discourse generally were: the mechanical tempo of a functioning clock, the astronomical logic of the Christian calendar and the biblical authority of the seven-day week. The opposition between 'regularity' and 'irregularity' is one example among several temporal dichotomies prevalent in colonial discourse which, combined, formed a familiar pattern of cultural negations and of positive versus negative attributes, the whole versus the incomplete, the human versus the savage, and ultimately, the Saved versus the Fallen. The following paradigm outlines some of the time-related dichotomies of colonial discourse which this book explores:

The Self	is to	the Other
as Time	is to	Time-less
as Regular	is to	Irregular
as Uniform	is to	Erratic
as Rational	is to	Irrational
as Modern	is to	Primitive
as Christian	is to	Heathen
as Knowledge	is to	Superstition
as Human	is to	Nature/the savage

As we will see in Chapters 2 and 4 – devoted to the British settler-colonies of Victoria and the Cape, respectively – the notion of the 'savage' was constructed partly upon the belief that to be 'human' entailed separating man's rituals and routines from the rhythms and cycles of nature. According to a similar logic, settlers' work and Christians' devotions were to a great extent set apart from the labour and lore of 'savages' and 'heathens' through the logic that ordered their rhythms: the former were idealised as uniform, regular and continuous; the latter as nature-oriented; and hence irregular, irrational and superstitious. Thus, portrayals of Indigenous populations as lacking, to varying degrees, the qualities of order and regularity and as ignorant of time, both as a measure of duration and as an object of value, helped construct an irregular Other against which Europeans could identify – invariably to their own advantage.

Here the book's approach is clearly indebted to Edward Said's deconstruction of otherness in his seminal text, *Orientalism* (1978), which has shown how images of the 'Other', in Said's words, 'help the mind to intensify its own sense of itself by dramatizing the distance and difference between what is close to it and what is far away'.[19] By way of comparison with other temporalities, colonists were able to craft and maintain their own sense of who they were. Whether British or Dutch, men or women, of working-class or bourgeois stock, the perception of the 'time-less' Other helped define their own civilities in relative terms of regularity, productiveness, modernity, etc. Time thus contributed to the construction of an evolutionarily distant 'Other'; for the gulf between the mechanical rationality of clocks and the nature-oriented calendars of Indigenous societies was perceived to be as vast as the epochs separating the Stone Age from the steam-engine. Europeans indeed came to associate a failure to keep time with an inability to keep up *with* time.

Representations of non-European people as lacking suitable practices and perceptions of time contributed to the establishment of the nascent nineteenth-century discipline of anthropology as 'a science of other men in another Time'.[20] Societies which became the objects of enquiry in the proto-anthropologies of European explorers, travellers and missionaries were depicted as belonging not so much to the present, of which Europe was sole denizen, as to a previous stage of development through which Europe had already passed. This 'denial of coevalness' – a term coined by Johannes Fabian in his seminal critique of contemporary anthropology, *Time and the Other* (1983) – was a means for Europe to reserve for itself terms such as 'modern' and 'progressed', allowing it to depict other societies as being in an embryonic, or immature, state of development, rather than as fully-fledged cultural systems in their own right. As we will see in Chapters 2 and 4, the perception that African and Aboriginal societies had failed to 'keep' time by mastering the science and language of abstract time-reckoning, contributed to their denial of coevalness and subsequent portrayal as 'primitive' and pre-modern. Lucien Lévy-Bruhl provided an early-twentieth-century example with his claim that 'the primitive's idea of time, which above all is qualitative, remains vague; and nearly all primitive languages are ... deficient in methods of rendering the relations of time'.[21]

But such discourses were circulating even before anthropology had established itself as a formal discipline. The idea of evolutionary time flowing along a single, unidirectional line (a trope already prevalent in biblical time-consciousness) was channelled and popularised through British society thanks to the theories of progress and evolution developed by eighteenth-century Enlightenment *philosophes*. Thus, according to the evolutionist theories popularised by Turgot, Adam Smith and other stadial theorists, all societies necessarily progressed through determined stages of economic and social development, each with greater divisions of labour and more complex social organisation: first, the Age of Hunters; second, the Age of Shepherds; third, the Age of Agriculture; and fourth, the Age of Commerce.[22] According to this world-view, Australia's Aborigines belonged to the first age and were thus classed as belonging to the distant, and thus most primitive, past. The mixed farmer–agricultural Xhosa-speaking peoples of the Cape Colony, on the other hand, who had 'progressed' on this fictive timeline to the 'Age of Agriculture', were understood as belonging to a more recent period of evolution, and thus a higher level of civilisation – though still distinctly pre-modern in relation to industrialised Europe. Naturally, according to the proponents of the stadial theories, the fourth stage of progress against which all other societies were measured, was exemplified by contemporary bourgeois Europe. (We still hear distinct echoes of this evolutionist world-view today when people talk of the 'developed' and the 'developing' world.)

Enlightenment ideas about progress and evolution underpinned notions of human perfectibility by characterising the growth of civilisation as advancement through time: a conquest of time itself. Civilisation and modernity could be understood in terms of a society's ability to husband, harness and cultivate not only animals and plants but also the resource of time. Since time was a marker of civilisation, certain societies were seen to possess a more developed sensibility towards it than others – i.e.: one that resembled that of its European advocates more closely. Thus, Europeans were better able to recognise evidence of a 'developed' time-consciousness in those societies oriented around pastoral and agricultural economies and their relative calendars. This is because, as William Grossin notes, 'there is a correspondence, a correlation between the economy of a society, the way on which labour is organized, the means used for the production of its goods and services and the representation of time in the collective consciousness'.[23] In societies that did not measure and 'keep' time, however, Europeans perceived a kind of *status naturae* as prevailing, since the degree of separation of human-time from nature's time operated as a measure of a society's progress in the quest to transcend natural limitations. Hunter-gatherer rituals and nomadic lifestyles were labelled as primitive and savage partly because they were seen as being guided not by a rational, linear and man-made calendar and clock but by 'unpredictable' and 'irregular' cues dictated by the natural environment: the rising of a specific star, the phases of the moon or the seasonal appearance of flora and fauna. ('Primitive man', an early anthropologist wrote, 'rises and goes to bed with the sun.'[24]) A distinctly European epistemology determined what counted as true and false time. According to this world view, the hunter-gatherer did not keep time at all; nature did – 'the savage' merely followed.

In colonial discourse, the ways in which non-European societies related to time became a measure of their humanity as well as their morality and civility. The Western humanist conception of time is aptly conveyed in the workings of the clock and the seven-day week – two quintessentially man-made inventions whose claim to superiority in their colonial observers' eyes, was their apparent abstraction and separation from the rhythms of nature. Consider how the clock acts as an intermediary between humans and nature in the computation of time: emulating the sun's diurnal passage across the sky, it communes with the human subject through a man-made interface, the *dial* – from the Latin *dies*, 'day' – a *memento* of nature which digital clocks abandoned entirely through the adoption of ciphers in the twentieth-century. In a similar vein – and despite its apparent, natural inevitability, as Zerubavel points out – the seven-day week is 'totally oblivious to nature, resting on mathematical regularity alone', an artificial unit of time which conveniently fills the gap between natural lunar-months and solar-days.[25] In the colonies, as we will see, the idea of the clock's civility and of the Sabbath's sacredness were forged in opposition to the 'savagery' and 'sin' of those societies whose rituals and routines were determined solely by nature's time.

These are some of the key themes explored in Chapters 2 and 4, which examine the manner in which colonial perceptions of 'Aboriginal time' and 'African time' shaped Europeans' attitudes to the societies they encountered in Australia and southern Africa, respectively. Drawing upon nineteenth-century discourses of race, human nature, modernity and civilisation, they explore how representations of supposedly anomalous attitudes to time across colonial locations helped to define and maintain a sense of the 'otherness' of Indigenous societies, whilst helping to forge a trans-colonial discourse of civilisation, Christianity and modernity. In turn, these chapters suggest some of the ways in which such representations advanced settler-colonial projects and missionary agendas by undermining the validity of 'alternative' temporalities. As we will see, discourses of 'Aboriginal time' and 'African time' would benefit their advocates by justifying the need to 'civilise the natives', whilst at the same time legitimising their dispossession.

However, it is important to note that neither chapter seeks to offer an anthropological commentary on Indigenous knowledge systems; the object is rather to understand how Europeans themselves viewed Indigenous temporalities. After all, colonisers were bent on reforming what they themselves had construed as 'Aboriginal time' and 'African time'.

Settler-colonisation: time, land and labour

Time is a dimension through which the fundamental tenets of a culture are learnt, disseminated and held to be true. As such it provided one of the key standards of knowledge and models of behaviour against which Europeans sought to reform their Others in the colonies – operating simultaneously as a category for establishing the cultural and racial inferiority of local populations and as a channel for reforming the latter into so-called modern, civilised and Christian subjects. Accordingly, whilst the first part of each case-study in this book deals with the 'othering' process produced by discourses of time, the second part goes on to consider time's role as a tool of colonial reform.

The colonisation of time, however, was not a uniform or homogeneous process; for the ways in which European agents sought to reform alternative temporal cultures in the two British colonies under consideration – the Cape Colony and Victoria – was determined to a significant extent by the structural relationship which framed the colonial encounter in each setting. It is important to note from the outset therefore that Britain's colonies in Australia – like others in Canada and New Zealand (and, to some extent, South Africa and the United States) – were characteristic of a particular colonial formation: that of settler-colonialism. As distinct from franchise colonial formations (e.g. India and the Dutch East Indies) and colonies based on chattel-slavery (e.g. the West Indies), where the relationship between colonisers and colonised was centered primarily on labour, the economic interest in settler-colonies was vested primarily in the *land*.[26] Settlers, as the word implies, had come to stay. This is not to imply that Indigenous labour was superfluous in these places. As we will see, Aboriginal labour was valued in Victoria on a seasonal basis, while the demand for African labour in the Cape Colony by far exceeded the supply. Nevertheless, in purely structural terms, the relationship between colonisers and colonised in both settings was centered primarily on the land. The primary logic of settler-colonisation, as historian Patrick Wolfe maintains, can therefore be characterised as one of 'elimination': settler-colonialism seeks to replace 'the natives' physically on their land.[27]

Chapter 3 examines how the colonial curtailment of Aboriginal

[13]

temporalities complemented this logic of elimination by helping to contain, absorb and effectively remove an Indigenous presence in the colony of Victoria. As Deborah Bird Rose points out, all the 'native' had to do to get in the way of settler colonisation was to stay at home.[28] To a very real extent, however, it was the rhythmical itinerancy of Aboriginal life which also defined 'home' and thus 'got in the way' of settler interests. Aboriginal migrations – guided as they were by seasonal rhythms which determined the availability of flora and fauna – implied a notion of 'home' that was defined temporally as well as spatially. Thus the sedentary logic of settler-colonisation, implicit in the very notion of 'settling' in a land, and the relatively perpetual movement that hunter-gatherers considered as the norm, placed the rhythms of these two civilisations onto a direct collision course. Colonisation was about temporal, as well as spatial, invasion and displacement.

Towards the second half of the nineteenth-century, when mission stations and government reserves were established to contain and control the surviving Aboriginal population of Victoria, missionaries and colonial authorities certainly emphasised the importance of reforming 'Aboriginal time' within the context of philanthropy. However, as Aboriginal labour was generally superfluous to colonial interests other than for seasonal demands, justifying their dispossession as a primitive culture characterised the primary function of temporal discourse in Victoria; whilst subsuming the presence of Aboriginal people within the colonisers' temporal landscape contributed to rendering the previous occupants of the land less visible within colonial space. In the institutionalised environment of the mission station, time served this agenda well: the calendars and schedules of pastoralism and agriculture were enforced, displacing the seasons of the hunter-gatherer economy; Sabbaths, Christmases, and Easters interrupted the regular flow of the rituals and routines which had renewed and reaffirmed Aboriginal family and kinship bonds; bells and seven-day weeks imposed curfews on, and boundaries between, work-time and leisure-time, which relegated Aboriginal modes of production to the status of pastimes. The overall process complemented the logic of elimination that underpinned settler-colonisation by suppressing and subsuming the vestiges of rituals and temporalities that confirmed the existence of a sovereign Indigenous presence – a presence which itself embodied a direct threat to the newcomers' claims of exclusive sovereignty over the land.

Whereas Victoria witnessed the frontier spreading swiftly across the land as settlers soon outnumbered the Indigenous population, the Cape Colony experienced a very different scenario. There the advancement of settlement was much slower – particularly on the eastern frontier, where Europeans would always be vastly outnumbered by African populations. Unlike their counterparts in Victoria who were quickly immured by the settlers' landed interests, British missionaries at the Cape effectively became the cultural vanguards of settler-colonisation, often operating well beyond the colonial frontier, surrounded by the people they aimed to evangelise and reform. Chapter 5 illustrates how, in these circumstances, time played a different but nevertheless crucial role in planting the first seeds of a European cultural order in that part of the world. As the sound of the bell was imported to places where it had never been heard before, and as the temporal jurisdiction of the seven-day Sabbath ritual was extended in so-called heathen lands, the rituals and routines of Christian time became a cultural frontier in themselves, precursors to the physical settler-colonial frontier. Daily and weekly, missionaries preached the gospels of work and the Sabbath, the virtues of sedentary life and agriculture, housing and hygiene, 'artificial wants' and – implicit in all of these – a new consciousness of time. In so doing, they helped to establish the institutional rhythms and ideological groundwork for the social order which would later be entrenched under formal colonisation.

Chapter 6 extends the African case-study in order to explore the continued significance of temporal reform among the Xhosa-speaking peoples, against the backdrop of the labour crisis which afflicted the Cape Colony during the second half of the nineteenth century, once the Xhosa had been dispossessed and forced into the colonial labour economy. Whereas in Victoria the labour power of Indigenous peoples was generally superfluous compared with the wealth derived from territorial acquisition alone, a vast demographic disparity between Europeans and Africans, and a heavy reliance on the agricultural (and later, mineral) wealth of the land, meant that the Cape Colony also came to depend to a large extent on the exploitation of Indigenous (as well as imported) labour. In this context, 'African time' was identified as a clear culprit amidst the chronic labour shortages which affected the Cape's economy. Part of the problem was one of guaranteeing the security of a colonial economy which had to operate all-year-round, even if 'the native' did not. The incentive to reform the time- and work-ethic of African workers in the Cape subsequently led to far more intensive, and expensive, attempts to reform Indigenous temporalities than it did in Victoria. Chapter 6 thus explores attempts to reform 'African time' in the missionary-run schools and industrial institutions that sprang up along the Cape's eastern frontier from the 1850s, focusing on one of the Colony's most famous schools – the Lovedale Institution – where it was hoped that a supposedly ineffective, inefficient and irregular population would be remoulded into a time-disciplined, clock-oriented African working class. The effects of institutional education on Indigenous time-consciousness were profound. However, little did missionaries and colonial authorities imagine that such education would also help nurture and empower a generation of African intellectuals and leaders who would one day lead the South African nation to democracy.

Bells, Bibles and the civilising mission

Missionaries deserve a special early mention given that they were key agents of cultural reform both in the Cape Colony and Victoria – playing a fundamental role in shaping domestic perceptions of Indigenous temporal cultures, as well as in attempting to reshape the latter around the order of the clock and the seven-day week. Often the earliest, and decidedly the most zealous, emissaries of a new order of time to the colonies, they were often seriously preoccupied with temporal matters – both existential and horological. Indeed, a penchant for temporal accountability, coupled with a passionate set of convictions as to the virtues and liberating potential of their way of life, placed them at the frontline in the colonisation of time.

By following the sound of bells on the missionary trail, we will gain a measure of understanding of how the order of the clock and the seven-day week were first introduced among Indigenous societies. If the clock was an avatar of Western time, the bell was its amplifier, and next to the Bible it became one of the missionaries' most practical instruments for establishing centralised temporal control – a function which the bell had long since played in Europe's monasteries, factories and schools, where it acted as a precursor to the clock. In a geographic act of temporal extension, the sounds of bells, which had been responsible for carrying the canonical hours of the day throughout Western Christendom during the middle ages, were transported to the rest of the world thanks to the work of Christian missionaries in the nineteenth century. Colonial missions became replicas of the medieval Benedictine monasteries, whose bells, timetables and temporal asceticism had left no corner of European society untouched. Symbolically, it was common for patrons and supporters of the missionary enterprise to donate bells as gifts once new mission stations were established in the colonies, making them one of the many cultural artifacts to be shuttled through the emerging networks of empire and Christianity during the nineteenth century. Thus the bell which tolled the hours of work and prayer for Aboriginal people at Ebenezer – a Moravian mission in Victoria – hailed from Saxony; while the bell calling the Khoikhoi to worship at the Wesleyan mission of Lily Fountain in the northern Cape was donated by a patron in Bristol. The Berlin Missionary Society at the Cape received two bells from Hamburg (their special status was even acknowledged by the Colonial Office, which waived the regular custom duties for their importation to the Colony).[29]

We have already noted some of the key interests and circumstances which framed settler agendas in the Cape Colony and Victoria. A different set of interests – both moral and economic – also inspired and motivated British missionaries in their quest to reform Indigenous temporalities. On the one hand, the great religious revival that had swept across England from the mid-eighteenth century led to a heightened sense of Christian vocation and to the subsequent birth and expansion of the non-conformist missionary movement: strict Sabbath observance and temporal austerity, as we will see in Chapter 1, became central tenets for leading virtuous lives, along with a desire to civilise and reform the calendars and rituals of supposedly popish, pagan and superstitious peoples – both in England and in the colonies. On the other hand, the missionary mandate in the colonies was deeply influenced by the liberal doctrines of Britain's leading Evangelicals who, during the 1820s and 1830s, had turned their attention from their anti-slavery campaigns in the West Indies to the rights of Indigenous peoples across the Empire. As an alternative to practices prevailing in the colonies, many of the leading missionary societies came to proffer an alternative, 'humanitarian' model of imperialism, premised on the *cultural* reformation of Indigenous societies instead of their coercion and enslavement. Christianity and civilisation, the Evangelicals argued, were the panacea that would reconcile Britain with the debt owed to the 'natives' for the trail of violence, destruction and dispossession left in the wake of its imperial expansion. Simultaneously, they would transform those same natives into producers and consumers who, motivated by the prospect of personal betterment, would make better workers and hence better profits for those who employed them.[30] As the *Report from the Select Committee on Aborigines (British Settlements)* put it in 1837, summing up the views of Britain's Evangelicals: 'We have had abundant proof that it is greatly for our advantage to have dealings with civilized men rather than with barbarians. Savages are dangerous neighbours and unprofitable customers'.[31]

As 'proof' of the benefits of the civilising mission, and as a measure of their success in converting 'savages', missionaries frequently cited their ostensible success in establishing 'regular' timetables and rituals – particularly the Sabbath – among their followers. The observance of the Sabbath (and, consequently, of the seven-day week) was treated as evidence of progress in the humanitarian mission in reports from across the Empire – from the Khoikhoi at the Kat River Settlement, to the

Maori on the North Island of New Zealand.[32] The River Credit Mission in North America was held up as another such model of acculturation: 'About ten years ago', the British Select Committee on Aborigines was told, the 'Indians' there had 'no houses, no fields nor horses ... Each person could carry all he possessed on his back, without being much burthened'. But after being Christianised and civilised they could be found living in houses replete with 'tables, chairs, bedsteads ... closets for their cooking utensils, cup-boards for their plates', and many other indicators of an improved manner of living: 'Some', the Committee was told, even 'have clocks and watches'.[33]

All such reforms were intended to transform 'natives' into producers and consumers of commodities – of which time was one. But not all colonial agents shared this view. Indeed, whilst missionaries and humanitarians attributed evidence of temporal acculturation to the redeeming effects of Christianity, their settler critics often discredited such achievements by popularising the stereotype of the incurably lazy 'native' – a stereotype so profuse in the colonial imagination that it hardly requires examples. Powerful settlers' interests across the British Empire generally deemed it more convenient and profitable to justify the dispossession and exploitation of Indigenous peoples by portraying the latter as irredeemable savages who were immune to the ameliorative effects of Christianity, civilisation and education. Accordingly, time became yet another dimension within the broader propaganda war of representations, as historian Alan Lester terms it, which was 'fought out across trans-imperial networks of communication ... over the definition and determination of "proper" relations between British colonists and their others'.[34]

In the light of all this, what missionaries ultimately aimed at in this process, was ideological conversion: a total remaking of culture, rather than merely a superficial reform. Theirs, in effect, was a quest for hegemony – to persuade rather than coerce the natives into becoming vassals of the clock. Missionaries and their metropolitan allies understood well that if the humanitarian vision of imperialism were to prevail – that is, if they were to prove to their critics that free labour and Christianity would be more productive and profitable than slavery and coercion – their converts would have to internalise the ideologies of middle-class, Protestant-evangelical culture truly. Only by ensuring hegemony could missionaries and humanitarians achieve their vision of sober and docile natives who would willingly accept their place in colonial society. Although not all missionaries were allied with the humanitarian cause, most perceived that true and lasting conversion to Christianity and civilisation entailed the internalisation of the clock's culture rather than its external imposition. Therefore, in their daily efforts to reform the time-consciousness of Indigenous peoples entirely, this ideological reorientation of the mind was their ultimate objective.

Resistance and hegemony

Time has long played a role as one of the channels through which defiance towards established order can be manifested. 'One recurrent form of revolt within Western industrial capitalism, whether bohemian or beatnik,' as E. P. Thompson points out, 'has often taken the form of flouting the urgency of respectable time-values.'[35] This also applied to colonial scenarios, where respectable time-values were regularly flouted, both in spectacular and in clandestine ways, as a means of expressing defiance towards the colonial presence; and where the colonisers' notions of order and regularity became particularly vulnerable to subversions, interruptions and delays at the hands of the colonised, whose unapproved breaches of temporal authority turned into an effective means of frustrating colonial and missionary order.

Undoubtedly, having been displaced from their lands, deprived of access to its resources and refused the same social and political rights as those enjoyed by white men, the vast majority of colonised peoples had little choice but to conform in some shape or form to the rituals, routines and regimes of the colonisers' temporal order. But obeying the visible order of the weekly ritual and the clock's regime did not necessarily entail imbibing the culture that came with them. (Time, as noted, is above all an *idea*.) Whilst colonial reformers often succeeded in imposing an outward appearance of order and uniformity, their mission to inculcate their specific ideas of time, order and regularity was widely challenged and determined by the resistance and agency of colonised peoples themselves. Therefore, the narrative of resistance which runs parallel with the colonisation of time can help us form a more complete picture by revealing the limitations, as well as the reach, of colonial power and agency. Indeed, the continuing existence of various forms of resistance towards the temporal mores of western European culture is a sign that the colonisation of time was an incomplete project – one which is accordingly best understood as a case of 'dominance without hegemony'; that is, of rule through coercion rather than consent.[36] A lack of success in terms of implanting the values of a middle-class, industrial-capitalist time-consciousness among colonised peoples meant that the clock's dominance would have to be introduced and maintained through coercion – whether direct or indirect.

Resistance towards the imposition of a new order of time manifested itself in numerous ways, sometimes overtly and confrontationally, at other times covertly and furtively. We tend to recognise resistance most clearly when expressed openly – and, as we will see, it often was: the history of colonialism is littered with damaged bells, broken curfews and desecrated Sabbaths – suggestive of the fact that time was a cultural arena in which the colonial struggle was consciously fought out. But 'resistance' also includes responses other than a straightforward refusal to march to the colonisers' drum. Colonisation was a process of intense cultural upheaval, and produced a range of responses among the colonised that was far more varied and complex than simply offering a choice between accepting or refusing new practices and beliefs. Time became a channel for negotiating compromises between new and old customs; Christian rituals and capitalist notions of time provided discourses that could be appropriated and redeployed in order to bargain for better working and living conditions. In short, time became not simply the conduit of colonial power and anti-colonial resistance but also provided avenues for people to forge bridges between the new and the old.

Colonisers, however, rarely interpreted such behaviour as signs of resistance or Indigenous agency. In order to lend credence to the extent of their hegemony, they habitually coded resistance within a discourse of the 'pathological', attributing refusals or reluctance to conform to their temporal demands to the racial inferiority of local populations. As discourses of madness and deviance were deployed in the metropolis to rationalise the working classes' aversion towards bourgeois timetables and schedules, so did discourses of 'superstition' and racial inferiority function as their counterparts in the colonial context, where – as Frantz Fanon observed – anti-colonial sentiments were routinely 'attributed to religious, magical, fanatical behavior'.[37] To recover narratives of resistance, therefore, we will need to read between the lines of colonial discourse: here, as Fanon hinted, the native's 'laziness' often emerges as 'the conscious sabotage of the colonial machine'.[38]

We conclude with a vignette, in which Frantz Fanon observed the whole process unfolding in a microcosm, in the medical rooms of colonial Algeria where he worked during the 1950s. There he witnessed how 'colonised Algerian' patients expressed their resentment of colonial domination by refusing to obey the temporal instructions issued by the French 'colonising doctors'. He noticed that 'the Algerian' had developed a reputation among doctors for being incapable of taking his medicine 'regularly', for taking the wrong doses and 'fail[ing] to appreciate the importance of periods of visits'; and, in spite of being told to return to the clinic at 'regular intervals', for refusing to meet the 'definite appointment with the doctor for a fixed date'.

> The patient, in fact, comes back five to six months or sometimes a year later. Worse still, he has failed to take the prescribed medicine. An interview with the patient reveals that the medicine was taken only once, or, as often happens, that the amount prescribed for one month was absorbed in a single dose.[39]

The French doctors interpreted the Algerian patient's intransigence as fanatical adherence to superstitious beliefs; but Fanon understood them as symptoms of the patient's struggle to reconcile two incompatible cultural spheres – in this case those of Western and traditional medicine. 'Sometimes the patient gives evidence of the fear of being the battleground for different and opposed forces', Fanon observed; psychologically he 'has difficulty, even here in the presence of illness, in rejecting the habits of his group and the reactions of his culture'. In the end, the patient opts for a practical compromise: he accepts the colonisers' medicine, but not the temporal instructions for administering it. 'Swallowing the whole dose in one gulp', Fanon concludes, 'is literally getting even with it.'

Such were some of the subtler ways in which time could act as one of the dimensions of life which colonised people inhabited: not solely as victims but also as agents who negotiated cultural compromises, grappling their way through the pressures and expectations of two often-conflicting worlds. Furthering our understanding of this process may help to explain why, amongst societies that experienced, and physically survived European colonisation, we find that 'alternative' attitudes to time still survive, despite being marginalised, maligned and targeted by continuing attempts to further their assimilation within the temporal landscape of the dominant, clock-governed society.

Notes

1 Eviatar Zerubavel, 'The Standardization of Time: A Sociohistorical Perspective', *American Journal of Sociology*, 88:1 (1982), 1–23, p. 2.
2 Émile Durkheim, *The Elementary Forms of the Religious Life* (1912), trans. Carol Cosman (Oxford: Oxford University Press, 2001), pp. 18–19.
3 Dan T. Nguyen, 'The Spatialization of Metric Time: The Conquest of Land and Labour in Europe and the United States', *Time and Society*, 1:1 (1992), 29–35; Maureen Perkins, *The Reform of Time: Magic and Modernity* (London: Pluto Press, 2001), pp. 19–25.
4 David Landes, *Revolution in Time: Clocks and the Making of the Modern World* (Cambridge. Mass.: Harvard University Press, 1983), pp. 1, 7.
5 John Comaroff and Jean Comaroff, *Of Revelation and Revolution, Volume 2: The Dialectics of Modernity on a South African Frontier* (Chicago, Ill.: University of Chicago Press, 1997), p. 35; Frederick Cooper and Ann Laura Stoler, 'Between Metropole and Colony: Rethinking a Research Agenda', in F. Cooper and A. L. Stoler (eds), *Tensions of Empire: Colonial Cultures in a Bourgeois World* (Berkeley, Calif.: Univer-

sity of California Press, 1997), p. 4.
6 The first academic studies to focus exclusively on time within colonial/imperial contexts are: Jean Comaroff, 'Missionaries and Mechanical Clocks: an Essay on Religion and History in South Africa', *Journal of Religion*, 71 (1991): 1–17; Frederick Cooper, 'Colonizing Time: Work Rhythms and Labor Conflict in Colonial Mombasa', in Nicholas B. Dirks (ed.), *Colonialism and Culture* (Ann Arbor, Mich.: The University of Michigan Press, 1992); and Dan Thu Nguyen, 'The Spatialization of Metric Time', all of which deal with different aspects of time's function as an instrument of colonial/ imperial control. Following this, there seems to have been a flurry of studies which probed deeper into the significance of time's role in the colonial context: Keletso E. Atkins' brilliant analysis of the reform of African time-discipline in Natal, *'The Moon is Dead, Give us our Money!' The Cultural Origins of an African Work Ethic: Natal, South Africa, 1843–1900* (London: Currey, 1993) is one of the only monographs dedicated exclusively to time in a settler-colony; Janet Hoskins in *The Play of Time: Kodi Perspectives on Calendars, History and Exchange* (Berkeley, Calif.: University of California Press, 1993) offers a perceptive ethnographic account of missionary impact on local time-consciousness and calendars on the island of Sumba (Indonesia); Graeme Davison's *The Unforgiving Minute: How Australia Learnt to Tell the Time* (Melbourne: Oxford University Press, 1993) is a very readable account of the clock's importation to Australia, albeit strangely devoid of explanations of how Aborigines supposedly 'learnt' to tell 'the' time. (Davison's choice of subtitle seems to imply that there was only one way of 'telling the time' – the colonisers'.) After decades of literature written *by* Europeans about the time of the Other, Joseph K. Adjaye's edited volume, *Time in the Black Experience* (Westport, Conn.: Greenwood Press, 1994), offers a welcome response from African scholars on the subject of time in Africa and the Black Diaspora. Mike Donaldson in *Taking Our Time: Remaking the Temporal Order* (Perth: University of Western Australia Press, 1996), is one of few authors to emphasise the resistance of Aboriginal people towards the colonisation of their time. Carol Greenhouse's *A Moment's Notice: Time Politics Across Cultures* (Ithaca: Cornell University Press, 1996), is a highly original ethnographic account of time, employing a comparative approach that often engages questions of imperial power. Another meticulous work is Mark M. Smith's *Mastered by the Clock: Time, Slavery, and Freedom in the American South* (Chapel Hill: University of North Carolina Press, 1997), framed in the context of plantation slavery of the antebellum American South. (Despite this, it curiously misses the opportunity to engage the question of how the clock impacted on Indigenous peoples in North America, whose notions of time preceded the arrival both of masters and slaves.) Aimed at a less academic readership, Jay Griffith's *Pip Pip: A Sideways Look at Time* (London: Flamingo, 1999) provides one of the most varied, entertaining and insightful analyses of time's role in the context of cultural imperialism. Finally, Maureen Perkins' *The Reform of Time* stands out for its brilliant postcolonial analysis on European discourses of the 'timeless cultures', and its enlightening comparative approach between colony and metropole. Several other studies have, of course, contributed to the field in less specialised ways and still other works which have focused on time and empire might not have come to my attention.
7 As a few examples among many, see the otherwise-meticulously written histories by Landes (*Revolution in Time*); G. J. Whitrow, *Time in History: The Evolution of Our General Awareness of Time and Temporal Perspective* (Oxford: Oxford University Press, 1988); and Anthony Aveni, *Empires of Time: Calendars, Clocks and Cultures* (New York: Kodansha Globe, 1989). Many sociological studies also tend to operate in a vacuum that is apparently impervious to narratives of colonisation. A few writers do of course stand out; Barbara Adam, for instance, in her *Time* (Cambridge, Polity Press, 2004), pp. 136–43, includes a section describing time's function as 'a most effective colonizing tool'.
8 Immanuel Kant, *Critique of Pure Reason* (1787), trans. Norman K. Smith (London: Macmillan, 1929), p. 77.
9 Isaac Newton, *Philosophiae Naturalis Principia Mathematica* (1689), trans. Andrew Motte (1729), in Florian Cajori (ed.), *Principia*, vol. 1 (Berkeley, Calif.: University of

California Press, 1934), p. 6.
10 Norman Mailer, *Cannibals and Christians* (New York: Dial, 1966), p. 267.
11 Alfred R. Radcliffe-Brown, *Structure and Function in Primitive Society: Essays and Addresses* (London: Cohen & West, 1952), p. 167; Mircea Eliade, *The Sacred and the Profane: The Nature of Religion* (1957) (Orlando, Fla.: Harcourt, 1987), p. 81; cf. Lewis Mumford, *The Myth of the Machine: Technics and Human Development* (London: Secker & Warburg, 1967), p. 62.
12 Barbara Adam, *Timewatch: The Social Analysis of Time* (Cambridge: Polity Press, 1995), p. 29. See also Edward T. Hall, *The Dance of Life: The Other Dimension of Time* (New York: Anchor/Doubleday, 1984); Donald Brown, *Human Universals* (New York: McGraw-Hill, 1991); Carol Greenhouse, *A Moment's Notice: Time Politics Across Cultures* (Ithaca, N.Y.: Cornell University Press, 1996). It is generally accepted that humans experience time culturally, for to speak of perceiving time in any physiological way immediately begs the question: which of our senses is responsible for the perception of time?
13 Karlheinz A. Geißler, 'A Culture of Temporal Diversity', *Time and Society*, 11:1 (2002), 131–40, p. 133.
14 See Perkins, *The Reform of Time*, p. 12; E. P. Thompson, 'Time, Work-Discipline and Industrial Capitalism', *Past and Present*, 38:1 (1967), 56–97.
15 Eviatar Zerubavel, *The Seven Day Circle: The History and Meaning of the Week* (New York: The Free Press, 1985), p. 22.
16 Johannes Fabian, *Time and the Other: How Anthropology Makes Its Object* (New York: Columbia University Press, 1983), p. ix.
17 Greenhouse, *A Moment's Notice*, p. 88.
18 John G. Wood, *Uncivilized Races of Men in All Countries of the World: Being a Comprehensive Account of their Manners and Customs, and of Their Physical, Social, Mental, Moral and Religious Characteristics* (Hartford, Conn.: J. B. Burr Publishers, 1878), vol. 1, p. 239.
19 Edward Said, *Orientalism* (New York: Pantheon), 1978, p. 55.
20 Fabian, *Time and the Other*, pp. 143, 147.
21 Lucien Lévy-Bruhl, *Primitive Mentality* (Boston, Mass.: Beacon Press, 1923), pp. 445–6.
22 P. Stein, *Legal Evolution: The Story of an Idea* (Cambridge: Cambridge University Press, 1980), pp. 24–36; R. L. Meek, *Smith, Marx and After: Ten Essays in the Development of Economic Thought* (London: Chapman & Hall, 1980), pp. 18–32.
23 William Grossin, 'Technological Evolution, Working Time and Remuneration', *Time and Society*, 2:2 (1993), 159–77, p. 160.
24 Martin Nilsson, *Primitive Time-Reckoning: A Study in the Origins and First Development of the Art of Counting Time among the Primitive and Early Culture Peoples* (Lund: Gleerup, 1920), p. 128.
25 Zerubavel, *Seven Day Circle*, p. 4.
26 Patrick Wolfe has been a key figure in theorising settler-colonisation as a land-based project. See his *Settler-Colonialism and the Transformation of Anthropology: The Politics and Poetics of an Ethnographic Event* (London: Cassell, 1999), p. 29; and his 'Land, Labour and Difference: Elementary Structures of Race', *American Historical Review*, 106:3 (2001), 866–905, pp. 867–70.
27 Wolfe, 'Land, Labor and Difference', pp. 868, 870.
28 Deborah B. Rose, *Hidden Histories: Black Stories from Victoria River Downs, Humbert River and Wave Hill Stations* (Canberra: Aboriginal Studies Press, 1991), p. 46.
29 KAB, CO 4105, Ref. S18, memo, C. M. Schwabe to Colonial Secretary, 'Duty on Bells at the Berlin Missionary Society', 10 Feb. 1858.
30 *The Report from the Select Committee on Aborigines (British Settlements) with the Minutes of Evidence*, British Parliamentary Papers, 1837, VII [hereafter: *Report from the Select Committee on Aborigines (British Settlements)*, 1837], pp. 3–15, 74–6; see also Julie Evans et al., *Equal Subjects, Unequal Rights: Indigenous Peoples in British Settler Colonies, 1830-1910* (Manchester: Manchester University Press, 2003), pp. 26–34. For the remarkable story behind the *Report* itself, see Zoë Laidlaw, '"Aunt

Anna's Report"': The Buxton Women and the Aborigines Select Committee, 1835-37', *Journal of Imperial and Commonwealth History*, 32:2 (2004), 1–28.
31 *Report from the Select Committee on Aborigines (British Settlements)*, 1837, p. 45.
32 *Ibid.*, pp. 53, 54, 71.
33 *Ibid.*, p. 47.
34 Alan Lester, 'Humanitarians and White Settlers in the Nineteenth Century', in Norman Etherington (ed.), *Missions and Empire* (Oxford: Oxford University Press, 2005), p. 64.
35 Thompson, 'Time, Work-Discipline and Industrial Capitalism', p. 95.
36 Following Guha – see Ranajit Guha, 'Dominance Without Hegemony and Its Historiography', in R. Guha (ed.), *Subaltern Studies IV: Writings on South Asian History and Society* (Delhi: Oxford University Press, 1994), pp. 281, 296–9, 307 – this study adapts Antonio Gramsci's concept of *egemonia* to the colonial setting, where hegemony is understood as being a condition of dominance such that rule through consent/persuasion outweighs the need for coercion.
37 Frantz Fanon, *A Dying Colonialism*, trans. H. Chevalier (London: Penguin, 1970), pp. 41, 102–10; cf. Guha, 'Dominance without Hegemony', pp. 265–6; Alamin Mazrui and Lupenga Mphande, 'Time and Labor in Colonial Africa: The Case of Kenya and Malawi', in J. K. Adjaye (ed.), *Time in the Black Experience* (Westport, Conn.: Greenwood Press, 1994), p. 115.
38 Frantz Fanon, *The Wretched of the Earth*, trans. C. Farrington (New York: Grove Press, 1963), p. 239.
39 Fanon, *A Dying Colonialism*, pp. 109–10.

CHAPTER ONE

Clocks, Sabbaths and seven-day weeks: the forging of European temporal identities

Shortly after arriving in Matabeleland in 1861, Emily Moffat – daughter-in-law of the famous British missionary to southern Africa, Robert Moffat – penned the following lines in a letter, reminding us that wherever the British went, by the mid-nineteenth century so too did mechanical timekeepers.

> You must know that today we have unpacked our clock and we seem a little more civilized. For some months we have lived without a timepiece. John's chronometer and my watch have failed, and we have left time and been launched onto eternity. However, it is very pleasing to hear 'tic tic tic' and 'ding ding'.[1]

In a society that had come to liken God to a watchmaker and the universe to a clock, a functioning timekeeper had become the embodiment of a universal time sense, a marker of civilisation. Being left without a timepiece was akin to being cut loose from the company of civilised society altogether: to be 'launched onto eternity'.

Consider now a second scene, featuring another Protestant missionary, the Reverend Barnabas Shaw (whom we will encounter again later) as he travelled on horseback in the Cape Colony. 'I was about to see what o'clock it might be,' Shaw recorded in his journal one day, 'but found I had lost my watch – the watch worth about £40 presented to me on leaving the Cape in 1837. I was in great anxiety, and set off to try whether I could discover it.' After retracing his steps for over two miles Shaw succeeded in recovering his precious instrument, which he had dropped in the middle of the road. 'Had any wagons come or had the strong S. East wind been blowing', he reflected, 'it would have been buried in the sand.'[2]

The sense of disquiet which accompanied the earliest clock-bearers to distant lands was palpable whenever their timekeepers were misplaced or failed to function. But how had it come to pass that

European men and women far from home became so reliant on their clocks and watches? What is the history of this society that shaped the clock and eventually became shaped by it instead? And why – we may well ask – were Christian missionaries so well equipped with watches as well as Bibles?

Europeans who travelled to and from the colonies – with or without clocks at their disposal – carried a set of internal temporal values and beliefs that were intrinsically connected to the convictions of their age. Indeed, by the mid-nineteenth century in the British metropolis, a wide cross-section of society had strongly correlated the notions of 'civilisation' and 'true religion' with the accurate measurement and profitable use of time. What came to constitute a 'profitable' use of time was itself a debated issue, as bourgeois identities were being crafted in opposition to working-class attitudes towards time, work and productivity. As this suggests, the idea of time was, and indeed remains, a subjective, contested and shifting notion, divided across lines of class, gender and race: the product of a complex and ongoing interaction between sacred and secular influences, new technologies and old ideologies.[3] This is reflected in the different vernaculars of time which travelled with Britons to the colonies. Settlers, planters, missionaries and officials – men and women – spoke about time in different ways, according to their specific circumstances. These discourses were by no means impermeable to each other, either; they also intersected across lines of class. Many early-nineteenth-century missionaries, for example, came from rural, working-class backgrounds, yet they spoke the middle-class language of time-thrift, 'rational recreation' and respectability. In sum, the colonisers' culture of time, whilst distinct from that of Indigenous populations in other parts of the world, was not itself homogeneous – and neither, presumably, was that of Indigenous populations.

Nevertheless, clocks *were* all the same, their utility and value precisely constituted by their increasing ability to preserve the flow of metropolitan time no matter where they were carried. Similarly, the ritual of the seven-day week was another unvarying manifestation of time that accompanied most Britons to the colonies. As such, clocks and seven-day weeks fulfilled an important cultural and synaptic function, by allowing their bearers not only to measure time and lines of longitude, but also to preserve a sense of connectedness with the metropolis and each other, whilst far from home. Indeed, through their particular expressions of time and their authoritative methods of establishing a sense of 'order' and 'regularity', these two manifestations of time came to function as powerful identity markers of Christianity, civilisation and modernity in the colonies, enabling their bearers to preserve both a feeling of belonging to a Christian, industrialised nation, and a sense of difference between themselves and the clock-less, Sabbath-less societies which they encountered abroad. In this chapter we investigate how, in their ability to generate a rhythm of life that was quite distinct from any other in the world, the clock and the seven-day week reinforced the colonisers' sense of who they were: a modern, God- and time-aware civilisation.

Clocks, conquest and civilisation

> It is therefore with the help of these clocks ... that longitude is found.
>
> Gemma Frisius, *De Principiis Astronomiae Cosmographicae* (1530)

Clocks played an important role from the earliest stages of European imperial expansion. Indeed, the so-called New World was brought within the purview of the Old largely thanks to the science of horology; for the exploration and charting of lands and waters along east- and westward meridians – or 'lines of longitude' – relied on the invention of clocks that could accurately keep time at sea. As first proposed by a Dutch cartographer, Gemma Frisius, the method for calculating longitude with clocks was, in theory, simple. There being 24 hours in a day, 360 degrees in a circle, and the sun moving across the sky at a rate of 15 degrees per hour, longitude is calculated by a simple equation involving the time at the point of observation in relation to that of a known (aka 'prime') meridian. The key to this method, however, depended on the clock's ability to provide the correct time at sea: thus, Frisius instructed, 'while we are on our journey, we should see to it that our clock never stops'.[4] Europe's capacity to rule the seas would depend largely on its ability to keep its clocks ticking accurately. And this was a serious problem in Frisius's day, for the to-and-fro movements of the ships and the variations in temperature, pressure and humidity encountered on long voyages inevitably caused the clocks of the day – with their unbalanced spring-mechanisms – to slow down or speed up, leading to significant errors in the computation of longitude.

The quest for a solution to the problem of longitude sparked a race between rival imperial powers to develop an accurate maritime timekeeper – a captivating story which has been narrated elsewhere, and a fitting prelude to other well-known scrambles for imperial possessions, both by land and sea.[5] Rather than explorers, armies and entrepreneurs, however, it occupied the finest minds in astronomy, clock-making and navigation and culminated in the mid-eighteenth century with the construction of the first accurate marine chronometer (dubbed 'H4'

1.1 Military technology: the 'K1' Larcum Kendall chronometer (1764)
The instrument that guided Captain Arthur Phillip and the First Fleet
to the shores of Australia in 1788.

after its inventor, John 'Longitude' Harrison, who eventually claimed the £20,000 prize held out by the Board of Longitude for the invention of an accurate method for calculating longitude at sea).

The stakes for dominance over time and space were certainly high, as was illustrated by the events that immediately followed the construction of Harrison's H4 chronometer. In late 1775, Captain James Cook of the Royal Navy had returned from his second voyage around the world, the most important secondary aim of which had been the scientific testing of the Larcum Kendall chronometer (code name: 'K1'), an exact replica of H4, which had been built to assess the accuracy of Harrison's original design. (The primary objective of the voyage, of course, had been to 'discover', chart and claim lands – a reconnaissance mission – for the British Crown.) The K1 chronometer was, in effect, military technology and had proved itself, according to Cook's report to the Admiralty, 'a faithful guide through all the vicissitudes of climates'. Accordingly, K1 was redeployed, and made its second trip to the south Pacific in 1787. On this occasion, however, it guided a fleet of eleven ships carrying a crew of over 1,400 colonists, including several convicts and marines. 'The First Fleet' – as it came to be known – arrived at Sydney Cove in January 1788, thus heralding the beginning of the British colony of New South Wales.

'The conquest of space', as Dan Thu Nguyen rightly observes, 'is intrinsically tied to the mastery of time.'[6] Indeed the clock was almost as essential to the colonisation of Australia as the tall ships which carried European settlers to its shores.

But even after distant lands had been 'discovered', seas charted and colonies established, clocks continued to play an indispensable strategic and cultural role. Maintaining an awareness of (clock) time allowed commercial depots, colonial outposts and Christian missions to assume and maintain their nodal position within the circuits of commerce, evangelism and communication which had begun to connect and sustain Britain's growing empire. The clock's ability to quantify time provided a powerful instrument of cognisance and conquest, both of 'undiscovered' lands and 'heathen' souls. Not by chance, the most important instrument David Livingstone claimed to carry on his travels, along with the sextant, was 'a chronometer watch, with a stop to the second hand – an admirable contrivance for enabling a person to take the exact time of observations'.[7] Along with their zeal for evangelising, missionaries brought with them a passion for measuring and quantifying things: times, distances, degrees (of temperature and longitude), altitudes and populations. Always with a timekeeper at hand, they were expert at recording times of events, coordinates and locations. Sometimes they did so in ways which are reminiscent of a soldier calling-in for an air-strike: 'From pretty correct observations', a letter from a missionary in southern Africa reads, 'we are but one hundred and ten miles from the eastern coast of Africa, in south latitude 28° 50', and east longitude 28° 30'. We have forty-four thousand people who are ready to receive the gospel'.[8]

A functioning clock became more than an instrument of conquest. As Emily Moffat suggested, it was also a symbol of civilisation – a means of maintaining a sense of what it meant to feel British and modern, even whilst far from home. This temporal sense of civility was forged in opposition to a perceived temporal primitivity among societies who lacked such devices – a 'defect' often associated with an absence of time itself, and so also seen as an absence of reason and rationality. As historian Michael Adas writes, Europeans' 'perceptions of the material superiority of their own cultures, particularly as manifested in scientific thought and technological innovation, shaped their attitudes toward and interaction with peoples they encountered overseas'.[9] Even the so-called more advanced civilisations in China and India, which employed the use of abstract units and mechanical clocks, were regarded as crude and inaccurate timekeepers by Europe's standards.

Clocks and watches assumed a powerful symbolic function, especially when they were paraded as artifacts of technological superiority in the presence of clock-less societies. On such occasions, the clock was calculated to make an impression on the minds of 'primitive' peoples – even though their reaction was not always one of wonder. Consider the case of John Campbell, an early British missionary to southern Africa, who decided to exhibit his pocket-watch to a group of 'Bushmen' during their very first encounter. The gesture was ostensibly intended to be conciliatory, but the results were quite the opposite. Upon observing its mechanical motion and ticking sound, Campbell related in his journal with amusement, '[the Bushmen] evidently concluded it must be a living animal, and my offering to hold it near their ears, to hear its sound, seemed to convince them it was some dangerous creature, by which I intended to injure them, for they almost overturned the hut in order to escape from the watch'.[10] On another occasion, the German traveller and botanist Heinrich Lichtenstein recorded an encounter with a Xhosa envoy, who was shown a watch and told that 'this instrument kept pace with the sun'. According to Lichtenstein, the man 'gave it back again without saying a word, almost as if offended that he should be told any thing so utterly incredible'.[11] An ability to elicit awe, fear and perplexity among 'the natives' made the clock a powerful psychological weapon.

Even more influential than the clock, however, was the *idea* of time which accompanied Europeans to distant lands: the concept of how time ought to be 'kept', counted and accounted for – in both a moral and a mathematical sense.

Consider the story of the legendary (fictional) castaway, Robinson Crusoe – in many ways a symbol of his age ('the true prototype of the British colonist', as James Joyce described him), who emblazoned the centrality of timekeeping in the English colonial imagination when he resolved to keep a track of the passing days, weeks, months and years on his desert island. Symbolically, the ever-resourceful castaway did not mark the flow of European time via a clock, for this was not one of the artifacts of European civilisation salvaged from the shipwreck that brought him to the island. Instead, the vessel which conveyed time to the island was the mind of the colonist himself. As Crusoe related:

> After I had been there about ten or twelve days, it came into my thoughts, that I should lose my reckoning of time for want of books and pen and ink, and should even forget the Sabbath days from the working days; but to prevent this, I cut it with my knife upon a large post, in capital letters, and making it into a great cross, I set it up on the shore where I first landed, *viz. I came on shore here on the 30th of Sept. 1659.* Upon the sides of this square post, I cut every day a notch with my knife, and every seventh notch was as long again as the rest, and every first day of the month as long again as that long one; and thus I kept my kalandar, or weekly, monthly, and yearly reckoning of time.[12]

With exceptional zeal, Crusoe kept track of the passing of the days, weeks and months as best he could, for more than a quarter of a century – or, to be exact, for 'eight-and-twenty years, two months, and nineteen days', as he was able to confirm in the log book of the ship in which he eventually left the island.[13] Such temporal accountability was the kind of energising myth of imperialism which inspired generations of British evangelical readers. So too was Crusoe's capacity to maintain the daily routines of civilised society by ordering his 'times of work ... time of sleep and time of diversion' and by observing the Sabbath, despite all adversities. Indeed, it was partly thanks to such temporal sagacity that Crusoe became king of the island and master of its inhabitants, and was ultimately delivered to salvation. Mastery of time allowed Crusoe to honour Christian Sundays and to name a savage 'Friday'. Prodigiously, after more than two decades of solitary life, Crusoe was still counting the days of the week; for when his fateful encounter with 'the savage' took place, he stated: 'I let him know his name should be Friday, which was the day I saved his life. I called him so for the memory of the time.'

Christian time and Christian names were elements of civilisation and knowledge which Europeans considered they themselves had brought to 'time-less', anonymous savages. True to this tradition, Crusoe invoked time's symbolic function as a dimension whereby colonisers were able to establish the relations of power between Europe and its Others. Indeed, immediately after naming the savage 'Friday', Crusoe stated: 'I likewise taught him to say Master; and let him know that was to be my name.'[14]

1.2 Robinson Crusoe's calendar, by N. C. Wyeth (1920)
'And thus I kept my kalandar, or weekly, monthly, and yearly reckoning of time'.

Sabbaths and seven-day weeks

> Remember the sabbath day, to keep it holy. Six days shalt thou labour, and do all thy work: But the seventh day is the sabbath of the lord thy God. In it thou shalt not do any work, thou, nor thy son, nor thy daughter, thy manservant, nor thy maidservant, nor thy cattle, nor thy stranger that is within thy gates.
>
> Exodus 20:8–10 (The Fourth Commandment)

'In the beginning', time belonged to God.

For millennia, the human experience of time has been inextricably bound up with nature and mythology. The seven-day week (the term itself deriving from the Old English *wice*: 'a turning', 'alteration', 'succession') is but one example of how humans have long sought to attribute symbolic meaning to the rhythms of nature in order to create institutional rituals that offered a sense of social order. Its origins can be traced back to ancient Babylonian astronomers, who first divided the year into twelve parts (forming the zodiac) and named the days in patterns of seven after their seven planet-gods.[15] Thus it was that the relationship between human time, mythical time and the visible rhythms of the sky was everlastingly preserved and enshrined in the seven-day cycle.

Over the centuries, other societies inherited the idea of the week, maintaining its fundamental order whilst infusing it with their own systems knowledge and mythologies, so as to make it their own. Thus one can trace, for example, how *Ishtar*, the Babylonian goddess of love, war and fertility (personified by the planet Venus) was carried over in the Latin of the Roman week as *dies Veneris* – 'the day of Venus', the goddess of love and desire in the Roman pantheon. As a result, the fifth day of the week is still known in Romance languages as *venerdì*, *vendredi*, and *viernes* – in Italian, French and Spanish, respectively. (The English language did not inherit this cognate owing to its Anglo-Saxon influences, but the mythological legacy of the seven-day cycle is nevertheless present in the English nomenclature of the week-days, in which the Norse goddess of beauty, fertility and death, *Freyja*, lends her name to 'Friday'.)

The Judeo-Christian week and its Sabbath ritual is no different in this regard. Its creators appropriated the same seven-day cycle and infused it with Old Testament lore, according to the belief that God had created the world in six days and rested on the seventh. Backed by the authority of Biblical scripture, the seven-day ritual was subsequently institutionalised as the collective regulator of society, enshrined in the concept of the *Sabbath* (the word itself deriving from the Hebrew,

שבת – *Shabbat*, 'to cease'). Centuries later, the influential nineteenth-century Quaker minister and banker, Joseph John Gurney, would describe the Sabbath as an 'institution founded on a divine pattern – on the recorded example of the Almighty himself', based on the belief that, 'in the march of time, God claims every recurring seventh day as peculiarly his own'.[16]

The Judeo-Christian week, as philosopher of religion Mircea Eliade described it, is 'an *imitation dei*': God had created man in his own image.[17] The early Christians, however, were Jewish, and accordingly imitated God by ceasing work on Saturdays – the seventh day of the Jewish week. The idea of *Sunday* as a day set apart from the rest became specific to Christianity only from the fourth century A.D. The story, recounted here in its barest details, is an apt example of time's ability to forge collective identities. It was Constantine I, the first Christian Roman emperor, who issued the earliest recorded Sunday law: 'On the venerable Day of the Sun', as his famous edict proclaimed in 321 A.D., 'let the magistrates and peoples residing in cities rest, and let all workshops be closed.'[18] Constantine's imperial decree marked the first of numerous laws which would set Sunday apart as a day of special importance for Christians, providing them with a 'portion' of time which was set aside – one with which they could collectively identify. In the process of being integrated into Christianity the Sabbath also acquired its own *raison d'être*: it now commemorated the day of Christ's Resurrection; hence, *dies dominica* ('the Lord's Day') – as it came to be known among Christians.

'One of the most effective ways to accentuate social contrasts', Eviatar Zerubavel reminds us, 'was to establish a *calendrical contrast*.'[19] Thus, as Christianity gained self-consciousness as a distinct group, the Sunday Sabbath came to mark the distinctive rhythm of the followers of Christ. In similar fashion, Islam would later claim its own distinct day for collective worship, *Yawm Al-Jumu'ah* (the 'Day of gathering'), which falls on Friday. Despite their emphasis on a different day of the week, all three of the great monotheistic religions share the underlying seven-day structure of the week, proving that even subtle variations in the organisation of time in society aid the establishment and separation of collective identities.

Time's pre-eminent role as a marker of religious (and, with the passing centuries, national) identity is demonstrated in no better way than by the bitterness and longevity of the conflicts which it subsequently generated – many of which are too intricate to be covered here. The debacle over the computation of Easter, for example, which emerged in the aftermath of the First Council of Nicaea (325 A.D.) when the early Christian fathers had agreed to separate the computation of Easter from that of the Jewish Passover – in what was yet another attempt to separate the ritual identities of Christians and Jews – created schisms which would reverberate across Europe for the next thousand years. This debacle culminated in a reform of the calendar in 1582 by Pope Gregory XIII, which, in turn, created fresh tensions across Post-Reformation Europe as Protestant nations fervently began to dispute not the science so much as the authority of the Catholic Church to alter time.[20]

One of the clearest and most fascinating examples of how calendars can define, and redefine, national and religious identities occurred in 1793, when Revolutionary France made one of its most dramatic breaks with the *ancien régime* by summarily ending the Christian chronology of time altogether and resetting the calendar to the year zero. Inspired by Enlightenment and Romantic ideals, the French Republican calendar proclaimed a new order of time, inspired by nature, mathematics and rationality as a new source of temporal authority. Accordingly, the seven-day week – that key marker of a Christian temporal identity – was completely eliminated by the purge and replaced by a ten-day week, renamed as *décade*. The day itself was divided into ten hours, hours were partitioned into 100 minutes, and minutes into 100 seconds. Meanwhile, a new breed of clocks was designed to mark the decimal hours (a few specimens of which survive today in museums, reminders of a failed revolution in timekeeping).

Even though the life of the Republican calendar was short – lasting only into its thirteenth year (i.e. 1806) – its memory endured for many decades in England among Protestant polemicists, who were provided with a seemingly inexhaustible source of theological ammunition for condemning the Revolution as a revolt against God Himself. 'Malicious design against the highest and best interests of true religion never developed more of the cunning of the old Serpent', one theologian wrote, 'than when the Sabbath was abolished in France and converted into a *Decade* devoted to sensual pleasure'.[21] In the wake of this temporal *coup*, the seven-day week and the Sabbath became even more of a shibboleth of Christian and British identity than it already was: Napoleon was said to personify in flesh and bone God's punishment upon France for its sin of abandoning the Sabbath, whilst rumours circulated in Britain that only a collective observance of the Lord's Day would spare the nation from a similar fate.[22] The logic was sometimes taken to extremes, with John Newton writing to Wilberforce: 'If the breach of the Sabbath was authorised by law, it would alarm me much more than to hear that fifty or a thousand French were landed or that our Grand Fleet was totally destroyed. I should consider it as a decided sign that God had given us up.'[23]

In these ways, time helped to reinforce a collective British, Protestant identity in relation to the calendars of the Other – whether it be the popish feasts of Catholic Rome, the revolutionary calendar of Republican France or the lunar calendar of the Jews.

In the colonies, as we will see, the seven-day week and the Sabbath constituted a pre-eminent symbol of Christianity and Britishness; as far abroad as the Pacific islands, a member of the London Missionary Society could proudly affirm: 'our native land has long been proverbial for Sabbath observance.'[24] In their unshakeable zeal and conviction, missionaries refused to recognise alternative Indigenous rituals – celebrations, feasts, corroborees – as anything but idolatrous superstitions, partly because, *inter alia*, they did not conform to this divine order of time. Such beliefs were founded on theological proclamations of the type: '[t]he division of our time into seven equal parts, and setting aside one out of the seven, for a general and sacred rest, is in itself considered, strictly moral. For if the sabbath is any thing, it is a positive law, and the observation of it must be considered as obedience to a peremptory command.'[25] Accordingly, missionaries who carried the law of the Sabbath from Europe to the colonies often did so under the assumption that it enjoyed a universal jurisdiction among all human societies; for, as Joseph Gurney stated, the Sabbath was deemed 'of universal applicability to our species'.[26] From this it followed, for some, that the *absence* of the Sabbath was a sign of sub-humanness altogether. 'If it should be objected that no foot-steps of it can be traced amongst the savage nations', as William Lewelyn wrote in his *Treatise on the Sabbath* (1783), 'these, in fact, have ceased to be men, and are become brutes.'[27]

Not by chance, as we will see, one of the very first steps that missionaries took in their attempts to 'civilise' so-called savages, was to teach them to count the days in groups of seven.

The monastic legacy

> As the prophet puts it, 'Seven times daily I have praised you.' This sacred number of seven will be performed by us if we carry out the duties of our service at Lauds, Prime, Terce, Sext, None, Vespers and Compline, for it is of these hours of the day that he said, 'Seven times a day I have praised you.'
>
> The Benedictine Rule, Chapter 16

The seven-day week was not the only ritual inspired by God that would profoundly shape the time-consciousness and temporal identity of western-European culture.

In the early years of the sixth century, St Benedict formulated a code of law for organising monastic life which became the model for all subsequent monastic Rules. In accordance with its mandates, the brethren lived a life of asceticism in isolation from the outside world, dedicating their days and nights to prayer, liturgical offices and manual labour, all of which were scheduled according to a strict hourly timetable inspired by a literal reading of the Bible. This daily routine was regulated by the seven periods of prayer, listed above – also known as the canonical hours (*horae canonicae*) – which were intended to act as reminders of the Passion (in which the high priests gather early in the morning; the crucifixion falls on the third hour; Jesus dies at the end of the ninth and is laid in the tomb at dusk).[28]

Acoustic signals (*signa*) were employed to announce the hours of the day, and the most common instrument for announcing the canonical hours was the *bell*. The ringing of the bell was a serious matter within the fortress-like walls of the monastery. As the Rule decreed, 'the indicating of the hour for the Work of God by day and by night shall be the business of the abbot. Let him either do it himself or entrust the duty to such a careful brother that everything may be fulfilled at its proper time.'[29] This complete authority assigned to the bell in the monastic *milieu* established a strong precedent for the centralised control of time that would be exercised centuries later in factories and schools – and also, as we will see, on colonial missions. As in factories and schools, the bell's tolls were given precedence over all other tasks and activities in the monastery: 'As soon as the signal for the Divine Office is heard', the Rule ordered, 'the brethren must leave whatever they have been engaged in doing, and hasten with all speed, but with dignity.'[30] This system resulted in collective punctuality becoming the specific focus of monastic life.[31]

According to David Landes, the fact that Christianity – alone among the great monotheistic religions – called for prayers at times defined in hourly terms explains why the Christian Church became the most active medieval institution backing the invention and perfection of devices that could measure time ever more accurately.[32] Indeed, monastic orders were, in Foucault's words, 'the specialists of time, the great technicians of rhythm and regular activities.'[33] However, before the invention of the first European mechanical clocks, monastic communities relied on a host of relatively inaccurate devices and contraptions designed to keep track of time: water clocks, shadow-tables, sand-glasses and sundials marked the hours of daylight; while star observation, candle-clocks and oil-clocks kept track of the hours at night. And in the mornings, it was still the cock's crow that provided the day's first temporal cue. Being dependent on natural variables and human agency, such technology was subject to frequent errors. But the Benedictine Rule compensated for this by promoting the internalisation of a general awareness of time as a *psychological* deterrent towards tardiness.[34] Indeed, given that lateness was effectively treated as a sin, and properly punished (the Rule clearly defined penalties, from small castigation to excommunication, for those careless enough to fall behind the prescribed routine), a neurosis about 'being on time' became a common anxiety within the monastic community. 'Run while ye have the light of life, lest the darkness of death overtake you', the Rule's Prologue exhorted the brethren. It was therefore in the early Christian monasteries that time-discipline was first coupled with a discourse of morality, and its waste explicitly associated with sin. 'Idleness is the enemy of the soul', was one of St Benedict's most famous pronouncements.[35]

Foreshadowing the veneration of uniform, coordinated behaviour which would later become iconic of the 'modern' and industrial era, the monasteries were the earliest European institutions to demonstrate the benefits of synchronising the activities of human subjects, both as a means of enhancing the collective power of prayer and also of increasing the efficiency of manual labour.[36] All this generated a rhythm quite distinct from that of the agricultural laity outside the abbey, where the pace of life was still that of 'an economy dominated by agrarian rhythms, careless of exactitude, unconcerned by productivity'.[37] Historian Nigel Thrift aptly describes medieval monasteries as 'islands of timekeeping in a sea of timelessness' – an image that we will encounter again in descriptions of colonial mission stations.[38] Gradually, however, as the monastic influence started to make itself felt among the adjacent lay communities, countryside and market-places, so too did the custom of marking the hours come to be associated with the sound of the bell. This was no small influence, for at the height of its success there were as many as forty thousand monasteries working under the Benedictine Rule.[39]

Much like the monastery, Christian missions in the colonies would be established as the providers of divinely-sanctioned time to peoples thought of as living beyond the pale of God and civilisation. Both institutions came to be portrayed by their respective communities as keepers of order and regularity amid the perceived spiritual and temporal 'wilderness' – their clock-governed rituals and routines functioning as a means of identifying and separating insiders from outsiders, the saved from the heathen. Indeed in their daily exertions, and in their quest to establish patterns of regularity in work and prayer, missionaries seem to have been inspired by the monastic model: the ringing of the mission bell, like the monastic bell, signalled the regular hours of the clock and its audible range provided surrounding peoples with a new means of orienting themselves in time. As a European traveller commented during a visit to the Moravian missionaries in southern Africa: 'All the communities of Brethren over the whole earth, at the same hour, morning and evening are united in singing the hymn appointed for that day'.[40] Through such veneration of synchronised activities, missionaries constituted a living link between the temporal culture of the medieval monasteries of western Christendom and the colonial outposts of Empire.

The secularisation of time

The centuries separating the age of the monastery from that of the factory witnessed a crucial shift in western European time-consciousness, characterised by the gradual secularisation of 'sacred time' through the influence of what Jacques Le Goff has called 'merchant's time'.[41] The rise of mercantilism from the thirteenth and fourteenth centuries successfully introduced a form of temporal materialism that challenged the hegemonic status previously enjoyed by the Church's sacred monopoly on time. In the process of this amalgamation, 'merchant's time' and 'God's time' gradually came to share the role of shaping the dominant culture of time in Western Europe.

It was during this critical period that the practical necessity for a more accurate method of keeping time set the scene for the entrance of the clock. The first reports of a European mechanical clock (the word 'clock' itself deriving from the German *glocken*, the French *cloche*, and the Latin *clocca*, all of which mean 'bell') appeared in the late thirteenth century (although this was not the world's first mechanical clock).[42] Its subsequent diffusion throughout Europe was triggered, according to Dohrn-van Rossum, by the rise of mercantile activity between 1300 and 1350, when the increased need for time-based transactions across growing urban centres, the reintroduction of money and gold coinage and the emergence of the first monetary fluctuations and inflationary market trends began to call for a more definite measure of time, leading to the erection of the first public clocks across the towns and cities of western Europe.[43] Placed high up on towers and opposite church bell steeples in towns and cities, their urban proliferation in the fourteenth century ensured an increasingly precise definition of time and of the collective notion of 'punctuality'.[44]

Importantly, the mechanisation of the clock heralded the first clear signs of man-made devices supplanting nature as the main provider of time to humans. During the age of the sundial, the lengths of days waxed and waned in unison with the earth's elliptical orbit around the sun, making the hours of the day appear shorter in winter and longer in summer. But the mechanical clock, based on a division of the day into twelve equal and unvarying parts, divorced itself from the visible oscillation of the planet around its star and began counting the hours even whilst the sun was out of sight. The gradual adoption of *equal-length* hours in the public domain which accompanied the rise of the mechanical clock, was nothing less than a revolution in human time-consciousness – one that became evermore common from the fourteenth century as trade and commerce in the rapidly growing urban centres of Europe became more complex, multifarious and increasingly circadian. Once abstracted in this way, clock-time could be subdivided into smaller abstract units: half, third and quarter hours, and – by the end of the sixteenth century – into sixty minutes.[45]

This abstraction of time from nature's rhythms would become yet another defining feature for European of the superiority of Western technology over societies for whom nature remained the sole provider of time. (Clock-time – as Emily Moffat implied – is civilised time, *par excellence*.) It was through this gradual separation from nature's rhythms that time was humanised and that humans were able to see timekeepers as avatars and reflections of their own Selves. It was not by coincidence that, during this period, clocks started to function as markers of identity and measures of technological progress in European society. The precision, craftsmanship and beauty of clocks quickly became symbols of status and prestige. 'From the beginning of the fifteenth century', Dohrn-van Rossum writes, 'possession of a public clock was part of a city's self-identity... [t]he expensive design of the public clock increased a city's renown and bolstered its self-confidence'.[46] The deep-seated relationship between clocks and identity, which caused such great importance to be placed on time as a measure of status, was fundamental to the formation of European temporal culture.

In the emerging temporal landscape that was gradually shaped by the mechanical clock, time also helped forge social boundaries within European communities. The acoustic range of bells, for example, helped construct the territorial identity of individual suburbs within cities. Thus, in the acoustically-dense environment of early-modern London, it was commonly known that the loudest of all church bells was that of St Mary-le-Bow. Such was its influence that it signalled the start and end of the workday for those living within its audible range (with any tardiness in its ringing prompting workers to complain, *'Clarke of the Bow bell with the yellow lockes,/ For thy late ringing thy head shall haue knockes.'*) According to historian Bruce Smith, the proverbial association between the Bow bell's acoustic range and 'your true Londoner' was already current by 1617, when Fynes Morrison stated that 'Londiners, and all within the sound of Bow-Bell, are in reproch called Cocknies, and eaters of buttered tostes'.[47] Indeed, 'the emotional impact of a bell', historian Alan Corbin suggests, 'helped create a territorial identity for individuals living always within range of its sound.'[48] As we will see, the bells' ability to define the territorial identities for populations living within their audible range would be of particular use to missionaries, as they sought to extend the influence of Christian time beyond settler-colonial frontiers.

However, the most profound impact on European temporality occurred once the bell and the clock were introduced into the workplace, where they gradually reshaped the fundamental rhythms of human labour and cycles of production. Prior to this, the work pattern of labourers in the agricultural and artisan centres of pre-industrial Europe had been characterised essentially by sporadic activity: it had always been a case of 'alternate bouts of intense labour and of idleness, wherever men were in control of their own working lives'.[49] This began to change as the rising mercantile classes introduced the work-bell into the workplace with the intent of monitoring the length of the working day and ensuring that workers did not cheat employers of their money. Starting in the fourteenth century in the textile-manufacturing centres of continental western Europe – the most developed industrial sectors of their time – and quickly spreading to the rest of Europe, the bell became the regulator of work rhythms in the factory and the workshop, backed by the increasing exactitude of the mechanical clock and enforced with ever more draconian penalties for the tardy. The rise of capitalism and the work-clock thus went hand in hand: time became a quantifiable measure of exchange-value in the marketplace for trading in the commodity of human labour, the currency in which the workers' lives – their time, reified – was bought and sold. (Thus 'the economy of work', as Marx observed, 'becomes the economy of time'.)[50]

Accordingly, the rising merchant classes made the objective of controlling work and production rhythms one of their top priorities. For, approaching the dawn of the industrial revolution even greater demands for clock-governed work rhythms were required: temporal uniformity became vital for the heightened degree of coordination between increasingly distant workers – workers at different stages of production, producing goods in different factories, in different towns. Attempts to re-orientate workers' rhythms towards the clock, rather than the task, implied a collective shift in time-consciousness, which intensified during the transition from agricultural to large-scale industrial society. Duly, unpunctuality became a potential threat, not merely to financial profits but to the very order of society: absenteeism and lateness threatened to undermine that order; and 'irregularity' – a quality which came to be (re)defined as deviant and troublesome – was targeted for elimination.

Collective obedience to the clock was not so much taught as imposed, upon the masses. Jacques Le Goff's and E. P. Thompson's seminal accounts of this process suggest that the collective shift in Europe towards an industrial-capitalist time-consciousness took the form of a cultural war waged against pre-industrial rhythms and patterns of work and life. This view bears strongly on the colonial scenario, where, as we will see, a similar cultural assault was launched against the perceived irregularity of Indigenous work patterns and lifestyles. In both settings, resistance and compromises played a part in stipulating the terms of life under the clock's regime. Indeed it was not long before European workers came to resent their bondage to the increasingly regimented timetables and the harsh laws and penalties being imposed upon them for lateness and sluggishness. Protests in the form of uprisings against the work-clock were not uncommon.[51] Gradually, however, the clock's dominant role as the 'keeper' of time in society was secured.

Even so, the struggle over time never stopped: time has remained the single most important issue in labour disputes ever since, with demands for shorter working days in the nineteenth century leading to the Factory Acts, Bank Holidays Acts, the forty-hour week and, in the twentieth century, to paid-overtime and time-off 'in lieu'. The definitive step had already been taken, however, from the moment at which workers began to talk about time, work and wages in the language of the clock, consenting to fight – as E. P. Thompson famously put it – 'not against time, but about it'.[52]

'Redeem the time': evangelical influence in nineteenth-century Britain

> Men of business are accustomed to quote the maxim that Time is money; but it is more; the proper improvement of it is self-culture, self-improvement, and growth of character.
>
> Samuel Smiles, *Self Help* (1859)

Coinciding with the age of colonialism, the fervent religious revival which swept across Great Britain from the mid-eighteenth gave rise to a number of key developments in time-consciousness which deeply shaped British society and consequently influenced much of the world over the course of the nineteenth century.

Evangelicalism, according to Ian Bradley, was 'never really a theological system so much as a way of life' – one that had an enormous impact on British society.[53] As a popular movement, it initially belonged to the working classes, the millions who had been neglected by the established Church amid the turbulent impact of the industrial age. In this context, Evangelical belief became, as one historian put it, 'the necessary religion for the Industrial Revolution'.[54] By the early nineteenth century, however, the broad principles of evangelicalism began to spread upwards in the social ranks, affecting the entire structure of British society. Inspired by the doctrine of the total depravity of man and of salvation through personal conversion, one of its strongest single characteristics during the early nineteenth century was the missionary movement, whose zeal for proselytising came to be directed towards both the English working classes and, through the spearheading of missions across the Empire, non-European societies.

One of the greatest preoccupations of Britain's middle-class evangelicals was time itself. Endlessly advocating the virtues of regularity and punctuality and obsessed with a millenarian belief in the Day of Judgment, when all men would be called forth to account for their actions on earth, middle-class evangelicals revived the monastic tradition of temporal asceticism by scrupulously accounting for every hour of the day. It became customary, for example, to keep a diary as an assurance that no time would go to waste.[55] 'I have lived twenty-two years', wrote Edward Bickersteth as he contemplated evangelical conversion in his youth, '[t]hat is nearly two hundred thousand hours and twelve million minutes; for the employment of every one of those minutes I am accountable to God ... what a mountain of iniquities does this at once discover.'[56]

All this meshed well with the world of banking, business and commerce, in which large numbers of the middle classes were profitably employed. As Ian Bradley comments, evangelical values of temporal accountability and thrift 'could almost have been designed deliberately for businessmen and financiers'.[57] By the end of the eighteenth century, Protestantism and capitalism – God and Mammon – had converged to a point of mutual agreement, as parish priests and members of the gentry came to resemble each other in the way they spent their time.[58] Accordingly, notions of time were often expressed in a hybrid discourse of sacred and merchant time; in terms of financial loss and divine profit: for time was a sacred trust from God – and God, Thomas Gisborne wrote, 'expects his own with usury'.[59]

The nineteenth-century fusion between the temporal materialism of capitalism and the temporal austerity of Protestant evangelicalism produced a distinctly obsessive culture of time. E. P. Thompson alluded

1.3 'Family Prayers', by Samuel Butler (1864)

to the nature of this merger when he wrote that, 'Puritanism, in its marriage of convenience with industrial capitalism, was the agent which converted men to new valuations of time; which taught children even in their infancy to improve each shining hour; and which saturated men's minds with the equation, time is money.'[60] As the sacred and secular influences of Christianity and industrial-capitalism combined, weeks, hours, minutes and seconds – *fiat* currency in a moral economy of time – assumed a commodified and a religious value in themselves. A fetishisation of time generated a fixation on how this currency was spent, used, saved, wasted, invested and redeemed. In the interests maintaining the established social and economic order, the ruling classes developed methods of enforcing its dominance and policing its use. Time was centralised and became increasingly ubiquitous; fenced-in, yet increasingly invasive. Children's time had to be disciplined, women's time had to be domesticated, and workers' time in general had to be counted, supervised and coordinated through timetables, schedules, clocks, bells and whistles – the ritual- and routine-compellers of civilised society.

The ways in which the ruling classes viewed time reflected the dominant ideals of British society. Thus, in middle-class circles, the Protestant ethic of work, moderation and temperance came to be

1.4 Working-class family prayers (1849)

appropriately reflected in the image of the clock; for the clock was the key symbol of correct proportions.[61] Likewise, the seven-day week was enshrined as the paradigm for the correct ordering of the days in society. 'Time then presents a perfect whole ... when it is shaped into a week', stated Sir William Smith's popular *Dictionary of the Bible* (1863); 'modelled on the six days of creation and their following Sabbath ... Six day's work and the seventh day's rest conform the life of man to the method of his Creator.'[62]

This suited the interests of the ruling classes, in whose eyes an ideal pattern had developed by the mid-1900s: ordinary people should work five full days, Monday to Friday, and one shorter day, Saturday.[63] The Sabbath was a convenient way of moralising the enforcement of such work rhythms: telling workers that the seventh day was a mandatory day of rest implied that the remaining six days should be seen as mandatory days of work. In recompense, the middle-classes promoted the moral benefits of Sabbatarianism. In the language of social improvement, its advocates referred to the Lord's Day as the 'light of the week', 'torch of time', 'pearl of days', 'heaven's antidote to the curse of labour', often blending religious and capitalist rhetoric to rather shameless extents. As one moral treatise reads:

> A seventh portion of our time – fifty-two Sabbaths in every year, and ten years of Sabbaths, or 3650 days, in a life of threescore years and ten – is thus redeemed from secular pursuits, and becomes the especial property of mind. Oh, what intellectual riches would the Sabbath hours of an average life, wisely husbanded, enable us to hoard![64]

Sunday legislation – previously dominated by theological rhetoric – gradually acquired a discourse of social welfare which was aimed above all at workers. Already in the mid-eighteenth century, as William Blackstone's *Commentaries on the Laws of England* declared, the observance of the Lord's Day was considered a matter of social significance. 'Besides the notorious indecency and scandal of permitting any secular business to be publicly transacted on that day in a country professing Christianity', Blackstone wrote,

> keeping one day in the seven holy, as a time of relaxation and refreshment as well as for public worship, is of admirable service to a state, considered merely as a civil institution. *It humanizes*, by the help of conversation and society, the manners of the lower classes, which would otherwise *degenerate into a sordid ferocity and savage selfishness* of spirit; it enables the industrious workman to pursue his occupation in the ensuing week with health and cheerfulness; it imprints on the minds of the people that sense of their duty to God so necessary to make them good citizens, but which yet would be worn out and defaced by an unremitted continuance of labour, *without any stated times* of recalling them to the worship of their Maker.[65]

In Protestant middle-class discourse, the Sabbath represented a moral pillar of the established social order, providing a lifeline to the 'lower classes' to avert an otherwise inevitable degeneration to the level of savages. (The latter, as we will see in the colonial setting, would be defined as such partly in lieu of 'stated times of recalling them to the worship of their Maker'.) Indeed, at a time when ideas of racial difference were finding popular acceptance in society, images of 'degeneration' and of 'sordid ferocity and savage selfishness' evoked the sense that to be human and civilised was to know the times appropriate to things. Accordingly, the Sabbath became a key factor in the forging of notions of race, class and gender. It represented the temporal nexus between the dominant secular and sacred rhythms of society, tying together the rituals of Christianity and the ethic of regular work and the uniform routines of industrial-capitalism, whilst also upholding the gendered order of bourgeois society by privileging the role of the male patriarch, upon whom the duty fell to ensure that prayer times and the Sabbath were observed among the women and children. (In the colonial setting, this role would be taken up by paternalistic missionaries ministering among the 'natives' whom they would, in turn, regard as children.)

A direct result of all this was that the language of social improvement – both in the metropolis and the colony – was often couched in the discourse of temporal reform, directed not merely at the sphere of work but particularly towards that of leisure. 'In mature capitalist society, all time must be consumed, marketed, put to *use*', writes Thompson; 'it is offensive for the labour force merely to "pass the time".'[66] The lifestyles of workers in the metropolis and 'natives' in the colonies were seen by the ruling classes to afford an excess of 'free' time which merely encouraged idleness – a privilege which the leisured classes were wont to reserve for themselves. The attack on leisure time called for a definitive break with pre-industrial culture – one which had never made such clear distinctions between 'work' and 'life'.[67] Workers' so-called 'free time' was increasingly 'colonised' as customary practices of popular recreation in Britain came under the reform and supervision of the ruling classes, who passed legislation against Sabbath-breaking, significantly shaping the social habits of British society well into the twentieth century. Thus ensued the proliferation of lobbies against secular activities targeting all pastimes and entertainments which desecrated the Sabbath: the Society for the Suppression of Vice – founded in 1802 – which clocked up 623 successful prosecutions for breaking the Sabbath laws in 1801 and 1802 alone; the Society for Promoting the Observance of the Sabbath (1809); and the Lord's Day Observance Society (1831) which outlawed trading, professional entertainment and sport on Sundays.[68] Simultaneously, the process of erosion of popular holidays in Britain was in full swing by the early nineteenth century, as Protestant England purged its public calendar of popular festivities, feasts, wakes and saints' days fostered by Catholicism – whose calendar was said to encourage idleness and laziness through its indulgent over-abundance of feasts and saints' days.[69]

As if the drastic curtailing of popular holidays and pastimes were not enough, attempts were also made to dictate the manner in which the working classes should spend their remaining time. According to evangelical ideals, recreation had to be ordered, disciplined, improving and educational. Missionaries took up the call and preached forms of 'rational recreation' to the working classes as a means of improving themselves and society; and for every increment in the workers' free time, it appeared necessary to fill the latter with moral, sober and self-improving activities.[70] The Yorkshire evangelicals who launched the Ten Hours Movement in 1830 secured vital reductions from the cruel, fifteen-hour workdays; but they also advocated the reinvestment of the newly acquired time in religious instruction.[71] Thus, in 1847, with the passing of the Ten Hours Bill, January Searle stated: 'now ... there is leisure enough for the working classes to get wisdom and understanding'.[72]

The Methodists, who sparked off the first great English evangelical revival in the late 1730s – and whose emissaries to the colonies in the nineteenth century we will encounter throughout later chapters – were particularly well-known for their temporal asceticism. Their leader, John Wesley, rose every morning at four until the age of eighty, ordering that the pupils at Kingswood School should do the same. (His sermons were clear in their condemnation of those who lay in bed for eight hours: 'all who indulge themselves in this manner are in the way to hell'.)[73] Methodism was successful in serving simultaneously as the religion of the industrial bourgeoisie as well as a wide proportion of the working-classes.[74] And whilst no single explanation can account for working-class adherence to Methodist values, indoctrination from a tender age was certainly a major factor: 'The pressures towards discipline and order', E. P. Thompson writes, 'extended from the factory, on one hand, the Sunday school, on the other, into every aspect of life: leisure, personal relationships, speech, manners.'[75]

Time-thrift propaganda was also rife: 'in early Victorian tracts and reading-matter aimed at the masses, one is choked by the quantity of the stuff'.[76] One of the great success stories of Victorian publishing was in fact Samuel Smiles' moral treatise *Self Help* (1859). Selling twenty thousand copies in the year of its publication and nearly a quarter of a million by the end of the century, it had a status second only to the Bible in many Victorian homes. One passage reads:

> Lost wealth may be replaced by industry, lost knowledge by study, lost health by temperance or medicine, but lost time is gone for ever ... An economical use of time is the true mode of securing leisure.[77]

And for the younger generation, Isaac Watts' *Divine Songs of Children* (1715) were taught at Sunday School for toddlers to sing.[78] 'Against Idleness and Mischief', was an old-time favourite:

> How doth the little busy bee
> Improve each shining hour,

And gather honey all the day
From every open flower!

Approaching the nineteenth century, as they became ever more common for the lower classes, schools gradually became incubators for new, clock-compliant generations of workers. Sunday Schools became one of the most effective institutions for inculcating submission to the clock and bell – whose signals children were taught to obey from an early age.[79] In words that echo Benedict's Rule, the regulations of one Methodist Sunday School decreed that, 'every scholar must be in the school-room on Sundays, at nine o'clock in the morning, and at half past one in the afternoon, or she shall lose her place the next Sunday, and walk last'.[80] The schools in York were known to fine even the teachers for unpunctuality.

Of course, working-class conformity to middle-class values was by no means total: 'drunkenness and uproar still often surged the streets'. By 1830, both the Established Church and the Methodists were meeting sharp opposition from freethinkers, Owenites, and non-denominational Christians. Strikes, idleness, lateness and truancy would always interrupt the bourgeois and Christian order of society; whilst St Monday continued to be venerated in some areas of England throughout the nineteenth century, as evinced by the many Victorian temperance tracts that targeted it.[81] Sundays became a site of struggle, too, with working-class spokespersons upholding with increasing confidence the right to a day of respite both from the church and the workplace: a reprieve from endless toil, and an opportunity to visit theatres, parks, the countryside, the pub or the races. George Holyoake, a well-known Owenite and member of the Birmingham Chartists, was a notoriously outspoken critic of evangelical Sabbatarianism. 'Why should it not be a day of pleasure?' was his response to local church ministers who had expressed 'intense concern' at reports of the newly re-constructed Crystal Palace remaining open on Sundays. 'The precept, "Keep the Sabbath-day holy,"' Holyoake declared during a public debate in 1853, 'we would interpret [as] keeping it healthfully, usefully, instructively.' Instead of prayers and austerity, the workers' Sabbath, 'would take, when necessary, the poor factory-jaded Sunday scholars into fields – that school-room of nature! It would throw open the Clyde on the Sunday to the Sunday steamer, that the poor Glasgow weaver might gaze on Ben Lomond on the Lord's-day. It would give the mechanic access to museums, and botanical gardens, and crystal palaces, and even to the theatre on that day.'[82]

Debates such as these over Sunday conduct were common during the nineteenth-century – a reminder that time was a site of social tension even within British society. Nevertheless, although society disagreed on *what* workers ought to be doing on Sundays, most people generally agreed over *when* they should be doing it. Few disputed the underlying order of the seven-day week. The result, by the mid-nineteenth century, was the institution of Sunday as a day apart from the rest, with the seven-day cycle emerging as commonly accepted ritual for most Britons.

Standard-time and modernity

> Have men not improved somewhat in punctuality since the railroad was invented? ... To do things 'railroad fashion' is now the by-word; and it is worth the while to be warned so often and so sincerely by any power to get off its track.
>
> Henry David Thoreau, *Walden* (1854)

The clock's dominant position in Western society having been secured, the nineteenth century witnessed the quest for uniformity and global centralisation to ensure that all clocks, and people, kept time together. Clock-synchrony was propelled above all by the speeding-up of life that accompanied the age of steam-driven transport and electric communication: 1825 was the year of the first passenger train and 1827 the first crossing of the Atlantic under steam power; 1836 witnessed the advent of the electric telegraph. As industrialisation started to kick into full-swing, the extent to which human patterns of work and life were standardised and harmonised with one another on a global scale increased dramatically. Temporal synchronicity would indeed become a defining feature of a sense of 'modernity'.

The mid-nineteenth century marked another watershed in the formation of a Western culture of time insofar as it witnessed a major step in the abstraction of human-time from nature's time. As we have seen, mechanical clocks already did not keep true solar time, but rather an approximation of the sun's position in the sky – that is, *mean* solar time. Nevertheless, prior to the standardisation of time in the mid-nineteenth century, it was common for each town to keep a *local* form of mean time, by setting public clocks according to the position of the sun in the sky as seen from each locality. Thus there were as many positions for the minute hands on Europe's dials as there were towns under the sun.[83] Moreover, different cities in Europe used different systems for talking about clock-time: Basel's day, for instance, began at noon (although it was called one o'clock, which meant that it always ran one hour ahead of its neighbours). Some localities divided the day into twenty-four hours (known as 'Italian time'), others halved it into twelve-hour rounds (known as 'German hours' in Bohemia and 'French hours' in Italy).[84]

But the coming of steam-driven transport and the galvanic telegraph meant that faster methods of travel and communication drastically reduced the distance between people and places, both in space and time.[85] And as the circulation of information and commodities through the railway, telegraph and faster mail services accelerated, a uniform definition of time soon became indispensable if passengers and goods were to depart from one locality and arrive at another safely and on time. Soon, the ability to know 'the' time depended on having access to an accurate watch. (Not surprisingly, watch production proliferated dramatically during the first three-quarters of the nineteenth century, with worldwide output increasing almost tenfold, from 350–400 thousand to 2.5 million pieces a year.[86]) During the process of this shift, the rhythms of society were gradually reoriented around a new source of temporal authority, driven by the exigencies of major business and mercantile interests – a new Chronos, of which the train was an apt symbol: fast, linear, unidirectional, and confident of its destination. Victorians 'took the train to be modernity's cutting edge', Ian Carter writes.[87] Indeed the train became a symbol of speed and efficiency, of man's triumph over the limitations of nature, providing a new paradigm for the concept of 'regularity'. For similar reasons, the telegraph became an icon of the modern era: its capacity to transcend time and space altogether provided the first glimpse of a cosmopolitan world. 'A cable lying far down in the depths of the Indian Ocean gives us the "planet's daily murmur",' wrote a missionary from the southernmost tip of Africa – 'not in the *London Times* but in the *Cape Times*, *Argus*, or *Mercury*: or we can have it at the rate of 9s 4d a word, if we choose to pay for it.'[88] This instantaneous transmission of 'intelligence' drew contemporary writers to compare it to the human nervous system (more than one quoted Job 38:35 – 'Canst thou send lightnings, that they may go and say unto thee, Here we are?').[89] The telegraph was also an indispensable tool for commercial and imperial expansion. By enabling the imperial centre to monitor its colonial peripheries, noted Sandford Fleming, Chief Engineer of the Canadian Pacific Railways, it 'subjects the whole surface of the globe to the observation of civilized communities'.[90]

Having broken the local-time barrier, the railways were the first to abandon regional timetables, gradually replacing them with a single standard-time across their networks. In England this took place in 1848 when all the rail stations agreed to set their clocks to London time, otherwise known as GMT. In order to achieve this level of temporal coordination, Britain's Astronomer Royal, George Airy, was actively campaigning by the end of the 1840s to connect the Greenwich Observatory to the telegraph network so as to relay the GMT time signal by galvanic current throughout Britain. From 1852, electrical clocks across England were being activated by electrical pulses transmitted along the telegraph laid alongside the major rail networks. (Suggestively, these remote-controlled clocks were known as 'slave' clocks, whilst Greenwich's were known as 'master clocks'.) Time-balls were activated by galvanic current in a similar way, providing a daily display of the official time by being raised and lowered at exactly one o'clock GMT thus allowing ship captains to adjust their chronometers to the recognised time standard. Rapidly, towns and cities across Britain followed suit by giving up their 'real', local times and setting their clocks to railway time, so that by 1855 nearly all public clocks were set to GMT – effectively placing all of Britain into a single 'time zone'.

Despite pockets of opposition, the same general pattern unfolded rapidly throughout Europe, where, by 1870, over 50,000 miles of railway lines stretched across the continent.[91] But nowhere was the annihilation of local time more evident than in the United States, where by 1869 the first trans-*continental* railway connected distant cities on the Pacific and Atlantic coasts. Thoreau sensed the shift taking place two decades earlier, from his quiet sanctuary at Walden Pond: 'The startings and arrivals of the [train] cars are now the epochs in the village day', he noted. 'They go and come with such regularity and precision, and their whistle can be heard so far, that the farmers set their clocks by them, and thus one well conducted institution regulates a whole country.'[92] Thoreau's vision was accurate enough: by 1883, all regional and local-time zones had been substituted by four standard-time zones, similar to those in use today. And, by the turn of the century, 'standard time' was effectively ubiquitous. 'To the degree that they thought about it at all', historian Michael O'Malley writes, 'most Americans came to understand standard clock-time as "Time" itself.'[93]

The age of temporal heterogeneity gave way to the age of standardised uniformity, a trend that was reflected across society as evinced by the drastic transformation of the calendar (still the most widespread guide to the passage of time in the middle of the century). Local almanacs in Britain, as Maureen Perkins has documented, were gradually discontinued and replaced by the new, 'universal' calendar, exemplified by *Whitaker's*, which first appeared in 1869. Divested of 'local colour' – feasts, wakes and weather predictions – *Whitaker's* was fit for being distributed throughout the country by the expanding railway network.[94]

The way it was measured and conceived had changed drastically, but one thing remained constant: time still operated as a marker of identity. 'There is sublimity in the idea of a whole nation stirred by one impulse', wrote Henry Booth, Secretary of the Liverpool and Manchester Railway; 'in every arrangement, one common signal regulating the movements of a mighty people!'[95] An efficient, reliable and coordinated railway system became (at least to the middle classes) a matter of national pride. 'We can, on an English railway, always obtain correct time', bragged George Airy, 'but not so on a French or German railway, where the clocks are often found considerably in error.'[96] The perception that the British were a punctual people was exported far and wide, thanks to the symbol of the railway. 'Punctuality is said to have been taught to English people by the railways, and no one may live in hope of being more regardful of time in South Africa', a white teacher told his African colleagues; 'but at present the Native people of this Colony are notoriously unpunctual.' Later in his lecture, the same teacher referred again to the railway analogy in order to convey the importance of punctuality in the classroom: 'If the train delayed until all intending passengers found it convenient to take their seats, it would stand in the station all day.'[97] The message was clear: humans had to keep time, not with one another, but with the clock; 'time waits for no man'.

The visions of uniformity which permeated bourgeois discourse in the metropolis reflected a sense of foreboding towards extraneous movements of people – both the peregrinations of gypsies and vagrants in Europe and the nomadic rhythms of Indigenous people in the colonies. In the age of centralisation and uniformity, as the maintenance of the established social order came to be geared around protecting the regular flow of clock-time, a failure or refusal to march to the drum of the clock was labelled ever-more explicitly as deviant and troublesome behaviour – even madness. 'Madmen' were included in the proscription of idleness, as Michel Foucault found; '[i]n the workshops in which they were interned, they distinguished themselves by their inability to work and to follow the rhythms of collective life'.[98] A discourse of temporal aberrance helped to entrench the sense that to be normal was to know the time proper to things. (And still today, from both a psychiatric and popular perspective, not knowing the day or date is considered a classical symptom of insanity.)

Against such anxieties, temporal uniformity and centralisation provided a comforting antidote, making the future more certain.[99] Indeed the science of forecasting flourished in the nineteenth century, becoming yet another defining feature of a sense of modernity in its ability to predict the unknown – from weather forecasts and eclipses to passing comets and unsighted planets. At the same time, tales of 'primitive' peoples paralysed with fear during an eclipse became imperial clichés for expressing the backwardness and irrationality of 'savages' (see figure 4.1).[100] As we will see in the following chapters, it was by way of opposition to the temporal cultures of so-called primitive and superstitious societies that European temporal technologies and attitudes helped to crystallise a discourse of modernity and civility; for time operated as a dimension of life through which European identities were forged during the colonial encounter.

―◆◇◆―

The trend towards the centralisation of time did not stop at the geographical borders of Europe but continued until it had encompassed the entire globe. It was Sir Sandford Fleming, Chief Engineer of the Canadian Pacific Railways, who, in 1876 (so the popular story goes), after missing a regional train connection in Ireland that cost him sixteen hours of 'monumental vexation', began to push for the adoption of a single definition of time for the whole world.[101] Fleming's vision for a more punctual world would be realised remarkably soon, although it would take several more decades before all countries and colonies adopted the new system. World time (or 'Cosmic Time' – Fleming's suggestion for the term) was established in 1884, when representatives of twenty-five nations convened at the International Meridian Conference in Washington, D.C. 'to devise a perfect system of time reckoning for the whole world' and to establish a common zero for measuring longitude.[102] The delegates represented the twenty-five independent nations recognised by the United States as 'civilised' – which of course excluded the vast majority of the world's people. Unperturbed by this level of under-representation, the delegates agreed by vote that the line of longitude passing through the British Royal Observatory at Greenwich would henceforth be adopted as the Prime Meridian of the world. As other nations one by one gradually adopted GMT as their official and public time standard, London effectively became the centre of the world as far as the definition of time was concerned.

Running parallel to the colonial conquest of territory was a powerful claim to the definition of a single notion of time, to which the nascent globalised world was expected to conform. Over the course of the following chapters, however, we will see that GMT represents only half the story of how that claim was asserted and enforced on the ground, amongst those societies which had never even heard of the fictitious Prime Meridian, let alone consented to being governed by its definition of time.

Notes

1. Emily Moffat to J. S. Unwin, 17 Mar. 1861, Nyati, Matabeleland, in J. P. R Wallis (ed.), *The Matabele Mission: A Selection From the Correspondence of John and Emily Moffat, David Livingstone and Others 1858–1878* (London: Chatto & Windus, 1945), p. 136.
2. Cory, CO, doc 08, mf 436, box 23/1&2, Barnabas Shaw, Journal, 10 Feb. 1844, section 4, folder 3, p. 64.
3. Richard Whipp and Barbara Adam, among others, have alerted us to the coexistence of many, often conflicting, permutations and discourses of temporal experience in society. See Adam, *Timewatch*; Richard Whipp, '"A Time to Every Purpose": An Essay on Time and Work', in P. Joyce (ed.), *The Historical Meanings of Work* (Cambridge: Cambridge University Press, 1987), pp. 210–307.
4. Quoted in Derek Howse, *Greenwich Time and the Discovery of Longitude* (Oxford: Oxford University Press, 1980), p. 9.
5. On the story of John Harrison and the quest for longitude see Dava Sobel, *Longitude* (London: Fourth Estate, 1996); Howse, *Greenwich Time*.
6. Nguyen, 'The Spatialization of Metric Time', p. 30.
7. David Livingstone, *Missionary Travels and Researches in South Africa Including Sketches of Sixteen Years' Residence in the Interior of Africa* (New York: Harper, 1858), p. 251.
8. Barnabas Shaw, *Memorials of Southern Africa* (London: Thomas Riley, 1841), p. 258.
9. Michael Adas, *Machines as the Measure of Men: Science, Technology, and Ideologies of Western Dominance* (Ithaca: Cornell University Press, 1989), pp. 4, 61.
10. John Campbell, *Travels in South Africa: Undertaken at the Request of the Missionary Society*, 2nd edn (London: Black, Parry & Co., 1815), p. 235.
11. Heinrich Lichtenstein, *Travels in Southern Africa in the Years 1803, 1804, 1805 and 1806* (London, 1812), trans. A. Plumptre, 2 vols (Cape Town: The Van Riebeeck Society, 1928), p. 308.
12. Daniel Defoe, *Robinson Crusoe* (1719), John Richetti (ed.) (London: Penguin, 2001), p. 52.
13. Defoe, *Robinson Crusoe*, p. 219.
14. Defoe, *Robinson Crusoe*, p. 163.
15. Zerubavel, *Seven-Day Circle*, pp. 1–26.
16. Joseph J. Gurney, *Brief Remarks on the History, Authority, and Use of the Sabbath*, (London, 1831), 2nd edn (Andover: Flagg, Gould and Newman, 1833). pp. 29, 31.
17. Mircea Eliade, *The Myth of the Eternal Return: or, Cosmos and History* (*Le Mythe de l'éternel retour: archétypes et répétition* (1949), trans. Willard R. Trask (Princeton, N.J.: Princeton University Press, 1974), p. 23.
18. *Codex Justinianus*, quoted in Philip Schaff, *History of the Christian Church*, vol. 3, 5th edn (New York: Scribner, 1902), p. 380, n. 1.
19. Zerubavel, *Seven-Day Circle*, p. 22. Germano Pàttaro, 'Christian Conception of Time', in L. Gardet *et al.*, *Cultures and Time* (Paris: Unesco Press, 1976), pp. 183–5.
20. Robert Poole, *Time's Alteration: Calendar Reform in Early Modern England* (London: UCL Press, 1998); Duncan Steel, *Marking Time: The Epic Quest to Invent the Perfect Calendar* (New York: Wiley & Sons, 2000), pp. 99–100.
21. Moses Stuart, quoted in Gurney, *Brief Remarks on the History, Authority, and Use of the Sabbath*, p. iv.
22. Doreen M. Rosman, *Evangelicals and Culture* (London: Croom Helm, 1984), p. 218; V. Kiernan 'Evangelicalism and the French Revolution', *Past and Present*, 1:1 (1952), 44–56.
23. John Newton quoted in Ian Bradley, *The Call to Seriousness: The Evangelical Impact on the Victorians* (London: J. Cape, 1976), p. 103.
24. Rev. W. W. Gill, Mangaria (Polynesia) to LMS, 1860, in *Report of the Congregational Missionary Society, Melbourne* (Melbourne: Goodhugh, 1861). (SLV, SLT204: Victorian Religious Pamphlets, 28.)
25. William Lewelyn, *A Treatise on the Sabbath* (Leominster: P. Davis, 1783), p. 15.

26 Gurney, *Brief Remarks on the History, Authority, and Use of the Sabbath*, p. 16.
27 Lewelyn, *Treatise on the Sabbath*, p. 15.
28 Gerhard Dohrn-van Rossum, *History of the Hour: Clocks and Modern Temporal Orders*, trans. T. Dunlap (Chicago, Ill.: Chicago University Press, 1996), p. 29.
29 Chapter 47, 'The Signal for the Work of God', in J. McCann (trans./ed.), *The Rule of Saint Benedict* (London: Sheed & Ward, 1976), p. 52.
30 Abbot Parry, OSB, and Esther de Waal (eds), *The Rule of Saint Benedict* (Leominster: Gracewing, 1990) Chapter 48: 'The Daily Manual Labour', p. 77.
31 Landes, *Revolution in Time*, p. 58.
32 *Ibid.*, p. 70.
33 Michel Foucault, *Discipline and Punish: The Birth of the Prison*, trans. A. Sheridan (London: Penguin, 1977), pp. 149–50.
34 Adam, *Timewatch*, pp. 64–5; Landes, *Revolution in Time*, p. 66; Eviatar Zerubavel, 'The Benedictine Ethic and the Modern Spirit of Scheduling: On Schedules and Social Organisation', *Sociological Inquiry*, 50:2 (1980), 157–69.
35 Parry and de Waal, *The Rule*, p. 77.
36 Lewis Mumford, *The Human Prospect* (Boston, Mass.: Beacon Press, 1955), p. 4; Lewis Mumford, *Technics and Civilization* (London: Routledge, 1934), pp. 12–14. The three great methods of the monastic community, according to Michel Foucault, were 'to establish rhythms, impose particular occupations, regulate the cycles of repetition – a ritual, in effect, that was soon to be found in schools, workshops and hospitals'.
37 Jacques Le Goff, *Time, Work, and Culture in the Middle Ages*, trans. A. Goldhammer (Chicago Ill.: University of Chicago Press, 1980), p. 44.
38 Nigel Thrift, 'The Making of a Capitalist Time Consciousness', in J. Hassard (ed.), *The Sociology of Time*, (London: Macmillan, 1990,) p. 106.
39 Landes, *Revolution in Time* (2000 edn), pp. 58–62, 283.
40 Lichtenstein, *Travels in Southern Africa*, vol. 1, p. 194.
41 Le Goff, *Time, Work, and Culture in the Middle Ages*, pp. 29–42.
42 J. Needham, *et al.*, *Heavenly Clockwork: The Great Astronomical Clocks of Medieval China*, 2nd edn (Cambridge: Cambridge University Press, 1986).
43 Paul Glennie and Nigel Thrift, 'Reworking E. P. Thompson's "Time, Work-Discipline, and Industrial Capitalism"', *Time and Society*, 5:3 (1996), 275–99, pp. 290–1; Dohrn-van Rossum, *History of the Hour*, p. 159.
44 Le Goff, *Time, Work, and Culture in the Middle Ages*, p. 36.
45 Alistair C. Crombie, *Augustine to Galileo: The History of Science, A.D. 400–1650* (London: Falcon, 1952), pp. 150–1; Dohrn-van Rossum, *History of the Hour*, pp. 282, 294.
46 Dohrn-van Rossum, *History of the Hour*, pp. 146, 140–50.
47 John Stowe and Fynes Morrison, quoted in Bruce R. Smith, *The Acoustic World of Early-Modern England* (Chicago, Ill.: Chicago University Press, 1999), p. 53.
48 Alan Corbin, *Village Bells: Sound and Meaning in the 19th-Century French Countryside*, trans. M. Thom (New York: Columbia University Press, 1998), pp. 95–7.
49 Thompson, 'Time, Work-Discipline and Industrial Capitalism', pp. 73 and 71.
50 Karl Marx, *Das Kapital*, vol. 1, MEW 23 (Berlin: Dietz, 1969), p. 339.
51 Le Goff, *Time, Work, and Culture in the Middle Ages*, pp. 43–52; Dohrn-van Rossum, *History of the Hour*, pp. 297–9; Hugh Cunningham, *Leisure in the Industrial Revolution, c.1780– c.1880* (London: Croom Helm, 1980), p. 57.
52 Thompson, 'Time, Work-Discipline and Industrial Capitalism', p. 85.
53 Bradley, *The Call to Seriousness*, p. 22.
54 Noël Mostert, *Frontiers: The Epic of South Africa's Creation and the Tragedy of the Xhosa People* (London: Cape, 1992), p. 285.
55 Bradley, *The Call to Seriousness*, p. 24; Rosman, *Evangelicals and Culture*, pp. 58–9.
56 T. R. Birks, *Memoir of the Rev. Edward Bickersteth* (London: Seeleys, 1851), vol. 1, pp. 9–10.
57 Bradley, *The Call to Seriousness*, pp. 156–7. See also: David W. Bebbington, *Evangelicalism in Modern Britain: A History from the 1730s to the 1980s* (London: Unwin

Hyman, 1989), p. 11; Thrift, 'A Capitalist Time Consciousness', p. 111.
58 Bebbington, *Evangelicalism in Modern Britain*, p. 11.
59 Thomas Gisborne, *An Enquiry into the Duties of the Female Sex* (1816) quoted in Rosman, *Evangelicals and Culture*, p. 58.
60 Thompson, 'Time, Work-Discipline and Industrial Capitalism', p. 95.
61 Gavin Lucas, 'The Changing Face of Time: English Domestic Clocks from the Seventeenth to the Nineteenth Century', *Journal of Design History*, 8:1 (1995): 1–9, p. 8.
62 Sir William Smith, (ed.) *A Dictionary of the Bible: Comprising its Antiquities, Biography, Geography, and Natural History* (Boston, Mass.: Little, Brown & Co., 1863), vol. 3, p. 1068.
63 Cunningham, *Leisure in the Industrial Revolution*, p. 143.
64 J. A. Quinton, *Heaven's Antidote to the Curse of Labour or The Temporal Advantages of the Sabbath, Considered in Relation to the Working Classes* (London: Partridge & Oakley, 1849), p. 68.
65 William Blackstone, *Commentaries on the Laws of England: In Four Books* (New York: William E. Dean, 1853), vol. 2, book 4 ('Of Public Wrongs'), p. 45. Emphasis added. See also Gurney, *Brief Remarks on the History, Authority, and Use of the Sabbath*, p. 99: 'Everyone who is accustomed to communicate, in our jails and other such places, with the refuse of society – with the most abandoned and profligate men', Gurney wrote, 'must be aware that Sabbath-breaking is, very commonly, a first step to every species of crime.'
66 Thompson, 'Time, Work-Discipline and Industrial Capitalism', pp. 90–1.
67 John Urry, 'Time, Leisure and Social Identity', *Time and Society*, 3:2 (1994), 131–49, p. 134; Tim Ingold, 'Work, Time and Industry', 4:1 (1995), 10–16; Eviatar Zerubavel, 'Private-Time and Public-Time', in J. Hassard (ed.), *The Sociology of Time* (London: Macmillan, 1990), pp. 169–70.
68 E. P. Thompson, *The Making of the English Working Class* (London: Victor Gollancz, 1963), p. 402.
69 On work, leisure-time and popular festivities in England see: Robert D. Storch, 'The Problem of Working-Class Leisure: Some Roots of Middle-Class Reform in the Industrial North, 1825–50', in A. P. Donajgrodzki (ed.), *Social Control in Nineteenth-Century Britain* (London: Croom Helm, 1977), pp. 138–62; Robert W. Malcolmson, *Popular Recreations in English Society 1700–1850* (Cambridge: Cambridge University Press, 1973); Nels Anderson, *Work and Leisure* (London: Routledge & Kegan Paul, 1961), pp. 52, 77; David Cressy, 'God's Time, Rome's Time, and the Calendar of the English Protestant Regime', *Viator: Medieval and Renaissance Studies*, 34 (2003), 392–406, pp. 394–5; Cunningham, *Leisure in the Industrial Revolution*.
70 Storch, 'The Problem of Working-Class Leisure', p. 145.
71 Bradley, *The Call to Seriousness*, p. 128.
72 January Searle quoted in Storch, 'The Problem of Working-Class Leisure', p. 145.
73 John Wesley, *The Works of the Rev. John Wesley*, vol. 7 (New York: Harper, 1826), Sermon XCIV, p. 77.
74 Thompson, *The Making of the English Working Class*, p. 355.
75 Thompson, *The Making of the English Working Class*, p. 401.
76 Thompson, 'Time, Work-Discipline and Industrial Capitalism', p. 90; See also Robert F. Wearmouth, *Methodism and the Working-Class Movements in England 1800–1850* (Clifton: Helley, 1972), p. 22.
77 Samuel Smiles, *Self Help: With Illustrations of Conduct and Perseverance* (1859) (London: IEA Health and Welfare Unit, 1996), p. 168.
78 Thompson, *The Making of the English Working Class*, p. 376.
79 Bradley, *The Call to Seriousness*, p. 44; Wearmouth, *Methodism*, p. 235.
80 *Rules for the Methodist School of Industry at Pocklington*, quoted in Thompson, 'Time, Work-Discipline and Industrial Capitalism', p. 84.
81 Thompson, *The Making of the English Working Class*, p. 427; Thompson, 'Time, Work-Discipline and Industrial Capitalism', pp. 74–6.
82 B. Grant and G. J. Holyoake, *Christianity and Secularism: Report of a Public Discussion Between the Rev. Brewin Grant, B.A. and George Jacob Holyoake, Esq.*

Held in the Royal British Institutional (London: Ward & Co., 1853), p. 26.
83 Jo E. Barnett, *Time's Pendulum: The Quest to Capture Time – From Sundials to Atomic Clocks* (New York: Plenum Trade, 1998), pp. 29, 127–37; Zerubavel, 'The Standardisation of Time', p. 5.
84 Landes, *Revolution in Time* (2000 edn), p. 98.
85 On the impact of the mail services' transformation under standard-time see Dohrn-van Rossum, *History of the Hour*, pp. 328–45.
86 Landes, *Revolution in Time* (1983 edn), p. 287.
87 Ian Carter, *Railways and Culture in Britain: The Epitome of Modernity* (Manchester: University Press, 2001), p. 8.
88 James Stewart, *The Educated Kaffir, Industrial Training, a Sequel* (Lovedale: Lovedale Press, 1880), p. 20. (UCT, MS BC106, item D28, James Stewart papers.)
89 Morus, 'The Nervous System of Britain', pp. 456–463. See also Hanna Gay, 'Clock Synchrony, Time Distribution and Electrical Timekeeping in Britain 1880–1925', *Past and Present*, 181:1 (2003), 107–40.
90 Sandford Fleming, 'Time-Reckoning for the Twentieth Century', *Smithsonian Report* (1886), pp. 345–66.
91 Howse, *Greenwich Time*, 81–113; Zerubavel, 'The Standardization of Time'; Barnett, *Time's Pendulum*, pp. 127–37.
92 Henry David Thoreau, *Walden and Civil Disobedience* (New York: Penguin, 1983), p. 163.
93 Michael O'Malley, 'Standard Time, Narrative Film and American Progressive Politics', *Time and Society*, 1:2 (1992), p. 195.
94 Perkins, *The Reform of Time*, pp. 25–33.
95 Henry Booth (1847) quoted in Thrift, 'Capitalist Time Consciousness', pp. 122–3. On opposition movements against the adoption of standard time in Britain see Howse, *Greenwich Time*, pp. 105–13. For a detailed examination of the global implementation of standard time see Ian R. Bartky, *One Time Fits All: The Campaigns for Global Uniformity* (Stanford, Calif: Stanford University Press, 2007).
96 George Airy (1865) quoted in Perkins, *The Reform of Time*, p. 23.
97 Mr. W. Hay, 'Example is Better than Precept', *Imvo Zabantsundu* (Xhosa, 'Native Opinion'), King William's Town, no. 17 (23 Feb. 1885), p. 4. (SANL, MP 1009.)
98 Foucault, *Discipline and Punish*), p. 178; Michel Foucault, *Madness and Civilization: A History of Insanity in the Age of Reason* (1961) (Abingdon: Routledge, 2006), pp. 53–4.
99 On the transformation of calendars and time-keeping in response to society's concerns about the future, see Perkins, *The Reform of Time*, pp. 19–39.
100 Katharine Anderson, *Predicting the Weather: Victorians and the Science of Meteorology* (Chicago, Ill.: The University of Chicago Press, 2005), pp. 19–22; Maureen Perkins, *Visions of the Future: Almanacs, Time and Cultural Change 1775-1870* (Oxford: Clarendon Press, 1996); Perkins, *The Reform of Time*, pp. 100–1.
101 Clark Blaise, *Time Lord: Sir Sandford Fleming and the Creation of Standard Time* (London: Phoenix, 2000), pp. 78–80; Bartky, *One Time Fits All*, pp. 50–1.
102 A. M'Dowall, 'The Intercolonial Survey Conference: Proposed Reform in Time-Reckoning', *Argus*, Melbourne, 22 Oct. 1892, p. 7. On opposition and debates regarding the choice of Greenwich as Prime Meridian see Howse, *Greenwich Time*, pp. 116–159; Bartky, *One Time Fits All*.

CHAPTER TWO

Terra sine tempore: colonial constructions of 'Aboriginal time'

The belief that 'progress' and 'civilisation' are correlated with the human capacity to transcend the limitations of nature is a mainstay of Western mythology and cultural commentary stretching back for centuries.[1] Time – being a marker of civilisation – was no exception to this trend in nineteenth-century European discourse: the more a society was considered to be 'civilised', the greater the extent to which its calendars, discourses and computations of time were 'reckoned without reference to any of the factors given by Nature'.[2] As anthropologist Martin Nilsson stated in his early-twentieth century study, *Primitive Time-reckoning* (1920), abstract temporal units such as weeks, hours and minutes were signs of civilised society: 'These artificial periods belong to a highly developed stage of time-reckoning'; whereas 'stellar science and mythology [are] wide-spread among the primitive and extremely primitive peoples, and attain a considerable development among certain barbaric peoples.[3] If, as this chapter argues, the ways in which non-European societies were understood to perceive and practise time were considered in Western scientific and popular discourse as markers of civilisation, then colonial understandings of Indigenous temporal cultures must have played a significant function in terms of determining which societies were thought to count as 'civilised' and which as 'primitive' (if, indeed, even 'human').

The original inhabitants of Australia already challenged the very limits of nineteenth-century European conceptualisations of humanity on a number of counts. 'With the exception of the bushmen of South Africa,' as a missionary in Australia wrote, 'some suppose the aborigines of this country are about the lowest type of humanity. As the lowest savages they lived, without clothes, without care, without trouble for temporalities, subsisting on the simple products of nature without let or hindrance.'[4] Aboriginal ideas about time, rituals, rhythms and discourses – structured as they were primarily around natural rhythms

– contributed to the portrayal of the Aborigine as a 'savage' – indeed as something other than human, 'where to be human was to be separate from nature'.[5] Given that in the nineteenth-century British metropolis, as we have seen, nature itself was generally coming to be regarded as a 'bad' timekeeper compared to the time provided by the railways, such closeness to nature resulted in the representation of Aboriginal societies as innately 'irregular' and 'erratic', evincing a sense of timelessness and aimlessness that implied a failure of understanding and a lack intelligence rather than an alternative way of ordering life.

Such representations of Aboriginal societies contributed to their depiction in terms of extreme deficiency, precisely at a time when European jurisprudence was busy interpreting such deficiencies as a justification for colonisation. This logic was manifested to its clearest extent in the Australian colonies, where representations of nomadic hunter-gatherers within frameworks of lack and absence constituted the 'legal' foundation for British occupation. Indeed, the legal doctrine of *terra nullius* (lit. 'no one's land'), which the British Crown had invoked in order to justify its occupation of the Australian continent, was couched primarily within a discourse of *lack* – in this case of property rights – since European jurisprudence did not regard land as 'owned' unless its inhabitants had visibly enclosed, developed, irrigated and thus 'improved' it through human labour.[6] If these criteria were not met, 'the inhabitants were not so much a society as legally transparent entities so that, for ownership purposes, the land belonged to nobody'.[7] Such views stemmed from a profound ignorance and disapproval of Aboriginal land-use, as well as of the rhythms that guided Aboriginal people as they moved over, and drew sustenance from, that land. Settlers staking a claim to the land, asserted that they could see no sign of permanent settlement, no evidence of ownership, no enclosure and no agriculture (*terra nullius*); but they also claimed that they could sense no rational rhythm and no regularity or periodicity in the nomadic life: *terra sine tempore* – a timeless land.

Australian historians Bain Attwood and Maureen Perkins have pointed out that the notion of Aboriginal societies as 'timeless cultures' reinforced the fiction of *terra nullius*: 'Time and space were intimately related,' Perkins writes, 'the absence of one a precondition for the absence of the other.'[8] In analysing colonial constructions of 'Aboriginal time', this chapter seeks to deepen our understanding of the ways in which colonial constructions of 'Aboriginal time' helped bolster the fiction of Australia as *terra nullius* by portraying its inhabitants as a natural, rather than a cultural, presence – with a tenuous and *temporary* attachment to the land.

'Aboriginal time' before the time of settlement

It is commonly said, even today, that the four seasons in Australia are the 'reverse' of those in Europe. But this is merely a symptom of the myth that time the world over is defined in relation to Europe. Australia's seasons are in fact not four in number. 'We have six seasons,' explains a member of the Mirrar people in Arnhem Land, in the north of Australia. 'But our seasons don't come regular like they do for the balanda [white people]. We know when it begins because Yamidji the green grasshopper, he call out that cheeky yams are ready.'[9] The six seasons of Arnhem Land, moreover, are different from the six seasons observed by the Noongar peoples in the southwest of the continent; different again are the five seasons in the northwestern Kimberley region and the eight others in the Cape York peninsula. In the southeast, where the city of Melbourne now stands, the Kulin peoples recognised seven seasons, each of a different length, according to the appearance of specific flora and fauna: Kangaroo-apple Season, corresponding roughly to the month of December, Dry Season (around January–February), Eel Season (around March), Wombat Season (approximately April–August), Orchid Season (September), Tadpole Season (October), and Grass-flowering Season (around November). Two longer, overlapping seasons were also recognised: fire (approximately every seven years) and flooding (approximately every 28 years).[10]

The fact that most Australians today are almost entirely unaware of the existence of such seasons in their respective parts of the continent is a symptom of the ongoing structures of colonisation; for only until very recently, the myth of *terra nullius* encouraged a denial of the existence of pre-colonial Indigenous institutions. The perception that Europeans had introduced time, calendars and seasons to Australia was forged during the infancy of British settlement. In actual fact, all that could be truthfully claimed is that, at the time of British settlement in 1835, there had been no clocks, watches and bell-towers in Victoria (or rather, the Port Phillip District of New South Wales, as it was known by settlers until its proclamation as a separate colony in 1851).

In spite of this, and although they were said to possess no equivalent words for the concept of 'time', the original inhabitants of southeastern Australia observed multiple, well-established and rigidly respected times for the holding of celebrations, the heralding of gatherings and the undertaking of journeys across the land. Such movements were based on an intimate knowledge of nature's rhythms, which allowed for groups to accurately estimate, among other things, the distances that were to be covered by foot, the seasonal availability of resources, the reproductive rhythms that determined the edibility or toxicity of the vegetation, and the feeding habits and migration patterns of the

2.1 Map of Victoria, showing approximate territories of Kulin nations (in italics) and other Aboriginal peoples mentioned in this book, at the time of the British invasion

fauna.[11] Indeed, pre-colonial time was coordinated by an understanding of social and ecological cycles and patterns that were by no means limited, haphazard or primitive.

Much of this can be gleaned from the reports of a handful of observant colonial writers, such as George Augustus Robinson, Chief Protector of Aborigines in the Port Philip District. Robinson described how 'the Natives of the Low Country and of the Mountains assemble in large numbers in the fine Season to collect the Bogong fly, a species of Moth [that is] extremely nutritious, and the Natives subsist during the season entirely upon them'.[12] One of Robinson's Assistant Protectors, William Thomas, recalls how the Kulin used to build 'very large barques and cross over Western Port to French Island at a certain season of the year after eggs'.[13] Edward M. Curr, a squatter in Victoria, described how members of the Bangerang people 'erected annually fishing weirs, at the proper season', during the flood-waters period.[14] Some of the more perceptive observers also noted that these events marked the times for Kulin social, economic and religious gatherings.[15] Thus events like the annual swarming of the Bogong moth in the Victorian Alps were also a time for initiation ceremonies, corroborees, trade, marriages and the settling of disputes. As William Thomas put it, 'in Australia there is not a month but some tree, shrub, or flower is in blossom – and for exact assembling they calculate and arrange time in the latter way'.[16]

Astronomical knowledge provided a fundamentally important means of marking the passage of time in pre-colonial Australia. James Dawson, a settler in the western District of Victoria – an area originally inhabited by the Djargurd Wurrung people – provided a perceptive description of the manner in which the movements of stars helped to configure the temporal landscape of pre-colonial life:

> Although the knowledge of the heavenly bodies possessed by the natives may not entitle it to be dignified by the name of astronomical science, it greatly exceeds that of most white people. Of such importance is a knowledge of the stars to aborigines in their night journeys, and of their positions denoting the particular seasons of the year, that astronomy is considered one of the principal branches of education ... For example, when [the star] Canopus is a very little above the horizon in the east at daybreak, the season for emu eggs has come; when the Pleiades are visible in the east an hour before sunrise, the time for visiting friends and neighbouring tribes is at hand.[17]

Symbolically, Australia's original inhabitants looked up at the same sky and stars as Europeans, but the ways in which they lined-up the dots in the sky were altogether different. The Boorong people in northwest Victoria, for example, looked at the Southern Cross and saw a ring-tailed possum sitting on a tree bough; Scorpius was a giant emu; Castor and Pollux, the twins in Gemini, were formed by *Wanjel* the tortoise and *Yuree*, the fantail cuckoo; and Orion's stars were aligned in the shape of two dancing men (*Kulkunbulla*). The two brightest stars in the sky, Sirius and Canopus, represented *Warepil* (the wedge-tailed eagle – known as Bunjil among the Kulin) and *Waa*, the crow. Combined, these two astral figures embodied the two moieties, or 'skin groups', according to which all creations are considered to be divided.[18]

Pre-colonial zodiacs have been said to demonstrate an encyclopedic oral knowledge of the night sky, 'a giant textbook' which could be used to regulate times for hunting and gathering, child-rearing, story-telling and more.[19] Thus the Boorong knew that the ground-birds' egg-laying season was at hand when *Neilloan* (the mallee fowl constellation) disappeared from the night sky; and that the spawning season of the murray cod had commenced when *Otchocut* (the great fish constellation) went out of sight. This knowledge did not apply to other more remote groups, however; for astronomical lore and constellations varied from region to region, reflecting the local changes in the flora and fauna and the various moiety systems across the continent.[20] Like its seasons, the calendars and temporal lore of pre-colonial Australia varied across the continent, according to its peoples, eco-systems and climate regions.

Diverse ecological calendars based on seasonal and cyclical events helped structure the annual cycle of pre-colonial Aboriginal life; but what of methods for establishing the times of more specific and singular events? Here, too, some colonial observers were perceptive enough to note how Aboriginal peoples marked events in time. William Thomas was struck, for example, by the manner in which an elderly Kulin man attempted to express the time at which his wife had passed away the previous night, by pointing to the sky and describing 'exactly the position of the moon when she died'.[21] Assistant Protectors of Aborigines, James Dredge, reported that whenever the Daung Wurrung people in the Goulburn district left the Protector's station, they would inform him of the length of their absence in terms of 'sleeps', or *'nangrys'*. On one occasion, Dredge recorded in his diary: a man 'brought me a stick with as many notches cut in it as they would be gone "nangrys", which he desired me to keep'.[22]

Expressions of longer periods were also recorded by settlers. Richard Sadlier found it of interest that, the natives 'seem to have some idea of measuring time, for they pointed out to [Thomas] Mitchell's party that white men (evidently Sturt's party) had passed there, pointing to the sun, six annual revolutions'.[23] The rhythms of the moon and sun clearly provided a common language of time which both parties could understand. Accordingly, in his attempt to inform the Daung Wurrung about the distance that separated England and Australia, James Dredge opted for the use of lunar timescales. In his diary he noted that, 'when I informed them of the great distance, that we were 5 moons without seeing anything but water, that we were sent on purpose to take care of them, they were amazed'.[24] (There is some ambiguity here as to whether the amazement was in response to the length, or the purpose, of the journey.)

Many of the observers who benefited from early, firsthand contact with Aboriginal people in Victoria clearly did not portray the latter as being ignorant of time. Indeed, Assistant-Protector of Aborigines, Edward Stone Parker, even regaled a Melbourne audience with an account of this very subject in 1854. 'The tribes and nations', he explained during a public lecture, 'maintain friendly relations with each other, by frequent meetings, at appointed times and places.'

> If the tribes on parting agree to meet again, the time as well as the place is duly fixed, and to maintain the remembrance of the engagement, a very original species of calendar is employed. One of the young men is selected, and a red pigment prepared. The number of days being fixed, each of these are duly marked on the body of the young man, beginning with the forefinger of the right hand, passing up the arm and over the head to the forefinger of the left hand, and as every joint of the finger,

and every minute division of the human body, have their characteristic names, there is space enough for a considerable number of days. It is the duty of the living calendar, so selected and marked, to keep the tribes informed of the lapse of time and the day of the meeting.[25]

To Europeans, however, such methods appeared fundamentally impractical and unreliable. By comparison with the clock, the 'living calendar' was as much an ethnographical curiosity as the practice of using a boomerang. The two timekeepers were not merely technologically different; they seemed to serve an altogether different purpose. Whilst the permanent and omnipresent clock kept time uniformly and invariably for everyone alike, the 'living calendar' only seemed to affect those individuals participating in an appointment. Its purpose having been served, the timekeeper itself could be simply disposed of. William Buckley's description of the Wathaurong system aptly conveys this sense of impermanence: 'Their method of describing time', he stated, 'is by signs on the fingers, one man of each party marking the days by chalking on the arm, and then rubbing one off as each day passes.'[26]

William Buckley's experience is worth citing briefly since it offers a rare case of genuine appreciation by a European regarding the extent to which time featured as a critical element of pre-colonial Kulin life. Following a narrow escape as a convict from the Sorrento penal settlement in 1803, Buckley very nearly succumbed to hunger and thirst as he struggled to survive in a foreign environment. A real-life Robinson Crusoe, Buckley was not nearly as enterprising and confident as Defoe's fictional castaway: rather than constructing a calendar to keep a tally of the days, he quickly lost track of time altogether. Shortly after his escape from the settlement he began to experience the first acute signs of temporal disorientation, having camped near an Aboriginal well where he 'remained more than a week, perhaps it may have been two or three, for I seem henceforward to have lost all record of time, except by return of the seasons, and the rising and setting sun'.[27]

Since the Sorrento penal settlement was disbanded in 1804, leaving Buckley behind, he became the only white man to walk on Kulin lands for the subsequent three decades. But even though his recollections of this period constantly refer to the sense of a *loss* of time (a time concerned with hours, weeks, months and years) they also imply the gradual acquisition of a new sense of time, tuned to the rhythms of the surrounding environment: 'It was necessary', Buckley stated, 'to consult the moon, so as to judge of the ebbing and flowing of the tides; for the fish, I ascertained[,] came and went accordingly.'[28]

The Wathaurong people who eventually adopted Buckley possessed an intimate knowledge of such rhythms, for in their company he never experienced such hardship again.[29] Buckley became fluent both in

[65]

the Wathaurong language and in their culture of time: he learnt their custom for fixing appointments in time – including the system of the 'living calendar' which would later be described by Edward Parker.[30]; and he was taught that the tapping of certain food sources called for a precise knowledge of the local seasonal calendars:

> We remained at the opposite side of the lake, until the approach of spring. Here [the Kurung] made their food principally of the large ants called the *kalkeeth* ... It is only for about one month in each year they can be had, for after that time they are transformed to large flies, and then fly away to die, or again change their shape or nature.[31]

Buckley's adventures ended in 1835, when, on the eve of settler-colonisation in Victoria, he encountered John Batman and John Helder Wedge at Indented Head, who were then busy surveying the country for their pastoral enterprises.[32] It is said that, when Buckley walked into the squatters' camp wearing a kangaroo skin and carrying Aboriginal weapons, he could barely remember his mother tongue, having lived without any contact with European civilisation for such a long period – though how long, even he did not know. 'Mr. Batman asked me many questions,' Buckley recalled, 'and I told him I arrived in a ship, the name of which I had forgotten; and, as I thought, about twenty years before – but that I could only guess, having lost all recollection of time.'[33] Buckley's estimation was out by twelve years. Clearly, however, the loss he experienced was not that of time in general, but specifically of European time.

'Aboriginal time', race and humanness

So far we have examined European portrayals of 'Aboriginal time' as it was understood by a number of early observers – including three of the Assistant Protectors, whose cultural contact with Aboriginal peoples in Victoria would have been significantly more extensive than that of most settlers. To shed some light on more general understandings of 'Aboriginal time' in mid-nineteenth century Victoria, however, we now turn to a different source of information on this subject – a source which is of particular interest to us, given that it brings into stark relief some of the connections between 'Aboriginal time' and nineteenth-century discourses of race, humanness and civilisation.

We owe the existence of this document to the emergence, during the early nineteenth century in Britain, of the 'Exeter Hall influence' and to the Evangelical philanthropists of humanitarian persuasion who had begun to demonstrate a distinct interest in the condition of (what were believed to be) the variations of the human races across the world. Much alarm was caused in humanitarian circles in 1839 when Britain's pre-eminent 'racial-scientist', Dr. James Prichard, published a paper entitled *On the Extinction of Some Varieties of the Human Race*, which suggested that a number of these 'races' – including Australia's Aboriginal peoples – stood on the verge of extinction. Such apprehensions led the recently established Society for the Protection of Aborigines to publish 'a set of queries to be addressed to those who may travel or reside in parts of the globe inhabited by the threatened races'.[34] The resulting document – *Queries Respecting the Human Race, to be Addressed to Travellers and Others* – came to constitute a list of eighty-eight questions, grouped under nine categories which reflected the traits and achievements that British science had identified as indicators of civilisation: 1. Physical Characters; 2. Language; 3. Individual and Family Life; 4. Buildings and Monuments; 5. Domestic Animals; 6. Government and Laws; 7. Geography and Statistics; 8. Social Relations; and 9. Religion, Superstitions &c.

The questions embodied the key features of social and cultural behaviour which were considered by British science as measure of a civilisation's state of advancement. ('Is there any prevailing disproportion between different parts of the body?'; 'What is the prevailing complexion?'; 'Is there any remarkable deficiency or perfection in any of the senses?'; 'At what age does puberty take place?'; 'Are there domestic animals in the possession of the people?'; 'What is the form of Government?' etc.) It is significant, therefore, that three of the queries in the list concerned the manner in which other societies measured and kept time – an indication that temporal aptitude was considered a significant factor in the formulation of such hierarchies. The fact that these time-oriented questions were grouped under the category of 'Religion, Superstitions, &c.', is also a reminder that both alternative Gods and temporalities could be interpreted as evidence of false religion/knowledge.

- Have they any sacred days or periods, fixed or moveable feasts, or religious ceremonies of any kind, or any form of thanksgiving or other observance connected with seasons?
- Are they in any way observed with reference to the division of the year, and how?
- If time is not divided by observation of these bodies, what other mode is adopted? And do observances connected with them rest with the priests or chiefs?

A version of these same *Queries* was adopted by the Victorian Parliament as a means of gathering evidence for a Select Committee in 1858 – the first inquiry of its kind which was appointed to ascertain

2.2 Phrenological report by P. Sohier, submitted as evidence to the Victorian Select Committee of 1858–59

In his attempt to diagnose Aboriginal group achievement, Sohier awarded points for various character and intellectual traits (note the score of '3' for the faculty of Time). There is no evidence that Sohier actually took any measurements of Aboriginal craniums. More than likely, his 'diagnoses' were based merely on popular prejudices.

the condition of the Aboriginal population in the colony.[35] In order to gather its evidence, the list of queries was circulated among settlers, missionaries and officials and all those deemed to be knowledgeable of Aboriginal customs and beliefs. The information gathered by such means came to form a compendium of European knowledge of local Aboriginal culture, described by the Select Committee as 'one of the most valuable historical documents extant connected with Victoria'.[36]

The importance which was attributed to this document is best understood when placed in the context of metropolitan developments, at a time when influential debates were circulating regarding the question of the origin of the human species. These debates reached a climactic point among scientists in the 1850s, when a major ideological shift occurred regarding the previous, widely accepted monogenist world-view (predicated upon a notion of a single origin of humanity in the creation of Adam and Eve) to polygenism (which argued a belief in separately constituted and biologically determined races). Darwin's findings in *The Origin of the Species* (1859) – published in the same year as Victoria's Select Committee *Report* – had not yet influenced the course of this debate. Britain's Evangelicals were thus still very much preoccupied with the task of collecting empirical evidence which corroborated their monogenist world-view. The question of the origins of humanity indeed had profound implications for their own ideology: monogenism confirmed Evangelical belief in the universal redemption of all humanity through conversion – a single origin of humanity supporting belief in a single destiny for all humankind.[37] If, on the other hand, polygenists were right and certain peoples belonged to different 'races' with innate biological qualities, all attempts to civilise and Christianise them could well be regarded as futile. The inclusion of the *Queries* in the Victorian Select Committee reflects this concern with 'scientifically' proving through empirical evidence that Aboriginal people belonged to the human family, albeit at its lowest state of development; whilst the presence of the three time-related questions highlights the relevance of time within such wider debates, underscoring its role as a marker of humanness and civilisation.

This is borne out with particular clarity by a craniological report which the Select Committee requested from Melbourne's leading 'professor' of phrenology, Philemon Sohier. The report's inclusion was no doubt an attempt to lend 'scientific' weight to the Committee's evaluations, for the study of phrenology enjoyed immense popularity during the mid-nineteenth century – even among monogenists – until it was eventually dismissed as a pseudoscience in the late 1870s.[38] Based on the belief that the skull was shaped by the capacity and power of the brain, phrenology sought to diagnose character traits and aptitudes by supposedly 'reading' the skull as if it were an accurate index of abilities and tendencies. Of course, Sohier's diagnoses – which were included as evidence with the Committee's *Report* – reveal nothing scientific at all. They do however provide a useful indication of popular racist prejudices in mid-nineteenth-century Victoria. One of Sohier's diagnoses, for instance, describes Aboriginal people as: 'extremely superstitious for and tenacious to old traditions and habits, rather deceitful, suspicious, slippery and time-servers, or dissemblers'.

A closer look at Sohier's report (see figure 2.2) reveals that 'Time' – defined as the 'Sense of duration, and the relative distance of time' – was one of the key measures of intellect which phrenology was able to appraise. According to Sohier's measurements, 'the Aborigine' scored a 3 (out of 7 points) for the faculty of Time, meaning that their sense of time was classed as: 'Moderate: rather below mediocrity; active only in a subordinate degree, and having only a limited influence over the mind and character.'[39] By contrast (and somewhat predictably), Sohier awarded seven points out of seven to the Aborigines for their sense of 'Locality', indicating an excellent understanding of 'the relative position of places and objects, roving desire, memory of places'. Sohier's report demonstrates how Western science itself lent spurious credence for a while to what would long remain a common stereotype in the colonial imagination: that the accurate perception of time was an innate handicap for Aboriginal people.

Returning now to the three time-related questions in the list of *Queries* adopted by the 1858–59 Select Committee: the first thing we note is that most of the informants on the mailing list returned the circular without answering these particular questions at all – a fact which the Committee appears to have foreseen – not because of the informants' unfamiliarity with the subject at hand, but rather on the basis of the prediction that not all the queries in the list would 'be deemed applicable to a race deemed so low in the scale of civilization as the Aborigines of this colony'.[40] Some respondents provided other reasons for not answering the queries. One settler from the area of Omeo replied: 'The tribe being extinct, no reply is necessary.'[41] Indeed, in the space of merely twenty years, settler-colonisation had wreaked such devastation among the Aboriginal population in Victoria, that the majority of colonists had barely had the opportunity, let alone the chance to develop an inclination, to learn more about Aboriginal culture. What remained of Aboriginal societies in Victoria was no longer seen to afford an ethnographically 'pristine' object of inquiry. As a settler described the situation to the Select Committee, one could observe remnants of a civilisation, 'but as a race their history is a tale of the past'.[42]

COLONIAL CONSTRUCTIONS OF 'ABORIGINAL TIME'

A small number of respondents did attempt to answer the time-related queries, however. Their testimonies, albeit brief, offer a useful insight into colonial understandings of Aboriginal ways of keeping time. (The responses are cited here in their entirety and will be evaluated in the next sections of the chapter.)

- **Have they any sacred days or periods, fixed or moveable feasts, or religious ceremonies of any kind, or any form of thanksgiving or other observance connected with seasons?**[43]

Mr. Shuter – I do not think they have.

Mr. Croke – No.

Mr. Beveridge – They have no sacred days or religious ceremonies of any kind.[44]

Mr. Strutt – They have certain general meetings, at which all the members of the tribe are expected to attend. But these meetings are at irregular intervals, and their object is not always known to Europeans.[45]

Mr. Thomas – They have no sacred days, or moveable feasts – unless it be when the Rains are procured from a fellow creature, when for three days continued Dancing and Rejoycing, their bodies are cleared from all appearance of Mourning, and rejoycing in its stead.[46]

C. J. Tyers – None.[47]

- **What ideas are entertained respecting the heavenly bodies? Have they any distinction of stars, or constellations? And if so, what names do they give them, and what do these names signify?**

Mr. Shuter – I cannot tell.

Mr. Beveridge – They have a name and legend belonging to every planet and constellation visible in the heavens, but it would take too much time and space to transcribe them here.

Mr. J. M. Allen – They have. The sun (*yarh yar*) and moon (*unnung*) they suppose to be spirits. "*Whycuhrl*" is their name for a star.

Mr. Thomas – They have names for the heavenly bodies. They have distinction of stars, some of them they maintain were once blackfellows, but for certain good acts were taken to heaven and made stars of.

C. J. Tyers – Cannot say.[48]

- **Are they in any way observed with reference to the division of the year, and how?**

Mr. Sherand – Yes. The Moon.

Mr. Beveridge – They are not connected in any way with the division of the year.

Mr. Thomas – They have accurate Notions, and have terms for the four seasons, which they determine by the Motion of the heavenly bodies.

W. McKellar – The division of the year is reckoned by the full moons, and also by what they term 'sleeps' (days).[49]

- **If time is not divided by observation of these bodies, what other mode is adopted? and do observances connected with them rest with the priests or chiefs?**

Mr. Croke – Seasons.

Mr. Beveridge – The only method they have of dividing the year is by heat & cold, or summer & winter.

Mr. J. M. Allan – They divide time by the seasons.

Mr. Godfrey – Their only mode of computing time, appears to be the moon – its full especially is noted; and now they have the advantage of dating from the "Nip Nip," or settlers' yearly regular shearing time. This seems to supply them with a mode of stating years, which before they had not. Months or moons then satisfied them.[50]

Mr. Thomas – Time is divided by the Motion of the heavenly bodies. They have also other modes, such as the blossoming of trees & shrubs. They can occasionally define the very Month by this method.[51]

Nature's time versus human time

In consideration of the fact that the vast majority of respondents did not address these time-oriented questions at all, the overall picture painted of 'Aboriginal time' was that of a crude element of pre-colonial Aboriginal life. This perception substantiated the overall framework of lack and absence which dominated colonial understandings of Aboriginal cultures. As the Report of the 1858–59 Select Committee concluded:

> The general tenor of the evidence will bear out the conclusion which your Committee have arrived at – that, while the Aborigines are endowed with keen perceptive faculties, there is a considerable deficiency in their reflective faculties, and a certain want of steadiness of purpose in their characters, which appears the great obstacle to be overcome in reclaiming them, and bringing them within the pale of civilization and Christianity.[52]

Whilst acknowledging the catastrophic effects of colonisation on the Aboriginal population, the Select Committee responded to the evidence it gathered by recommending policies for the gradual containment of the survivors on a number of mission stations and reserves. Here, under the charge of lay or clerical missionaries, they would be taught to combine agricultural and gardening activities with small-scale pastoral activities and be induced 'to take an interest in the occupations of civilized life'. According to this plan, the Committee predicted, 'the remnants of the Aborigines may be both civilized and Christianized'.[53] As we will see in Chapter 3, part of this process would witness missionaries and station-managers making the first systematic attempts to re-orientate Aboriginal temporal consciousness away from nature and around a new order of time.

As we have seen, virtually all the responses to the list of queries depicted Aboriginal understandings of time as being virtually synonymous with nature's time. Moons, stars, rains and the blossoming of trees and shrubs were the clocks of pre-colonial Australia – and its original inhabitants had mastered their language. Whilst today some might be inclined to interpret 'Aboriginal time' as a romantic alternative to the regime of the clock, nineteenth-century Europeans generally conceived such closeness to nature as calling into question the very humanity of those who practised it. As it was understood by many early settlers, 'Aboriginal time' confirmed the sentiment that Aboriginal societies were more like flora and fauna than owners and inhabitants of the land. This was partly determined by the fact that Enlightenment values and ideals had come to associate the idea of 'humanness' with man's transcendence and domination over nature; and its corresponding opposite – savagery – as a mode of life that existed 'closer *to* nature'.[54]

Max Weber noted that a similar belief was channelled through Puritan discourse, which valorised rational conduct over *status naturae* as a means of freeing 'man' from his dependence on the base impulses (both inner and outer) of the natural world, and delivering him towards *status gratiae* – salvation.[55] There is of course more than a hint of irony in the colonisers' conviction that 'savages' were enslaved to the rhythms of nature, given that clock-time itself demanded nothing less than their complete compliance, leaving little room for deviations, even of minutes. The paradox of perceiving themselves as free from *status naturae* whilst effectively enslaved to *status horologii* was resolved through ideological rationalisation. To do things 'by the clock' was not an act of submission to the machine, but rather evidence of a human transcendence of nature's limits; for what came to be conceived of in humanist thought as a 'movement out of nature' consisted partly in the ability of societies to substitute the clock for nature as the prime source of temporal authority in society.

This should not be taken to imply that nature's demand for 'punctuality' is less severe and rigid than that of the clock. Neither the clock nor nature freed human societies from the need to keep up with an external source of temporal authority; indeed, nature could sometimes be just as strict a timekeeper as the clock. The only comparison being made in this book between nature's time and clock-time, relates to the ways in which these two different modes of relating to time were perceived, and to the values and beliefs with which they were associated, by nineteenth-century colonial observers.

And when we look closer at the representations of hunter-gatherer societies which were presented to the Victorian Select Committee of 1858–59, we start to understand the manner in which such perceptions had a profound impact on the portrayal of Aboriginal peoples at the time of British occupation. Just as the practice of agriculture and the domestication of stock demonstrated to Europeans a higher stage of progress, the capacity to abstract time from nature demonstrated the ability to domesticate time and thereby cultivate the Self. As they were, however, Europeans perceived Aboriginal people as creatures passive before the imposed rhythms of nature, their ceremonies and feasts taking place on dates *dictated* by the occurrence of events beyond their control. 'They trust to the bounty of a Providence they do not appreciate,' William Thomas remarked – echoing Locke's definition of the 'state of nature', which was said to be found in those societies still reliant on the 'spontaneous hand of Nature'.[56]

If absence of cultivation and enclosures suggested the absence of land ownership, a supposed lack of providence and foresight suggested to Europeans a state of immature cultural development, reflected in Aboriginal peoples' apparent disregard for the ethic of regularity and future planning. 'One of their principal characteristics is indolence,' a Victorian settler reported to the Select Committee, 'and a total disregard for the future, so that their immediate wants are supplied'.[57] This kind of prodigality was closely associated with the belief that there was little or no order separating human movements from those of common animals. As a prominent Victorian settler, Edward Curr, wrote:

> It is a noteworthy fact with the Bangerang, and indeed, with the whole aboriginal population that, as they neither sowed nor reaped, so they never abstained from eating the whole of any food they had got with a view to the wants of the morrow. If anything was left for Tuesday, it was merely that they had been unable to consume it on Monday. In this they were like the beasts of the forest.[58]

To rely entirely on nature's time was to be childishly dependent on chance and providence; it was to lead an existence, as anthropologists Baldwin Spencer and Frank Gillen wrote at the turn of the century, without 'the slightest thought of, or care for, what the morrow may bring'.[59] The perceived absence of care for the future, coupled with the absence of a historical chronology, gave rise to beliefs that, for Aboriginal people, there was no future to speak of at all. 'Without a history,' as an Adelaide journalist would write in 1879, 'they have no past; without a religion they have no hope; without the habits of forethought and providence, they can have no future.'[60]

The belief that events in Aboriginal societies were dictated by nature also influenced colonial understandings of Aboriginal lore and religion. As we observed in Chapter 1, the timing of religious rituals played a fundamental role in European society in establishing centralised authority. ('The more accurate a calendar could be made to seem', writes historian Michael O'Malley, 'the more legitimate its authority over daily life.')[61] Christianity relied on a complex system of rituals which helped define a Christian temporal identity by demanding regular and synchronised days and times of prayer and devotion (the Sabbath being a prime example). Accordingly, Aboriginal peoples were portrayed as lacking a religious identity, partly because the rituals they performed failed to display an adequate respect for time. The absence of a religious schedule and a special day set aside for rest and worship, along with the lack of a collective ritual that evinced clear demarcations between times of worship and secular activity, supported claims regarding the lack of a spiritual dimension to Aboriginal life. As a settler, Peter Beveridge reported to the 1858 Select Committee, the Aboriginal people had 'no sacred days or religious ceremonies of any kind'.[62]

Rather than ceremonies or rituals, settlers frequently referred to corroborees as 'modes of amusement in vogue amongst the aborigines'; as remnants of religious observances; or as 'games' and 'native festivals'.[63] Beveridge, even more critical, believed that the corroborees '[were] just so many grotesque jumps and not worthy the name dances'.[64] Several aspects of the corroboree, other than a perceived temporal aberrance, contributed towards eliciting such feelings among Europeans; but time was certainly one of these. The occurrence of the corroboree did not appear to obey a visibly set rhythm and thus failed to conform to the colonisers' standards. 'They have certain general meetings at which all the members of the tribe are expected to attend', Mr. Strutt stated in his response to the query regarding observance of religious events. 'But these meetings are at *irregular intervals*', he specified, 'and their object is not always known to Europeans.'[65]

Settlers and missionaries did occasionally witness what was in fact the highly structured nature of Aboriginal ceremonies: 'the blacks are rigidly observant of their duties,' one settler reported to the Select Committee. 'The order of the ceremony is distinct,' he added, 'and no native would deviate from it in any particular'.[66] Nonetheless, the order which they followed was clearly not the 'correct' order, by Christian standards. Indeed, even when Aboriginal groups were reported to corroboree at regular, appointed times, the periodicity of such ceremonies failed to relate to 'proper' sources of temporal authority. These criticisms reflected the fundamental dislike for alternative sources of temporal authority in society – especially those oriented around nature. As one Victorian settler reported:

> [The Aborigines'] great corroborees are only held in the spring, when the Pleiades are generally most distinct, and their corroboree is a worship of the Pleiades, as a constellation which announces spring. Their monthly corroboree is of the moon. The whole of the ceremonies and the custom of the lubras [women] doing up of the possum rug and beating it, is precisely that of the Greeks and of the ancient nations, which observances the Israelites were warned to avoid ... The last corroboree I ever saw was on the old punt bridge ... [I] then particularly noticed that, after so many genuflexions, they looked at the moon and bowed, clasping their hands.[67]

Conveying a distinct sense of paganism, the above description echoed common anxieties among social reformers in the British metropolis, where – as Perkins has documented – 'the nineteenth century saw a concerted campaign ... to suppress 'superstitions' associated with timing according to the phases of the moon'.[68]

Missionaries, whilst never doubting the authenticity of their own ritual – according to which every seventh day called for prayer and abstinence from work and worldly pursuits – described Aboriginal rites, taboos and ceremonies as categorically superstitious. This was in spite of the fact that certain similarities appeared obvious to at least some of the Aboriginal people of Victoria. In 1838, for instance, after performing his first Sunday service among the Kulin, the Reverend Francis Tuckfield reported the reaction of the locals to the spectacle of the Sabbath ritual. 'They said: 'Merigig, Mr. Tuckfield, Merigig you woo deolyal – woodeolyal corrobory that is very good you plenty plenty plenty corrobory you' – comparing my preaching with their native corroboories, or assemblies for harangue, feasting, dancing, etc.'.[69] To most missionaries, however, such parallels were invalid: the corroboree was not worthy of being a religious rite. 'It has been thought by some that their corroborees are a sort of religious ceremony,' reads a religious pamphlet from Victoria in 1861; '[b]ut this is not likely, as they appear destitute of any act of devotion whatever.' The pamphlet made this distinction in part by drawing its readers' attention to the corroboree's supposed lack of a formalised schedule, thereby implying its apocryphal character: they 'are generally held in summer, when fish and other kinds of food are more plentiful'.[70]

To the critics of Aboriginal religion and spirituality, the issue was one framed partly around the significance of temporal authority; for, in establishing the times proper to things in their own context, 'Aboriginal time' was effectively nature's time, and thus no human time at all. Given that the clock and the seven-day week had come to represent the temporal standard against which Europeans measured all other forms of social organisation, Aboriginal customs and their lore and land-ownership could be denied, partly on the basis the belief that they took inadequate account of the passage of time. Such beliefs were deeply ingrained within the colonial consciousness and gradually found their way into mainstream historiography and anthropology, where they were further disseminated in society. Thus, in 1907 for instance, the *Historical Geography of the British Colonies* could authoritatively inform its readers that 'the traditions of [Aboriginal] totems take no note of time'.[71]

Regularity versus irregularity

Maureen Perkins notes that the term 'walkabout' entered Australian colonial discourse around 1828, and soon became a common expression for describing the perceived irregularity inherent in Aboriginal life.[72] Aboriginal people who moved about land without the purpose of seeking employment elsewhere, or who left their work outside of the approved periods of leave, were commonly said to have gone 'walkabout' – a term which implied the perceived extraneousness of Aboriginal life, evoking images of a culture that was guided by 'another' calendar, or by no calendar at all. To 'wander' (from the Germanic, *wend* – 'to turn') connoted the idea of non-linear movement; of aimlessness and lack of direction. Migrant workers could move from place to place without raising suspicion because they did so according to the calendars and seasons of approved forms of labour and industry. But Aboriginal people and 'vagrants' were said to 'wander' about the country, since their movements were not guided by an accepted source of temporal authority. The term 'walkabout' is indeed 'a reminder', Perkins notes, 'that at the very heart of representations of indigenous people as timeless is a deep abhorrence within western European culture to the practice of nomadism'.[73] As such, it echoed similar prejudices towards nomadic populations in other colonial spaces, as well as the fears and suspicions which were generally felt in Europe toward gypsies, vagrants and other itinerants.

The use of time-conscious attributes such as 'wandering' and 'irregular' to describe Aboriginal peoples' movements reveal the deep-seated aversion amongst settlers towards populations guided by untamed (and un-timed) nature, and can be traced back to the earliest colonial observations of Aboriginal societies. The general manner in which nomadic movements were conducted evoked a sense of indolence and irregularity often appeared to European observers as forms of indulgence. 'As a rule they are lazy travellers,' Richard Brough-Smyth commented. 'It is generally late in the morning before they start on [their] journey, and there are many interruptions by the way.'[74] A perceived lack of discipline was reflected in the general appearance of family relations and daily life: 'the children are not educated in the slightest degree,' a settler stated in his reply to one of the queries posed by the 1858–59 Select Committee. 'Their parents have not the slightest control over them'.[75] As the responses given to Question 38 in the list of queries suggest, settlers were not able to perceive any sense of regularity even in the most basic aspects of pre-colonial Aboriginal life:

- **What number of meals do they have and what is their capacity for temporary or sustained exertion?**

  Mr. Murray – The prevailing food was originally chiefly animal, for which they trusted entirely to Nature for supply ... Their meals are very irregular.

  Mr. Smith – They have no regular number of meals, but eat when they have the opportunity, principally, however, in the mornings and evening.

  Mr. Cooke – They are too idle to cultivate for themselves ...They have no regular time for their meals, but seem to be always eating and sleeping, except when they are out hunting.[76]

This chronology of activities portrayed 'the wild life' as being (mis)guided by an erratic and haphazard timetable, suggesting a failure to appreciate the advantages of a uniform, predictable and repetitive timetable. 'Irregularity' was seen to have induced many of the hardships that supposedly afflicted Aboriginal people. 'The irregularity and uncertainty of their diet would be fatal to a white man', one settler wrote. 'They often remain at their huts in a listless state for days and nights together, when suddenly some of them will undertake a long and fatiguing journey travelling night and day, or other violent exercise, as the corrobboree, hunting, &c' [sic].[77] The logic was taken to extremes by claims that infanticide (and subsequent cannibalistic feeding upon murdered infants) was a consequence of their failure to plan for the future.[78]

In later years, on the missions and reserves, it became common to blame Aboriginal deaths and illnesses on the refusal to abandon the seasonal calendar of nomadic life, rather than on the devastating consequences of colonisation (including the introduction of alcohol and disease). In a report from one of the missions, for instance, the station manager reported that five cases of fatal illness had occurred during the past year alone. But 'I would have it known', he specified, 'that four out of the five who died were old blacks, of wandering propensities and dissipated habits, who would never remain on the station for any length of time.'[79]

The ubiquitous notion of 'irregularity' is a powerful and rather unquestioned aspect of colonial discourse which demands greater recognition for its role in bolstering the denial of Aboriginal peoples' attachment to the land. Regularity was fundamental to effective nomadic land uses: Aboriginal peoples made cyclical use of tracts of land within a larger, defined territory for a determined period and then proceeded to move on, keeping pace with the seasonal changes in their environment.[80] Successful hunter-gatherer economies required regularity and order – 'proof', historian Henry Reynolds argues, 'of their exploitation or "enjoyment" of the land'.[81] In practice, however, such land-uses were not recognised as sufficiently evident, especially given that (or perhaps, precisely because) the recurrence of such movements was based, once again, upon an understanding of time and regularity that was oriented around nature – not by a predictable and structured calendar or by the exigencies of an industrially and agriculturally oriented economy. In a Lockean sense, therefore, the regular calendars of agriculture and pastoralism could legitimately displace the irregular seasons of nomadic hunter-gatherers, subsuming them within the temporal order of a more 'civilised' relationship with the land.[82]

Constant seasonal migrations undertaken at the times determined by the availability of food, water and better climates failed to satisfy the prerequisite conditions for land ownership partly because those who described them as haphazard and irregular failed to understand, or refused to value, *inter alia*, the temporal order guiding and coordinating such movements – but also because it simply suited settlers to believe as much. Indeed, when staking a claim to soil that was 'unoccupied' at the time of their arrival, most settlers did not usually consider the fact that, with the changing of the local seasons and the regeneration of flora and fauna, the same land would be visited once again by its regular inhabitants. This kind of denial of nomadic land ownership was repeated over and over again. Thus, in what would have been one of numerous such occasions, when a group of settlers formally petitioned the Victorian government in 1858 to sell the 'empty' land set aside as the Aboriginal reserve of Mordialloc – now a suburb of Melbourne – their request was granted. This took place in spite of vehement protests from Assistant Protector William Thomas, who opposed the motion on the grounds that the land was still seasonally used by Aboriginal people.[83] On another occasion, the influential settler Edward Curr, who was eager in the late 1870s to vacate land around Melbourne for pastoralism and settlement, justified the proposal to remove the residents of one of Victoria's most vibrant communities (Coranderrk) by hinging his argument on the seasonal nature of their ancestors' tenure over the land: 'They only went there in the summer time,' Curr responded to his critics. 'They never lived in the mountains; they went there occasionally ... It was not at any time the head-quarters of a tribe.'[84]

Recent history has shown that such misrepresentations of Aboriginal culture still carry enough power to ensure the continuing denial of Aboriginal land-rights in parts of Australia. In 1998, Edward Curr's representations of Aboriginal life and customs in his memoir, *Recollections of Squatting in Victoria* (1883), were adopted as a key source of evidence to support Federal Court Justice Olney's ruling on a Native Title claim by the Yorta Yorta people. Whilst in the nineteenth century the law had refused to recognise the temporal ties of nomads to their lands, in the twentieth century, this logic was reversed. Given that the Yorta Yorta no longer led 'traditional' elements of 'Aboriginal' life (instead of nomads, for instance, they had become sedentary and urbanised) they did not meet the requirement, under native title law, that claimants must be able to demonstrate a continuing connection to the land through the continuity of tradition with pre-colonial times. Even as a metaphor, time could be redeployed to justify the continuation of dispossession. Symbolically, Justice Olney ruled that the Yorta Yorta claim to native title had been 'washed away by the tide of history'.[85]

―⋘⋙―

Europeans brought with them new rhythms and rituals to settler colonies such as Victoria. The introduction of a developed European industry, full-scale pastoralism and sedentary agriculture loudly drummed out a new 'beat', which at times complemented, and at times conflicted with, the older, pre-colonial rhythms of Aboriginal societies. As one settler noted in his reply to the Queries of the 1858–59 Select Committee, the Aboriginal population of Victoria had begun to respond to the introduction of these new pastoral rhythms by incorporating, and to a certain extent accommodating, them within their pre-existent mode of temporal reckoning: 'now they have the advantage of dating from the "Nip Nip," or Settlers' yearly regular shearing time. This seems to supply them with a mode of stating years, which before they had not.'[86] These 'new rhythms', however, would prove to come into direct conflict with the pre-colonial rhythms and ways of life. The settlers' 'yearly regular shearing time', which embodied the new rhythm of colonial Australia, was a commercial time driven by the exigencies of capitalist enterprise, whose most distinctive feature was precisely that constructed quality of 'regularity' by means of which it differentiated itself so starkly from the 'erratic' pace of life which it sought to supplant.

The Aboriginal peoples of Victoria were not a static culture, however, and adapted to the new rhythms remarkably quickly, given the force of the impact with which these were introduced following the onset of British colonisation. Already by the mid-nineteenth century, the surviving Aboriginal population began to respond by integrating colonial-time within their temporal horizon. What the encounter with colonial society thus inevitably entailed was a shift from one source of external temporal authority to another. As Michael O'Malley states with reference to the same shift characterising western European society during the expansion of industrial capitalism: 'The crucial change ... came not in a fall from some "task-oriented" state of Arcadian grace, but rather from a redefinition of time's authority. As the symbols, artefacts and ideas used to embody time's passage changed, they offered new models for social and political organization.'[87]

The manner in which this transition was enforced and negotiated in settler-colonial Victoria comprises the subject of Chapter 3.

Notes

1 Kay Anderson, *Race and the Crisis of Humanism* (New York: UCL Press, 2007).
2 Nilsson, *Primitive Time-Reckoning*, p. 128.
3 *Ibid*, p. 128.
4 John B. Gribble, *Black but Comely, or, Glimpses of Aboriginal Life in Australia* (London: Morgan & Scott, ca. 1844), p. 20.
5 Anderson, *Race and the Crisis of Humanism*, p. 29.
6 Barbara Arneil, *Locke and America: The Defence of English Colonialism* (Oxford: Clarendon Press, 1996), p. 210; Alan Frost, 'New South Wales as Terra Nullius', in S. Janson and S. Macintyre (eds), *Through White Eyes*, (Sydney: Allen & Unwin, 1990), pp. 65–76; Henry Reynolds, *The Law of the Land* (1987) (Melbourne: Penguin, 2003), p. 25.
7 Wolfe, *Settler Colonialism*, p. 26.
8 Attwood, 'The Past as Future: Aborigines, Australia and the (dis)course of History', in Bain Attwood (ed.), *In the Age of Mabo: History, Aborigines and Australia* (St Leonards: Allen & Unwin, 1996), p. ix; Perkins, *The Reform of Time*, p. 95; see also Rod Macneil, 'Time after time: temporal frontiers and boundaries in colonial images of the Australian landscape', Lynette Russell (ed.), *Colonial Frontiers: Indigenous-European Encounters in Settler Societies* (Manchester: Manchester University Press, 2001), pp. 47–65.
9 Quoted in Donaldson, *Taking Our Time*, p. 145.
10 Alan J. Reid, *Banksias and Bilbies: Seasons of Australia* (Moorabbin: Gould League Victoria, 1995). 'Seven Seasons of the Kulin People', Museum Victoria (www.museumvictoria.com.au/forest/climate/kulin.html – accessed 15 Jan. 2011).
11 Geoffrey Blainey, *Triumph of the Nomads: A History of Ancient Australia*

(Melbourne: Macmillan, 1975), pp. 153, 189, 202–8; Broome, *Aboriginal Australians*, p. 68; Mike Donaldson, 'The End of Time? Aboriginal Temporality and the British Invasion of Australia', *Time and Society*, 5:2 (1996): 187–207, pp. 191–2; Josephine Flood, *Archaeology of the Dreamtime: The Story of Prehistoric Australia and its People* (Sydney: Angus & Robertson, 1996), pp. 238–40, 247.

12 SLV, Rare Books Collection, 'George Augustus Robinson's Journey into South-Eastern Australia, 1844', in G. Mackanness (ed.), *Australian Historical Monographs*, vol. xix (New Series) (Sydney: D. S. Ford, 1941).

13 William Thomas, quoted in *Report of the Select Committee of the Legislative Council on the Aborigines together with the Proceedings of the Committee, Minutes of Evidence, and Appendices*, PPV 1858–59 (hereafter: *Report of the Legislative Council, 1858–59*), vol. 1, 'Replies to Circular Letter, With List of Queries', p. 68.

14 SLV, Rare Books Collection, Edward M. Curr, *The Australian Race: Its Origin, Languages, Customs*, vol. 1 (Melbourne: John Ferres, 1886), p. 65.

15 Richard Brough-Smyth, *The Aborigines of Victoria, with Notes Relating to the Habits of the Natives of Other Parts of Australia and Tasmania*, 2 vols (Melbourne: George Robertson, 1878), vol. 2, p. 295; Donaldson, *Taking our Time*, p. 136; Michael F. Christie, *Aborigines in Colonial Victoria, 1835–86* (Sydney: Sydney University Press, 1979), pp. 17–18.

16 William Thomas, *Report of the Legislative Council*, 1858–59, 'Replies to a Circular Letter, with List of Queries', pp. 25–79.

17 James Dawson, *Australian Aborigines: The Languages and Customs of Several Tribes of Aborigines in the Western District of Victoria, Australia* (Melbourne: George Robertson, 1881), pp. 98–9.

18 Patricia Christies and Martin Bush, 'Stories in the Stars: The Night Sky of the Boorong People', Museum Victoria, 2005 (www.museumvictoria.com.au/pages/6927/stories-in-the-stars.pdf – accessed 3 Mar. 2010).

19 John Morieson, quoted in Guy Healy, 'Good Heavens, an Australian Zodiac', in *The Weekend Australian*, 24–25 Oct. 1998; J. Morieson, 'The Night Sky of the Boorong: Partial Reconstruction of a Disappeared Culture in North-West Victoria', M.A. thesis, University of Melbourne, 1996.

20 See Serena Fredrick, 'The Sky Knowledge: A Study of the Ethnoastronomy of the Aboriginal People of Australia', M.A. thesis, University of Leicester, 2008.

21 PROV, VPRS 4467, mf reel 4, item B/59/2702, William Thomas to Hon. Commissioner of Land Surveys, 25 May 1859. William Thomas also recorded a vocabulary of Kulin languages which included eighteen temporal adverbs. See *Report of the Select Committee of the Legislative Council of Victoria*, Appendix D, pp. 91–92 ('Succinct Sketch of the Aboriginal Language').

22 SLV, MS 11624, box 16/4, Diary of James Dredge, 29 Oct. 1839, p. 42.

23 Richard Sadlier, *The Aborigines of Australia* (Sydney: Government Printer, 1883), p. 21.

24 James Dredge, Diary, 27 Jan. 1840, p. 85.

25 SLV, MS 7881, mf 200, Edward S. Parker. 'The Aborigines of Australia: A Lecture Delivered in the Mechanics Hall, Melbourne, Before the John Knox Youngmen's Association, May 10th, 1854'.

26 John Morgan, *The Life and Adventures of William Buckley, Thirty-two Years a Wanderer Amongst the Aborigines* (1852), C. E. Sayers (ed.) (Melbourne: Heinemann, 1967), pp. 28–9, 47.

27 Morgan, *William Buckley*, p. 11. On reports of settlers losing track of time in the Australian outback see: Davison, *Unforgiving Minute*, pp. 30–1 and Perkins, *The Reform of Time*, p. 14.

28 Morgan, *William Buckley*, p. 65.

29 *Ibid.*, p. 38.

30 According to Buckley's narrative, 'a Bihar, or messenger, came to us; he had his arms striped with red clay, to denote the number of days it would take us to reach the tribe he came from; and the proposed visit was for us to exchange with them eels for roots. The time stated for this march would be fourteen days, and the place was called Bermongo, on the Barwin River.' *Ibid.*, p. 38.

31 *Ibid.*, pp. 56–7.
32 *Ibid.*, p. 92.
33 *Ibid.*, pp. 89–90.
34 Aborigines Protection Society, *Queries Respecting the Human Race, to be Addressed to Travellers and Others* (London: R. & J.E. Taylor, 1841), p. 3.
35 *Report of the Legislative Council*, 1858–59, vol. 1.
36 *Report of the Legislative Council*, 1958–59, 'Replies to a Circular Letter, with List of Queries' (hereafter: 'Replies to a Circular Letter'), p. 25; see also *Report of the Legislative Council*,1858–59, p. v.
37 Brian Stanley, 'Christianity and Civilization in English Evangelical Mission Thought, 1792-1857', in Brian Stanley (ed.), *Christian Missions and the Enlightenment* (Grand Rapids, Mich.: William B. Eedmans Publishing Company, 2001), pp. 169–76. On how monogenist/polygenist debates played out in colonial and missionary contexts see also Jane Samson, 'Ethnology and Theology: Nineteenth-Century Mission Dilemmas in the South Pacific', in Stanley (ed.), *Christian Missions and the Enlightenment*, pp. 108–22.
38 Adas, *Machines as the Measure of Men*, pp. 294–300.
39 PROV, VPRS 2599, box 11, original manuscript version of the 'List of Queries regarding Aboriginal matters', p. 66.
40 'Replies to a Circular Letter', p. 25.
41 Mr. Willis, 'Replies to a Circular Letter', p. 32.
42 W. H. F. Mitchell (J.P.), Kyneton, 'Replies to a Circular Letter', p. 85.
43 All quotations in this section are taken from 'Replies to a Circular Letter', pp. 71–2, unless otherwise noted.
44 Peter Beveridge, Caretaker of the Aborigines, on the Lower Murray (1866).
45 C. E. Strutt, Honorary Correspondent of the Board for the Protection of Aborigines at Echuca (1866).
46 William Thomas, Guardian of the Aborigines (1849-60); previously Assistant Protector of Aborigines (from 1839 to 1849).
47 C. J. Tyers, Commissioner of Crown Lands, Alberton, 'Replies to a Circular Letter', p. 77.
48 'Replies to a Circular Letter', p. 77.
49 W. McKellar, Broken River, 'Replies to a Circular Letter', p. 79.
50 F. R. Godfrey, elected Vice Chairman of the Board for the Protection of the Aborigines in 1876.
51 'Replies to a Circular Letter', pp. 25–79.
52 *Report of the Legislative Council*, 1858–59, p. vi.
53 *Report of the Legislative Council*, 1858–59, p. v.
54 Anderson, *Race and the Crisis of Humanism*, pp. 29, 13.
55 Max Weber, *The Protestant Ethic and the Spirit of Capitalism*, trans. T. Parsons (London: Unwin, 1970), pp. 118–19.
56 Thomas, 'Replies to a Circular Letter', p. 56; John Locke, *Two Treatises of Government*, quoted in Anderson, *Race and the Crisis of Humanism*, p. 47.
57 Mr Huon, 'Replies to Circular Letter', p. 52.
58 Curr, *Recollections of Squatting in Victoria* (1883), H. W. Forster (ed.) (Melbourne: Melbourne University Press, 1965), p. 122.
59 Walter B. Spencer and Francis J. Gillen, *The Native Tribes of Central Australia* (London: Macmillan, 1899), p. 53.
60 J. D. Woods, *The Native Tribes of South Australia* (Adelaide: E. S. Wigg & Son, 1879), p. xxxviii.
61 Michael O'Malley, 'Time, Work and Task Orientation: A Critique of American Historiography', *Time and Society*, 1:3 (1992): 341–58, p. 347.
62 Beveridge, *Report of the Legislative Council*, 'Replies to a Circular Letter', p. 70.
63 'Replies to a Circular Letter' pp. 56–7, 69, 78; George A. Robinson, 'Journey into South-Eastern Australia', p. 30.
64 'Replies to a Circular Letter', p. 57.
65 C. E. Strutt, 'Replies to a Circular Letter', p. 70. Emphasis added.
66 Mr Rusden, 'Replies to Circular Letter', p. 69.

67 William Hull, *Report of Legislative Council*, 1858–59, *Minutes of Evidence*, p. 9; cf. McKellar, 'Replies to Circular Letter', p. 79.
68 Perkins, *Visions of the Future*, p. 89.
69 Rev. Tuckfield, 27 Sep. 1838, quoted in Michael Cannon (ed.), *Historical Records of Victoria* (Melbourne: Victorian Government Printing Office, 1983), 2A, pp. 108–9.
70 SLV, Rare Books Collection, *4th Annual Report of the Melbourne Church of England Mission to the Aborigines of Victoria* (Melbourne: Mason & Firth, 1861), pp. 10–11.
71 J. D. Rogers, *A Historical Geography of the British Colonies*, vol. 6 (Australasia) (Oxford: Clarendon Press, 1907), p. 27.
72 M. Perkins, 'Timeless Cultures: The "Dreamtime" as Colonial Discourse', *Time and Society*, 7:2 (1998): 335–51, p. 346.
73 *Ibid.*, p. 347.
74 *Ibid.*, p. 125.
75 Peter Beveridge 'Replies to Circular Letter', p. 28.
76 'Replies to a Circular Letter', pp. 54–6.
77 Philip Chauncey (J.P. District Surveyor at Ballarat), 'Notes and Anecdotes of the Aborigines of Australia', quoted in Brough-Smyth, *The Aborigines of Victoria*, vol. 2, p. 243.
78 See Brough-Smyth, *The Aborigines of Victoria*, vol. 1, p. 8.
79 AAV, B333, box 2, Robert Thwaites to Captain Page, Framlingham Station Report for the years 1882–83, in *19th Annual Report of the Board for the Protection of Aborigines*, (hereafter: BPA), Appendix 2.
80 N. M. Williams, *The Yolngu and Their Land: A System of Land Tenure and the Fight for its Recognition* (Canberra: Australian Institute of Aboriginal Studies, 1986); Donaldson, 'The End of Time?', p. 192.
81 Reynolds, *Law of the Land*, p. 16.
82 For what it was worth, nomadic peoples' property rights had been addressed in European law, when the eminent philosopher Christian Wolff stated that nomadic people could not legally be dispossessed simply because their patterns of land-use were different from those of agriculturalists. 'For the purpose of assuring cattle or for some other purpose, the intention of wandering, which is governed by that intended use, gives sufficient evidence of the occupation of the lands subject to that use, although they have not established a permanent abode on them.' (Christian Wolff, *The Law of Nations*, (1740–49), quoted in Reynolds, *Law of the Land*, pp. 15–17).
83 PROV, VPRS 4467, mf reel 4, items c/58/1340, c/5/420, William Thomas, 'Aboriginal Affairs Records'.
84 Edward M. Curr, *Report of the Board Appointed to Enquire into, and Report Upon, the Present Condition and Management of the Coranderrk Aboriginal Station*, P.P. Victoria, 1881 (hereafter: *Report on Coranderrk Inquiry*, 1882), in *Minutes of Evidence*, p. 120.
85 *The Members of the Yorta Aboriginal Community v The State of Victoria and Ors* (1998) at para 126 per Olney J. For a critique of Olney's use of Edward Curr's evidence in the above case, see: Samuel Furphy, 'Edward Micklethwaite Curr's *Recollections of Squatting*: Biography, History and Native Title', in P. Edmonds & S. Furphy (eds), *Rethinking Colonial Histories: New and Alternative Approaches* (Melbourne: University of Melbourne, History Department, 2006), pp. 33–48.
86 Godfrey, 'Replies to a Circular Letter', p. 71.
87 O'Malley, 'Time, Work and Task Orientation', p. 355.

CHAPTER THREE

Cultural curfews: the contestation of time in settler-colonial Victoria

> Pretty strict rules, you know. The Aboriginal Protection Board, they called it at the time. Yeah. And your families couldn't come to visit you, unless they had to go to the managers first and say who they were and put down names and what time they got there and how long they were gonna stay ... You only had a time limit, you know, on your stay, your visits, while you were there. Really depressing.
>
> Uncle Colin Walker (Yorta Yorta), 2004.[1]

As the memories of contemporary Aboriginal people who were born and raised on Victoria's missions and reserves in the early-twentieth century can testify, temporal control was part of everyday life during the process of colonisation. Indeed, from the mid-nineteenth century, as colonial policies for dealing with Victoria's rapidly declining Aboriginal population shifted from confrontation to containment and subsequently to assimilation, time played a key role in exercising and maintaining control over the land and its original inhabitants.

'One of the primary objects of discipline is to fix; it is an antinomadic technique,' wrote Foucault; 'it arrests or regulates movements ... it dissipates compact groupings of individuals wandering about the country in unpredictable ways.'[2] What this chapter illustrates is that discipline and the control of human movements were channelled in a temporal as well as a spatial manner. In the colony of Victoria, missions and reserves sought to confine Aboriginal people within an unseen matrix of temporal control, imposing curfews and restrictions which interrupted the regular flow of pre-colonial patterns, rituals and calendars, much as they attempted to prevent their observers' movements across space. Spatially segregating the Indigenous population within missions and reserves inside the colony was a way of curbing and controlling the movements of a society whose rhythms conflicted with those of the newcomers. But the object and consequence was also the normalisation, and later assimilation, of Aboriginal people within the cultural geography of the settler-colony. The act of imposing the colonisers' idea of 'regularity' was another way of eliminating the presence of an Indigenous population, of making its 'irregular' presence less noticeable within colonial society. Given time's role as a marker of culture and identity, attempts to reform the fundamental rhythms of Aboriginal life were tantamount to a denial of Aboriginal identity. This had more than 'merely' cultural implications. In the light of the central economic imperative of settler-colonisation – to assume exclusive control over the land – the very category of indigeneity carried a heightened significance in terms of its inherent claim to prior ownership. Although framed within the rhetoric of philanthropy, therefore, temporal reform complemented the process of territorial dispossession by helping to erase the cultural footprint of an Indigenous presence in Australia. Not by chance, the temporal patterns of cultural behaviour which had previously defined a sense of Aboriginality were explicitly targeted for interruption, abolishment and removal (as were kinship ties, languages and children) – as part of the process of disempowering communities and severing the bonds which connected them to their land and to each other.

'The fate of the Aborigines', historian Graeme Davison writes, 'was to collide with a people whose conceptions of time had lately undergone a mighty revolution, and who were seized with an ambition to subject the whole world to the rule of the clock.'[3] This chapter pauses to reflect on how this process unfolded; how the rule of the clock (and of the seven-day week and the European seasons) was introduced and the ways in which Aboriginal societies responded to such changes. As we will see, rather than simply colliding, people found ways of opposing, contesting and negotiating their way through the new (daily, weekly and annual) rhythms of life.

The war on 'erratic liberty'

The colonisation of time and space in Victoria unfolded in three general phases in relation to the Aboriginal population: confrontation, containment and assimilation.[4]

The first phase began in the mid-1830s, as pastoralist entrepreneurs, squatters and convict workers rapidly invaded and took possession of lands around Port Phillip Bay, then part of the colony of New South Wales. They brought with them herds of cattle and sheep, as well as firearms and new diseases, which wreaked destruction among the local inhabitants on a level of genocidal proportions. The Kulin nations inhabiting the region around Port Phillip Bay were the first to experience the impact of invasion. In offering physical resistance, once it became clear that settlers had no intention of leaving, they suffered heavy casualties amid numerous clashes, leading to a frightening reduction of the Aboriginal population from several thousand to a few hundred survivors, with few attacks on settlers taking place after the first decade of settlement.[5]

Events moved swiftly during this phase: pastoral patterns of land use clashed sharply with the cycles of nomadic life, which the nascent colony sought to shut down aggressively and peremptorily. In the absence of a fixed frontier, the same pattern of elimination and dispossession was repeated again and again across the land as many other Aboriginal peoples of Victoria experienced the impact of colonisation and were soon pushed to the very edge of survival, leading to the belief among Europeans that they would soon simply die out.

The violent dispossession of Indigenous peoples in the Australian colonies (and elsewhere across the British Empire) was sternly denounced during this time by Britain's leading Evangelicals, most notably in the *Report from the Select Committee on Aborigines*, 1837, whose calls for moderation led to the establishment of an official Protectorate in Victoria, which was charged with the task of defending the interests of Aborigines and of imparting unto them the principles of Christianity and civilised life. In 1838, Chief Protector George Augustus Robinson arrived in Melbourne together with his four Assistant Protectors – three of whom had previously been Methodist schoolmasters (William Thomas, James Dredge and Edward Stone Parker).[6] The humanitarians' calls were answered by several other missionary societies, the earliest of which, however, enjoyed but limited success due to the level of interference caused by the voracious pace of white settlement. As fast as missionaries and Protectors gained a foothold, the settler frontier overtook them. And although missionaries and Protectors sought to shield Aborigines from the physical assault of settler-colonisation, they also perceived the 'irregularity' of nomadic movements as a hindrance to their mission. 'While they continue to wander,' an early Wesleyan missionary reported, 'our labours to a very great extent must be lost upon them'.[7] 'The first efforts of missionaries, therefore,' declared Assistant Protector, Edward Stone Parker, 'should be directed to the removal of this excitement of wandering.'[8]

While unnecessary human movement was also viewed with suspicion in Britain at this time, fixing nomadic people to a single location was a common preoccupation of colonial governments, for nomadism posed, in the words of a Victorian settler, 'an insurmountable obstacle to anything approaching centralisation'.[9] The nomads' 'logic of unending travel', as historian Geoffrey Blainey described it, had to

THE COLONISATION OF TIME

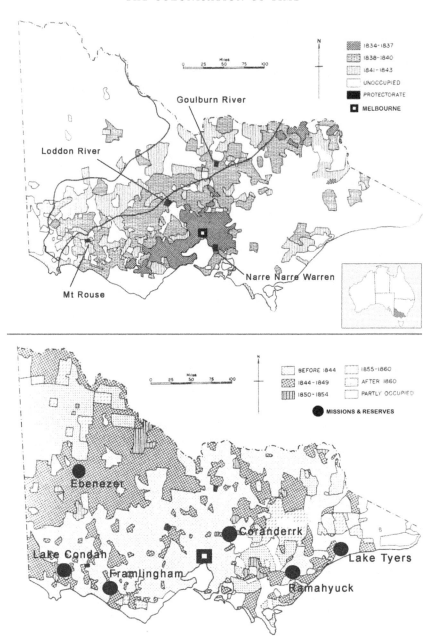

3.1 Map of Victoria, showing rate of European pastoral expansion
from 1834 to 1843 (*above*); and after 1843 (*below*)
In the absence of a fixed frontier, settler-colonisation spread rapidly across the land.

[88]

be reformed into the settlers' logic of sedentary locality.[10] Thus the early missionaries and Protectors began to itinerate with Aboriginal clans, entreating the people they met to abandon their 'wanderings' and settle down in places set aside for them, to cultivate both the soil and their souls, observe the Sabbath and allow their children to be educated in school. The desired goal was to curb 'their erratic liberty', as a cleric in New South Wales put it.[11] In view of this the earliest missionaries were urged to dedicate utmost 'attention to system, order and regularity in all the details of the mission Establishment,' as the Reverend Joseph Orton emphasised in a memorandum to the Wesleyans at the Buntingdale mission. 'I can scarcely conceive that you can spend too much time or patience, in the observance of order among so undisciplined a race of our fellow beings.'[12] In 1836, with similar intent, Governor Bourke established the first school for Kulin children on the banks of the Yarra river: an operation that was placed under the care of an Anglican catechist, George Langhorne, who believed that 'the first aim must be gradually to reconcile them to fixed hours of labour and school'.[13]

At the same time, the rapid expansion of colonial settlements meant that Aboriginal populations rapidly faced insurmountable difficulties in maintaining the rhythms of movement upon which their economy relied. Cattle and sheep alone were responsible for the destruction of native vegetation and fouling of water-sources, thus abruptly curtailing long-established cycles and hunter-gatherer patterns of land use. Under these circumstances, missionaries and Protectors soon became one of the only sources of provision for several displaced Aboriginal groups who, compelled by hunger, settled temporarily on stations and followed the missionaries' directives in exchange for rations.[14] This situation was both acknowledged and exploited by missionaries in order to establish 'order and regularity'. The Wesleyan missionaries at the Buntingdale mission, for example, were under orders that 'the principle of remuneration for service ought to be observed as rigidly as possible, that such provision may operate as an incentive to habits of industry rather than encourage their proneness to indolence'.[15] A similar system was implemented by Assistant Protector William Thomas at the Narre Narre Warren station, where he began dispensing rations only to 'regular adults', as he called them, in order 'to inculcate the idea of locality'.[16] By 1841, a similar strategy had been implemented at all of the Protectorate outposts surrounding Melbourne. (St Paul's maxim that 'He who will not work, neither shall he eat' literally afforded a divine mandate in the execution of this system.)

Indirect coercion was also used to introduce the Christian order of time among Aboriginal peoples in Victoria. As the Wesleyans readily

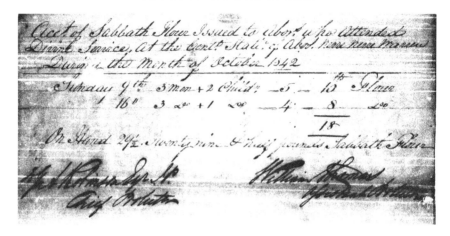

3.2 'Account of Sabbath Flour issued to Aborigines who attended Divine Service ... in the month of October 1842', signed by William Thomas, Assistant Protector of Aborigines

admitted, rations were handed out, 'not only to those who are employed on the mission premises, but to all who come on the Sabbath; an expedient which is desirable according to the present state of things, as they are almost in a state of starvation and can only obtain food day by day, by begging or hunting'.[17] Among William Thomas's correspondence files, we indeed find an account for aptly named 'Sabbath Flour' (see figure 3.2), which the Protectors dispensed to those Aborigines who consented to stop and honour the Sabbath on Sundays.[18]

The Kulin peoples of Victoria were not so much taught to observe the Lord's Day as they were compelled to do so by necessity. Indeed, given their dire circumstances, it was not long before they had learnt to recognise the seven-day pattern of the coloniser's weekly ritual. As Joseph Orton wrote in 1839 – less than five years after the British occupation of Victoria:

> Many of those who have been in the habit of associating with the missionaries begin to comprehend some of the great principles of religion ... They know well the return of the Sabbath, on which occasions they are in the habit of assembling in considerable numbers and proceeding with the mission family to the place where European service is held ... Not only do they know the return of the seventh day, but some of them have an idea of the sacredness of the day.[19]

The inculcation of order and regularity was not pursued solely by missionaries. In 1839, as a means of implanting notions of uniform and regimented behaviour, Captain Alexander Maconochie submitted a proposal to the New South Wales Governor for employing Aboriginal people in a trained police corps. Apart from 'secur[ing] them against want and idleness', Maconochie claimed, the Native Police would help establish the fundamental tenets of disciplined behaviour which might one day qualify Aborigines for white employment: 'A knowledge of, and taste for European manners and civilization, would be thus extensively yet silently implanted, and the habits of order, concert, and decorum learnt and practised in the field, would probably sooner pervade their huts and family stations than is now thought possible.'[20]

The Native Mounted Police was officially assembled in 1842. Its daily routine was organised as follows: a trumpet call at 5.30 a.m. signalled the hour of rising (6 a.m. in winter); 8 a.m. was breakfast; '10 a.m. saw the men and horses parading in the paddock; drills lasted for two hours after that, and continued for another two hours after lunch; 4 p.m. was the hour for taking the horses to drink.'[21] The punishment for lassitude ranged from withholding pay to outright dismissal, and the Day Book of the Native Police shows that several troopers were brought before the officer in charge for offences such as 'neglect of duty' and 'idleness'.[22] In his *Recollections of Squatting in Victoria* (1883), Edward Curr provides a descriptive account of the troopers' ritual of dismounting, their un-slinging of carbines and removal of cloaks, etc.:

> The uniformity practised in such matters by the troopers, and their systematic clock-work-like mode of managing matters which civilians are apt to look on as trifles, did not fail to elicit, *sotto voce*, uncomplimentary remarks from some of my men [ex-convicts], to whom such methodical ways brought back unpleasant reminiscences of prison days.[23]

But all this was merely a prelude of things to come. During the first two decades of settlement, the colonisation of time unfolded rather ineffectively and unsystematically: the Native Mounted Police reached its greatest number of (sixty) troopers in 1851, but was disbanded shortly thereafter. All other missionary societies which commenced operations during this period (the Baptists at Merri Creek, the Moravians at Lake Boga; the Church of England at Yelta) were short-lived. Indeed, despite the increasing challenges posed by off-station life, the greater part of the Aboriginal population treated the missions and Protectorate stations merely as interim shelters and depots, refusing to settle permanently and preventing them from becoming stable communities. With dwindling members, general settler hostility and a lack of funding and government support, it was not long before all the early missions, and the Protectorate itself, were disbanded.[24]

3.3 Time-ball tower in Williamstown, Melbourne (*ca* 1900)

This provided ships' captains with a daily signal for setting their chronometers in Melbourne (where the tower still stands). It is depicted here in a postcard celebrating Christmas—another ritual introduced to Victoria by Europeans.

A new order of time: on the missions and reserves

As the settler population grew dramatically in the wake of the discovery of gold in western Victoria, and as settler-colonisation spread rapidly across the land, the sound of European time grew correspondingly bolder and louder. The growth of Melbourne as a major commercial node in the trade network of Empire, following the discovery of gold in western Victoria in 1851, was reflected in the proliferation of clocks. In 1841, *Kerr's Melbourne Almanac listed* only four clockmakers in Melbourne; a decade later there were seventeen and by 1854 the number had more than doubled. The sounds of bells began to fill Melbourne's aural landscape by announcing the order of clock-time to all those within its audible range: the city's first peal was the six-bell peal installed in St James' Old Cathedral in 1852.

With the clock came other key developments portending the extension of Britain's temporal culture to Victoria. The first railway terminus was established in 1854, with scheduled services for passengers and goods along the four-kilometre track between Flinders Street and Port Melbourne, and soon it was extended to connect the city centre with St Kilda, Richmond and Hawthorn. The following year, the Williamstown astronomical observatory was completed at Point Gellibrand, its main function being to provide Melbourne's longitude and a time service to the ships in Hobsons Bay. In 1861, a time-ball was erected above the Williamstown lighthouse (see figure 3.3) to replace the old light-and-shutter time signal, thereby plugging Melbourne's clocks into the GMT spatio-temporal matrix which was connecting all important coastal towns in the Empire at this time. As in many other British ports located around the world, the time-ball was lifted and dropped at one o'clock each day – local mean time – so that ships' captains could correct their chronometers by it before sailing out with their cargo. Soon, telegraph signals would activate the time-ball remotely and link communications between Melbourne and Geelong (1854), as well as Ballarat and other central Victorian gold towns by 1856.[25]

As the aural frontier of colonial time was amplified, Kulin-time became correspondingly less audible. By 1858, many of the settlers described the general state of Victoria's Aboriginal population as 'quiet': 'They are perfectly quiet; and I am not aware of any depredation having been committed against life or property for many years back.' 'Quiet' was a sinister euphemism for describing the dismal aftermath of British occupation with its alarming decline of the Aboriginal population. The new sounds of the land were increasingly those of the agricultural and pastoral industries, regulated by the calendars and seasons of labour. 'The aborigines in this district ... are quiet,' one settler reported; 'They

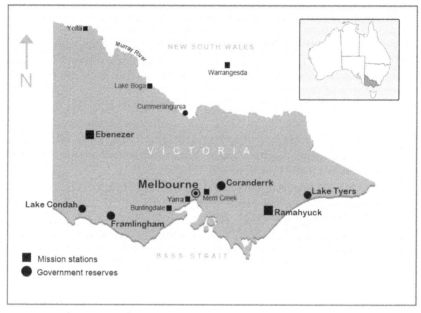

3.4 Map of Victoria, showing approximate locations of mission stations and Government reserves

are employed for sheep-washing, harvesting, and cutting wood; and are paid in money for such services.'[26]

It was around this time that the Government of Victoria began to consider ways of dealing with the surviving Aboriginal population in the colony. In 1856, a group of settlers had gone so far as to petition Parliament to relocate all the survivors to one of the islands in the Bass Strait. With a staff of Protectors and teachers to oversee them, the petitioners proposed that the natives' 'restless roving disposition, and the difficulty of getting them to apply their minds steadily for any length of time ... would in great measure be overcome'. An Alcatraz-like setting would prevent anyone from escaping the regimentation of time, the petition recommended. 'The blacks would be compelled to go for their meals at stated hours, and the foundation of the habits of regularity, which would be of infinite service when their mental culture came to be attempted, would be laid'.[27]

No such removals took place in the end. Instead, the same logic of isolation and temporal control was effectively deployed on the mainland, when, following the recommendations of the recent 1858–59 Select Committee (discussed in Chapter 2), Victoria's Parliament deployed the Aboriginal reserve and rationing system. So began the era of separation in Victoria, which was designed to achieve the gradual confinement of Aboriginal peoples in a number of reserves and missions – and, simultaneously, the further vacating of Aboriginal lands for the use of pastoralists and settlers. By the end of the 1860s there were six main stations in place. Three of these were Christian missions – Lake Tyers (Anglican), Ebenezer (Moravian), and the Presbyterian and Moravian mission at Ramahyuck – while the other three were government-controlled reserves: Coranderrk, Lake Condah and Framlingham.[28] (See figure 3.4.) Further Parliamentary legislation in 1869 saw the creation of the Board for the Protection of the Aborigines, vested with new coercive powers enabling it to prescribe where Aboriginal people could reside, the work contracts in which they could be engaged, the manner in which their earnings might be distributed, and how the care and custody of their children should be managed.[29] By the late 1870s, as a census reveals, almost half of the Aboriginal population (which amounted to merely 1,067 individuals) was living on missions and reserves.[30] While small groups of people might still be found resisting insulation and captivity on the reserves, moving on and off the stations as they pleased, the majority already had some experience of station life. By the 1870s, Bain Attwood suggests, the mission effectively 'dominated the Aboriginal milieu'.[31]

The mission environment confined the inmates both temporally and spatially through rules and regulations which privileged the timetables of agriculture, pastoralism and Christianity, whilst curtailing the 'irregular' movements, calendars, rituals and economies of precolonial society. The Board for the Protection of Aborigines (henceforth, 'the Board') prescribed a clock-governed division of activities for all the inmates: children would be made to progress through the day with 'a certain number of hours to labour, and a certain number of hours to attendance in the school ... leaving them, however, a proper amount of time for play and rest.'[32] Curfews and timetables were a significant part of the rules and regulations imposed on reserves. At the Coranderrk station in 1864 the daily timetable for children stipulated:

1. The hours of attendance at school shall be for children from half past one o'clock p.m. until three o'clock p.m.; and for men, from six o'clock p.m. until eight o'clock p.m. throughout the year.

2. All the Aborigines shall be mustered at eight o'clock every morning and they shall be inspected by the Master and Matron.[33]

Once most Aboriginal people in Victoria came to be confined on reserves, and as off-station alternatives diminished, missionaries and station managers could easily afford to make a clearer distinction than their predecessors in dispensing rations; between those who spent their time industriously and to those who worked sporadically. 'I give those who work regular one pound (1lb) daily,' reported John Green, Coranderrk's relatively benevolent manager, in 1871, 'but those who will not work regular I give them only six or seven pound'.[34] Several rolls of attendance, or 'Time Books', which note the hours worked and the equivalent rations or wages dispensed, attest to the use of this system.[35] The Moravian missionaries at the Ebenezer mission were praised by the Board for keeping 'a very interesting diary, showing the occupation of the blacks on the station from sunrise to sunset'.[36]

The reform of time and work-ethic were part of the same process; civilising and Christianising went hand in hand; and missionaries and station-managers applied themselves not only to evangelising but equally to supervising the regular flow of work and prayer. The aim was not simply to induce people to work, however, but to work in a regular and uniform manner, for a specific period of time per day. 'Regularity', rather than productivity, was the sought-after objective. So much can be inferred from a statement of the Reverend Stähle on the Lake Condah reserve: 'Though the hours of labour are short, ... regularity in keeping at the work shows its effect by the station constantly improving.'[37] Similarly, praise was directed by the Board towards Coranderrk in the 1860s, much being said regarding the beneficial effects of 'the system of regular industry introduced and adopted amongst the adults,' and the 'order and regularity ... everywhere apparent'.[38] On Victoria's missions and reserves, it was often this vision of order and regularity that was viewed with satisfaction rather than the productivity of the labour itself. An official memo to Coranderrk's manager in 1876, for example, expressed the Board's concern with the outward appearance of work-discipline, rather than the productiveness of the labour itself: 'Attention should be particularly directed to inducing the people to go about their work in a heartier manner', it recommended, 'in a less listless way than now.'[39] A similar logic applied to the Christian order of time, with more satisfaction being expressed for the visual display of Sunday conduct than the extent to which the people actually understood, or indeed believed, the spiritual significance of the Sabbath. 'They have evidently been carefully taught', an inspector reported after witnessing the 'orderly, quiet, almost solemn manner' in which the Aborigines had conducted themselves during the Sunday Services at Coranderrk. '[I]f they but faintly understand the object and purpose of the service which they attend every morning and evening, the effect on their minds cannot be small.'[40]

A common belief among both missionaries and settler-colonial society was that the surviving population of Aborigines might eke out a living by becoming a landless proletariat. In this case, as William

Thomas had predicted, 'the highest pitch the Aborigines could ever arrive to would be that of a hired labourer'.[41] Aborigines would in fact make substantial contributions to the pastoral industry; during the labour shortage that followed the gold rush of 1851, for example. As Henry Reynolds notes, however, the primary objective of reformers was generally to teach Aborigines to conform to the *notion* of how the working classes should ideally behave, rather than to transform them into the *actual* working class.[42] In the Cape Colony, as we will see in following chapters, the centrality of labour in the relationship between colonisers and colonised was such that the project to reform 'African time' witnessed a much greater emphasis on inculcating among Africans the temporal mores of capitalist ideology. But in Victoria, where the primary aim of settler-colonisation was to replace Aboriginal people on their land, time served first and foremost as a means of substantiating settler claims of superiority and of absorbing the Indigenous presence within settler space. If Aboriginal labour subsequently proved useful, this was a bonus, but not an expectation.[43]

The order of the day: the mission bell

Colonisation in Victoria witnessed the imposition on Aboriginal peoples of a new order of events and rhythm of life, right across the spectrum of social time – from annual seasons and calendars to weekly and daily routines. The imposition of the new temporal regime ultimately sought to jostle the pace of family time and to interfere with kinship systems (as we saw in the opening quote of this chapter). In this sense, the mission and reserve environment was at times that of a total institution, seeking to subordinate all aspects of life to a centralised authority. In this environment, clocks were instated as the new authorities of colonial time; while bells became their acoustic heralds, punctuating the order of the day and providing a new referent for people to orient themselves in time.

Bells were certainly omnipresent on Victoria's stations, not as mere ornaments but rather as essential instruments involved in the timing of daily activities. References to their utilitarian function are relatively scant in the historical archive – an omission that belies the extent to which these instruments featured in the daily experience of mission life. But they did often feature in missionary narratives (not just in Victoria but across the British Empire), as a symbol of Christian conversion – often accompanied by images of Christianised natives punctually responding to its 'call'. 'It is cheerful', the Reverend John Bulmer reported from the Lake Tyers mission, 'to see them at once following the sound of the church bell to go to the house of God.'[44]

3.5 'Group of Aborigines at Coranderrk mission', with manager's house and bell-post in background (*ca* 1903)

We know that a bell was used at the Moravian station of Ebenezer: it had been expressly sent to Australia all the way from Saxony and sounded the mission's official opening in 1860. So powerfully did the bell prefigure as a symbol of religious conversion in the mind of the local missionary, the Reverend Friedrich Hagenauer, that he even penned an ode to it in later years: 'Ebenezer Bell' –

> Where lately nought was rife but sin and sadness,
> A little bell rings out in tones of gladness –
> A welcome to the service of the Lord,
> A call to raise the voice with one accord
> In Ebenezer.
>
> Ah yes! That little Ebenezer bell
> Could now a tale of stirring interest tell,
> Of hopes and prayers and longings for the hour
> When Christ, the Sun, should rise in glorious power
> In Ebenezer.[45]

Such panegyric imagery conveys little about how bells also functioned as tools for exercising control. But a closer look at mission and station life reveals the amount of authority with which they were endowed.

3.6 Coranderrk: 'Going to morning prayer' (1904)
Inset: the bell, captured in action.

As surviving photographs of missions and reserves illustrate, the bell-post was usually located in a central, elevated and commanding position; on the Coranderrk station, the order and direction of each day's activities were issued directly beneath it.[46] Within the planned mission environment, the location of the bell on the mission grounds was a clear indication of its centralising authority, a reminder that the control of time was paralleled by geographies of spatial power – as Jane Lydon has documented in a detailed study of Moravian missions in Victoria.[47] More than a century later, the sound of the same bell resonates clearly in the memory of a contemporary Kulin Elder, recollecting her time spent as a youth at Coranderrk: 'They also had this bell,' Aunty Joy Murphy Wandin recalls, 'the traditional bell that you pull, the cord that you pull and it rings. And that was the wake-up call in the morning for everyone to go to church to say prayers, and from there that day would begin. So it was very much an everyday part of life.'[48]

The bell was part of every-day life on all the mission stations in Victoria. As a visiting journalist noted during a visit to the Moravian mission of Ramahyuck in Gippsland, the result was a fairly regimented order of activities. 'From the early hour at which the men gather at the store to obtain their daily rations of meat until evensong ... everything goes on regularly as on board ship.' In ensuring such regularity, it was often necessary for bells to be rung at fairly close intervals. Thus, alongside the larger fixed bells in the church spire, the Reverend Hagenauer also adopted the use of smaller handbells as a supplementary means of urging the tardy to their duties.[49] In Hagenauer's grip, the small handbell served as a constant reminder of the punctuality demanded on the mission – as well as the coercive nature of its temporal regime. As the same journalist remarked, half in jest: 'none dares be indolent or insubordinate here, for my good-tempered-looking host [Hagenauer] has a mighty arm as well as a large heart'.[50]

One of the effects of this strict temporal *milieu* was to familiarise mission and station residents with the language of clock-time. Thus, when requested to describe a day in the life at Coranderrk, James Edgar – one of five youths examined before the 1877 Royal Commission on the Aborigines – demonstrated fluency in the clock-governed discourse which regulated each day's events. The exchange is worth citing in full:

> Will you tell me what you do; what is your usual work on the station; how do you begin the day; are the blacks called together in the morning every day in the schoolroom? – To go to work.
>
> Before they go to work? – The bell rings at nine o'clock.
>
> What happens then? – They go to work.
>
> How long do you work? – Three hours in the forenoon and three in the afternoon, six hours.
>
> What do you do before work, before nine or after work, when you knock off? – We do not do much after we knock off.
>
> You do what you like? – Yes; at five o'clock the bell rings, at five in the afternoon.
>
> And after that you can do what you please, amuse yourselves, and do anything you like? – Yes.
>
> And what is done on Sunday? Do you have any service there? – Yes.
>
> What time? – Eleven.
>
> Is any school held? – Yes, on Sunday.
>
> For the children? – Yes, for the children.
>
> Do you have service in the afternoon after that? – We have service at seven o'clock.[51]

The progress being made by Aboriginal youths in terms of their acquaintance with Western notions of time was of significance to colonial authorities during the 1877 Royal Commission, in which a number of Aboriginal people were called to testify. The Commissioners even quizzed some of the latter on their basic maths skills, whilst testing their ability to speak of time and money as exchangeable commodities:

> If you had a shilling a day, how much would you have at the end of the week? – That would be only six bob.
>
> At the end of the month, four weeks, how many 'bob'? – (After thinking for some time) – Twelve. No, twenty-four.[52]

Writing about language, Frantz Fanon noted that, 'to speak means to be in a position to use a certain syntax, to grasp morphology of this or that language, but it means above all to assume a culture, to support the weight of a civilization ... To speak a language is to take on a world, a culture.'[53] Hours, weeks, months, Sabbaths, work seasons, years and ages were significant cultural components of the colonisers' language, reminders that Europeans carried with them to the colonies a temporal vocabulary of time which they expected everyone to accept and internalise as their own. Consider how the following exchange, between the Commissioner and another Aboriginal youth, brings this into relief in terms of the choice of words used to define the concept of 'age':

> How old were you when you came [to Coranderrk]? – I have no idea.
>
> Do you know how old you are now? – *I am supposed to be* about twenty-two.
>
> Then you must have been about ten when you came in? – I was a boy then, but I have no idea how old I was then.
>
> You had no whiskers then? – No, I had no whiskers then.[54]

The first generation of people living on missions in Victoria were told what age they were 'supposed to be', much as they were given a new – Christian – name which they were supposed to go by. As exemplified by Crusoe's symbolic naming of 'Friday', the conferral of new names and ages was subliminally linked to the instatement of Christian time: a new concept of age imparted a 'civilised' identity in the place of a 'savage' one, replacing the Aboriginal concept of age – defined by the calendars of Aboriginal rituals and initiations – with one defined by the colonisers. In the above exchange, however, the two languages of time – not arriving at a common agreement – were forced to settle on a neutral definition of age: the biological time of the human body (a temporal *lingua franca*).

As these vignettes imply, pre-emptive efforts to inculcate a new sense of time was directed with the greatest of intensity towards youths, for children were commonly regarded by colonial authorities as a *tabula rasa*, and more promising subjects than their 'irreclaimable' parents. Consequently in what became one of the darkest chapters in Australia's history, unknown numbers of children were systematically separated from their parents throughout the nineteenth century (and the twentieth), and placed on missions or settler households with the explicit intent of facilitating their assimilation into white society. Part of this process entailed, once again, raising children to be conditioned to orienting their lives around the authority of the clock. 'Having myself brought up and educated an aboriginal boy from the time he was six years old,' one settler reported to the Board in 1861, 'I found that it conduced greatly to his habits of regularity and cleanliness to make him wash himself all over at a stated time every morning.'[55] The objective was what historian Michael O'Malley refers to as 'a redefinition of time's authority'; the substitution of the clock for nature as the prime model for social organisation.[56]

The order of the week: work and leisure

Western society demands a strict and very particular demarcation between work time and leisure time, in a way that distinguishes it from many other cultures in the world. A glimpse of the endeavour to enforce these temporal boundaries among Aboriginal peoples comes to us from 1865, when Lucy Edgar, daughter of the Superintendent of an Aboriginal reserve at Merri Creek (now an inner-city suburb of Melbourne) witnessed the arrival of the first group of children recently removed from their families. 'Not the faintest idea of figures had the poor fellows,' she wrote; 'they could not count their fingers, nor tell how many moons it was since they left the bush.' What was more, she noted with implied disdain, 'they were greatly surprised that they should not be allowed to dawdle about all day long, get their meals when they pleased, and smoke, sleep, or bathe in the rivers as the fit seized them'.[57]

Lucy Edgar's words portended great changes for the children, and the new life on the mission quickly sought to curtail such irreverent conduct. Being 'civilised' entailed recognising not only the appropriate behaviour for certain occasions but also the appropriate time for each and every action – work, leisure or prayer. It was precisely in drawing the ideological line between what counted as 'work' and what as 'leisure' that another fundamental step was taken in the process of reforming and absorbing Aboriginal rhythms. For by enforcing this distinction, the activities that previously constituted the very modes of production of society were relegated to the secondary category of pastimes and recreations. This process was achieved in part through the medium of temporal control, for such activities were permitted only during 'residual' time slots in the week.

In an attempt to replicate the ideal temporal order of British society, station managers and missionaries attempted to ensure, as a rule, that all men and women carried out a five-day, or a five-and-a-half-day, working week. A 'good day's work' at Coranderrk consisted of eight hours per day – from nine till one and from two till five, with Saturday being a 'holiday' on which rations were dispensed.[58] Moreover, work had to be of a pastoral or agricultural nature , and not of 'native' ilk. Thus, hunting, fishing and – worse still – the holding of corroborees, were strictly prohibited during the normal days of the week. What time was not taken up by the necessary labours and devotions came to be known as 'time off', and it was these periods which were set aside for other 'traditional' Aboriginal activities – e.g. hunting, fishing, spear-making, tree-climbing, basket-making, boomerang-throwing, game-playing, etc. Though it was recorded with approval by some station managers that such activities were gradually becoming 'lost arts' amongst the Aborigines, hunting and fishing continued to be tolerated, provided that these pursuits respected the temporal boundaries set aside for 'recreation'. The Reverend Hagenauer reported with satisfaction from Ramahyuck: 'Some of the old blacks are still hunting native game and the enjoyment of fishing [sic], in which all join on their free afternoons or holidays.'[59] Likewise, the women were encouraged to undertake basket-making in their 'spare' time.

These mundane forms of temporal control placed temporal barriers – a permanent curfew in effect – which reduced pre-colonial economic activities to the level of sports and pastimes, disempowering and thus subsuming them within the new dominant order of schedules of events. 'Many of the Aborigines gladly employ themselves in their leisure hours in fishing,' the Board's Secretary, Richard Brough-Smyth, recorded; 'and the streams near Coranderrk are certainly such as to tempt *sportsmen* to indulge in this *pastime.*'[60] Similarly, Hagenauer reported in 1891, 'The Blacks like occasionally to hunt and fish here, though not for the sake of getting supplies, but for pleasure.'[61]

Hunting and gathering were no longer regarded as harmful or threatening to settler society once they were demoted from their previous status as economic modes of production to that of pastimes and leisure activities. This process was achieved largely through temporal control, by assigning specific days for work, rest, pastimes and prayer – and specifically through the institutionalisation of the seven-day week as the dominant ritual of life. The system is reported on every mission and reserve in Victoria:

THE COLONISATION OF TIME

3.7 A vision of order: Warrangesda mission (New South Wales)
Scene depicting the bell, the flag, and the ideal separation between the spheres of work (*left*) and leisure (*right*).

At Ebenezer: 'Saturday and, when work is slack, Wednesday are allowed for fishing and hunting, of which both young and old are fond.'[62]

At Ramahyuck: 'Fishing and hunting receive proper attention on days set aside for that purpose.'[63]

At Framlingham: 'The men continue to hunt native game, and to fish during the season. Every Saturday is occupied by them in hunting.'[64] 'Have they any stated times for hunting? – Saturday.'[65]

At Coranderrk: 'Have they not some spare time during the week in which they can hunt? – They have every Saturday.'[66]

At Lake Tyers: 'The blacks still hunt native game on the proper hunting days, as there is not sufficient meat to supply all they require.'[67]

At Lake Condah: 'Do they have any part of the week to go hunting? – Yes, the whole of Saturday.'[68]

'Saturday is always a holiday, and, when the natives have done a special piece of work particularly well, an extra holiday is occasionally given to enable them to go fishing or hunting.'[69]

The cyclical pattern of the seven-day week was institutionalised across the mission *milieu*, and enforced through threats of punishments, fines, curtailing of rations, wages and even banishment and separation from family members, for those who stepped out of line. An Aboriginal man at Coranderrk, for example, forfeited his rations and was forced to leave the station for twelve months, when it was discovered that he had gone fishing on a Tuesday. As the man in question reported during the 1881 Government enquiry into the management of Coranderrk, 'I had not enough meat to keep me so ... I went out fishing one day, on a Tuesday, upon the Yarra, and came back again, and got my rations stopped.'[70] The culprit had transgressed the order to the week; for the mission's rules decreed that all the men should work on weekdays; and fishing, as we have seen, was not classified as 'work', but as a pastime which (at Coranderrk) could only be engaged in on Saturdays.

Whilst framed in the rhetoric of improvement, the intent of such curfews was to confine Aboriginal people within the limits established by settler-colonial society. Vestiges of pre-colonial Aboriginal life were tolerated, provided that they accepted 'their place' in time within the new dominant order of society.

Whilst attempts to establish the regular alternation of work and leisure comprised one side of the order of the week, the religious side of this process consisted in punctuating the end of each week with a Christian Sabbath. Thus the temporal regimes of both religion and economy complemented and reinforced one another, for the same bell that called people to work also became the device for heralding times of prayer. At Ramahyuck, 'religious ordinances on the Sabbath day are strictly observed,' Hagenauer announced in his annual report. 'Altogether the Sabbath is kept as a day of rest for the body and enjoyment for the heart and soul.' Such enjoyment was *mandatory*, however, as Sunday attendance was subject to a thorough regime of surveillance and accountability, whereby 'if one is absent without cause, inquiry is made for the reason of such absence.' For, as Hagenauer explained, 'to attend at the house of God at the beginning of the day, and to be present at conclusion at sunset, belongs to the order of the daily life'.[71]

The order of the year: redefining the seasons

One of the key differences between the four, equal-length seasons of northern Europe, and the heterogeneous, unequal-length seasons which pre-dated the British occupation of Australia, consists in their respective sources of temporal authority. Both European and Aboriginal calendars function within their respective cultural and geographical contexts; in each case, they are recognised as possessing a cyclical rhythm, a property any time-correlation device must provide in order to prove useful.[72] But whilst Aboriginal seasons are tied to their local environments, Europe's are tied to astronomical cycles and thus decontextualised from local natural variables, by virtue of which they can effectively be exported from their original context. This abstraction of time from its local environment literally permitted Europeans to carry the four seasons with them, superimposing them on local seasons wherever they went around the globe. This did not mean, however, that the four seasons – winter, spring, summer and autumn – were geographically suited to the Australian environment and its weather patterns. The simple act of reversing the order of the seasons does not make them compatible with local, antipodean climates and cycles, nor does it alter the fact that they are a fundamentally alien calendar which was introduced by superimposition over nature, rather than in response to it.

The fact that the four European seasons are still commonly observed in Victoria, and elsewhere across Australia, exemplifies the ongoing and structural nature of settler-colonisation, which continues to displace local seasons and cycles in much the same way as the peoples who observed them continue to be displaced from their lands. Whilst this daily reality occasionally surfaces into public consciousness, it is seldom acted upon in any practical way – no doubt because of how deeply entrenched time is in society. 'We are cultural imperialists and we have just said what we want the weather to be,' a spokesperson for the New South Wales Weather Bureau complained in 1995. 'We came out here and said that there are four seasons in Europe so four seasons there should be here. Why should there be four seasons in Australia just because there are four seasons in London?'[73] By now the answer to this question should be clear: time, calendars, season, rituals and so forth are a deeply ingrained aspect of cultural identity; preserving continuity with familiar (in this case, northern hemispheric) patterns of time rather than adopting Indigenous ones, allowed the colonisers to retain a sense of who they were in the antipodes.

It was the antipodeans, however, who were expected to adjust to the new seasons of the colonisers. Thus, the four seasons and the calendars associated with the new economy – whaling, sealing, shearing, planting, harvesting, etc. – introduced a new pattern of life which effaced pre-colonial rhythms on the longer end of the timescale: the Kulin fire-stick seasons, for instance, which for millennia had comprised the local method of farming the land and maximising the replenishment of natural resources, were extinguished by the new dominant calendars and economies of time/land management.

As all missions and reserves in Victoria came to pursue some form of cultivation of specialised crops in a bid to generate income, the calendars of agriculture arguably helped to familiarise Aboriginal people with European years, seasons and months, more than anything else. The Ramahyuck mission, for example, started cultivating and preparing arrowroot hops from 1876, as well as experimenting with cotton cultivation and basket willows for a basket-making venture. Lake Condah cultivated potatoes, hops, and oats for hay. At Coranderrk, where men were employed seasonally in hop-picking, workers were soon familiarised with the hops-calendar: a month to dig, a month to prune, and a month to pole – followed by a month of rest before the hops were ready for picking.[74] Such rhythms mirrored England's seasonal agricultural activity, where hop-picking was an established form of itinerant seasonal labour.

In the pastoral sector too, Aboriginal men were widely employed in mustering, horse-riding, shearing, and sheep washing. The shearing industry exerted a particularly strong temporal influence on workers; it required not merely a daily timetable of activity but also a highly structured year-round calendar. Indeed, given the seasonal nature of the work, the shearing industry effectively tied large groups of male workers to single locations for specific periods of time. This also impacted on their families, as the occupation was often passed on from father to son and it was not unusual for all the men in a family to be shearers. All these changes did not exclusively affect the men – who were in many ways colonised differently from Aboriginal women.

The latter were generally consigned to indoor domestic chores (which generally went unpaid) and in other seasonal forms of labour – including their sexual labour, which male settlers also valued on a seasonal basis.[75]

In turn, the feasts and holidays which punctuated the pauses of the working year for white workers gradually became holidays for Europeans and Aboriginal men and women alike, gradually supplanting yet another aspect of pre-colonial life with the rituals and calendars of European society. As the Reverend Stähle described from Lake Condah towards the end of the century, 'some of the men were away shearing, and, as is always the case, they returned in time to spend the Christmas season at home with their dear ones'.[76]

This control over space was intimately connected to control over time. Movements between reserves were tolerated provided they took place in response to the seasons sanctioned by the pastoral and agricultural calendars. This explains why the only instance in which Aboriginal people were encouraged to move across the colony, from one station or mission to another, was if their intent was to take up regular employment at their destination. Missionaries and station managers happily issued 'passes' for travel across the colony during the shearing and harvest seasons, for example – but not during the hunting and fishing season, and certainly not for the corroboree seasons. Movements in response to these calendars were categorised as instances of 'itinerant labour' rather than 'wandering' and 'going walkabout'. Time which generated money was worth more than time which used it up – a doctrine clearly invoked by the Reverend John Bulmer in his report for the Lake Tyers station: 'I think the blacks begin to show a more settled disposition,' he wrote. 'The only time they have wandered during the year was at hop-picking. For this there is some excuse, as they like to earn money.'[77]

Most essentially, this epitomised the full extent of the 'colonisation of time': the enforcement of a collective ideological shift in the understanding of what constituted the permissible time for each and every activity, including moving through the land. It was by monopolising time – at the yearly, weekly and daily level – that all extraneous Aboriginal activities and movements were further confined and assimilated within settler-colonial society. The seasonal calendar of agriculture, for instance, effectively dominated the movements of people on and between the stations, as described by Uncle Albert Mullett, a contemporary Koorie Elder who experienced life on the Lake Tyers reserve in the mid-twentieth century:

> Only time our mob was allowed money was outside when they got a permit to go off and work outside doing the season's work ... In later

years that happened and a lot of the families came off Lake Tyers during the bean picking season and the peas and winter-time they go back to Lake Tyers. They might come out for a couple of months or more ... All depends on the season you know.[78]

Indeed, 'it all depends on the season'. But whose seasons? As territorial needs for agriculture and pastoralism displaced and curtailed nomadic and hunter-gatherer movements spatially, so too did the accompanying calendars and routines begin to dislocate Aboriginal calendars of migration, trade and lore. By the 1870s, Aboriginal people still to be found moving outside of missions and reserves were doing so increasingly in accordance with agricultural or pastoral calendars of economic events. As a settler reported to the Board, 'as a rule they do not care about work except at shearing time'.[79] In turn, itinerant work gave rise to patterns of movement that actually came to resemble those of pre-colonial times. They 'lead, the greater part of the year, a vagabond or gypsy-like life,' a settler reported, 'moving in small parties from station to station, as chances of obtaining food from the settlers offer; and ... during the shearing season some of these assist in shearing sheep'.[80]

Aboriginal people in Victoria were able to adapt to this new, often hostile, environment with remarkable success, maintaining elements of cultural continuity by alternating between one world and the other.[81] The story of 'Gnaweeth' – as recorded by a sympathetic settler, James Dawson, in the 1850s – illustrates this well. Gnaweeth was an Aboriginal sheep herder in western Victoria, who had applied for leave from his white employer in order to attend an important meeting of Aboriginal clans. His request, however, was denied: Gnaweeth was told that the farm could not do without him because the recent discovery of goldfields nearby had resulted in a local shortage of shepherds.

But when the time of the meeting arrived, Gnaweeth disappeared. From the farmer's perspective, he had gone 'walkabout'. As Dawson described the event:

> Having thus broken his engagement, [Gnaweeth] considered he had forfeited all claim to payment for the work which he had before faithfully performed; and, therefore, deposited at the back door of the house a bundle containing his clothing, blankets, gun, and every other article that had been given to him for his long services. He gave all his property rather than disobey the summons. Many months passed over ere he was heard of; and it was only after repeated invitations and assurances of welcome that he returned. He then explained, that, had he neglected the summons to attend the meeting, his life would have been forfeited.[82]

Although Dawson cited this story as evidence of the Aborigines' exacting obedience to tradition, the subtext clearly evokes the sense that many Aboriginal people were often caught between the temporal exigencies of two worlds. In order to keep alive their cultural rituals and calendars, Aboriginal men and women often risked losing their jobs, wages and reputations in settler society. Learning to navigate the straits between these two orders of time was not easy: on the one hand stood the Scylla of destitution; on the other, the Charybdis of cultural alienation. In such dire straits, resistance to the new order of time had to be negotiated carefully.

Resistance and negotiation

Although it can take several forms, we tend to recognise resistance most clearly when expressed overtly. And sure enough, during the first decades of settlement in Victoria, a total refusal to conform to the new order of time was common. Often, such resistance was directed against the Sabbath, the key ritual of Christianity, which became a natural arena wherein conflicting rituals could play out their dialogues and battles. By example, the diary of James Dredge contains a simple but unequivocal report of his failure to persuade the Daung Wurrung to recognise the sanctity of the day: 'This evening there was a grand Korroberry [sic] – I endeavoured to dissuade them, telling them that it was Sunday – but they said "black fellow no Sunday".'[83]

Evidence of resistance towards the Christian Sabbath is scattered throughout the records of early colonial Victoria, revealing that the imposition of Christian temporal order was one of the missionaries' greatest challenges. Not surprisingly, some of the missionaries often lost their traditional composure over this impasse. The Wesleyan missionary, Francis Tuckfield, for example, vented about such difficulties in his diary, after failing yet again to induce the local peoples to observe the Sabbath:

> Sun[day] 12th ... notwithstanding I have given them an extra quantity of food & all my talking to them I have not been able to prevent them from breaking the Sabbath. May God Almighty put this law into their heads and write it upon their hearts!!![84]

Resistance was even more overt when Aboriginal people intentionally staged their corroborees – nemeses of the Sabbath – *on* Sunday. Keeping in mind that religious rites serve, in the words of Radcliffe-Brown, to 'reaffirm and strengthen the sentiments on which the social order depends,' such acts can be interpreted as evidence of an intent to assert a separate, sovereign identity from Christianity, as well as to confront and disrupt the rituals and routines underpinning the colonisers' social order.[85] From the journals of Assistant Protector William

Thomas alone, it appears that such examples of sabotage occurred frequently, and that it often succeeded. On Sunday 15 December, for instance – ten days before Christmas and despite Thomas's explicit prohibition of the event – the women on the Narre Narre Warren station staged a large dance during the day, while the men held a corroboree of their own that same night ('Awful day this,' Thomas recorded in his journal).[86] Far from emerging as triumphant in their early efforts to establish Sabbatarianism, missionaries and protectors seemed to be losing their own God-given right to the enjoyment of the revered day of rest. 'What a life,' William Thomas complained after a desecrated Sabbath day; 'I cannot say "welcome sweet day of rest."'[87] The same sentiment was echoed by Tuckfield: 'Oh, how different is spending the Sabbath at home in England from spending it on a Mission Station like this.'[88] (Interestingly, the harm was often calculated in terms of squandering precious time: 'How awful to behold the hallowed hours pass thus', the methodist in Thomas lamented after yet another defiled Sabbath.[89])

Aboriginal people continued to exercise their sovereign rhythms during the first decade of colonisation. In 1839 at the Narre Narre Warren station, according to the diary of William Thomas, the Sabbath sermon was abruptly curtailed when an Aboriginal man suddenly appeared at the camp to inform the people that a meeting was about to take place between the local tribes. The congregation was immediately up on its feet preparing for the journey, whilst William Thomas was 'much vexed and showed it' – but to little effect. The tenuous authority of the Christian ritual during the earlier stages of colonisation, is demonstrated by the frequency with which the missionary was hustled through his sermon in order to accommodate the sovereign rhythms of Aboriginal time. 'I was forced rather abruptly to finish the service,' recorded a dispirited Thomas. '[I] gave them after the service rice and sugar. Scarcely had I finished doling out before all was on the move, even the old man whose foot was so bad.'[90]

Missionary texts, as Anna Johnston notes, are notorious for placing emphasis on positive evangelical achievements whilst overlooking the more spectacular failures.[91] However, the reports of early missionaries and Assistant Protectors of Victoria consistently make an exception to this rule, for their labours were quite undeniably marked by significant setbacks and failures. ('When I reflect on the past year's labour', a dispirited Tuckfield wrote in his journal, 'it seems to me that I have scarcely done anything.'[92]) Missionaries in Victoria possessed a clear *idea* of the world they wanted to recreate but were unable to do so in its entirety, because, as Bain Attwood writes, 'the cultural order they brought with them was disembodied'.[93] Christmas in Australia, as James Dredge complained, 'can never seem like Christmas in such a climate'. The idea of a 'well-spent Sunday' was above all an idea; one which relied on a whole range of signifiers which were often absent. This was a constant cause of discontent to James Dredge and some of the other, less-weathered migrants to Australia: 'Sunday 15th: A day of extreme mental dejection', Dredge complained. 'A Sabbath, but no Ordinances, no multitude keeping holy day, no songs of praise from well tuned hearts and voices ... all is Solitary and lonely, an awful silence reigns around.'[94]

From the 1860s, however, as many numbers of Aboriginal people were gradually contained on missions and reserves, such forms of explicit resistance towards the law of the Sabbath became less of a viable option. Here, their wellbeing came to depend increasingly on rations and the goodwill of their overseers and supervisors, both of which remained contingent on the observance of the Sabbath ritual and obedience to the bell. Aboriginal people at the Ebenezer station were given a clear demonstration of this arrangement when they refused to respect the Sabbath in protest against the missionary. One Sunday, angered by Reverend Hagenauer's conduct towards a member of the community, the men and women on the mission refused to attend prayers when the missionary rang the bell for Service; 'they only laughed and scoffed at him, saying "Pray to-morrow"'. The response to this effrontery reveals how the balance of power had shifted dramatically by the latter half of the century: the following Monday, when 'the blacks applied as usual for work and for rations', Hagenauer noted in his diary, he sent them away with the same rebuff: 'Rations, to-morrow.'[95]

The order of Christian time was nevertheless frequently contravened even if it meant suffering hefty consequences. Reports of defiance continued well into the late nineteenth century – defiance not only towards the rituals of Christianity but also against the regimented routines of sedentary life and regular work. Despite attempts to control every aspect of their lives, as a settler commented in 1877, 'Aborigines are only inclined to stop their own time.'[96] The Protection Board frequently received reports of managers' inability to stop people from leaving the station unless authorised. 'They have all been here,' one correspondent declared as late as 1879, 'but not caring to be under any restraint and discipline, however mild, have gone away again.'[97] Missionary and reserve coercion never achieved the total hegemonic results desired, partly because neither the rhythms of the market economy nor the promise of wages ever seemed to represent the governing motivation for Aborigines to leave the stations for work. 'They mainly left "in order to be free and without control"', writes Bain Attwood, 'getting away from the paternalistic missionaries and the closely-ordered regime of the mission stations – asserting their independence.'[98] Station managers and missionaries often simply resigned themselves to seeing some people come and go as they pleased (although they occasionally attempted to save face by maintaining that the people had left with their permission).

Despite the reformers' best efforts in converting Aboriginal people into 'good' workers there would always remain a temporal distinction in colonial discourse between the rhythms of white and black labourers. 'I only know two or three who hire themselves like white men,' one settler reported. 'They are trustworthy and truthful ... but I cannot with any certainty name the time they may stop.'[99] The lack of a black 'work ethic' was frequently denounced for what became known as its distinctive irregularity: 'They are generally wandering around from place to place', another settler stated, 'often employed by settlers, but very seldom for a year, mostly for two or three months at a time.'[100] 'To be always at work is hardly in accordance with the black disposition', another declared; 'they may work one day without stopping, but not on another.'[101] Just as demands for regularity, punctuality and order did not go uncontested by the working classes in Britain, the new order of time was regularly flouted by Aboriginal peoples in Victoria. The parallel was evident to some as early as 1842, when William Thomas recorded in his Journal that 'this morn scarce a Black would work. In fact I find generally that the Blacks are lazy on the Monday like English Cobblers. I fear they will keep Saint Monday.'[102]

The order of the bell was not immune from becoming the victim of insubordination either. One man's persistent insubordination at Ebenezer frustrated the Reverend Kramer to the point of lodging an official complaint to his superiors: 'I had not unfrequently [sic] to hunt about for him all over the place an hour after the bell had rung for work,' he complained to the Board, 'and then would perhaps find him playing in one of the houses.'[103] It was typical of the missionary to conclude, as he did, that the man was simply 'very lazy'. (However, laziness, as Frantz Fanon believed, was also 'the conscious sabotage of the colonial machine'.[104])

The supposed inability to conform to colonial demands for punctuality and regular work were commonly attributed, rather than to anti-colonial sentiments, to racial inferiority. In 1881, for example, at a time in which the Aboriginal population of Coranderrk was explicitly protesting against the Board's management of Coranderrk by refusing to carry out work and regular duties, the station manager, Reverend Strickland, preferred to attribute such behaviour to racial factors: 'In the pure aboriginals', he explained when asked about the Aborigines'

3.8 '*Dolce far niente*: an Aboriginal interpretation', *ca* 1900
Europeans rarely interpreted opposition towards colonial timetables
and schedules as signs of resistance.

unwillingness to work, 'it is the absence of a sense of duty to work; in the half-castes, I think it is indolence.'[105]

As for the attempted imposition of a separation between work time and free time, during everyday activities on Victoria's missions and reserves there was often a patent refusal to conform fully to the clear-cut distinction between labour and leisure. Harvest time on the hop fields at Coranderrk, for instance, was a period of holiday as much as for working; women and children joined the men in the field and infused the work time with their own pace of life, making time for eating, drinking, kinship, festivities and amusements.[106] Even in the course of the normal workday, it was habitual for the men also to put down their tools and 'take a spell'. 'Smoking time', as it came to be known at Coranderrk, took place each day at 10 a.m. and again at 3 p.m., when workers conceded themselves a quarter-hour break – without permission. The practice appears to have been part of a mutual *entente*, in which workers had supposedly agreed with the farm manager as to the specific time and duration for the 'smoking time' in exchange for reprieve. But the practice was not officially endorsed by the farm manager, who openly acknowledged that he could not have prevented it from happening among the older men even if he had wanted to.[107]

In such ways, time was redeployed by Aboriginal people as a negotiating tool, for bargaining compromises between new and old rhythms, and for maintaining a degree of independence from their self-styled reformers. Indeed, both colonisers and colonised found it necessary to make room for concessions in order to coexist. For many Aboriginal people in Victoria, oppressive as they were, missions and reserves were the only refuge and sometimes the only means of remaining close to Country. For some missionaries, too, compromise and negotiations over daily timetables came to characterise the general temporal landscape of mission life. This was at least evident to Thomas Goodwin, manager of the Yelta mission in northern Victoria, who, after entreating the Aborigines to postpone a hunting expedition until after the Sabbath, reported as follows:

> I did not anticipate what I said would deter them from going, but was pleased to find on leaving the room that they at once decided not to start until [Monday]. They now generally wait until after prayers before they start on their expeditions. If I know they are desirous of going, I have prayers somewhat sooner, *to accommodate them*.[108]

It was through a process of mutual compromise – rather than of outright imposition or assimilation, or of resistance or defiance – that the conflicting rhythms of colonial and Aboriginal life were forced to share a mutual timescape. Negotiations, on both sides, allowed colonial reformers to achieve a degree of conformity as regards their vision of order and 'regularity' whilst affording Aboriginal people both a level of continuity with pre-colonial rhythms and a sense of independence and autonomy from the regime.

Precisely because it was such a strong factor in the formation of cultural identity, time continued to offer Aboriginal people in Victoria an important channel for asserting a sense of cultural autonomy. This would have been particularly so in the wake of the miscegenation policies which were introduced towards the end of the century – such as the 1886 ('Half-caste') Act, which sought to eliminate the category of 'Aborigine' altogether, with the intent to 'breed them white'.[109] Amid policies aimed to assimilate Aboriginal people culturally and biologically within settler-society, the continuing practice of 'alternative' rhythms of life and labour across Australia offered a way of maintaining a meaningful connection with elements of Aboriginal life, culture and identity.

Rather than being assimilated within the rhythms of the colony's economic calendar, historian Mike Donaldson observes, many Aboriginal peoples in rural parts of Australia in fact continued to incorporate their traditional patterns of movement within those of the pastoral industry during the twentieth century; 'stopping when there was a demand for their labour, on stations that were part of their territory; shearing, mustering, droving and doing domestic work; while maintaining their links with the people and the land, [to ensure] the continuation of the cycles of regeneration and rebirth'.[110] As similar evidence of the continuation of Aboriginal temporalities in southwestern Australia, Sally Hodson writes that 'Nyungar time' continued to constitute a barrier to assimilation well into the twentieth century.[111] Indeed – right across present-day Australia – as Maureen Perkins points out, 'it is a widely repeated nostrum of mainstream culture that there is "blackfella" time, one which is oblivious of (or resistant to?) white temporal schedules'.[112]

In Victoria, as elsewhere across the British Empire, the temporal dimension of colonisation at best entailed dominance without hegemony. The temporal order of settler-colonial society would always rely more on the coercion rather than the consent of Aboriginal peoples. Even as workers eventually agreed to carry out the material and mechanical tasks associated with labour in the settler-colonial economy, they could still circumvent the temporal consciousness that came with such tasks, like the division between work time and free time, and the demand for yearly work and 'regularity'. 'While they might handle the tools of the labourer,' Henry Reynolds writes, 'they were reluctant to accept the discipline that went with them.'[113] Moreover, Aboriginal workers quickly learnt to argue with their reformers in their own master language, managing to adopt, adapt and exploit the discourse of time to their own ends. As Bain Attwood writes, they 'began to speak the language of the middle class and "respectability" and of the working class and trade unionism, demanding fair wages, bonuses and shorter hours'.[114]

Already by 1881, we may observe clear indications of a remarkable adaptation: during the controversial inquiry into the management of Coranderrk that year, the Aboriginal community (under the guidance of the Wurundjeri leader, William Barak), turned the tables on their reformers and accused the Board and the station manager of negligence, unpunctuality and irregularity in distributing wages, clothing and rations.[115] This form of agitation for justice implied a radical shift from the type of resistance that characterised earlier confrontations. However, it was part and parcel of the compromises and negotiations which ensured cultural survival.

In the face of the adverse cultural transformations that deeply and unavoidably altered their way of life, Aboriginal people in Victoria became active cultural brokers and agents in the creation of their own identities. Despite the rhetoric, few of their self-styled reformers can be given credit in making that transition an easy one.

Notes

1 Interview with Uncle Colin Walker, remembering his experience of growing up on the Cummeragunja reserve, where he was born in 1935. ('Mission Voices' website, 2004, pp. 3–4). Note: this chapter contains a number of excerpts taken from the *Mission Voices* website (www.abc.net.au/missionvoices), a web-based archive of interviews with Aboriginal (Koorie) Elders from across Victoria. Most of the interviewees were born in the 1920s and 1930s on stations, missions and reserves such as Coranderrk, Cummeragunja and Lake Tyers. Given the paucity of Aboriginal voices in the historical archive, it is important to consider these memories and accounts as a valuable source of oral history, offering an Aboriginal perspective on the experience of life on Victoria's missions. All use of twentieth-century sources is clearly signalled in the main text. The term 'Koorie' derives from the word for 'people' and is the current term used for group self-description among many people of Aboriginal descent living in Victoria and in south and central New South Wales. 'Auntie' and 'Uncle' are Koorie titles of respect. Permission to quote these voices was formally obtained from all the individuals quoted.
2 Foucault, *Discipline and Punish*, pp. 218–19.
3 Davison, *The Unforgiving Minute*, p. 9.
4 Wolfe, *Settler Colonialism*, p. 168; Wolfe, 'Land, Labor, and Difference', p. 871.
5 Noel Butlin, *Our Original Aggression: Aboriginal Populations of South-Eastern Australia, 1788–1850* (Sydney: Allen & Unwin, 1983), p. 146; Henry Reynolds, *The Other Side of the Frontier: An Interpretation of the Response to the Invasion and Settlement of Australia* (Townsville: James Cook University, 1981), pp. 98–9. Diane Barwick, 'Changes in the Aboriginal Population of Victoria, 1863–1966', in D. J. Mulvaney and J. Golson (eds), *Aboriginal Man and Environment in Australia* (Canberra: Australian National University Press, 1971), p. 288; John Chesterman and Brian Galligan, *Citizens Without Rights: Aborigines and Australian Citizenship* (Cambridge: Cambridge University Press, 1977), pp. 12–13; Beverley Blaskett, 'The Level of Violence: Europeans and Aborigines in Port Phillip, 1835–1850', in Janson and MacIntyre (eds), *Through White Eyes*, pp. 69–94.
6 *Report from the Select Committee on Aborigines (British Settlements)*, 1837, pp. 82–3; Richard Broome, *Aboriginal Victorians: A History Since 1800* (Sydney:

Allen & Unwin, 2005), p. xxiii; Lester, 'Humanitarians and White Settlers', p. 76.
7 SLV, MS 12699, box 3504/9, Letters, J. Orton to Wesleyan Methodist Missionary Society (hereafter: WMMS), 14 Jan. 1840.
8 SLV, MS 7881, mf 200, Lectures, E. S. Parker, 'The Aborigines of Australia', 1854.
9 PPV, 1877–78, III, *Royal Commission on the Aborigines, Report of the Commissioners Appointed to Inquire into the Present Condition of the Aborigines of this colony, and to Advise as to the Best Means of Caring for, and Dealing with Them, in the Future, Together with Minutes of Evidence and Appendices*, 1877 (hereafter: *Royal Commission on the Aborigines,* 1877), *Minutes of Evidence*, Appendix C, no. 41, Peter Beveridge, p. 115.
10 Blainey, *Triumph of the Nomads*, p. 185.
11 *Report from the Select Committee on Aborigines (British Settlements)*, 1837, *Minutes of Evidence*, vol. 1, Archdeacon Broughton, p. 13.
12 Memo, Rev. J. R. Orton to Rev. Hurst and Rev. Tuckfield, June 1839, in Cannon, *Historical Records of Victoria*, 2A, p. 126.
13 G. M. Langhorne to Colonial Secretary, 14 Aug. 1837, in Cannon, *Historical Records of Victoria*, 2A, p. 173.
14 Rev. J. Orton to WMMS, 13 May 1839, in Cannon, *Historical Records of Victoria*, 2A, p. 122. See also William Thomas, Journal, in Cannon, *Historical Records of Victoria*, 2B, p. 554; James Dredge, Diary, 4 Sept. 1839, pp. 2–3.
15 Rev. J. R. Orton to Rev. Hurst and Rev. Tuckfield, June 1839, in Cannon, *Historical Records of Victoria*, 2A, p. 124.
16 PROV, VPRS 11, item 392, William Thomas to Chief Protector, G. A. Robinson, 11 Sept. 1841; See also William Thomas, Journal, 26 Oct. 1839, in Cannon, *Historical Records of Victoria*, 2B, p. 554-5.
17 Rev. Orton to WMMS, May 13th, 1839, in Cannon, *Historical Records of Victoria*, 2A, p. 122.
18 PROV, VPRS 11, mf 8, unit 2, item 463, William Thomas to Chief Protector, G. A. Robinson, Oct. 1842.
19 Rev. Orton to WMMS, May 13th, 1839, in Cannon, *Historical Records of Victoria*, 2A, p. 122.
20 *Extracts from the Papers and Proceedings of the Aborigines Protection Society*, no. 4 (Aug.–Sept. 1839) (London: Ball & Co., 1839), art. V, 'Captain Maconochie's Plan for the Organisation of the Natives of Australia as a Police', pp. 108–16 (University of Melbourne Library, Special Collection). Cf. *Ibid*, no. 5 (Oct.–Nov. 1839), pp. 132–3.
21 Marie H. Fels, *Good Men and True: The Aboriginal Police of the Port Phillip District, 1837–1853* (Melbourne: Melbourne University Press, 1988), pp. 67–8. See also: Christie, *Aborigines in Colonial Victoria*, pp. 72–7; Broome, *Aboriginal Victorians*, pp. 43–6.
22 PROV, VPRS 90, unit 1, Victoria, Police Department, 'Day Book of the Native Police Corps, Narre Narre Warren 1845-53'.
23 Edward M. Curr, *Recollections of Squatting in Victoria* (Echuca: Rich River Printers, 2001 edn), p. 187.
24 Bain Attwood, *The Making of the Aborigines* (Sydney: Allen & Unwin, 1989), pp. 5–6; Broome, *Aboriginal Victorians*, p. 121.
25 Andrew Brown-May and Shurlee Swain (eds), *The Encyclopedia of Melbourne* (Cambridge: Cambridge University Press, 2005), pp. 41, 68, 155, 588–9, 709–11, 722; Davison, *The Unforgiving Minute*, pp. 36–8.
26 *Report of the Legislative Council*, 1859–59, 'Replies to a Circular Letter', Mr Crooke, Mr Aitken, Mr Ormond, p. 35.
27 *A Plea on Behalf of the Aboriginal Inhabitants of Victoria* (Geelong: The Advertiser, 1856), pp. 8–9 (SLV, Rare Books Collection).
28 Framlingham (previously an Anglican mission) came under government control in 1866; the Yelta mission closed down in 1869. This left three mission stations and three government reserves in Victoria by 1870. See: Broome, *Aboriginal Victorians*, pp. xxiv, 126.
29 Chesterman and Galligan, *Citizens Without Rights*, pp. 16–17; Broome, *Aboriginal*

Victorians, pp. 130–1, 146.
30 *Royal Commission on the Aborigines*, 1877, *Minutes of Evidence*, p. 95.
31 Bain Attwood, 'Off the Mission Stations: Aborigines in Gippsland, 1860–1890', *Aboriginal History*, 10:2 (1986), p. 132.
32 PPV, 1872, *Eighth Report of the Board for the Protection of Aborigines* (hereafter: *Report of the BPA*), Appendix II, Richard Brough-Smyth (Secretary of the BPA), p. 10.
33 PPV, 1864, *Fourth Report of the Central Board Appointed to Watch Over the Interests of the Aborigines in the Colony of Victoria* (hereafter: *Report of the CBPA*), p. 6.
34 AAV, B313, box 11, item 182, correspondence, John Green to Brough-Smyth, Coranderrk, 5 Jan. 1871.
35 See *Report of the Coranderrk Inquiry*, 1882, *Minutes of Evidence*, p. 93
36 PPV, 1862, *Second Report of the CBPA*, Rev. Spieseke, p. 6.
37 PPV, 1898, *Thirty-fourth Report of the BPA*, Rev. Stähle to Rev. Hagenauer, Lake Condah, 11 Aug. 1898, Appendix II.
38 PPV, 1869, *Sixth Report of the BPA*, statements by R. Brough-Smyth and John Mackenzie, pp. 4, 18.
39 AAV, B313, box 11, item 186, memo, BPA, 'Suggestion for running of Coranderrk station', 29 Feb. 1876.
40 PPV, 1864, *Fourth Report of the CBPA*, p. 5.
41 Mitchell Library, MSS 214/8, Journal of William Thomas, 18 Sept. 1841; Henry Reynolds, 'Aborigines and European Social Hierarchy', *Aboriginal History*, 7:2 (1983), p. 124; Attwood, 'Off the Mission Stations', p. 132.
42 Henry Reynolds, 'Aborigines and European Social Hierarchy', pp. 124, 132.
43 Robert Foster, 'Rations, Coexistence, and the Colonisation of Aboriginal Labour', *Aboriginal History*, 24 (2000), 1–26, p. 1; Peggy Brock, 'Pastoral Stations and Reserves', in A. McGrath, K. Saunders and J. Huggins (eds), *Aboriginal Workers* (Sydney: Australian Society for the Study of Labour History, 1995), p. 102.
44 *Annual Report of the Church of England Mission of Victoria to the Aborigines*, no. 27 (1881) (Melbourne: The Mission, John Bulmer, Lake Tyers), p. 7 (SLV, Rare Books Collection).
45 The full poem can be found in Susan Robertson, 'The Bell Sounds Pleasantly: Ebenezer Mission Station', *Timely Essays*, no. 3 (Luther Rose Publications, 1992), p. 79. (Originally published in the Yearbook of the Lutheran Church Australia, 1977.)
46 Elizabeth Shaw, *Early Days Among the Aborigines: The Story of Yelta and Coranderrk Missions* (Melbourne: W. & J. Barr, 194(?)), p. 16. (SLV, Rare Books Collection.)
47 Jane Lydon, 'Space, Power, and the Mission House', in Jane Lydon, *Fantastic Dreaming: The Archaeology of an Aboriginal Mission* (Lanham: Altamira, 2009).
48 'Mission Voices' website, interview with Auntie Joy Murphy (1933–) in 2004, p. 3.
49 SLV, MS 9556, G. Mackenzie, 'A Tale of Two Bells', in *The Missionary Chronicle of the Presbyterian Churches of Victoria, South Australia, Tasmania, Queensland and Western Australia*, 63:6 (1969), p. 15.
50 SLV, MS 9556, newspaper cutting, 'Picturesque Victoria: Ramahyuck', *Argus*, Jan. 1886.
51 *Royal Commission on the Aborigines*, 1877, *Minutes of Evidence*, James Edgar, pp. 26–7.
52 Ibid., Martin Simpson, p. 30.
53 Frantz Fanon, *Black Skin, White Masks*, trans. C. L. Markmann (New York: Grove Press, 1967), pp. 17–18, 38.
54 *Royal Commission on the Aborigines*, 1877, *Minutes of Evidence*, Martin Simpson, p. 29. Emphasis added.
55 PPV, 1861, *First Report of CBPA*, Appendix II, pp. 18–19.
56 O'Malley employs this perspective to describe the transformation of time-consciousness which occurred in white American society during the nineteenth century. See O'Malley, 'Time, Work and Task Orientation', p. 355; Michael O'Malley, *Keeping Watch: A History of American Time* (New York: Viking, 1990).

57 Lucy A. Edgar, *Among the Black Boys: Being the History of an Attempt at Civilising Some Young Aborigines of Australia* (London: Emily Faithful, 1865), pp. 5–6. (SLV, Rare Books Collection.)
58 *Report of the Coranderrk Inquiry*, 1882, Minutes of Evidence, pp. 2–3.
59 PPV, 1877, *Thirteenth Report of the BPA*, Appendix III, Rev. Hagenauer, Ramahyuck Mission Report (July 1877), p. 7.
60 PPV, 1871, *Seventh Report of the BPA*, R. Brough-Smyth, p. 8. Emphasis added.
61 PPV, 1891, *Twenty-seventh Report of the BPA*, Appendix IV, Rev. Hagenauer to the General Inspector of Aborigines, Ramahyuck, 7 July, 1891. See also: PPV, 1893, *Twenty-ninth Report of the BPA*, Appendix III; and PPV, 1894, *Thirtieth Report of the BPA*, Appendix II, Rev. Stähle.
62 PPV, 1877, *Thirteenth Report of the BPA*, Appendix V, C. W. Kramer, Ebenezer, July 1877, p. 9.
63 PPV, 1894, *Thirtieth Report of the BPA*, Appendix III, Rev. Hagenauer, Ramahyuck, 20 July, 1894.
64 PPV, 1876, *Twelfth Report of the BPA*, Appendix VI, W. M. Goodall, Framlingham, Dec. 1875, p. 14.
65 *Royal Commission on the Aborigines*, 1877, Minutes of Evidence, William Goodall, Framlingham, May 1877, p. 65.
66 Ibid., Hugh Hamilton, Coranderrk, May 1877, p. 33.
67 PPV, 1882, *Eighteenth Report of the BPA*, John Bulmer, Lake Tyers, July 1882, p. 10.
68 Ibid., Carl Kramer, Lake Condah, May 1877, p. 59.
69 PPV, 1899, *Thirty-fifth Report of the BPA*, Appendix II, Rev. Stähle to Rev. Hagenauer, Lake Condah, 28 July, 1899.
70 *Report of the Coranderrk Inquiry*, 1882, Minutes of Evidence, Martin Simpson, p. 10.
71 SLV, MS 9556, Bay 9/6c: box 1, folder/booklet, Rev. F. A. Hagenauer, 'Aboriginal Mission Station, Ramahyuck: Report for 1885', p. 1.
72 Anthony Aveni, *Empires of Time*, pp. 176–7.
73 Steve Symonds, quoted in J. Woodford, 'Spring May Be Sprung in the Fall of the Four Seasons', *Sydney Morning Herald*, 27 May 1995, p. 5.
74 *Report of the Coranderrk Inquiry*, 1882, Minutes of Evidence, Thomas Harris, p. 89.
75 Davison, *The Unforgiving Minute*, p. 90; Christine Choo, *Mission Girls: Aboriginal Women on Catholic Missions in the Kimberley, Western Australia, 1900–1950* (Perth: UWA Press, 2001), pp. 98, 112; See also Sally Hodson, 'Nyungars and Work: Aboriginal Experiences in the Rural Economy', *Aboriginal History*, 17:1 (1993), p. 75; Broome, *Aboriginal Victorians*, pp. 62, 148; Attwood, *The Making of the Aborigines*, pp. 33, 45.
76 PPV, 1898, *Forty-third Report of the BPA*, Rev. Stähle, Lake Condah, 2 Jan. 1898, pp. 6–7.
77 PPV, 1878, *Fourteenth Report of the BPA*, Appendix V, John Bulmer, Lake Tyers, p. 9; Cf. PPV, 1884, *Twentieth Report of BPA*, Rev. Kramer to Capt. Page, Ebenezer, 22 Sept. 1884.
78 'Mission Voices' website, interview with Uncle Albert Mullett (1933–) in 2004, p. 5.
79 PPV, 1871, *Seventh Report of the BPA*, W. L. Ker, July 1871, p. 18.
80 Reynolds, 'Aborigines and European Social Hierarchy', p. 128.
81 *Select Committee of the Legislative Council*, 1858–59, 'Replies to a Circular Letter', C. W. Carr, Warden at Anderson's Creek, p. 77.
82 Dawson, *Australian Aborigines*, pp. 78–9.
83 MS 11625, box 16/4, James Dredge, Diary, 16 Feb. 1840, p. 100.
84 MS 7667, loc. 655, Rev. F. Tuckfield, Journal, 12 Jan. 1840, pp. 108–9.
85 Radcliffe-Brown, *Structure and Function in Primitive Society*, p. 167.
86 William Thomas, Journal, 15 Dec. 1839, in Cannon, *Historical Records of Victoria*, 2B, p. 567.
87 Ibid.
88 Tuckfield, Journal, 12 Jan. 1840, p. 108.

89 William Thomas, Journal, 24 Nov. 1839, in Cannon, *Historical Records of Victoria*, 2B, p. 567.
90 *Ibid.*, p. 567.
91 Anna Johnston, *Missionary Writing and Empire, 1800–1860* (Cambridge: Cambridge University Press, 2003), p. 7.
92 Tuckfield, Journal, p. 106.
93 Attwood, *The Making of the Aborigines*, p. 1.
94 James Dredge, Diary, 15 Sept. 1840, pp. 113–14; 25 Dec. 1840, p. 179.
95 *Facts Relating to the Moravian Mission: First Paper* (Melbourne: Wm. Goodhugh, 1860), pp. 7–8. (SLV.)
96 *Royal Commission on Aborigines*, 1877, *Minutes of Evidence*, Appendix C, part II, Jas Finely (settler), p. 120.
97 AAV, B313, title 95, doc. 37, Anon., letter to Capt. Page, 11 Nov. 1879.
98 Attwood, 'Off the Mission Stations', pp. 143–4; Reynolds, 'Aborigines and European Social Hierarchy', pp. 127–8.
99 *First Report of the CBPA*, Appendix II, Mr David Edgar, p. 14. See also *Report of the Legislative Council*, 1858–59, *Minutes of Evidence*, Appendix, William Hull, Esq., JP, p. 9; *Royal Commission on the Aborigines*, 1877, *Minutes of Evidence*, Christian Ogilvie, p. 10.
100 *First Report of the CBPA*, Appendix II, Cecil P. Cook, p. 14.
101 *Royal Commission on the Aborigines*, 1877, *Minutes of Evidence*, C. E. Strutt, Esq., police, p. 19.
102 William Thomas, Journal, 1 Feb. 1842, quoted in Reynolds, 'Aborigines and European Social Hierarchy', p. 126.
103 AAV, B313/file 95/doc. 28, Rev. C.W. Kramer to Capt. Page, 3 Sept. 1879.
104 Fanon, *Wretched of the Earth*, p. 239.
105 *Report of the Coranderrk Inquiry*, 1882, *Minutes of Evidence*, F. P. Strickland, p. 1.
106 Attwood, *The Making of the Aborigines*, pp. 75–6.
107 *Report of the Coranderrk Inquiry*, 1882, *Minutes of Evidence*, Thomas Harris, pp. 87, 96.
108 *Seventh Annual Report of the Melbourne Church of England Mission to the Aborigines of Victoria*, Mr T. H. Goodwin to Rev. C. Chase, 5 Nov. 1860, Yelta, pp. 7–8. (SLV.) Emphasis added.
109 John McCorquodale. 'The Legal Classification of Race in Australia', *Aboriginal History*, 10:1 (1986), pp. 10–14; Wolfe, 'Land, Labor, and Difference', p. 87.
110 Donaldson, *Taking Our Time*, pp. 140–41.
111 Hodson, 'Nyungars and Work', pp. 75–84.
112 Perkins, *The Reform of Time*, p. 94.
113 Reynolds, *The Other Side of the Frontier*, p. 115.
114 Attwood, *The Making of the Aborigines*, p. 65. See also Comaroff, 'Missionaries and Mechanical Clocks', p. 16.
115 *Report of the Coranderrk Inquiry*, 1882, *Minutes of* Evidence, p. 7.

CHAPTER FOUR

'The moons are always out of order': colonial constructions of 'African time'

On 31 March 1847, in the vicinity of a remote Wesleyan mission station, north of the Cape Colony, the Reverend Benjamin Ridsdale announced to his African converts that a lunar eclipse would occur that night.[1] Armed with an almanac, a portable watch, and foreknowledge of when the event would occur – *ca* 9.30 p.m. – the missionary planned the event with care: this was a unique opportunity, he must have thought to himself, for demonstrating the undeniable supremacy of true, rational knowledge over the superstition which had shrouded Africa in darkness for so long.

Ridsdale's captive audience was composed of the 'God-less' and clock-less Namaqua, a Khoisan people whom the missionary had come to Christianise and 'civilise'. Amongst them, however, Ridsdale was most anxious to impress one individual: Old Tonnis, the wagon-driver, who had been a *toovenaar* or 'wizard', prior to his conversion. Given his past, Old Tonnis represented an alternative method of interpreting reality and 'seeing' the future – that of rain-makers and witchdoctors – whose belief system missionaries had quickly identified as a serious impediment to the spread of both Christianity and 'modernity' in the colonies. Ridsdale thus took extra care to educate Tonnis about the eclipse, being 'very anxious to uproot all his superstitions with regard to witchcraft, and to make him feel the superiority of real wisdom and knowledge to superstition and mere trickery'. As the time of the eclipse approached, Old Tonnis was no longer merely a member of the audience in Ridsdale's narrative but an actor cast in the role of the ignorant sceptic. '"Tonnis,"' Ridsdale addressed the old man with a hint of ridicule, '"it does not look as if the moon would be eclipsed tonight, does it?" "No, Sir," he said, "it won't be eclipsed;" almost laughing in his incredulousness at the idea.' '"Ah, but it will,"' Ridsdale replied prophetically, '"only it's too soon yet."'

It is important to note that the views of missionaries such as Ridsdale

4.1 Columbus predicts lunar eclipse of 1509 in Jamaica

One of the most famous illustrations of how Europeans were able to exploit foreknowledge of eclipses occurred when Christopher Columbus successfully predicted the lunar eclipse of 1509. The eighteenth-century populariser of astronomy, James Ferguson, noted with approval that the eclipse 'accordingly fell on the day he had foretold, and so terrified the Barbarians, that they strove who should be first in bringing him all sorts of provisions; throwing them at his feet, and imploring his forgiveness' (Ferguson, *Astronomy Explained Upon Sir Isaac Newton's Principles*, p. 303).

had not just an impact on the societies they sought to evangelise but also a huge influence on British perceptions of places like Australia and southern Africa and of the societies which inhabited them. Their representations of Indigenous peoples also travelled across the colonies, channeled through the imperial networks which were forged during the nineteenth century, thus influencing colonial perceptions of Indigenous peoples elsewhere.[2] The theatre-like narrative which frames the Reverend Ridsdale's account of the 1847 eclipse is therefore a fitting introduction to this chapter, which brings into relief the central role of time as a dimension of power within European discourses and displays of technological and cultural superiority.

Missionaries, of course, did not have to wait for the planets to align in order to stage demonstrations and attacks against African 'superstition': they were committed to this project on a daily basis, casting themselves in the role of the exporters of modernity and rationality to pre-modern and superstitious Africa in a 'theatre of the everyday' (to borrow one of John Comaroff's metaphors).[3] Their attack on superstition consisted in more than just debunking alternative spiritual beliefs: it also included attempts to refashion African understanding of material reality, including their conception of time; for 'superstition' conveyed not merely a sense of 'false religion' but also a set of understandings about cause and effect in the natural world that flowed 'from confused ideas of invisible agency', as the Reverend John Philip put it.[4] Missionaries sought to usher Africans into the 'modern' world by presenting them with technologies and truths which were calculated to explode their previous conceptions of reality.[5] And there were few instances as opportune as an eclipse for inducing this epiphany, for the science of forecasting was one of the most powerful manifestations of modernity in the nineteenth century; and missionaries knew very well that Africans, in their veneration of diviners and rain-makers, admired the capacity to predict the future just as much as Europeans did. Predicting the day *and* time of an eclipse provided missionaries with a valuable opportunity of winning over followers to their enlightened European ways.

It was in this spirit that Ridsdale – prompted by the cue of his watch – invited Old Tonnis to turn his eye to the moon. 'At about half-past nine he looked again, and said, "It seems as if one side of the moon was cut off!"' The two sat together in silence for a while watching the phenomenon unfold. The moral of the story would be revealed in the morning, when, according to Ridsdale, Old Tonnis approached the missionary with excitement, saying:

> 'Ah, Sir, I sat up till the eclipse was all over, and the moon became round and full again as when it rose; and everything came to pass *exactly* as you had said.' 'Well,' I said, 'I told you of this some time before it took place, and the time when it would begin and end. There was no trickery there; you know I could not get up there and draw a veil over the face of the moon.' 'No, Sir,' he at once replied. 'Well, you see how much better knowledge is than sorcery! Clever men calculate everything concerning eclipses to the minute, days, months, and years beforehand, and publish it to the world, so that men may have the opportunity of testing the truth of what they say.'[6]

Ridsdale's performance was not aimed solely at the Namaqua: it was directed just as much at a metropolitan readership, for whom Old Tonnis was the embodiment of the world of magic, astrology and superstition – a world which had become the target of rational reform in England.[7] This was a dramatisation, then, of the universal struggle between good and evil, of true knowledge versus superstition – the energising myth that propelled the missionary and modernist dream. And, in this particular act, we can see how the mastery over time could help the emissaries of modernity to win their battles on the ground.

The watch was a tool that did more than just keep the time; it presented Europeans in the colonies with a way of crafting their sense of the modern Self in opposition to a primitive, superstitious Other. Superstitious beliefs regarding time and the laws of nature were, according to Europeans, one of the flaws which had prevented Africans from developing the technological and intellectual capacity to reach the present, 'modern' era – let alone predict the future. As the early ethnographer and missionary (of the LMS) William Willoughby stated, 'Till a century or two ago, all nations regarded comets and eclipses as harbingers of calamity, and backward races are still of that opinion'.[8] By employing European standards to evaluate African time-reckoning, calendrical and forecasting technology, the African mind could be portrayed as inferior; and by comparing the sources of temporal authority which guided their rituals and ceremonies with the Christian calendar, alternative belief systems could be dismissed as superstitions.

Whether in relation to the hunter-gatherer 'Bushmen', the pastoralist Khoikhoi, or the mixed farmer-agriculturalist Xhosa, Europeans developed a set of prejudices against 'African time' that would become hallmarks of colonial discourse, portraying it as an aberrant and defective element of African life, a reflection of innate laziness and superstition. In turn, the apparent lack of temporal knowledge among Africans would help Europeans justify the need for the redemptive and civilising influences of Christianity and civilisation whose moral and material virtues were encoded in their culture of the clock and the Sabbath. An historical account of the colonial construction of 'African time' will thus enable us to define the discursive boundaries and ideological context wherein colonial reformers set out to remould African temporal cultures.

First impressions of Africa

In documenting the manner in which Europeans perceived 'African time' we ought to note that travellers to the colonies were themselves undergoing profound cultural changes in the process of adjusting to a new life. For all Europeans, whether sailing for Africa or Australia, the colonial experience invariably began with embarking on a ship; and there were good chances that, well before arriving at their destination, travellers would have experienced some degree of confusion and unfamiliarity with their new temporal surroundings. On-board ship, time and place themselves became a source of uncertainty. Time – or its perceived absence – played an important role in forging the earliest impressions of life away from the motherland; for, out of sight of land, the clock was no longer the omnipresent and punctilious harbinger of order that dominated the cities and workers of Europe. For those nineteenth-century passengers who did not possess accurate chronometers, the ship's bell was the only temporal reference during the long, monotonous days and weeks at sea. 'The first bell rings at half-past eight, dinner at half-past two o'clock, and tea about 6 p.m.', Isabella Turner recorded in her diary en-route from London to Melbourne.[9] For middle-class passengers in particular, the long passage to the Cape Colony (and the even longer passage to Australia) often involved sharing the company of lower-class individuals – whether crew or fellow passengers – and having to endure what were generally regarded as questionable practices and behaviour. At sea, the rituals and routines that formed the dominant experience of time in Britain were disrupted, if not eclipsed, by frequent interruptions of regular prayers and by refusals to observe the Lord's Day.[10] And all this was before arriving among the 'heathen'

Having reached their final destination at Cape Town, newly arrived migrants faced further discomfort and annoyance due to the inevitable effects of 'culture shock'. We are particularly interested in the first impressions regarding the pace of life in the colony, for this seems to have provided a common source of interest to newcomers, many of whom commented on the deliberate and unhurried pace of life in Africa, not only among the 'natives' but also among seasoned European settlers. The Reverend John Mackenzie light-heartedly described the 'indulgent' custom among the Cape Town storekeepers of taking a siesta after their midday meal:

> I made my appearance one day at a shop at this sacred hour, to complete some purchase, and was astonished to find everything shut, except one half of the adjoining house-door, at which stood a little black girl. In answer to my demand for the storekeeper, this sentinel said, in a low tone, 'Baas slaap' – 'the master is asleep.'

Having only recently disembarked in Cape Town, Mackenzie could not refrain from measuring this leisurely custom against the standards of thrift and industriousness that had been so heavily impressed on his mind in Britain. He amused himself by wondering: 'What would be the result to this easy going man of business were he borne by genii, while asleep, and laid gently down and left to awake on London Bridge or Cheapside!'[11]

If time appeared slightly distorted in the busy port of Cape Town, it took on an altogether new meaning once newcomers departed on their journeys into the interior. In so doing, several described the sense that they were on the verge of leaving time and civilisation behind them altogether. 'We were still on the Cape Flats, the grand outline of Table Mountain was still in view,' Benjamin Ridsdale wrote on the first day of his outbound journey 'the sound of the nine o'clock gun, fired every night at the castle, fell heavily on our ear, and made us still feel that we were within the reach of civilised life.'[12]

Travelling in African landscape was a trying experience for new arrivals, not least in terms of the new rhythms it imposed on them. The Reverend John Edwards became considerably exasperated at what he perceived to be the intolerable disorganisation of his African guides:

> The mode of traveling involved great loss of time, and often the preliminaries connected with trekking nearly cost me the surrender of my patience, and temper too ... It was provoking, when we were about to inspan the oxen, to see one man sit down composedly to mend his *veldschoen* (shoe); another rectifying a rein; while a third would be tying up something, and a fourth rolling up his scanty bedding ... Hours were often wasted in this manner. It was very trying for one just from England, where everything was orderly ... Just such were the natives of that country then, and just such were the impressions of a man who had lately opened his eyes upon Africa.[13]

Even seasoned missionaries found it difficult to maintain regular timetables. The lack of clocks and watches among the African people beleaguered the Reverend William Shaw's task of coordinating religious meetings: 'How are they to know the exact time when the Preacher can come...?' Conventional mail could not be relied upon to give notice of the missionary's arrival: 'The letter may reach him in three days, or it may be in three weeks'. In England, by contrast, itinerant preachers could rely on their Plans and well-regulated Circuits: 'Very different here!' Shaw exclaimed; 'the Preacher must in some instances wait a day at a place, before the people from various parts in the neighbourhood can be collected.'[14] The very terrain of the African landscape seemed to be hostile towards any attempt to fix meetings in place and time. The speed at which African wagon-travel progressed – the average rate being about three miles an hour, according to one observer – was perceived as painfully slow.[15] 'We thought we had made a good day's journey,' the Reverend W. J. Davis wrote of his first travel experience, 'when, a little after sunset, we found ourselves near a trading station on the Umtemtu River having accomplished fifteen miles in the day!'[16] Impatience and frustration naturally followed, for the equation between time-spent and distance-travelled by such 'primitive mode[s] of locomotion' appeared excruciatingly unprofitable compared with European standards.[17] From the mid-nineteenth century, the train had become the benchmark against which all other forms of speed and movement were compared, including that of local fauna. 'We have a speed of twenty-six miles per hour,' David Livingstone recorded as he timed an ostrich in full sprint with his sophisticated chronometer stop-watch. 'It cannot be very much more above that,' he added, 'and is therefore slower than a railway locomotive.'[18]

The rapid expansion of the railway system had transformed the Victorian travel experience into one of punctuality, efficiency and velocity. And the children of modernity found the transition from the velocity of steam-powered travel to the lethargy of the African ox-wagon to be a source of pure agony. Not all could easily bear it:

> I hope those who in England think a train slow that runs at thirty miles an hour, will feel sympathy with South African Missionaries when they hear that they have to curb in their impetuosity and submit to a whole day being spent in getting over fifteen miles! It is more trying than can be *conceived of*, it must be *felt* to understand the depressing effect it has on all energy of action. The wonder is, that it does not sap and drain out all the vigour of European activity, and cause the supineness of the Asiatic to take its place.[19]

In some cases lethargy did appear to be infectious. Acculturation, when it came to the pace of life, was sometimes characterised by a two-way process which saw Europeans being affected by the very sluggishness they attributed to the people they claimed to reform. As the Reverend Mackenzie wrote in another of his perceptive portraits of life at the Cape:

> The fact is, there is a certain steady, deliberate current, – or rather placid lake, – of action in South Africa, which is disturbed only by the newly arrived European. Whether he is farmer, merchant, or artisan, he is sure to be at first shocked with the 'slow' ways of the inhabitants. But, owing either to the atmosphere, or to the African mutton, or to some other occult cause – in a year or two the bustling 'uitlander' or foreigner himself succumbs.[20]

The pace of life in the colony was certainly different from that which was experienced in the bustling urban centres of Britain. However, whilst missionaries and middle-class settlers often complained of the carelessness towards time-thrift in the colonies, colonists of a lower social standing often welcomed this as a positive change. To the working-class settler, colonial life may have offered an increased amount of free time and the opportunity of working at a more relaxed pace than had been the case in the metropolis. Such was the experience of a Grahamstown mechanic, who thanked God for delivering him to the colony, 'because he was used to work eight days out of six in England, and could hardly keep body and soul together, *here* three days work will keep me drunk for four.'[21]

Three civilisations of time

Whilst the idea of a 'timeless land' could be upheld with ease in the Australian colonies, it became difficult for Europeans to apply such a uniform schema to the African context. Europeans in the Cape Colony recognised at least three cultural groups, which – although neither as rigid nor as impermeable as they imagined – practised significantly different economic, linguistic and social customs. Under the names designated them by contemporary colonial discourse, these were the 'Bushmen' (nomadic hunter-gatherers who originally inhabited all of southern Africa), the 'Hottentots' (the Khoikhoi: semi-nomadic pastoralists who inhabited the western and northwestern areas of the Cape Colony at the time of Dutch colonisation), and the 'Caffres/Kaffirs' (the Xhosa-speaking peoples: semi-nomadic, mixed pastoralists and agriculturalists occupying the areas east of the Cape Colony).[22]

As we might expect, notions of 'time-lessness' abounded in depictions of the Bushmen, who – having been classed in the same evolutionary period as Australian Aborigines – were portrayed as virtually deprived of all but the slightest regard for the passage of time. But the Xhosa, who employed stellar and agricultural calendars to regulate their seasons for planting, harvesting and feasting activities, evinced a more promisingly structured lifestyle, wherein Europeans were able to recognise rhythms and patterns more similar to their own. Colonial notions of 'African time', then, could not be exploited as easily as the diametrically opposed concept of 'Aboriginal time'. In the African context, the preservation of a sense of superiority indeed required a more carefully nuanced grammar of temporal difference, predicated on a set of terms that would maintain the inferiority and pre-modernity of 'African time'.

In order to account for these differences, colonial understandings of 'African time' were implicitly ranked in a hierarchical schema which roughly corresponded to these societies' progress through certain predetermined stages of evolution.[23] The distinctions between 'Bushman-time,' 'Hottentot-time' and 'Kaffir-time', however – like the stages through which these societies were thought to progress – were never as rigid as this schema might imply. Relative notions of 'time-lessness' were commonly elided with qualified depictions of inadequacy and deficiency in measuring or communicating the concept of time, so that colonial observers generally resorted to homogenising within the broader category of 'African time' anything that fell short of the standards of order and regularity which characterised Western time. Thus, whether among the 'primitive' Bushmen, the 'prodigal' Khoikhoi, or the pre-'modern' Xhosa, local calendars and conceptualisations of time were still seen to reflect the backwardness of Africa in relation to Europe. Nevertheless, Europeans did sense that hunter-gatherer, pastoralist, and agricultural societies in southern Africa practised and perceived the concept of time in different ways – generally in accordance with their economies and supposed level of progress on the scale of civilisation. This provides us with a valuable opportunity of refining our analysis of how European concepts of time reinforced, reflected and legitimatised the colonisers' evolutionist worldview.

'Bushman-time'

'The ignorance of this people concerning any division of time,' the missionary Barnabas Shaw wrote, is equal to that of the lowest orders of humanity. 'Indeed, if it be possible, they are altogether more ignorant and degraded than any of their neighbours.'[24] That the Bushmen were viewed in fundamentally similar terms to the Indigenous inhabitants of Australia is suggestive, not necessarily of the fact that these two societies were similar, but rather that colonial observers viewed both these societies from the same ethnocentric perspective. It was in relation to a distinctly European taxonomy that 'Bushmen' and 'Aborigines' were regarded as sharing the lowest state of development as well as the title of 'time-less cultures'.

This 'time-lessness' was related, as we have seen in Chapter 2, to a deep-seated intolerance among most Europeans towards the underlying logic of the hunter-gatherer economy, which was understood as a primitive dependence on chance and a prodigal, escapist attitude towards the demands of work. As Walter Gisborne informed the 1837 Select Committee on Aborigines in Britain, it was widely acknowledged that 'if [a Bushman] steals a horse today, he sits down and eats it, and never keeps any provision for a future time'.[25] In the European imagination, this supposed lack of concern for a future state was as a widely-recognised symptom of primitive mentality. Already by the eighteenth-century, as historian Anthony Pagden writes, 'it had become a commonplace to appeal to the savage's supposed inability to look beyond the satisfaction of his immediate wants as a sign of his unredeemable inhumanity'.[26] Even sensitive colonial observers perceived but a tenuous margin separating the humanity of Bushmen from the savageness of the fauna which they pursued. As David Livingstone described during his encounters in the Kalahari, the hunters' integration with the natural environment was such that the Bushmen virtually 'blended in' with nature: 'They are so intimately acquainted with the habits of game that they follow them in their migrations, and prey upon them from place to place, and thus prove as complete a check on their inordinate increase as the other carnivora.'[27] Europeans seldom acknowledged Bushman 'time-reckoning', other than to evoke its intimate and somewhat romanticised relationship with nature's time. The Reverend J. Campbell, for instance, recorded the story of a Bushman who had diagnosed the condition of a man wounded by a poisoned arrow, predicting that the victim would die 'immediately on the going down of the sun'. 'And he certainly did,' Campbell confirmed; 'for the sun had not dipped under the horizon five minutes before he breathed his last.'[28]

Despite such intimate acquaintance with the rhythms of flora and fauna, colonial observers seldom perceived such knowledge as evincing a life guided by well-established patterns of time, rhythm and ritual. The general consensus was that a reliance on nature had made 'wanderers' of these intractable nomads, leaving them 'without any system of order or government.'[29] Similarly, the supposed uncertainty and irregularity of nomadic life precluded proper rituals, calendars and religious ceremonies from being institutionalised. As in the Australian context, the perceived absence of times of worship was understood as the absence of religion altogether. As the Reverend John Mackenzie wrote:

> And as to religion, if I am not greatly mistaken, the Bushmen are the most 'superstitious' race in Southern Africa. The fact that they are so peculiarly dependent for subsistence upon what is beyond their control will perhaps account for this. With other natives the chief season of praying and necromancing begins when they have sown their corn, and stand in need of rain. *But all seasons are the same to the Bushman.*[30]

What Mackenzie articulated was a common prejudice among agricultural societies towards the rhythms of the hunter-gatherer economy. (The latter, as anthropologist Richard Borshay Lee observes, comprised 'steady work and steady leisure throughout the year, with no single season of peak effort, such as the harvest season of farming peoples'.[31]) This supposedly arhythmic economy, as Mackenzie implied, deprived the Bushmen of a regular chronology needed to establish rituals according to a recognisable pattern – a *civil* calendar. As in Australia, the lands where the Bushmen roamed were thus another case of *terra sine tempore*. And again, as in Australia, prejudices towards nomadic temporalities – and variations on the related themes of perpetual scarcity and the inefficiency of 'stone-age' economies – were incredibly powerful in terms of the cultural prejudices which they helped to fuel. Indeed, many of these prejudices have survived intact and are present in contemporary discourse, revealing their deep entrenchment in the imagination of agricultural societies – both European and African.

It was only in the 1970s that Western anthropology began to reconsider the logic of the hunter-gatherer economy in a more open-minded manner. In his seminal essay, 'The Original Affluent Society', anthropologist Marshal Sahlins first proposed an alternative explanation for the hunter-gatherers' indifference to the agricultural logic of surplus: rather than a lack of foresight or a symptom of irredeemable improvidence, the hunter-gatherers evinced 'a trust in the abundance of nature's resources,' Sahlins argued – 'a confidence which is the reasonable human attribute of a generally successful economy.'[32] Couched in these terms, counting and hoarding time was, in a sense, something which the Bushmen – unlike agricultural and capitalist societies – could afford to do without.

'Hottentot-time'

Europeans generally perceived Khoikhoi ('Hottentot') peoples as occupying a slightly higher stage of civilisation than the Bushmen. This was reflected in the principal mode of production practised by these societies: the Khoikhoi were herders, who tended to their domesticated stock and thus moved according to 'more regular' and predictable, transhumant patterns. Their practice of regular animal husbandry demonstrated to Europeans that the Khoikhoi possessed a keener sense of appreciation for deferred gratification than the Bushmen, and an ability to cope with more structured patterns of work. Of course, the idea of 'work' assumed very different meanings in the worlds of colonisers and colonised. Among British colonists, anything associated with cattle was not considered 'work': for, by affording African people a choice as to whether or not they wished to sell their labour to white employers, the cattle economy was thought to encourage an 'idle' existence.[33]

Despite their elevated state relative to the Bushmen in colonial discourse, the 'Hottentots' – which included various Khoisan subgroups such as the Namaqua, Hessequa, Outeniqua, Korana, etc. – were regarded as possessing an appreciation of time which was radically inferior to that expected of 'civilised' peoples. Compared with European standards of precision, Khoikhoi systems of reckoning and denoting time were clearly viewed as inadequate. As the Reverend Barnabas Shaw stated:

Concerning the divisions of time, as marked by the heavenly bodies, the Namacqua is in utter ignorance ... The periods which have passed away, he can only express by saying they were before or after some memorable event. The season of the year is generally indicated by its being so many moons before or after *uyntjes tyd*, or the time that the roots which they are accustomed to eat are in season.[34]

The German travel-writer Heinrich Lichtenstein used different words to the same effect:

The Hottentots understand no other mode of measuring time but by lunar months and days; they have no idea of the division of the day into hours. If a man asks a Hottentot how far it is to such or such a place, he either makes no answer, or points to a certain spot in the heavens, and says: 'The sun will be there when you get to it.'[35]

As a manifestation of these defects, Europeans pointed to the supposed lack of work-ethic among the 'Hottentot', their tendency to 'waste' time, a 'disposition to indolence', and a listless mode of life, all of which were understood as being biologically inherited maladies. Lichtenstein, during his visits to the Moravian missions at the Cape, felt that there was a correlation between race and slothfulness. The only 'natives' who had been worthy of baptism at Genadendal, he noted, had been those of mixed descent, 'since, among the pure Hottentots, exhortation alone cannot produce a sufficient effect to induce them to throw aside their careless and indolent ways.'[36] Although milder in their criticisms, missionaries reinforced the notion of the 'Hottentot' as naturally adverse to regular and protracted work. A member of the Berlin Missionary Society outpost at Zoar, Meyfarth, for example, expressed his belief that although 'Hottentots' were not lazy, they – 'true to their "hottentottischen Natur" – only worked as long as they wanted to work and did not do anything that took effort or sweat'.[37] The Reverend John Edwards, described the Griqua as 'naturally a vacillating people'.[38] Such indictments mirrored the English gentry's criticisms of the sporadic, pre-industrial labour patterns of the working classes, who were similarly regarded as lazy and averse to regular and constant labour. 'A Hottentot's motto might very well be "A feast and a fast,"' wrote the English traveller and botanist, William Burchell.[39]

Though he used the general appellation 'Hottentot' to describe the community at Klaarwater, the people who Burchell met were in fact the Griqua – descendants of the colony's so-called 'Bastard' population, the progeny of Dutch-speaking colonists, imported slaves and Khoisan, who lived as separate polities on the Cape's northern frontier.[40] Whilst the Griqua had inherited horses and guns from the Dutch Boers, Burchell's description suggests that they had obviously not inherited a correspondingly 'civilised' time-consciousness or a disposition towards sustained labour, implying that a century of cultural contact with the Dutch had done very little in the way of contributing to a reorientation of time-consciousness among the Khoikhoi (a view which was probably just as much an indictment of Boer culture; for British commentators often stereotyped Boer farmers themselves as being fat, lazy and unmotivated[41]). Indeed, Barnabas Shaw, who founded the first Wesleyan mission in the Cape in 1816, was similarly shocked to find that the Namaqua in the Khamiesberg had not internalised the most basic ideas of European time, even after so lengthy a period of contact with Dutch settlers.

> One day during the last week I called upon the young people together to question them not on the subject of religion, but *such things as are necessary for them to know*. To my great astonishment not one in the place could inform me how many days there are in a week. Two or three could count to one hundred. Some to 18 or 20 and others to five, while one could go no further than two.[42]

It is interesting to note that Shaw regarded the week – a specifically European construct – to be one of the things 'necessary for them to know'. It certainly also came to be understood as necessary to the Khoikhoi, once they realised that their work contracts with white farmers were based around this discourse of time. Indeed, disputes between settlers and servants often originated from a disagreement over the amount of time that had expired since the commencement of work contracts. Whilst visiting the Kat River valley during his six-month tour of the Cape, Lichtenstein was a firsthand witness to one such argument – a dispute which went so far as being brought to the attention of the Commissary-General, J. A. de Mist, who happened to be present and decided to adjudicate. The somewhat peculiar incident is of particular interest to us given that Lichtenstein decided to record the servant's side of the story, immortalised under the somewhat satirical title, 'A Hottentot's manner of explaining the proportions of time':

> A Hottentot in particular engaged our attention, by the simplicity with which he told his story. After he had harangued for a long time in broken Dutch, we collected so much as that he had agreed with a colonist to serve him for a certain time at fixed wages, as herdsman, but before the time expired, they had parted by mutual agreement. The dispute was how much of the time remained, consequently how much wages the master had a right to deduct from the sum which was to have been paid for the whole time. To illustrate this matter, the Hottentot gave us the following account. 'My Baas,' said he, 'will have it that I was to serve so long,' and here he stretched out his left arm and hand, and laid his right, with the little finger directly under the arm; 'but I say that I only agreed to serve so long,' and here he laid his right hand upon the joint of the left.

Apparently, he meant to signify, that the proportion of the time he had served, with that he had agreed to serve, was the same as the proportion of what he pointed out of the arm to the whole length of it. At the same time he shewed us a small square stick, in which at every full moon he had made a little notch, with a double one at the full moon, when he quitted the colonist's service.[43]

Ironically, De Mist's verdict expressed a typically middle-class disdain both for the 'Hottentot' and the farmer in question. As Lichtenstein relates: 'the conclusion was, as is very commonly the case, that both the master and the servant were somewhat in the wrong; that the one reckoned too much of the time expired, the other too little, and that according to the Hottentot's mode of measuring, the time expired came about to the knuckle.' The passage reminds us that Indigenous peoples who entered into work contracts with Europeans were simultaneously oppressed *and* empowered by the colonisers' language of time. As Shaw had intimated, the language of weeks, months and years was a necessary one, for it allowed workers to demand shorter or more precise periods of contract, thereby allowing them to negotiate the way in which they sold their labour rather than to submit to indefinite contracts that were tantamount to slavery.

'Kaffir time'

The Xhosa-speaking peoples who inhabited the lands to the east of the Cape frontier practised pastoralism and agriculture, and were consequently regarded by Europeans as one of the more 'progressed' civilisations in southern Africa. The way in which they related to time was consonant with this perception, for agricultural rhythms influenced and permeated Xhosa calendars, rituals and routines. The most patent sign of the close relationship between time and agriculture was demonstrated by the name which the Xhosa gave to the constellation of the Pleiades: Isilimela, which comes from the word *ukulima* – meaning 'to dig', 'cultivate'. Given its importance to Xhosa society, the annual rising of *Isilimela* announced the beginning of the Xhosa New Year and the start of the digging season. While the rising of another star, *uCanzibe* (Canopus), signalled the close of the year and the start of the harvest season.[44]

The Xhosa calendar's orientation around agricultural activities would have suggested a number of positive signs to European observers, such as the existence of defined seasons of work and rest, which in turn meant that social rituals and schedules were structured and oriented around calendars based on human labour, as well as on nature's time. Because of this, the language of Xhosa-time could be 'translated' into the colonisers' terms. Consider the following observation of the Xhosa, by the two French missionaries, Thomas Arbousset and Francis Daumas: 'the men and the women shoulder their *mogumas* [i.e.: hoes] ... [i]n the month of August, or *to speak in the language of the country*, two moons after harvest'.[45] This level of dialogic compatibility between agricultural calendars meant that, even after missionaries introduced the system of dividing the year into twelve months, the Xhosa were able to retain their own calendrical names and terminology for those months. The following translation of the British calendar into Xhosa terms, recorded by the Xhosa convert and missionary, John Henderson Soga, demonstrates this.

> January: *Eyom-qungu* (Of the tall grass), i.e. the ripening of the Tambooki grass;
> February: *Eyom-dumba* (Of the pod), when pod-bearing trees are carrying pods;
> March: *Eyo-kindla* (harvest month), i.e. earliest ripening of the grain;
> April: *U'tshaz impuzi* (when the pumpkins become frost-bitten);
> May: *U-Canzibe* (Saturn [sic]), when this 'star' makes its appearance;
> June: *Isi-limela* (The Pleiades), when this constellation appears. This is the beginning of the Xhosa year;
> July: *Eye-ntlaba* (Aloe month), when the aloe bursts into flower;
> August: *Eye-tupa* (Month of buds), when the trees begin to bud;
> September: *Eyo-msints* (Kafirboom) i.e. when the tree *Erythrina Caffra* blooms;
> October: *Eye-dwara* (Rag-wort, small variety), when it is in blossom;
> November: *Eye-nkanga* (Rag-wort, large variety), when in bloom;
> December: *Eyom-nga* (Mimosa month), when the acacia is in full bloom.[46]

For Europeans, the semi-sedentary lifestyle of agriculturalists also evinced key signs of a positive predisposition towards sustained effort and a heightened appreciation of the benefits of deferred gratification. The domestication of animals and plants, as we have seen, went hand in hand with the husbandry of time. This was an important distinction for Europeans, for whom the social organisation of time was one of the measures of civilisation. Thus the Xhosa were seen to reflect a higher level of work-ethic and time-discipline: 'The Kaffer and Boochuana [i.e. Tswana] tribes are decidedly more provident and economical than the Hottentots', wrote the Reverend Stephen Kay. 'Whilst the latter, with comparatively few exceptions, thoughtlessly kill and eat as long as their stocks last, or carelessly squander away their scanty pittance as soon as they get it; the former, on the contrary, uniformly labour to keep in hand a store of something or other.'[47] Concurring with such a comparison, Arbousset and Daumas commented: 'The bechuana female would by her diligence put the bastaard [Griqua] female to shame. The former is active and laborious, the latter is indolent in the extreme.'[48]

Europeans clearly perceived cultures such as the Xhosa, Tswana, Zulu and Ndebele to possess a higher degree of temporal sophistication than the Khoikhoi and Bushmen, largely due to the fact that their social and political lives were structured around an agricultural calendar, with specific periods set aside for work, feasts, ceremonies, dances and meetings. 'As a rule there are no specified times or places for holding these meetings', Sir Theophilus Shepstone stated when asked whether African tribes were capable of holding assemblies at specified times and places. 'But, with such highly organised tribes as the Zulus and Matabele,' he added, 'times are recognised when such general assemblies are held: for instance, among the Zulus the annual celebration of the first fruits is usually attended by work of this sort.[49]

Compared to 'Western time', however, 'Kaffir-time' was understood by Europeans as evidence of a state of immature cultural development. Such a perception was in great part based on a perceived *inaccuracy* of their computations of time. The Xhosa may have employed lunar and stellar calendars for gauging the seasons of planting, seeding and harvest, and their rituals and ceremonies; but they also took many of their cues from 'particular signs of nature', which were not always astronomically oriented. 'The shooting flower of the Kaffer-bloom is regarded as the signal for planting their first crop of maize', the Reverend Kay recorded during his observations of the Xhosa calendar. 'When the wild plum-tree puts forth its blossoms, they then put in their millet,' he continued; 'and upon observing the willow's aspect changed by the advance of spring, they count it high time to sow in their last crop of Indian corn'.[50] The tying of the social calendar to such natural phenomena resulted, according to an early anthropologist, in 'frequent confusion and difference of opinion as to which month it really is ... [A]s all these events may vary in time, the astrologers are frequently at sixes and sevens as to which moon they have'.[51]

To Europeans, the Xhosa were not so much 'primitive' in their way of reckoning time, as 'pre-modern' – having failed to take the necessary step towards modernity, by developing a language of time that could operate independently of nature's rhythms. 'No artificial means of recording time exists,' critics pointed out, 'and in dark or cloudy weather they are quite at a loss to tell the time even approximately'.[52] In technological terms, 'Kaffir time' belonged to a previous stage of Europe's own past, for European astronomers had long since devised systems for intercalating lunar and solar calendars. A supposed failure to develop a mathematical language of time became one of the explanations for the inability of many non-European societies to unveil, predict and thereby 'conquer' nature's laws. 'These moons are always out of order', the Reverend Eugène Casalis noted of the Basuto calendar, so that events 'which ought to appear in September [are] not seen till October'.[53]

These supposed calendrical defects provided proto-anthropologist like Casalis with a means of casting Africans in an immature state of cultural and technological development, suggesting a failure to progress beyond the technological discoveries of Biblical times in the European historical continuum. Writing in the 1920s, for instance, William Willoughby, declared:

> Of the astronomical lunar month, the Bantu [i.e. Africans] know nothing ... their year is measured, in practice by the recurrence of the seasons, and in theory by the rising of the Pleiades after sunset; and, to add to the confusion, they name their months after such a particular species of antelope, or the seasonal tasks of the farmer ... From the time of the Exile, Jews have mitigated this inconvenience by inserting an extra lunar month into their calendar about every third year; but Bantu tribesmen, ignorant of the discoveries of Babylonian or other astronomers, cannot make out why their lunar months will not keep step with the Pleiades and the bursting forth of bud and blossom.[54]

When he became the first headmaster of a school established in 1904 among the Tswana, Willoughby found an opportunity to 'modernise' the Bantu, by educating pupils about lunar months, solar years and seven-day weeks.[55]

The absence of temporal units in the Xhosa computation of time was another source of constant wonder to colonial observers. Harriet Ward's diary, for instance, records that 'Neither Fingoes nor Kaffirs seem to take much note of time; they sing and dance when hungry and thirsty. Days, weeks, months, and years pass by unnoticed, and uncounted.'[56] Lichtenstein concurred: 'They are very little capable of calculating time: a period of more than a few months they know not how to describe.'[57] As manifestations of these defects, colonial observers pointed to the supposedly inherent lethargy of African peoples – their custom of wasting time in idle talk, gossip and lounging around. Clearly, it was solely ever with reference to the Khoikhoi and Bushmen that the Xhosa and other agricultural societies were described as 'laborious', 'provident and 'economical'. When compared with Europeans, the Xhosa were victims of the same criticisms. To members of a developed industrial-capitalist society – not to mention Methodists and middle-class observers – it was unthinkable that time could be so scantily accounted for, or that society could function outside a temporal grid that regulated and coordinated the activities of the day. As William Shaw recorded in his journal on New Year's Day in 1829:

[The Natives] do not distinctly apprehend the accuracy of those calculations by which we determine the close and commencement of a year. Indeed, our division of time into minutes, hours, weeks, months, years, is a great puzzle to them. Notwithstanding this *defect*, we had a good watch night service, [and] the congregation filled the chapel.[58]

As is commonly the case, such accounts reveal more about their authors than the subjects in question – in this case the ethnocentric perspective through which Europeans understood the experience of time, according to which all non-mathematical methods of calculating and expressing the passage of time were perceived as 'defective,' flawed, and imprecise. Not even the Xhosa's manner of expressing their own ages escaped such criticisms. Captain Ludwig Alberti's provides one of countless examples:

It is not possible to determine the greatest age which these Kaffirs usually attain … To examine this, adequate comprehension of numbers and chronology would be required, which one does not find among these Kaffirs. At all events, they do not possess the aptitude to assemble and add up so many units as would be required to merely express a youthful age in months, which is their principal mode of determining it.[59]

Alberti recorded that the Xhosa practice for expressing the age of a child was to hold out a flat hand above the ground 'to indicate his height and to deduce his age from that', while a Xhosa woman might say that 'she is one, two, three, or more children old', meaning that she has given birth to that number of children. Such methods evidently sufficed to meet the needs of Xhosa society. But by the linear, progressive standards of European time, such simplicity was interpreted as another sign of African impracticality. Indeed, Alberti concluded, 'both methods of indicating the age [are] very unrealistic and apart from this, are only applicable in the case of children or women. The Kaffirs do not know at all how to indicate a greater age.'[60]

As these and other accounts of 'African time' circulated through Europe, they ended up shaping and reinforcing metropolitan ideas about the African subcontinent, supposedly peopled by natives who were ignorant, not merely about time but even their own ages. Of course, the Xhosa were not ignorant of their own age at all, but merely of the Europeans' manner of expressing it. During the course of missionary and medical work in the Cape, for instance, the Reverend Arthur Brigg learnt that the Xhosa expressed a person's age by other means than calendar years. When asked to state their age, his Xhosa patients would reply according to a local chronology of events within living memory. Brigg could then translate these into western European dates, as follows:

'He was born before the first Kafir war' (that is 1818); or, 'after the arrival of the British settlers' (1820); or, 'about the irruption of the Fecani under Matiwane' (1827); or, 'he was so big in the war of Hintza' (1835); or, 'during the Fingoe emancipation' (same year); or, 'on the abolition of slavery in the Cape,' (1838 [sic]); or, during the 'war of the axe' (1846); or, 'the war of Umlanjeni' (1850), etc.[61]

Interestingly, the Xhosa did also express concepts of age with reference to astronomical calendars, although very few Europeans realised this during the nineteenth century. Following the initiatory ritual of male circumcision, the Xhosa indeed counted 'the years of manhood' – not by the passage of the sun, but by the rising of *Isilimela*, the Pleiades, which were central to the Xhosa agricultural calendar. This practice was immortalised by the celebrated Xhosa *imbongi* (praise poet), S. E. K. Mqhayi, in what became one of the most famous poems in the Xhosa canon – 'A Silimela':

> Summon the nations, let's apportion the stars:
> ...You Britons, take Venus,
> To divide with the Germans and Boers,
> Though you are folk who don't know how to share.
> We'll divide up the Pleiades, we people of Phalo [i.e.: Xhosa]
> That great group of stars,
> For they're stars for counting off years,
> For counting the years of manhood[62]

The poem does not merely demonstrate the limited scope of the colonisers' comprehension of Xhosa culture but also shows that the Xhosa, like Europeans themselves, drew powerful and symbolic connections between time, calendars and sovereign identities. For decades to come, 'A Silimela' would in fact resonate with thousands of Xhosa people as a powerful statement of Xhosa national identity. When, in 1937, Mqhayi visited the Healdtown school, he recited 'A Silimela' to a class of young Xhosa students, amongst whom was a young Nelson Mandela. After Mqhayi had delivered the final verse, Mandela recalls: 'I felt such intense pride at that point, not as an African, but as a Xhosa.'[63]

'African time' in settler and missionary discourses

The depiction of African societies as lacking in a valid system of measuring and expressing time was a powerful feature of settler and Christian discourse. Unfavourable depictions of 'African time' were discursively applied in a number of ways to reinforce settler, as well as missionary, claims to cultural superiority. As we have seen in the case of Victoria, the notions of time-less nomads and erratic wanderers could be invoked to weaken the perceived attachment of Indigenous people to their lands. It was harder to sustain such arguments in relation to the Xhosa, whose developed patterns of agricultural land-use satisfied European understandings of land ownership. Nevertheless, by appealing to the perceived lack of calendars and chronologies among the Xhosa, settlers in the Cape were able to couch arguments and justifications for their dispossession, too. As a settler's statement illustrates, the absence of a written history and of precise dates quickly translated into a lack of historical consciousness and territorial entitlement:

> This cry of 'the land', in connection with these barbarian outbreaks, is misleading. It gives an air of patriotism to the violence and bloodshed and rapine of these people. It makes it appear as if they had sacred attachments to the land, like unto those of a people who have a history, and memories of their fathers worthy of being cherished. 'Their fathers!' Why, they cannot tell where their fathers lived two generations ago.[64]

It is interesting to note that we gain a very different perspective on such matters when we consult the observations of missionaries, whose objectives were less oriented towards territorial acquisition and more towards the conversion of souls. John Mackenzie's description of the rather extensive chronologies preserved by the Xhosa directly contradicts the above statement:

> The Kaffirs living to the east of the Cape Colony would seem to have given the greatest attention to genealogical questions. Some tribes among them reckon up to eleven ancestors, others fourteen; whilst the oldest or parent tribe, the Abatembu or Tembookies [i.e.: Thembu], treasures in its memory as many as eighteen chiefs – taking us back, according to recent computation, to about A.D. 1400.[65]

But settlers were not the only parties to employ a discourse of absence and stake a claim upon a dominant temporal consciousness. Missionaries popularised the notion of a *theological* timelessness, which served to substantiate their own assertion that African societies were bereft of religious institutions and thus in need of spiritual intervention. Whilst Christians annually re-enacted and reinforced religious doctrine by offering remembrance to the most important of biblical events – on Easter, Christmas and the Sabbath – the Xhosa, as William Willoughby wrote, possessed no such ritual calendar: their 'holy days' were 'not worshipped as a matter of routine on fixed dates', and their spirits were 'approached only when the soul of the community [was] disturbed by ... its need of supernatural aid'.[66] Compared to biblical time, the genealogies of Xhosa chiefs appeared to missionaries as vague histories that merely reached as far back as the fifteenth century.

Khoisan groups, on the other hand, who possessed no such chronology at all, were regarded as altogether devoid of a historical consciousness. According to the Reverend Stephen Kay, in questioning them about their practices of ancestor-worship and shamanism, 'the only plea they attempted to set up in justification of their system was, as usual, "that such had been the custom of their forefathers from time immemorial".'

> How melancholy the reflection! From time immemorial, millions have thus made their only refuge in times of trouble! from time immemorial, whole nations of men have thus been sinking in the vortex of delusion! Yea, from time immemorial, one generation of immortal beings has been thus blindly following another, and all literally 'perishing for lack of knowledge'.[67]

Missionaries presented Christianity to Indigenous peoples as a time-conscious religion, whose truth and continuity were legitimated by the supposed precision with which they were anchored to a linear, historical narrative. Biblical time, they explained to their converts, was permanent and all-encompassing, spanning from Genesis to Judgment Day. The missionaries' objective might not have been that of replacing the Xhosa on their land, but it clearly aimed to substitute their previous ideas of time, history and identity through a new understanding of the past, present and future. To impress upon their converts the legitimacy and authority of the Christian message, it thus became a practical necessity for missionaries to impart an understanding of the Christian calendar. William Shaw deemed it appropriate to conduct this lesson on Christmas Day:

> As the natives reckon time only by the moons and the years, and have no method of distinguishing days, we find it exceedingly difficult to give them even an idea on what plan we form our Chronology. The idea of any occurrence before the day of Togu [ca 1686], (who is the first Caffre chief of whom they have any tradition, and who must have lived less than 200 years ago) is to them a matter of astonishment. They can therefore form no idea of the length of time that has elapsed since our Lord Jesus Christ came into the world, nor indeed can the number of years of the Christian era be easily expressed in their language, so as to be understood.[68]

Ironically, whilst Shaw was busy reforming the calendars of his Xhosa converts in Africa, the dominance in society of the biblical chronology was itself in the process of being threatened by European scientists' discovery of 'geological time'.

The absence of detailed chronologies and written records and the orientation of Indigenous rituals around natural, instead of human (or 'divine'), events helped cast a discursive shroud of 'superstition' over

African belief systems, challenging their legitimacy. The portrayal of African rituals as pagan and superstitious no doubt operated on a multitude of layers, seizing upon the use of idols, fertility rituals, witchdoctors, divination, polygamy and many other signs associated with 'false religion'. But the manner in which ceremonies and rituals were ordered in time – the sources of temporal authority which determined and guided African religion – played an equally important role in their being labelled as 'heathen' customs. William Shaw's views on the Xhosa calendar were cemented when he discovered that 'the word which expresses [their priesthood's] initiatory process, *ukutwasa*, means "renewal", and is the same that is used for the first appearance of the new moon, and for the putting forth of the grass and buds at the commencement of spring'.[69] From this, Shaw deduced, 'the Kaffir cannot properly be said to possess any RELIGION; but they practise a complicated system of SUPERSTITION, which interweaves itself with all the principal transactions of their social life.'[70]

As Jean and John Comaroff write, Europeans 'were wont to reserve the term "religion" for systems that accorded with a modernist Protestant sense of faith and worship'.[71] Embodied in the timing of African rituals, missionaries saw evidence, not of *other* religions and other ways of interpreting the world, but of 'magic' and 'superstition', vestiges of Old Testament rites. The fact that African rituals did not make as clear a distinction between sacred and secular times (the Lord's Day being a clear point of contrast in this regard) was a key point of difference. Missionaries associated the lack of the concept of a seven-day week with the belief in a complete dearth of religious sentiment among Indigenous societies. The absence of the Sabbath implied the absence of a specific day of rest and worship, which in turn implied ignorance of the scriptures: 'Every day of the week had been alike to them,' the Wesleyan Reverend Edwards commented of the Griquas – 'they were purely children of nature.'[72] Likewise, the Wesleyan Reverend Broadbent remarked of the Tswana people: 'When we went there, the people had no religion. They had sorcerers, and witchcraft, but they had no God, no temple, no Sunday, no worship ... In a word, their minds were blank on spiritual and eternal subjects.'[73] Such accounts were echoed by the Wesleyan Reverend Thomas Hodgson, who referred to the Tswana as 'a people who hold no Sabbath and who appear to have no kind of religious worship.'[74]

Missionaries ascribed such 'defects' as the absence of the Sabbath to spiritual savageness; they saw African magic and rituals as pre-Christian residues which had failed to evolve into full-blown religion. Remnants of institutional rhythms resembling the Sabbath were said to be found among 'heathen' peoples, providing evidence that they too had once practised the ritual. 'Although *the recollection of the institution of the Sabbath* is lost among these people,' Eugène Casalis wrote of the Basuto, 'they have preserved the ideas that certain solemn and important circumstances demand the consecration of certain days of repose.'[75] This was a significant point, for it lent credence to the premise of the evangelical mission, predicated on the fundamental unity of humanity and the universality of the Christian narrative. The appeal to the idea of a common origin in itself constituted a reason to restore to 'the heathen' those aspects of religion and humanity which Africans had supposedly lost and forgotten as a result of sin.

The deeper a people had sunk in sin, the more missionaries perceived them as having misinterpreted and perverted the law of the Sabbath. 'There is no stated day of rest in any part of this country,' wrote Livingstone, as he probed deeper into the African interior, 'except the day after the appearance of the new moon, and the people then refrain only from going to their gardens.' To a Christian readership, such observations regarding the timing of rituals provided suggestive imagery. Visions of savages planning their 'false Sabbath' according to the lunar calendar evoked unpalatable images of witchcraft and diabolical proclivity. And if such allusions were not sufficient, other unsavoury details surely completed the picture: 'They watch most eagerly for the first glimpse of the new moon,' Livingstone continued, 'and, when they perceive the faint outline of it after the sun has set deep in the west, they utter a loud shout of "Kuà!" and vociferate prayers to it.'[76]

Given its discursive role in helping to construct notions of African superstition and savagery, time became one of the natural mediums through which missionaries and colonial reformers sought to reform and modernise their Others. If sinfulness was understood as a spiritual time-lessness, evinced by the absence of a recurring day dedicated to God, the process of redeeming Indigenous peoples came to be associated with imparting knowledge of the 'true' ritual – the Christian Sabbath. This was pithily forecast by the Wesleyan missionary, Stephen Kay, when he wrote that '[a]ll days were alike common to them while they lived "without God, and without hope in the world." But the word of God creates a Sabbath wherever it comes'.[77]

The advance of nineteenth-century European colonisation was therefore equated as much with the triumph of science and reason over the forces of superstition and ignorance as with the advancement of Christian time over the lands where heathen time prevailed. In this sense, the 'colonisation of time' constituted an important bridge between colonial projects of modernisation and Christianisation, both of which were premised on the exclusion of alternative technologies and rituals of time.

Notes

1 Benjamin Ridsdale, *Scenes and Adventures in Great Namaqualand* (London: T. Woolmer, 1883), pp. 272–3.
2 See Alan Lester, *Imperial Networks: Creating Identities in Nineteenth Century South Africa and Britain* (London: Routledge, 2001); Catherine Hall, *Civilising Subjects: Colony and Metropole in the English Imagination, 1830–1867* (Chicago, Ill.: Chicago University Press, 2002), p. 301; Thomas, *Colonialism's Culture*, p. 126.
3 John L. Comaroff, 'Images of Empire, Contests of Conscience', in Cooper and Stoler (eds), *Tensions of Empire*, pp. 181–2; see also the Comaroffs' discussion of 'the everyday as epiphany' in Comaroff and Comaroff, *Of Revelation, Vol. 2*, pp. 29–35.
4 John Philip, *Researches in South Africa; Illustrating the Civil, Moral, and Religious Condition of Native Tribes...* (London: James Duncan, 1828), vol. 2, p. 116.
5 See Jean Comaroff, 'Missionaries and Mechanical Clocks', p. 8.
6 Ridsdale, *Scenes and Adventures in Great Namaqualand*, pp. 272–3.
7 See Perkins, *The Reform of Time*; Perkins, *Visions of the Future*.
8 William Willoughby, *The Soul of the Bantu, A Sympathetic Study of the Magico-Religious Practices and Beliefs of the Bantu Tribes of Africa* (London: Student Christian Movement, 1928), pp. 121–2.
9 Isabella Turner, 1868, quoted in Andrew Hassam, *Sailing to Australia: Shipboard Diaries by Nineteenth Century British Emigrants* (Melbourne: University Press, 1995), p. 137.
10 E.g.: Cory, Doc 08; mf 436, box 23/1, 2, Barnabas Shaw, Journal, section 3, folder 1 of 2, p. 14; Hassam, *Sailing to Australia*, pp. 2–8, 59–98.
11 John Mackenzie, *Ten Years North of the Orange River: A Story of Everyday Life and Work Among the South African Tribes from 1859–1869*, (1871), 2nd edn (London: Frank Cass & Co., 1971), p. 8.
12 Ridsdale, *Scenes and Adventures in Great Namaqualand*, p. 8.
13 John Edwards, *Reminiscences of the Early Life and Missionary Labours of the Rev. John Edwards, Fifty Years a Wesleyan Missionary in South Africa*, W. M. C. Holden (ed.) (Grahamstown: T. H. Grocott, 1883), p. 46. (Cory Collection.)
14 William Shaw, *The Story of My Mission in South-Eastern Africa: Comprising some Accounts of the European Colonists; With Extended Notices of the Kaffir and other Native Tribes* (London: Hamilton, Adams & Co., 1860), p. 203.
15 William Moister, *Memorials of Missionary Labours in Western Africa, the West Indies, and at the Cape of Good Hope* (London: W. Nichols, 1866), pp. 512–15.
16 WMMS, *Missionary Notices of the Wesleyan Methodist Missionary Society and Papers Relating to the Wesleyan Missions, and to the State of Heathen Countries* (hereafter: *Wesleyan Missionary Notices*), 6:1 (1874), W. J. Davis, 12 Nov. 1873, p. 60.
17 Moister, *Memorials of Missionary Labours*, p. 512.
18 Livingstone, *Missionary Travels and Researches*, p. 172.
19 WMMS, *Wesleyan Missionary Notices*, 6:1 (1874), W. J. Davis, p. 60.
20 Mackenzie, *Ten Years North of the Orange River*, pp. 60–1.
21 *Graham's Town Journal*, 1:3 (13 Jan. 1832), p. 10. The editor added: 'So far the sentiment was by no means singular, though our readers may deem the reason not quite so satisfactory.'
22 For details regarding the names of peoples, please refer to the note on terminology (p. xvi).
23 On the stadial theory of evolution, see: Stein, *Legal Evolution*, pp. 24–36; Meek, 'Smith, Turgot and the "Four Stages" Theory', in Meek, *Smith, Marx and After*.

24 B. Shaw, *Memorials*, p. 47.
25 *Report from the Select Committee on Aborigines (British Settlements)*, 1837, *Minutes of Evidence*, vol. 1, Walter Gisborne, p. 365.
26 Anthony Pagden, *European Encounters with the New World: From Renaissance to Romanticism* (New Haven, Conn.: Yale University Press, 1993), p. 152.
27 Livingstone, *Missionary Travels and Researches*, p. 55.
28 B. Shaw, *Memorials*, p. 45.
29 *Report from the Select Committee on Aborigines (British Settlements)*, 1837, *Minutes of Evidence*, vol. 1, Andries Stockenstrom, p. 184.
30 Mackenzie, *Ten Years North of the Orange River*, p. 135.
31 Richard B. Lee, *The !Kung San: Men, Women, and Work in a Foraging Society* (Cambridge: University Press, 1979), p. 118.
32 Marshall D. Sahlins, *Stone Age Economics* (Aldine-Atherton, New York: 1972), pp. 28–9.
33 Jeffrey B. Peires, *The House of Phalo: A History of the Xhosa People in the Days of Their Independence* (Berkeley: University of California Press, 1982), p. 107.
34 B. Shaw, *Memorials*, p. 40.
35 Lichtenstein, *Travels in Southern Africa*, vol. 2, p. 90.
36 *Ibid.*, pp. 193–4.
37 Cory, pamphlet box 150, Hans Heese, 'Khoisan in Kannaland: Observation by the German Lutheran Missionaries from 1838 to 1938', in *Khoisan Identities and Cultural Heritage* (University of the Western Cape & South African Museum, 1997).
38 Edwards, *Reminiscences*, p. 61.
39 William Burchell, *Travels in the Interior of Southern Africa* (London: Longman, 1822), vol. 1, p. 365.
40 See Newton-King, *Masters and Servants*, pp. 133–4; Timothy J. Keegan, *Colonial South Africa and the Origins of the Racial Order* (Charlottesville: University Press of Virginia, 1996), pp. 21–4, 170–1.
41 Lester, *Imperial Networks*, pp. 15–16.
42 B. Shaw, Journal, 1 Nov. 1817, section 1, folder 1, p. 27. (Cory.) Emphasis added.
43 Lichtenstein, *Travels in Southern Africa*, vol. 2, p. 90.
44 Peires, *House of Phalo*, p. 7.
45 Thomas Arbousset and Francis Daumas, *Narrative of an Exploratory Tour of the North-East of the Colony of the Cape of Good Hope* (Cape Town: C. Struik, 1968), pp. 34–5. Emphasis added.
46 John H. Soga, *The Ama-Xosa: Life and Customs* (Lovedale: Lovedale Press, 1931), pp. 417–18.
47 Stephen Kay, *Travels and Researches in Caffraria: Describing the Characters, Customs, and Moral Condition of the Tribes Inhabiting that Portion of Southern Africa...* (London: John Mason, 1833), part 1, p. 145. (Cory Collection.)
48 Arbousset and Daumas, *Narrative of an Exploratory Tour*, pp. 11–13.
49 KAB, CCP, 4/1/2/1/1, *Report and Proceedings, with Appendices, of the Government Commission on Native Laws and Customs*, 1883, *Minutes of Evidence*, Theophilus Shepstone, 7 Sept. 1881, p. 4.
50 Kay, *Researches in Caffraria*, p. 371.
51 James Macdonald, 'Manner, Customs, Superstitions, and Religions of South Africa Tribes', *Journal of the Anthropological Institute of Great Britain and Ireland*, 19 (1890), p. 291.
52 *Ibid.*, p. 291.
53 Eugène Casalis, *The Basutos: Or, Twenty-three Years in South Africa* (1859) (London: James Nisbet, 1861), p. 164.
54 Willoughby, *The Soul of the Bantu*, p. 220.
55 See William Willoughby, *Tiger Kloof: The London Missionary Society's Native Institution in South Africa* (London: London Missionary Society, 1912).
56 Harriet Ward, *The Cape and the Kaffirs: A Diary of Five Years' Residence in Kaffirland* (3rd edn) (London: Henry Bohn, 1851), p. 36. (Cory Collection.)
57 Lichtenstein, *Travels in Southern Africa*, vol. 1, p. 346.
58 NLSA, MSB 435, 1/1, William Shaw, Diary, 1 Jan. 1829, p. 87. Emphasis added.

59 Ludwig Alberti, *Ludwig Alberti's Account of the Tribal Life and Customs of the Xhosa in 1807*, trans. William Fehr (Cape Town: Balkema, 1968), p. 43. (Cory Collection.)
60 Alberti, *Account of the Tribal Life and Customs of the Xhosa*, pp. 43–4. Similarly, in relation to the Tswana, see Mackenzie, *Ten Years North of the Orange River*, p. 377.
61 Arthur Brigg, *'Sunny Fountains' and 'Golden Sand': Pictures of Missionary Life in the South of the 'Dark Continent'* (London: T. Woolmer, 1888), p. 211.
62 S. E. K. Mqhayi, excerpt from 'Silimela son of Makinana', quoted in Jeff Opland, *Words that Circle Words* (Johannesburg: Donker, 1992), pp. 235–7.
63 Nelson Mandela, *Long Walk to Freedom* (London: Abacus, 1994), pp. 47, 49.
64 Anon., *A Plea in Vindication of the Colonists* (Grahamstown: Richard, Slater & Co, 1878, p. 5). (Cory Collection, PR 4787.)
65 Mackenzie, *Ten Years North of the Orange River*, pp. 483-4. On Xhosa genealogies see Peires, *House of Phalo*, p. 17.
66 Willoughby, *The Soul of the Bantu*, pp. 179–80.
67 Kay, *Researches in Caffraria*, p. 482.
68 W. Shaw, Diary, 25 Dec. 1826, p. 56. John Henderson Soga's chronology of Xhosa Chiefs suggests that Togu died around 1686 (Soga, *The Ama-Xhosa*, p. 421).
69 W. Shaw, *My Mission*, p. 447.
70 *Ibid.*, p. 444. Emphasis in the original.
71 Comaroff and Comaroff, *Of Revelation*, Vol. 2, pp. 74–5.
72 Edwards, *Reminiscences*, p. 60.
73 Samuel Broadbent, *A Narrative of the First Introduction of Christianity Amongst the Barolong Tribe of Bechuanas, South Africa...* (London: Wesleyan Mission House, 1865), p. 203. (NLSA Collection.)
74 R. L. Cope (ed.), *The Journals of the Rev. T. L. Hodgson: Missionary to the Seleka-Rolong and the Griquas, 1821–1831* (Johannesburg: Wits University Press, 1977), p. 153.
75 Casalis, *The Basutos*, p. 261. Emphasis added.
76 Livingstone, *Missionary Travels and Researches*, p. 255.
77 Kay, *Researches in Caffraria*, part 2, p. 426.

CHAPTER FIVE

Empire of the seventh day: time and the Sabbath beyond the Cape frontiers

By the close of the nineteenth century, a number of literate Xhosas had emerged from the missionary schools of the Eastern Cape. Among them was Isaac Bud-M'Belle who, in 1903, published a historical account of Xhosa languages, customs and beliefs: *The Kafir Scholar's Companion*. The third chapter, entitled 'Division of Time', recounts how the Xhosa came to adopt the seven-day week:

> In their uncivilised state the Natives knew only the difference between light and darkness, *i.e.* day and night. The first missionaries found them in this state. To teach them the seven days of the week was therefore no easy task. The first day which the missionaries taught them to observe was Sunday, the Christian Sabbath Day. Various ways were adopted to make them understand this.[1]

This was the version of history taught in missionary schools in the latter half of the nineteenth century: Christianity had brought civilised conceptions of time to the Xhosa, delivering them from ignorance and superstition and teaching them to name and order the days according to God's law. The opening gambit in the missionaries' attempt to reshape the modes of perception and practice of African culture was indeed to establish a new tempo of life, governed by the law of the Sabbath. At their earliest convenience – which often meant the day of first encounter – missionaries set the example of Christian conduct by establishing the principle that 'not all days were alike'. God himself (the missionaries informed all those whom they met) 'had appointed one day in seven to be kept holy by refraining from worldly occupation'.[2]

The Sabbath was a ritual of power and identity; individuals and entire nations – as we have seen – were labelled as believers or heathens, 'civilised' or 'uncivilised', according to whether or not they hallowed the seventh day of rest. Its adoption, therefore, indicated the spiritual transition of natives from savages into Christians and British subjects – a simple but emphatic affirmation, in the missionaries' eyes, of spiritual and moral conversion. Thus reports of Sabbath observance were treated by Britain's humanitarians as official evidence of missionary success in planting the seeds of Christianity, commerce and civilisation in places as far apart as the Kat River Settlement, in the Cape Colony, and New Zealand.[3] Likewise, missionary societies regularly published reports of the number of peoples who had been newly inducted into the seven-day regime as a means of providing their metropolitan supporters and patrons with a measure of their progress. For instance, shortly after the establishment of a new mission among the Namaqua people in 1816, the following letter from the Reverend Barnabas Shaw appeared as an excerpt in the *Missionary Notices of the Wesleyan Methodist Missionary Society*: 'AT THAT TIME,' Shaw reported, 'they knew nothing of Christian Sabbaths; but they have NOW learnt to make a Sunday and reverence the sacred day of rest. THEN they were without CHRIST ... and without GOD in the world; but NOW in CHRIST JESUS they are made nigh [etc ...]'.[4]

Thanks to missionaries, the Sabbath was probably the earliest element of European time to have been introduced to the Indigenous peoples in southern Africa. And once the concept of Sunday had been established, it was only the next logical step that the other days of the week should follow. As *The Kafir Scholar's Companion* narrates:

> The missionary *inter alia* explained the 'great day' and told the assembly that to-morrow would be Monday when they could resume their work, hence the term *u-Mvulo*, the opening. (The Zulus were told to call it *u-Msombuluko* – the Unfolding.) The second day, Tuesday, was named *olwesi-Bini*, Wednesday *olwesi-Tatu*, Thursday *olwesi-Ne*, and Friday was called the Fifth day ... Saturday (the sixth day) was [termed] *um-Gqibelo*, the Finishing. Thus they know that the next day would again be the 'great day' or *i-Cawa*.[5]

Whilst Bud-M'Belle was correct in ascribing to missionaries the introduction of the seven-day week among the Xhosa, there is clearly more to the story than what *The Kafir Scholar's Companion* lets on. This chapter revisits the quest to establish the dominance of the seven-day ritual in the Cape Colony, exploring the significance of its cultural impact and of the ways in which it was received, resisted and reinterpreted by Christian converts. In Chapter 3 we saw how the order of the week, the Sabbath and the bell were imported to Victoria swiftly and boldly in the wake of a rapidly advancing settler-colonial frontier. There, the colonisation of Aboriginal temporalities was contained within the *milieu* of mission stations and the reserves – institutions which were swiftly surrounded and physically restricted by white settlement. In the Cape, however, during the first half of the nineteenth century (the period dealt with in this chapter) many of the early missions were located well beyond the official limits of the colony, often far from the protection of their government and patrons. This created a fundamentally different set of circumstances for missionaries in the two fields. An obvious distinction was the demographic disparity between white and black – a colour dynamic which was geographically reversed in the Cape, where white enclaves and mission stations were surrounded by black populations. Secondly, the advancement of the Cape's settler frontier was much slower than in Victoria, providing missionaries with the opportunity to evangelise their converts without the same level of physical interference from settlers.

In these circumstances, missionaries at the Cape effectively became the cultural vanguards of European time, introducing concepts of discipline, order and regularity well ahead of formal colonisation. As the Reverend Dr John Philip of the LMS described it in 1828, 'our missionaries, beyond the borders of the colony of the Cape of Good Hope, are everywhere scattering the seeds of civilization, social order and happiness, they are, by the most unexceptional means, extending British interests, British influence and the British empire'.[6] One of these seeds of civilisation was the colonisers' idea of time.

Missionaries at the frontiers of time

By the time the Reverend John Philip surveyed the field, European colonisation in the Cape Colony had already been under way for over 150 years. Beginning in 1652, the Dutch East India Company had taken strategic possession of the Cape of Good Hope in order to provision its annual fleet en-route to the East Indies. As in the Australian colonies, the threat of dispossession had seen Indigenous groups offering resistance but eventually succumbing to the colonisers' superior military technology.[7] The introduction of distilled liquors and consecutive waves of smallpox epidemics accelerated social breakdown among the Khoikhoi so that, by the end of the eighteenth century, most had become bonded labourers (essentially de-facto slaves) within Dutch colonial society. These, together with a sizeable population of imported slaves, came to provide the economic basis of the Colony.

The Bushmen, on the other hand, many of whom continued to resist invasion and mounted small-scale raids on the farmers' stock, faced brutal retaliation from Dutch farmers, who led regular extermination parties against them, driving the survivors inland. As in the Australian colonies, the prospect of coexistence between European settlers and hunter-gatherers was impossible: the hunters' way of life was threat-

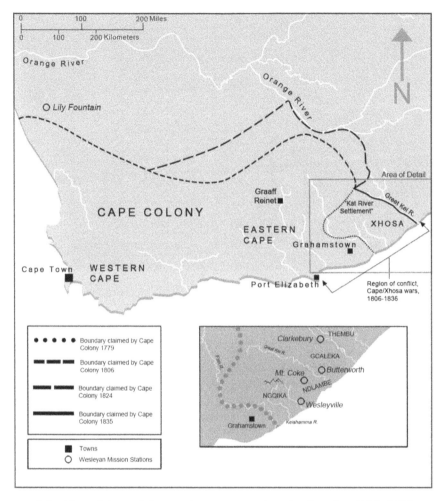

5.1 Map of Cape Colony: advancement of settler frontier, 1799–1835

ened to its very core by the advancement of cattle and farming activities on their lands.

Following a process of expansion by Dutch Trekboers in the 1770s, the area lying between the Orange River in the north and the Fish River in the east had come largely under white control by the end of the eighteenth century. This eastward expansion soon brought Europeans into contact with another Indigenous people occupying the land to the east of the Cape: the Xhosa-speaking nations, who were composed of various subgroups – the Ngqika, Gcaleka, Ndlambe, Thembu, Mpondo (and later other immigrant groups such as the Mfengu). Although sepa-

5.2 Moravian mission of Genadendal, Cape Colony, showing belfry at heart of village

During his visit in 1816, Christian Ignatius Latrobe (Secretary of the Moravians in Britain) reported that 'the sound of the bell may be heard a good way down the valley. It is used for every purpose of call, to church, to school, or to meals, and consequently is sometimes rung eight or nine times in the day' starting at 5:30 in the morning (*A Journal of a Visit to South Africa*, 1, pp. 90–2).

rate polities, these mixed farmer-agriculturalists collectively formed a large group of people whose westward expansion in search of pasturage, water sources and arable land placed them in direct competition with European farmers. Moreover, their iron-forged spears and well-developed warfare capacities posed a significant military obstacle to the advancement of the 'Eastern Frontier', as it came to be known.

When the British took possession of the Cape from the Dutch, they continued the eastward encroachment upon Xhosa lands.[8] The first frontier war (1779–81) had already been fought and won by the Dutch; but Xhosa military resistance was not easily overcome and the Eastern Frontier would see no fewer than another eight such wars fought against the Xhosa by the 1870s. One frontier war at a time, British settler-colonialism progressively moved eastwards, annexing all Xhosa lands through either conquest or cession by treaty following each successive war. By the end of the nineteenth century, white settlers had taken possession of vast tracts of land, the Xhosa gradually becoming servants on white-owned farms or working in the towns of the eastern Cape.

Although Christianity had arrived at the Cape with the first Europeans, the mission activities of the Dutch Reformed Church during most of the eighteenth century were minimal. The pioneers of the missionary movement in South Africa were the Moravians, who established the Cape's first permanent mission to the Khoikhoi in 1792, at Baviaans Kloof (later Genadendal). One of the most significant aspects of the Moravian mission – and indeed of the many non-Moravian missions that followed – was that, although it did not criticise the colonial hierarchy, it offered a place of spiritual comfort to many dispossessed Khoikhoi and a means of escaping a life of servitude on white farms. By the mid-nineteenth century there would be three successful Moravian missions in the western Cape: Genadendal (see figure 5.2), Elim and Groenekloof. Combining religion and agricultural industry, the Moravians set an example which other missionary societies at the Cape would follow, not least in terms of temporal discipline. 'Regularity is one of the most striking characteristics of the Moravian system', Thomas Pringle observed during his travels in the Cape, 'and a love of order, even to excess, pervades every part of their economy'.[9]

It was not long before British missionaries arrived at the Cape to carry the Gospel beyond Cape Town's hinterland and to evangelise the Xhosa as well as the Khoisan. By 1816, twenty LMS missionaries had arrived in the Colony, in which year they were also joined by the first representative of the Wesleyan Methodist Missionary Society (WMMS) and, shortly after, by missionaries of the Glasgow Missionary Society. The latter established themselves at a mission in the Tyumie valley among the Xhosa, and later built a school nearby: Lovedale – which will be the subject of the Chapter 6. Meanwhile, the Wesleyans, under the guidance of the Reverend Barnabas Shaw, established a mission for the Namaqua at Lily Fountain, beyond the northern frontier of the Cape Colony.

Within a few months of Shaw's arrival at Lily Fountain in 1816, set times were organised for religion and for manual labour. Shaw demonstrated the Protestant work-ethic, 'from necessity as well as for the sake of example, [since] like the other tribes of South Africa, the Namacquas are an indolent people'. The work paid off: by the end of the first year, the station was producing butter, soap and candles, and the benefits of industriousness and agriculture were being demonstrated. Time was scarce, but it had been husbanded well. As Shaw wrote in his memoirs – quoting one of John Wesley's hymns: 'Never before could I say with so much propriety:

> With us no melancholy void,
> No moment lingers unemploy'd,
> Or unimproved below.[10]

THE COLONISATION OF TIME

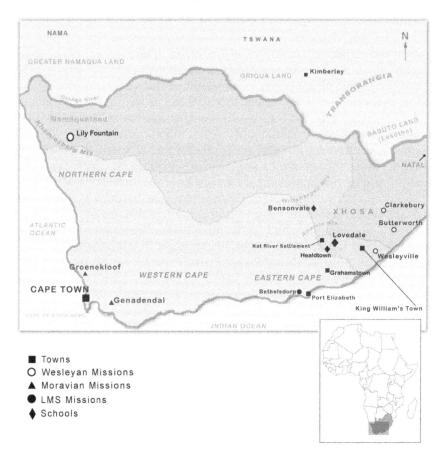

5.3 Map of Cape Colony, showing approximate locations of missions and schools mentioned in the book

Missionaries and settlers in the Cape Colony, particularly during the first half of the nineteenth century, often pursued different projects for the transformation of Indigenous peoples and their landscapes. Of all the societies in the Cape, the LMS played the most divisive and controversial role, since several of its leading members promoted a radical evangelism that overtly criticised the oppressed status of Khoisan labour within the Colony. Indeed, whilst British settlers had been forbidden to own slaves, a system of pass-laws, anti-vagrancy legislation and compulsory apprenticeships ensured that, during the transition from Dutch to British rule, the Khoikhoi remained practically – even if not legally – enslaved.[11] By championing the cause of Indigenous peoples, however, the LMS and its humanitarian allies in

London inevitably clashed with settler society, whose material prosperity and security relied on the coercion of Khoisan labour and the dispossession of the Xhosa. Such tensions within the colonisers' ranks eased from the mid-1840s as the humanitarian lobby gradually began to lose its influence over matters of colonial governance.[12]

However, not all missionaries in the Cape backed the humanitarian cause. This was particularly the case with the Wesleyan Methodist missionaries, many of whom derived from settler stock. The Reverends William Shaw and John Ayliff, who arrived in Algoa Bay together with the '1820 settlers' and established themselves around Grahamstown on the Eastern Frontier, were of this ilk. Whilst they were conscientious proselytisers, as Timothy Keegan notes, the Wesleyans 'never forgot that their first political allegiance was to the British settlers, from whom they drew their personnel and monetary support'.[13] They ministered to settlers, soldiers and Africans alike and were careful not to antagonise settlers and government officials by campaigning for the economic rights of Indigenous peoples. Indeed, William Shaw, who was also the WMMS's Superintendent in the eastern Cape, became a spokesperson for settler causes against the humanitarian missionary wing.

Moreover, the Wesleyans' readiness to act as government agents among the Xhosa allowed them to effectively spearhead the planting of missions beyond the Eastern Frontier. Here, in the words of Noël Mostert, they began 'to lead the great and sustained assault upon Xhosa culture and customs, upon the whole sense and way of Xhosa life'.[14] From the 1820s, with Governor Somerset's consent and under William Shaw's leadership, the Wesleyans embarked on an ambitious project to establish a chain of missions stretching across Xhosa-land, from the Cape to Natal. Mission outposts soon sprang up among the various Xhosa nations: at Mount Coke in 1824 among the Ndlambe Xhosa; at Butterworth in 1827 among the Gcaleka; at Morley and Buntingville in 1829 and 1830 among the Mpondo; at Clarkebury in 1830 among the Thembu; and, by 1834, at three other stations in Transorangia, among the Griqua and Tswana people.

In focusing primarily on the Wesleyan mission, this chapter brings into relief the way in which the introduction of Christian time acted as a vanguard to formal colonisation. Indeed, whilst it can be argued that many missionaries generally served as *unwitting* 'agents of a pervasive economic and cultural imperialism', the Wesleyans seem to have done so quite consciously.[15] Clearly, they regarded the establishment of the Christian order of time as paving the way for British colonisation, something which was explicitly conveyed by their custom of flying the British flag on the Sabbath. 'The natives know nothing of our English national flag,' one of the Wesleyan missionaries reported, 'but when ours is hoisted, they understand the signal. They are aware it is then God's day, and, as such, they pay some respect to it.'[16] As it turned out, the permanent introduction of the British flag did not lag far behind that of the seven-day week.

However, it is important to remember that the agents and models of Christianity which confronted Indigenous people were never identical. In the Cape Colony, as historians have emphasised, significant political splits occurred between – and even within – missionary societies.[17] We cannot really talk about 'missionaries' and 'Africans' without generalising and simplifying the picture somewhat. Nevertheless, even though the non-conformist, Anglican and Moravian models of Christianity may not have agreed about theological teachings and colonial policies, they certainly shared a number of axiomatic principles. The importance of the family unit and proper gendered divisions of labour, for example, were values regarded as universally sacred. Similarly, the Sabbath, the seven-day week, the authority of the clock and the moral value of time were elements ingrained at a deeper level than the ideals spawned by Reformation or imperial politics. Despite their affiliations, most Protestant missionaries embodied the temporal idiosyncrasies spawned by the current evangelical revival and the will to inculcate such mores within their converts.[18] Even at the Bethelsdorp mission – the separatist enclave established by the more radical LMS evangelists – the regular, institutional rhythms of Christian rituals and routines were upheld.[19]

Ultimately, missionaries were a product of their age, strongly influenced and often inspired by the technological breakthroughs of the nineteenth-century – from the railway to the telegraph. In their veneration of uniformity, regularity and punctuality they exuded the spirit of modernity. And whilst many of the younger generation of missionaries did not always match the zeal and determination of their predecessors, they certainly brought with them better timekeepers and a heightened sense of intolerance for imprecise clocks, watches and calendars.[20] Thus the simple sundial which Barnabas Shaw – the first Wesleyan missionary to the Cape – had mounted on a pedestal at the Lily Fountain mission, appeared outdated a decade or so later to a fellow Wesleyan who passed that way. It was 'an excellent dial', the Reverend Benjamin Ridsdale commented regarding his predecessor's work. However, he added, 'as it is not exactly adapted to the latitude of the place, it is only at the hour of noon that it shows true solar time, which, when the equation of time is applied, gives the time by the clock'.[21]

'The word of God creates a Sabbath wherever it comes'

'We arose on ground where the Sabbath was never before kept,' the Reverend Stephen Kay announced one Sunday morning, 'amongst a people to whom this divine institution had hitherto been altogether unknown. From their infancy, therefore, they had invariably spent it as other days'.[22] This solemn proclamation of arrival in heathen lands is a familiar adage of missionary travel-literature, for the absence of the Sabbath provided a useful means of marking the destination of the missionary's journey: heathendom and wilderness were seen to begin where the Christian order of time ended.

Thus it was that missionaries announced the law of the Sabbath:

> All stood amazed when told that it was the day of the Lord, and that his word enjoins upon us to do no manner of work therein, but to rest, keep it holy. Of this the King himself was informed ... Thus, therefore, was proclaimed the first Sabbath in Temboo-Land.[23]

The same process unfolded wherever missionaries gained a foothold. Among the Griqua, as the Reverend John Edwards described it:

> Every day of the week had been alike to them; but now by attending our service on the Sunday, and listening to our singing and preaching, they soon realized the truth that one day out of seven was differently observed to others, and to it they gave the name in their own language of *Tsatsi le le kulo*, which is equivalent to *Day the Great*. The people soon learned to understand the great design of the Christian Sabbath.[24]

Once they had proclaimed the Sabbath, missionaries embarked on a process of constant vigilance in order to ensure that the regime was maintained, issuing reminders and admonishments to those who transgressed the seven-day regime. 'This being new to them,' wrote Samuel Broadbent whilst evangelising the Tswana, 'frequent instances of forgetfulness of the day occurred, and persons would bring things for sale or barter. But when we told them that we did not transact such business on that day, as it was the Lord's day, they would immediately apologize, and say they did not know, or had forgotten.' Eventually, through sheer persistence and positive reinforcements, the Sabbath came to be collectively known and respected: 'Indeed, in less than twelve months,' Broadbent recorded, 'there was a quietness and stillness on that day which served to remind us of the Lord's day in our native land.'[25]

In their quest to familiarise their converts with the Sabbath, missionaries laid the temporal foundations for the doctrine of regular work, since regular prayer and regular work-ethic were encoded in the spirit of the Sabbath law: *Laborare orare est*. Teaching people that the seventh day was a day of rest, implied that the remaining days were to be considered days of work (not surprisingly, Genesis was one of the first stories taught and translated). This precept was demonstrated clearly when, on one occasion, a convert approached the Reverend John Ayliff, saying: 'You *mynheer* are a missionary to our souls – you have nothing to do with working.' Ayliff was quick to correct him; taking up the Bible in his hand he replied: 'This Book says "six days shall thou labour" [sic] and "if a man will not work neither shall he eat."'[26] British humanitarian and settlers-capitalist visions of colonisation differed strongly regarding the best means of obtaining African labour, but both agreed that the African ought to be engaged in regular work.

Such was the Sabbath's connection with both Christianity and civilisation that not only missionaries but also conscientious travellers and explorers felt it their duty to observe the ritual when in the presence of African people. 'I am not afraid of being laughed at,' Alexander Wilmot stated whilst travelling beyond the Cape frontier in the 1830s, 'when I tell you that I think it most important, wherever we may be during our travels, to keep the Sabbath holy.' To which another member of the travelling party added: 'even we may be of service to the good cause if, as we pass through the land, the natives perceive that we respect the Sabbath as the missionary has requested them to do. We are white men, and considered by them as superior; our example, therefore, may do good.'[27] Such 'performances' of Sabbath observance seem to have been consciously intended to reinforce the importance of the weekly ritual as being conducive to the establishment of order in colonial society. Thus William Burchell declared that his intention in attending the Sabbath during his stay among the Griqua was not for his own benefit, but rather – 'being an European, whom many of these poor creatures look up to as knowing what is right' – to 'encourage them, as far as [he] could ... to listen to, and respect, their teachers'.[28]

The Sabbath also allowed missionaries to subvert any competing ritualised activities; for theirs was a mission to enforce a Christian monopoly of time at seven-day intervals. Thus the Wesleyans sought to secure promises from local Xhosa chiefs that their people would exclusively observe the Lord's Day on Sundays. William Shaw, for instance, sent a message to Pato and various neighbouring chiefs one Sunday in 1827, 'desiring them to recollect' that the next day was 'the Sabbath and at least postpone their intended ceremonies until Monday'.[29] Shaw demonstrated that he was prepared to physically interrupt the flow of Xhosa rituals and festivities if such demands were not met. Thus it was that, on another Sunday, the missionary walked straight into the midst of a women's village dance, interrupted the ritual and asked the revellers 'whether it would not be very wrong to dance, and sing the

Devil's songs on the Great Day, when all ought to be at worship'.[30]

The importance of the Sabbath was such that when missionaries were actively requested by local chiefs to reside among them, one of their standard demands was a pledge that they would respect the Sabbath. Xhosa requests for missionaries were common, for the latter were seen as useful go-betweens with colonial authorities, as traders and teachers of new technologies, as status symbols for chiefs and as protectors in ongoing power struggles among Indigenous groups themselves. Thus, when a Xhosa chief expressed his wish to have a mission station established among his people, the missionary's immediate response was first to secure his assurance for a collective observance of the Sabbath: 'I asked them if they would, *as a people*, keep the Sabbath holy, if a Missionary came'.[31] It is important to give due attention – in the above case, and also in general – to the missionary's particular concern with a collective respect for the Sabbath (note the use of the phrase, 'as a people').

The seven-day week was not the only temporal pattern to be introduced during the early phase of evangelical encounter. The adoption of agriculture was a central component of the civilising mission and likewise required a reorientation of temporal rhythms and calendars.[32] Thus when it came to reforming the calendars of the pastoralist Khoikhoi, missionaries brought with them, in addition to clocks, Bibles and Sabbaths, a variety of garden seeds, spades and other agricultural tools. The introduction of agriculture among pastoralist societies was seen as an essential step to promoting not only progress in 'civilisation' but also an ethic of constant work and sedentary life; for it was generally felt that a reliance on pastoralism had made the Khoikhoi lazy, indolent and improvident (in other words, it provided them with a means of subsistence which obviated the need to work for Europeans); whilst pastoral migrations, or transhumances, also evoked uncomfortable images of shifting populations.

Barnabas Shaw's work at Lily Fountain provides a good example of the missionaries' attempts to introduce the calendars and rhythms of agriculture amongst a pastoralist society. Shaw earned the recognition of his peers when a report was published in *The Missionary Gazetteer* (1832) informing readers that 'a large part of the tribe of the Little Namaqua Hottentots have been reduced from migrating habits to the cultivation of the ground'.[33] In actual fact, Shaw never entirely effected this transformation of the Namaqua into sedentary cultivators. Although they did learn to cultivate, the Namaqua continued to maintain their pastoralist rhythms and to move with their herds and flocks to the lowlands in the cold winter months. It was initially the missionary who had to move with them – an outpost named Bethel having been established specifically so that the missionary could accompany them at these times.[34] Shaw's endeavours were the beginning of a process, however, which aimed to re-orientate the temporal axis of life for the Namaqua around the agricultural calendar. This process was continued by his successors, who later sought to control and limit the times of such movements by establishing a formal timetable which clearly prioritised the agricultural calendar over transhumant pastoralist rhythms. In 1858 they issued a code of conduct – the 'Rules and Regulations of the Wesleyan Missionary Institution called Lily Fountain'. Part of it reads:

> It being necessary for all the people to move from Lily Fountain to Bethel every winter, they shall do so at such a time as the Council directs, after the usual ploughing season, and return again to Lily Fountain *at such time in the spring as the Council may think proper to fix for getting in the harvest*, and to prevent the destruction of the standing crops.[35]

From the 1850s, following developments in the rest of the Cape Colony, Lily Fountain became a training Institution geared around industrial education and schooling. Under its 'Rules' (the monastic legacy is overt), all children above the age of five were required to attend school during the week as well as Sunday School. In turn, as colonisation became more firmly entrenched even in the more remote parts of the Colony, the temporal regimentation on mission stations became more formally institutionalised; the hours of the day, and the days of the week, headed by the Sabbath, became one of the mandatory laws for all those wishing to reside at Lily Fountain. 'Every family residing on the Institution', the Rules stated, 'shall attend Divine Service on the Lord's Day, unless they are herding cattle or otherwise necessarily engaged; but all trading and other unlawful employments are strictly prohibited.'[36]

Missions and their spheres of temporal influence

The visible effects of the Sabbath provided missionaries with a tangible means for gauging and conveying the extent of their influence on the lands and its peoples. 'One of the first and most striking indications of a good moral impression having been made by the preaching of the gospel in heathen lands,' as the Reverend William Moister explained, 'is to be seen in the regard which is generally paid to the holy Sabbath in the neighbourhood of our mission-station.'[37]

It appears from missionary narratives of the early nineteenth century (that is, when British territory in the Cape did not as yet formally include the lands on which many of the missions were erected) that missionaries employed the Sabbath as a metaphysical means of gauging their own frontiers of influence over Indigenous society as much in terms of a temporal, as of a spatial, hegemony. These frontiers were effectively demarcated by an imaginary boundary surrounding the missions, within whose perimeter converts were recognised by their industriousness and collective observance of the Sabbath. The Reverend Arthur Brigg's panegyric of the mission (portrayed here as the provider of temporal authority and focal point of a Christianised Xhosa society) provides a vivid image:

> Some years ago, having climbed to the summit of the nearest considerable height of the Wittebergen, I was much interested in the bird's-eye view of my Circuit, which lay mapped out below me. Innumerable roads and foot-paths were perceptible for miles round the station, all converging to it, and plainly indicating that *there* was the centre of attraction. Along these roads and paths are to be seen, on the Sabbath, companies of decently clad natives cheerfully wending their way to the chapel.[38]

The concept of a sphere of temporal influence naturally required a focal centre, a function that missionaries ascribed to the mission station, which sought to act as the epicentre of temporal authority for surrounding populations. Thus, when the Commission on Native Affairs (1865) enquired about missionary success in stimulating respect for the Sabbath day, respondents referred to the spatial degree of temporal control over the outlying regions. One missionary in British Kaffraria, for example, reported that on the Sabbath, 'for many miles round the station labour [was] abstained from'.[39] Another used a similar image to describe the status of the Sabbath in the Clarkebury district: 'The Station *is in the centre of Christian influence*,' he declared; 'The peaceful observance of the Sabbath is not without its moral benefit on those around.'[40] Such reports were of interest to settler-colonial authorities precisely because they provided an indication not only of Christianisation but also of acculturation to British customs, mapping out a centralised geographic relationship that essentially prefigured the dynamics of twentieth-century urban South Africa.

For missionaries, the extension of this sphere of temporal influence was of great importance and assumed a quasi-military tone in missionary rhetoric. 'As civilization advanced,' the Reverend Brigg observed, 'heathen customs and superstitions fell into abeyance. The Sabbath was very generally observed, at least as a day of rest, even by the heathens.'[41] In their correspondence, missionaries often gauged and communicated the Sabbath's sphere of influence in a discourse of boundaries and perimeters, conquest and advancement. ('Mission', as Johannes Fabian observes, 'serves as a common term for military and evangelizing purposes.'[42]) This military logic was reflected in their field duties, which included the regular patrolling of the temporal frontiers of the station's sphere of influence in order to maintain the flow of Christian time around the stations. Ensuring that neighbouring villages observed the Fourth Commandment was often the principal purpose of such journeys; and on such occasions, missionaries made it clear that their visits were tied to the Christian order of time: 'I remember commencing a conversation by asking the people if they knew what day it was', Brigg recorded during one inspection. 'They all replied that it was the Sabbath, and therefore they had not gone to work in their fields.'[43] Occasionally, as the Reverend Stephen Kay discovered, people living outside the mission's sphere of temporal influence were 'entirely ignorant of the Sabbath' and engaged in worldly pursuits. On such occasions, it was the duty of the missionary to rectify the situation. Thus, Kay continued, 'the greater part complied with my request, and immediately ceased working, after its inconsistency with the sacredness of the day had been explained to them.'[44] Other populations, however, were less compliant: 'Some pretended they forgot it was Sunday', the Reverend Francis Palmer reported after riding out to a *kraal* during Circuit duties; 'and others objected that we paid them nothing for their attendance.'[45]

Missionaries were keenly aware of the range of Sabbath observance around the station; for, just as a show of respect for the Christian order of time identified successful converts, its disregard marked out those populations who lived outside the missions' sphere of influence. Thus, as he rode out one Sunday to a village a fair distance from the mission, the Reverend John Ayliff found that the people there were openly engaged in profaning the Lord's Day. 'When I would ask how they could work on the "Icawe" – the Sabbath – they would reply – "Yes we know that it is the Icawe but then the Icawe is a thing only for the Mulunga [white man] – it is not our thing."' Unable to enforce the Fourth Commandment, Ayliff turned around and headed home. On approaching the neighbourhood of the mission, however, he noticed that: 'When I got within 10 miles of the station I saw a marked difference – not a man, woman or child was to be seen in any direction at work.'[46]

In order to maintain the rhythms of Christian time over such a large area, the Wesleyans had to exercise a coordinated system of regular surveillance. Their custom of itinerant preaching was well suited to the purpose and led to a settled system of extensive itinerancy in the Cape similar to the method of proselytising which had been adopted by John Wesley and his successors in England. Given the scattered state of the African populations, however, such journeys could cover extensive areas of land; a day's travel might see the missionary completing a distance of fifty or sixty miles on horseback.[47] For this to occur, Kay recommended that no station distant from the colony 'ought to have fewer than two or three missionaries upon it'. These, he explained, were 'requisite to give stability and regularity to the work'.[48] 'Native agents' were also regularly engaged to keep the flow of time going in the missionary's absence. In some areas, they manned entire networks of sub-stations and small satellite outposts surrounding the missions, which helped to extend the Christian message and its order of time, both beyond the practical travel limitations facing the missionary and deeper within Xhosa society. Missionaries were greatly aided in their quest to control the rhythms of society. As Brigg related, 'no set and formal services were held until, by the blessing of God, little churches had been formed, and the places became regular sub-stations'.[49] Thanks to such systems, missionaries found that nearby communities had begun to observe the Sabbath of their own initiative:

> I found ... that [the Mfengu] were in the habit of meeting in this house every morning at daybreak for prayer ... that on the Sabbath day they met in like manner, after which they held Sunday school and two services for adults. These services were conducted by four of their number in rotation, two of them going round every Sunday to all the kraals in the neighbourhood, to exhort the people, while the other two attended to the work on the spot.[50]

The Wesleyans' Circuits – as they were known – were effectively connected with one another across space through the Christian order of time. The very term 'Circuit' paints an apt picture of missions, sub-stations and *kraals* virtually connected via the Sabbath ritual – not merely with one another but also with British and Dutch congregations, who worshipped and conducted affairs on the basis of the same weekly pattern. Jean and John Comaroff provide an evocative image of mission stations as 'nodes in a global order, pegging out a virtual Empire of God'. This imagery certainly applied to the order of time which connected all missions across the expanding networks of Christianity. It is an image that would have been entirely consonant with William Shaw's dream of an unbroken chain of 'Christian fortresses' spanning the ever-shrinking area between the British frontiers of the Cape Colony and Natal.[51] Or with Cecil Rhodes's own version of that dream: a British railway spanning the entire African continent, linking Cape Town to Cairo.[52]

Temporal control and uniformity was fundamental to the realisation of all of these visions of empire. And whilst Africa was not painted quite as red as Rhodes had hoped, William Shaw lived to see his own vision come to fruition: 'the formation of a complete line of Stations from the border of the Eastern Province to Port Natal'; the network of missions extending over a distance of about four hundred miles, 'through a country in which', Shaw reminded his readers, 'the whole body of the people ... [was] shrouded in the deep darkness of an unmitigated Paganism'.[53] In the Wesleyans' own minds, the Sabbath had played a vital role in this process. Sure enough, the Cape's military frontier had moved inexorably eastwards in its wake, as foreshadowed by the missionaries' rhetoric of temporal conquest and advancement. Thus, in the words of a Wesleyan evangelist who surveyed the view from the Eastern Frontier in 1849:

> In Kaffraria the Sabbath has become known. Time was when that holy institution was unheard of in South Africa; and but thirty years ago no Sabbath sun arose upon the wretched Kaffir, but every day to him was just alike. But Kaffraria has her Sabbaths now. Soon after Mr. Shaw's introduction among the Congo tribes, the Chiefs made proclamation amongst their people, that the day of the Lord should be observed; and, accordingly, within the neighbourhood of the Mission village all unnecessary labour was then suspended on the Sabbath, and the inhabitants given to understand that it was God's day, and that they were to leave their work, and repair to the station to be instructed. At first this seemed strange; and well it might. Sometimes many of the people would forget when the day returned; and now and then an individual would come to the Missionary in the middle of the week, and inquire if it was the Sabbath; for the Kaffirs had not been accustomed to such a division of time. But the practice began soon to be understood; and now, on all our Mission institutions in Kaffraria, from the Great Fish River to the Umzimvoobo, and within a circuit of several miles around them, this sign of Christianity is set up and recognised – a day of rest.[54]

The mission bell: a powerful symbol

Next to the Bible, bells were one of the most symbolic and powerful instruments at the missionaries' disposal. Given that their primary function was to herald times of prayer and meetings on the mission, they became key symbols of the new order of time that was introduced by Europeans. In Chapter 3, we saw how bells were introduced on Victorian missions and reserves as a means of imposing a new order of time over Aboriginal people. There, the bell's acoustic power was channelled inwards, regulating the daily rituals and routines of an enclosed community that was virtually immured by white settlement. The sound of bells extended from Europe also to the Cape Colony thanks to the earliest missionaries; but, unlike their Victorian counterparts, on African missions they also served an outwardly expansionist function – especially during the early period of colonisation. Here, the missionaries' followers were often dispersed around the mission stations and Christianity was often perceived to radiate as far as the audible sound of the bell, for it was within these regions that the Christian order of time could be made known among the surrounding populations.

'The range of a bell', as Alan Corbin observes in the European context, 'served to define territory that was haunted by the notion of limits as well as the threat of their being transgressed.'[55] It was in accordance with this logic that the Reverend Arthur Brigg was able to express the number of converts under the influence of the mission station: 'there were living within sound of the station-bell: 2035 persons'.[56] Thus, the missions' sphere of temporal influence was maintained, not only through local Sabbath observance, but also through the acoustic authority of these devices responsible for heralding the times of work, rest, and prayer.

Conversely, the absence of the bell's sound functioned as a useful means of identifying those communities living beyond the pale both of time and Christianity. Many a missionary fondly quoted the famous English poet, William Cowper, who first immortalised the bell's absence as a symbol of a spiritual wasteland and a temporal wilderness. 'Our situation', as Barnabas Shaw wrote in 1816, setting out from Cape Town to seek a place to establish his first mission, 'vividly called to recollection the words of the poet Cowper –

> The sound of the church-going bell
> These valleys and rocks never heard;
> Never sigh'd at the sound of a knell,
> Or smiled when a sabbath appear'd.[57]

Missionaries capitalised on the imagery of the bell as an evocative means of rallying support for their cause. Thus, on his arrival among the Tswana, Stephen Kay lamented what he considered to be 'the moral and destitute condition of the multitudes around him. 'Here was a town containing, at least, thirteen or fourteen thousand souls, amongst whom the "sound of the church-going bell", had never been heard; who were, to a man, ignorant of their own immortality; who had not the most distant idea of a final judgment, or of a future state of reward or punishment.'[58] And on another occasion, with particularly emphatic imagery:

> O Britons! Christian Britons! I entreat you to remember poor Africa! Remember that while ye are literally exalted to heaven with privileges, her benighted nations are sinking into hell for want of them ... no spires or steeples are seen there; no 'church-going bell' is heard; nor was the warning voice ever sounded in many of those regions of death.[59]

No. CIV.   JUNE, 1846.

PAPERS
RELATIVE TO
THE WESLEYAN MISSIONS,
AND TO
THE STATE OF HEATHEN COUNTRIES.
(PUBLISHED QUARTERLY.)

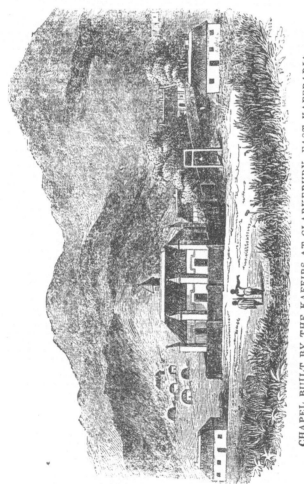

5.4 Front page of *Wesleyan Missionary Notices magazine* (1864), depicting the Clarkebury mission. Note the (size of) the central bell-post.

Although the early missions did not always possess the instrument itself, a substitute – whether a wagon whip, a suspended pit saw, a horn, a 'gong', a disused cart-wheel tire, a ship's bell salvaged from a wreck an old drum or even a waving flag – was always employed.[60] At a newly established 'Hottentot village' near the Kat River, for instance, Stephen Kay called the people to prayer by hanging-up a ploughshare and using it as a substitute bell. Judging by the response, the Khoikhoi had obviously become highly familiar with the procedure: 'Nearly one hundred and fifty persons, inclusive of children, were hereby called and assembled together in the course of a few seconds'.[61] At Lily Fountain, a cross-cut saw was suspended and struck with a hammer; later, a large wagon-whip was used; and sometimes a young man would climb the roof of the chapel and sound a large bullock's horn.[62]

The point was that an audible signal, taking its cues from the missionary, was always employed on mission stations to communicate the regular times of worship. As William Burchell noted during his visit to a mission for the Griqua, the bell was the necessary means for communicating time within the audible range of the mission.

> On Sundays the service commenced at nine in the morning, and again at four in the afternoon: at each time a bell gave the inhabitants a half-hour's notice, and also tolled when the prayers began. This notice was the more necessary, as some of the huts were scattered a mile from the church; and, from the openness of the situation, the bell could be heard at a great distance.[63]

Given the importance of establishing a temporal order on and around the station, the audible range of such devices was of considerable concern to missionaries, and was frequently mentioned in their narratives and correspondence. Barnabas Shaw referred to the sonic horizon covered by the sound of the various devices which served as 'bells'. He observed that the whip, 'when used by an expert wagoner, caused the mountain caverns to echo, and was heard at a considerable distance'.[64] As the population at Lily Fountain began to grow, Shaw became sufficiently concerned about this to warrant an official request for a bell: 'We also need a bell to call our people to service, [as] many of them live at a considerable distance, and have no clocks or watches', he informed the WMMS back in Britain. 'We now make use of a large beast-horn, which is blown at the appointed season for worship; but the blast is too weak to make all hear.'[65] Whilst waiting for the bell to arrive, Shaw compensated for the short-range of the bell's sound by requiring prayer meetings to be carried out in separate locations. Not to be deterred by the lack of a more sonorous clarion call, he set out to familiarise people with the idea of time's omnipresence:

THE COLONISATION OF TIME

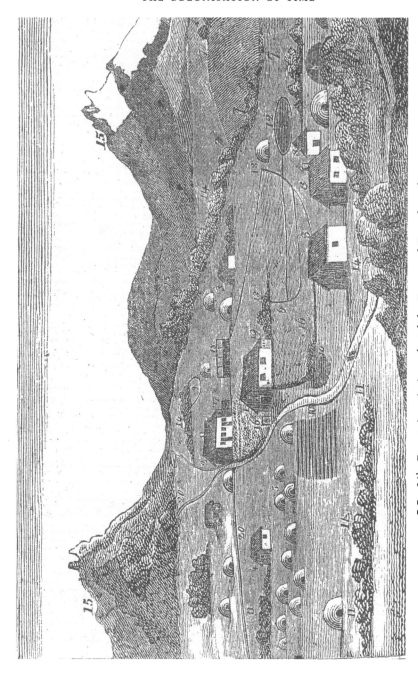

5.5 Lily Fountain mission: sketch by Reverend Barnabas Shaw. Among the features pointed out in Shaw's key to the sketch, are: (1) The Chapel and (16) 'The Bell, sent by Mr. Irving of Bristol'.

The bell being rung about seven in the evening, the people gathered to the seven places appointed for prayer and thanksgiving. This method has been adopted, not only with a view to their present growth in grace, but also to accustom them to holding Divine service among themselves: that, when dispersed with their cattle, they may in every place keep up the worship of God. All the meetings being held at the same time ... made it peculiarly solemn and delightful.[66]

5.6 Lily Fountain mission grounds (*ca* 1900)

5.7 Lily Fountain chapel, showing bell-post (*ca* 1900)

Ecstatic at the success of his experiment, Shaw's zeal reminds us that such displays of uniform behaviour fulfilled the old monastic ideal of order and coordinated behaviour. 'Standing by our dwelling-house, three distinct congregations might be heard worshipping', Shaw noted; 'the other four were at the same time engaged, though somewhat further from us, so that we could not distinctly hear, truly joy and gladness was found in our lofty mountains.'[67] Finally, in 1825, Shaw's request for a more sonorous means of reaching people within the required radius was fulfilled when John Erving Esq. of Bristol graced the mission by donating a bell. This, Shaw promptly reported, was duly 'fixed in a commanding situation, and daily calls of these hills to worship'.[68]

At Lily Fountain, as on other colonial missions, the bell soon became established as a divine icon of God's work. After it had been deployed in this position for some time an eminent member of Shaw's congregation, Jan William, is said to have publicly declared: '*Als its in de Bergen zy*, [when I am in the mountains,] and hear the sound of the bell I consider it as the voice of God, calling me to worship. Alas Alas! Should a time ever come again, when the Bell shall be silent, how awful will be our situation.'[69] Back in Britain, and across the Empire, supporters of the missionary enterprise would read of numerous such anecdotes in regular magazines, where the missions' progress was regularly conveyed through the imagery of bells, their influence depicted as extending over the surrounding peoples and their lands. As Shaw was proud to report:

> On their fathers a sabbath had never smiled, and they could remember the time when all their days were days of darkness, and when the shadow of death was brooding over them. But now, at the sound of the church-going bell, they poured from their huts to the house of prayer, and the sabbath was a day of joy and thanksgiving.[70]

The bell soon became a familiar symbol of Christianity beyond the colonial frontier – as evinced by the fact that some of the Tswana had come to refer to Sunday as *Tstasi ya tshipi* – the 'Day of the Bell'.[71] It was not symbolic to missionaries and their supporters alone, however: African converts saw in the bell symbols and meanings of their own, which could be appropriated and redeployed in ways that reflected the spiritual transition from one belief system to another.

The phenomenon is nowhere more apparent than in the hymns of the venerated Xhosa prophet Ntsikana (*ca* 1780–1821), whose interpretation of Christian belief and practice emerged as one of the dominant Xhosa responses to the missionary presence in the nineteenth and twentieth centuries.[72] It is thought that Ntsikana's conversion was influenced by LMS missionary, Johannes van der Kemp in the early 1800s. Nevertheless, as Janet Hodgson suggests, Ntsikana's four hymns are regarded as an authentic African interpretation of Christianity, and essentially one of the origins 'of an indigenous theology in Southern Africa'.[73] Of specific interest for our present purposes is the hymn, *Intsimbi Ka Ntsikana* ('Ntsikana's Bell'), originally written in the Xhosa vernacular. Tradition has it that Ntsikana would stand in front of his hut at dawn, chanting this very hymn to call the people to worship whilst 'ringing' a 'bell-stone' (*intsimbi*), whose percussion produced various notes with a tone that was similar to a church bell and audible over the same distance.

> And all ye children come!
> Ahom, ahom, ahom, ahom, ahom!
>
> It has fenced in, it has
> surrounded,
> This land of your fathers,
> He who obeys it by responding
> Will be blessed.
> Ahom, ahom, ahom, ahom, ahom!
>
> Sele! sele!
> Ahom, ahom, ahom!
> Respond ye! respond ye!
> To this call that comes from
> Heaven,
> Ahom, ahom, ahom, ahom, ahom![74]

Ntsikana's appropriation of one of the most symbolic of the objects associated with Christianity illustrates how Christianity could be received and redeployed by colonised peoples. As colonial aggression and evangelical persuasion effected sweeping changes in the Xhosa universe, Ntsikana's interpretation of the Christian message offered his people 'new sources of symbolic meaning and power', crafting a bridge between elements of Xhosa and Christian tradition.[75] Ntsikana's bell represented a symbolic mode of appropriating the new sources of centralised authority – including temporal authority – which had begun to reshape the temporal patterns of Xhosa society. It is clear that the sound of the bell-stone, like that of the mission bell, was vested with divine symbolism; it too was likened to the voice of God himself (*this call that comes from Heaven*). Ntsikana's message of continuity and cooperation with Christianity surfaces through the authority with which he credited the bell (*He who obeys it by responding will be blessed*). But the most revealing image of all – for our purposes at least – is that conveyed by the *spatial* ambition ascribed by Ntsikana to the bell (*It has fenced in, it has surrounded, this land of your fathers*) – an image which embodied Ntsikana's underlying message of compliance with the new cultural order of Christianity. Ntsikana had indeed prophesied that Xhosa land would be 'divided out to white men, and cut up into roads'.[76]

Echoing the missionaries' prophecy of spiritual conquest, as epitomised by their depictions of the mission bell, Ntsikana's hymn confirmed that the bell was indeed a powerful symbol.

Resistance and reinterpretation

The Christian order of time was unable to reform the pace of African life without regularly being contested, sabotaged or appropriated in ways which were beyond the missionaries' control. From the earliest encounters, attempts to establish Christian time as dominant over Indigenous rituals and routines met with a range of responses – from outright refusal to conditional acquiescence. Indeed, as long as the structure of Xhosa society and the chiefs' authority remained intact, the capacity of missionaries to establish the dominance of Christian rituals and routines beyond colonial frontiers depended largely on the chiefs' willingness to sanction their interferences and interruptions of the flow of Xhosa time. The essence of cultural relations and the balance of power between Christian and Xhosa rituals during this period was framed primarily in terms of compromise. The Xhosa chief, Ngqika, for instance, was unequivocal about maintaining a temporal balance which would respect his sovereignty. As he clearly told the LMS missionary, Joseph Williams:

> You have your manner to wash and decorate yourselves on the lord's day and I have mine the same in which I was born and that I shall follow. I have given over for a little to listen at your word but now I have done, for if I adopt your law I must surely overturn all my own and that I shall not do. I shall begin now to dance and praise my beast as much as I please, and I shall let all who see who is the lord of this land.[77]

Most of the early missionaries soon realised that circumstances in the Cape were such that they would have to accept whatever compromises they could, rather than expect immediate conformity to the law of the Sabbath.

The more stubborn among them, however, learned the hard way. Consider the following vignette, in which John Ayliff attempted to prevent a Xhosa feast from taking place on the Sabbath. To Ayliff's chagrin it was only with manifest reluctance that the people ceased their singing and dancing at his request. The revelers, equally vexed, encircled Ayliff and told the meddling missionary in the plainest of words that, 'they loved dancing, and that if [he] had anything to say to them *[he] must say it quickly as they wanted to go again'*. Both the Xhosa and the missionaries clearly understood that imposing temporal limits was a powerful means of exercising control. Rather than submitting to Ayliff's demand, therefore, the Xhosa attempted to subordinate the Christian order of time to that of their own ritual; thus they imposed upon the missionary a time limit of their own. To this ultimatum, Ayliff – a man of confirmed insensitivity in matters of cultural diplomacy – responded by declaring his unwillingness to be hustled through his sermon: 'I told them *I could not speak God's word in a hurry.*'[78] Within this exchange we can observe a microcosmic example of the encounter between two cultures of time, with each side attempting to situate the other within its own ritualised world. The result of this cultural impasse would essentially determine who would wait for whom; and on this occasion it was the Christian ritual that would come off second-best. Since Ayliff refused to compromise, the Xhosa returned to their singing and dancing with even greater defiance, and the missionary was left to mime the Gospel amid the clamour – 'The more earnest I was the more they Shouted, Danced & Laughed.'[79]

It may very well be that, during evangelical encounters, the struggle over time took place more commonly on Sundays than on any other day of the week. Given that it was such a powerful bearer of meaning, this particular day became a natural arena within which conflicting rituals could play out their dialogues and/or battles. Whilst outright resistance to the Sabbath was not the only alternative to compliance, it is important to note that outright defiance against the Christian order of time did in fact occur, this being one of the clearest ways in which a free people could express their opposition towards a colonising presence. Such explicit resistance greeted the Reverend Stephen Kay when he inspected a village one Sunday and found the people there 'painting their bodies; others dressing hides; a third class preparing garden pots; and a fourth engaged in idle chit-chat'.

> No argument whatever being sufficient to induce a cessation of labour, I at length determined to commence preaching, whether they would 'hear, or whether they would forbear.' A few then sat down, but the greater part continued talking, working, or mocking, almost the whole time.

The struggle over the timing of events afforded an opportunity, even during the most mundane exchanges, for expressions of resistance and negotiation between Christian and Xhosa rituals. Witness a short but telling exchange which occurred when the Reverend Brigg thought it appropriate to admonish an elderly Mfengu woman for carrying a load of wood on her head on a Sunday. Her response was pithy: *'Hai andingumtu!'* (according to Brigg's translation: '"I'm not a person" – meaning that she was now so old as to be of no account, and [that] it was no use trying to teach her other ways than those to which she had been accustomed.'[80])

In the struggle to ensure dominance over the ritual dimension of life, however, resistance and acceptance were merely polar extremes: time was above all the site of negotiation and mutual compromise. Xhosa chiefs, for their part, were often willing to meet the missionaries half way by diplomatically conceding to their insistence that every seventh day belonged to God. Most, in fact, were interested in having a missionary among them for strategic and secular rather than spiritual reasons.[81] If having a missionary entailed sacrificing some autonomy at seven-day intervals, it was a bargain which many of them were prepared to make – but also one they sought to *enforce* when necessary. Thus Maqoma, in expressing his wish for a missionary, was specific in stating that he did not want one who 'prayed more than one day in seven'.[82]

The struggles and tensions over the introduction of the Sabbath and the seven-day week highlight with particular clarity some of the ways in which colonised peoples sought to negotiate the terms of their relationship with the colonisers. Most Xhosa quickly learned that by accepting the law of the Sabbath, for instance, they could place limits on the missionaries' demands for attention on the other days of the week. Consider the following account, recorded by Arthur Brigg, in which two 'native evangelists' rode into a Xhosa *kraal* on a *Monday* attempting to call the people together for prayer:

> But the heathen party replied, 'We don't know you; we know the missionary and the local preachers, who come regularly to hold service at Manxeba's kraal, on the Sunday; but we don't know you, and besides this is not Sunday! we have heard that the Malay's [i.e.: Muslim's] Sabbath is on Friday, and the Jew's Sabbath is on Saturday, and we know the Christian's Sabbath; but we never yet heard that Monday was anybody's Sabbath, so we shall not gather together to hear you to-day.'[83]

Not impervious to the irony of the episode, Brigg quipped: 'Our two zealous brethren were obliged to leave these very punctilious people, and pass on in hope of finding others more accessible to gospel preaching on a Monday.'[84] Africans were quick to appropriate the discourse of Christian time when it offered a means of preserving and reaffirming their own temporal and cultural boundaries. Clearly, the power dynamic of Christian time did not always flow in one direction from colonisers to colonised: it could also be reversed and appropriated to strategic effect.

African workers in particular found out early on that the Sabbath offered one of the few laws which they could cite in order to justify their refusal to work for settlers. Witness the following exchange between Jacob Links – a devout Namaqua convert at the Lily Fountain mission – and a Dutch farmer, who had requested his services on a Sunday. The episode is recounted by Barnabas Shaw as evidence of Jacob's strength of faith.

> Jacob hesitated in obeying the command, and the Boor became angry. Jacob quoted the law on the subject, 'Remember the sabbath day to keep it holy;' the Boor said, 'I dare say you will not object eating on Sunday, and why not go with me as usual.' Jacob then answered with firmness, '*Ik zal niet gaan*, (I shall not go,) master; we ought to obey God rather than men ... Had you come yesterday, I would have accompanied you. If you will come to-morrow I will go; but this is the Lord's *day*, and not ours. I will not, therefore leave the house and worship of God on this day.'

Shaw reported that, ever since Jacob had confronted the farmer, the latter 'came no more to seduce the Namacquas from the worship of God on the sabbath'.[85] Not surprisingly, while the Sabbath became one of the many locations of tension between missionaries and settlers, African workers also came to find a source of refuge in it. These accounts suggest that African converts often embraced the Sabbath with greater devotion than many Europeans. On a number of occasions, they even had to reprimand the latter for breaching their own native ritual. For example, the day on which British troops began expelling Maqoma's people from the Kat River, Stephen Kay captured a somewhat Pythonesque scene of a Xhosa man asking one of the officers: '"Is this thing good, burning houses down on God's day!" "Bless my soul," cried one of the (English!) officers, "I'd forgotten that it was Sunday."'[86]

Just as it often succeeded in interrupting the flow of Xhosa time, the Sabbath often had to make allowances of its own to alternative rituals and routines. During the period of male initiations, for example, it was virtually impossible to secure regular church attendance; and – as even John Ayliff realised – there was little the missionaries could do about it.[86] The gendered divisions of Xhosa society also affected the rhythms of mission life. Since it was common for women to be absent at prayers during the seasons of intense agricultural activity, if the missionary wanted to preach the Gospel among them during this period, he would have to join them in the corn fields.[88]

An interesting question is whether Sunday as a day of rest was read by Indigenous interlocutors as a form of taboo. It is likely that the missionaries' preoccupation with the proscription of Sabbath work would have been consonant with Indigenous practices of identifying people and places as impure, requiring special ritual actions over specific periods of time. The French missionary Eugène Casalis, for instance, noticed that the Basutos observed 'days of sacrifice, or great purification,' and 'certain days of repose' which proscribed all public labour. 'Hence it is that the law relative to the repose on the seventh day', Casalis observed, 'so far from finding any objection in the minds of the natives, appears to them very natural, and perhaps even more fundamental, than it seem to certain Christians.'[89]

The Sabbath was the complex site of symbolic and political power, and missionaries were well aware of this. As we have seen, it allowed them to conceptualise the reach of Christianity by demarcating a spatial frontier and distinguishing their followers from the rest. Whilst we can only surmise the ways in which Xhosa chiefs viewed this spatio-temporal encroachment on their sovereignty, the evidence suggests that its imperialist connotations did not escape them. Consider as an example the events which took place one Sunday in 1832, when the Xhosa paramount, Hintsa, walked into the Butterworth mission and witnessed John Ayliff baptising several Mfengu. Furious at this sight, Hintsa is said to have left the mission crying: 'How dare Ayliff throw water on my dogs. I will make him take it off, and then I will kill him.'[90] Ayliff later claimed that Hintsa's hostility had been motivated by envy 'in seeing so many of his people attend on the Sabbath', and by the fear that he would subsequently 'lose their Services'.[91] Indeed, by involving himself with the Mfengu, Ayliff had interfered directly with Hintsa's affairs: the Mfengu were refugees who had recently fled the turmoil of internecine war in the east – the *mfecane* – and had come to Hintsa seeking his protection, willingly assuming a position of clientage among the Gcaleka Xhosa according to established practice.[92] Hintsa's reaction was a reflection of his indignation at Ayliff's interference in Xhosa politics, for the rituals of baptism and the Sabbath – both of which were generally performed on Sundays – were powerful symbols of Christian identity. Hintsa's words echo the anxieties of rural Dutch farmers who similarly feared that baptising slaves and the Khoisan would undermine their distinction as heathens – an identity boundary which had hitherto justified their exploitation.[93] What Hintsa witnessed that Sunday at Butterworth was in fact an omen of the threat which the Wesleyans posed to Xhosa independence in the early 1830s. And Hintsa was not mistaken either, for the alliance which the Mfengu had begun to form with the Wesleyans – and thus with the British – would ultimately facilitate the invasion of Gcaleka country in the upcoming frontier war.[94]

In the events which followed the ensuing fray, Ayliff managed to escape with his life; but the Butterworth mission was not so fortunate. When British troops arrived at the scene they found the station burned to the ground by Hintsa's men. Symbolically, the mission bell – that temporal symbol of Christian influence over the land – had been broken over a stone.[95]

The Sabbath was not only the site of conflict between Africans and Europeans; it also found its way into the war of representations that was fought out during this period between settlers and humanitarians.[96] Reports of Indigenous converts observing the Sabbath were cited by the latter as evidence that the 'natives' were indeed redeemable from barbarism; and that social order, discipline and civilisation could be attained by peaceful means. The Kat River Settlement was held up as a model of missionary success in this regard during the House of Commons' Select Committee on Aborigines (British Settlements) of 1837, where reports were heard of devout Khoikhoi converts cultivating the soil and regularly observing the Sabbath.[97] Settlers, however, could also employ the same logic to demolish such visions of Christian order: they did so by representing Xhosa hostility towards the Sabbath as evidence of their rejection of civilisation itself. A pertinent example comes from the settler-polemicist, Robert Godlonton, who, in recounting his version of the events leading to the outbreak of the 1834–35 frontier war, blamed Hintsa for having committed the first 'unequivocal outrage' against the British. This outrage consisted in having sanctioned the murder of a white trader: an 'atrocious deed worthy of record' – Godlonton took care to emphasise this for his readers – 'inasmuch as ... this unfortunate man was butchered in cold blood on the plea of refusing to violate, by trading, the sanctity of the Christian Sabbath'. The issue of murdered traders became yet another debacle in the overarching 'propaganda war' between settlers and humanitarians – with the latter seeking to lay the blame on the traders' own misconduct towards the Xhosa. 'Sweeping charges of this kind can seldom be met,' retorted Godlonton, who stressed the point that the trader in question had done nothing wrong: 'On the contrary, we find him forfeiting his life through a punctilious regard for a Christian ordinance.'[98]

Undoubtedly, however, the most spectacular power struggles were played out between missionaries and the spiritual authorities of Xhosa society, in ways which challenged the temporal symbols and rituals of both belief systems. 'They disputed every inch of ground with us,' William Shaw reported during the Select Committee on Aborigines, 'and were not willing to receive any dogma until it was proved to their satisfaction.'[99] Amidst the fray, the key symbols of Christianity came in the direct line of fire. Shaw himself described one of the most illuminating examples of this during the same Select Committee. His narrative recounts the story of a public debate between Shaw and an eminent rain-maker, Gqindiva, during a time of severe drought. Orchestrated by the local chief Pato and attended by several thousand Xhosa, the debate was intended to ascertain whether the missionary or the rain-maker possessed the real 'truth' about bringing rain. Considered as a battle between 'truth' and 'superstition', the event is a fascinating illustration of the clash of symbols and the 'contest of consciousness' that defined the evangelical encounter.[100] Witchdoctors and rain-makers were, as noted earlier, the missionaries' arch-nemeses – 'our inveterate enemies,' as Robert Moffat described them – 'uniformly oppos[ing] the introduction of Christianity amongst their countrymen to the utmost of their power'.[101] The feelings were undoubtedly mutual: rain-makers, in turn, saw the missionaries as direct threats to their own source of power and authority in Xhosa society. Not surprisingly, therefore, Gqindiva accused Shaw of having caused the drought, claiming that his charms had been ineffective ever since the missionary had entered the land: 'I would give rain ... and I have been trying to get it for some time', Gqindiva cried as he pointed a finger accusingly at Shaw with the view of exciting the people against him. 'I would give it now, but you are the hindrance!'

'How do I hinder the rain falling?' Shaw responded; to which Gqindiva replied: 'It's that thing you brought into the country, and set up upon a pole that stands near the great house where you have the talk (meaning the chapel)'.

> 'I have slaughtered cattle, and offered to the spirits; I have often burned herbs. When the clouds come up from the sea, and spread over all the land, and the rain is ready to fall, *that thing* which you have brought into the country and set up on a pole on the hill at Etwecu,' (Wesleyville,) 'goes *tinkle – tinkle – tinkle*; and immediately the clouds begin to scatter, they disappear, and no rain can fall.'[102]

Clearly, the presence of bells as well as Bibles – both key signifiers of Christianity's attempts to reshape the cultural axis of Xhosa life – represented a threat to the traditional authority figures in African society.

Such was the magnitude of this symbolic struggle that even as the drought intensified, the rain-maker and the missionary remained locked in steadfast adherence to their respective symbols of faith.

Shaw, despite being urged by some of his more cautious converts to cease ringing the bell, decided 'to give no countenance to the prevailing superstition by yielding the point'. Instead, he ordered a day of fasting and prayers on which the bell was rung at regular intervals throughout the day to gather the people for prayers. And at the end of that day – according to Shaw's account – rain began to pour so copiously that the riverbanks overflowed. 'Truly,' Shaw wrote with a sense of unconcealed accomplishment in defending the bell's reputation, 'all acknowledged that this was "GOD'S RAIN"'.[103]

It is tempting to interpret such clear-cut antagonisms as representative of the overall encounter between Christianity and Indigenous peoples. More often than not, however, there was no such clear distinction between Indigenous acceptance of, and resistance to, the bell, the Sabbath and the Christian calendar.[104] Through his condemnation of the bell, Gqindiva articulated the Xhosa's outright rejection of Christianity; but, as we have seen, Ntsikana embodied another reaction which took the shape of appropriation of Christianity and its symbols. Gqindiva's and Ntsikana's different relationships with the bell suggest that there were a range of ways in which the Xhosa responded to the colonisation of time.

Explicit resistance to the symbols and rituals of Christian temporality did occur – far more consistently, probably, than the archives let on – but ultimately, as Richard Elphick notes, 'two systems of thought do not "collide"; rather, real people negotiate their way through life, grasping, combining, and opposing different elements'.[105] Indeed, overt resistance was not always the most effective method for a people to retain a degree of cultural autonomy in response to the upheavals caused by settler-colonisation and internecine warfare. As Elizabeth Elbourne points out, the Khoikhoi were better able to sustain aspects of nomadic/pastoralist life, 'including mobility at will, the gathering of roots, bulbs, and honey, and the accumulation of stock' by exploiting the protection and opportunity provided by the mission environment.[106] The mission station was a refuge where families and children could avoid exploitation and 'apprenticeships' on white farms while the men sought work. To Mfengu refugees, as we have seen, it became a source of political patronage, which they successfully exploited to better their own position in the transition to colonial society. Precisely because an adoption of a Christian order of time was often mandatory as a precondition for residence rights on the mission, we should view its adoption by converts not simply as submission or genuine spiritual conversion, but, equally tenably, as a form of Indigenous use of Christianity.

This does not imply that Indigenous adoption of Christian beliefs and practices was always solely instrumental. Conversion was in some cases lasting and genuine. But even when they did earn converts to their faiths, missionaries could not always ensure that the Christian message was received by Indigenous peoples in the way they had intended. Rather, as Andrew Porter writes, 'a constant process of mutual engagement and two-way translation' took place.[107] By the late 1860s, for instance, Tswana followers of the LMS mission at Shoshong had successfully been taught to observe the Sabbath. Throughout the whole town of some thirty thousand inhabitants, the Reverend John Mackenzie reported, 'there were now very few who did not pay a certain deference to the "Letsatsi ya Morimo" – the Day of God, as the Sunday is called'. But the motivation behind such a disciplined adherence to Christian law, it turned out, was entirely different from that which the missionaries had intended. Indeed, on being questioned by Mackenzie, the women claimed to observe the Sabbath as a day of rest, stating: 'We observed ... that if one of our number injured herself with her hoe, it was always the Great Day; so we gave up working on that day.' A Tswana man expressed a very similar belief: 'A man may hunt with success all the week', he told Mackenzie; 'but if he goes out to shoot on Sunday, he gets nothing for his trouble. He meets with a lion, or lames himself with a thorn, or his gun bursts.' 'These ideas', Mackenzie was careful to stress, 'have not come from the missionaries. They were never threatened with such things if they broke the Sunday'.[108]

By the mid-nineteenth century, the seven-day week and the Christian Sabbath had become widely known among Indigenous peoples; and missionaries had played by far the greatest role in spearheading this process, well before formal colonisation had begun. However, the ways in which they were adopted and applied did not always correspond with what the missionaries had intended. This holds true for the entirety of the Christian message, as Elbourne writes – 'they "heard" the message in accordance with their own needs and existing situations'.[109] Time, like colonialism in general, was not coherently imposed, nor coherently resisted; it functioned, rather, as one of the many sites of cultural exchange, tension and negotiation which came to characterise nineteenth-century relations between colonisers and colonised across the British Empire.

—◆◆◆—

This chapter has explored some of the ways in which missionaries functioned as a conduit for the establishment of new time-structures among the Xhosa. By the year 1865, when the region was formally incorporated into the Cape Colony, a missionary was able to report from British Kaffraria that the Christian Sabbath was 'universally known'.[110] Indeed, the efforts of the missionaries to promote the dominance of the distinctive, seven-day ritual on and beyond the colonial frontier were not without success.

But this was merely a prelude to a far more intensive assault on African time, and the African psyche. From the middle of the nineteenth century, when the colony was by then firmly and permanently established in Xhosa territory, British missionaries were able to turn their attention to reforming African time at a deeper level – that of the mind. This approach was inaugurated through a number of government-funded schools and industrial institutions, which were established to train the labour force so desperately needed to sustain the colonial economy.

Notes

1 Isaac Bud-M'Belle, *The Kafir Scholar's Companion* (Lovedale: Lovedale Press, 1903), pp. 12–13.
2 Broadbent, *Narrative of the First Introduction of Christianity Amongst the Barolong*, p. 86.
3 *Report from the Select Committee on Aborigines (British Settlements)*, 1837, pp. 53, 54, 71.
4 WMMS, *Wesleyan Missionary Notices*, vol. 12, no. 4, B. Shaw to WMMS, 14 Nov. 1816. Emphasis in the original. (SANL Collection, P4631.)
5 Bud-M'Belle, *The Kafir Scholar's Companion*, pp. 12–13.
6 Philip, *Researches in South Africa*, vol. 1, pp. ix–x.
7 Shula Marks, 'Khoisan Resistance to the Dutch in the Seventeenth and Eighteenth Centuries', *Journal of African History*, 13:1 (1972), 55–80, pp. 68–78.
8 The first period of British occupation began in 1795 and lasted eight years. In 1803, following the Truce of Amiens, the Cape was handed back to the Dutch, only to be re-appropriated by the British in 1806, this time permanently.
9 Thomas Pringle, *African Sketches* (London: Edward Moxon, 1834), pp. 211–12. On timetables at Genadendal see Bernhard Krüger, *The Pear Tree Blossoms: The History of the Moravian Church in South Africa 1737–1869* (Genadendal: Moravian Book Depot, 1966), pp. 296–9.
10 B. Shaw, *Memorials*, pp. 76-83; John Wesley, *Works*, vol. 7, Sermon XCIV, p. 32.
11 Martin Legassick, 'The State, Racism and the Rise of Capitalism in the Nineteenth-Century Cape Colony', *South African Historical Journal*, 28 (1993), 329–68, pp. 333, 339–42.
12 Hall, *Civilising Subjects*; Lester, 'Humanitarians and White Settlers', pp. 64–5, 80–4.
13 Keegan, *Colonial South Africa*, pp. 67, 132.
14 Mostert, *Frontiers*, p. 593.
15 Keegan, *Colonial South Africa*, p. 133.
16 *Wesleyan Methodist Magazine for the Year 1849*, vol. 72 (May 1849) (London: J. Mason, 1849), Rev. Samuel Palmer, quoted on p. 451. See also reports of the flag being hoisted on the Sabbath in Janet Hodgson, 'A Battle for Sacred Power: Christian Beginnings among the Xhosa', in Richard Elphick and Rodney Davenport (eds), *Christianity in South Africa: A Political, Social, and Cultural History* (Berkeley, Calif.: University of California Press, 1997), p. 75.
17 Elizabeth Elbourne, *Blood Ground: Colonialism, Missions, and the Contest for Christianity in the Cape Colony and Britain, 1799–1853* (Montreal: McGill-Queen's University Press, 2002), pp. 312, 316–44; Keegan, *Colonial South Africa*,

pp. 87–90.
18 Monica Wilson, in Monica Wilson and Leonard Thompson (eds), *The Oxford History of South Africa* (Oxford: Clarendon Press, 1975), vol. 2, pp. 49–50; 73.
19 Elbourne, *Blood Ground*, p. 141.
20 Anna Johnston provides an excellent analysis of such intergenerational conflicts over time in her analysis of the intervention into the Polynesian calendar by the young LMS missionary, Lancelot Threlkeld, and the subsequent tensions which it generated with his superiors. (Anna Johnston, 'A Blister on the Imperial Antipodes: Lancelot Edward Threlkeld in Polynesia and Australia', in Alan Lester and David Lambert (eds), *Colonial Lives Across the British Empire: Imperial Careering in the Long Nineteenth Century* [Cambridge: Cambridge University Press, 2006], pp. 66–73).
21 Ridsdale, *Scenes and Adventures in Great Namaqualand*, pp. 31–2.
22 Kay, *Researches in Caffraria*, part 2, pp. 296–7; Cf. B. Shaw, *Memorials*, p. 253; Broadbent, *Narrative of the First Introduction of Christianity Amongst the Barolong*, pp. 86–7.
23 Kay, *Researches in Caffraria*, part 2, pp. 296–7.
24 Edwards, *Reminiscences*, p. 60.
25 Broadbent, *A Narrative*, pp. 86–7.
26 John Ayliff, Journal, 22 Nov. 1822, quoted in Peires, *House of Phalo*, p. 107.
27 Capt. Frederick Marryat, *The Mission, or, Scenes in Africa: Written for Young People* (London: Longman, Brown, Green & Longmans, 1845), vol. 1, pp. 199–200.
28 Burchell, *Travels*, p. 356.
29 SANL, William Shaw, Diary, 22 Mar. 1827, Wesleyville, p. 65.
30 WMMS, *Wesleyan Missionary Notices*, 120 (Dec. 1825), W. Shaw, p. 2.
31 WMMS, *Wesleyan Missionary Notices*, 32 (June 1828), W. J. Shrewsbury to WMMS, Butterworth, 30 Sept. 1827, p. 4. Emphasis added.
32 See Jean and John Comaroff's analysis of the introduction of agri*culture* in southern Africa: *Of Revelation, Vol. 2*, pp. 123, 119–65.
33 *The Missionary Gazetteer: Comprising a Geographical and Statistical Account of the Curious Stations of the American and Foreign Protestant Missionary Societies of All Denominations; With their Progress in Evangelization and Civilization* (Boston, Mass.: William Hyde & Co. 1832), p. 282.
34 Moister, *Memorials of Missionary Labours*, p. 532.
35 Cory, mic 447/2, box 52 ('Methodist Church of South Africa'), 'Rules and Regulations of the Wesleyan Missionary Institution called Lily Fountain, Khamiesberg, Namaqualand' (Rondebosch: Wesleyan Mission Press, 1858), pp. 6–7. Emphasis added. (The Lily Fountain 'Rules' were officially endorsed by the Cape's Governor in 1871.)
36 *Ibid.*, p. 4.
37 William Moister, *Missionary Anecdotes: Sketches, Facts and Incidents Relating to the States of the Heathen and the Effects of the Gospel in Various Parts of the World* (London: Wesleyan Conference Office, 1875), p. 297.
38 WMMS, *Wesleyan Missionary Notices*, 179, 3rd series (Nov. 1868), A. Brigg to WMMS, Wittebergen, 13 Aug. 1868, p. 180. Emphasis in the original.
39 KAB, CCP 2/2/2/3; G35A-'65, *Proceedings of, and Evidence taken by, the Commission on Native Affairs*, Grahamstown, 1865 (hereafter: *Native Affairs Commission*, Grahamstown, 1865), Appendix 1, 'Circular Letter with Questions and Answers Issued by Native Commissions Office in Grahamstown', Rev. John Gordon, p. 186.
40 WMMS, *Wesleyan Missionary Notices*, 104 (June 1846), Rev. Gladwin, 5 Aug. 1845, p. 3.
41 Brigg, *Sunny Fountains*, p. 146.
42 Johannes Fabian, 'Religious and Secular Colonization', in J. Fabian, *Time and the Work of Anthropology: Critical Essays 1971–1991* (Philadelphia, Pa.: Harwood Press, 1991), pp. 157–8, 166.
43 *Ibid.*, 134.
44 Kay, *Researches in Caffraria*, part 2, p. 301.
45 Samuel Palmer, diary excerpts quoted in F. P. Gladwin, 'Memoir of the Rev. Samuel

Palmer, Late Missionary in South Africa', in *The Wesleyan-Methodist Magazine for 1849* (May 1849), p. 453.
46 KAB, MS A80/2, John Ayliff, Journal, Haslope Hills, July 1839. For a similar account by Robert Moffat, see his *Missionary Labours and Scenes in Southern Africa* (1842) (New York: Carter & Brothers, 1850), p. 202.
47 W. Shaw, *My Mission*, pp. 205, 381.
48 Kay, *Researches in Caffraria*, part 2, p. 340.
49 Brigg, *Sunny Fountains*, p. 131.
50 *Ibid.*, p. 44.
51 Comaroff and Comaroff, *Of Revelation*, Vol. 2, p. 12. William Shaw is quoted in Hodgson, 'A Battle for Sacred Power', p. 75.
52 Paul Maylam, *The Cult of Rhodes: Remembering an Imperialist in Africa* (Cape Town: David Philip, 2005), pp. 88, 99, 148.
53 W. Shaw, *My Mission*, pp. 519, 468, 338.
54 Rev. Thornley Smith, 'Sketches of South Africa', *The Wesleyan-Methodist Magazine for 1849*, p. 507
55 Alan Corbin, *Village Bells*, pp. 95–7.
56 Brigg, *Sunny Fountains*, p. 109.
57 B. Shaw, *Memorials*, p. 73; (William Cowper, 'Verses').
58 Kay, *Researches in Caffraria* , part 1, pp. 235–6.
59 WMMS, *Wesleyan Missionary Notices*, 46 (Dec. 1831), Kay to WMMS, p. 4.
60 See, for example: WMMS, *Wesleyan Missionary Notices*, 49 (Sept. 1819), B. Shaw to WMMS, 2 Sept. 1819, p. 216; John Ayliff, Journal, 16 July 1820, p. 48; B. Shaw, Journal, 8 June 1817, section 1, folder 1, p. 16 ('An instrument', Shaw described the gong, 'the sound of which is exceedingly melodious, and which is used instead of a bell at our last out-post').
61 Kay, *Researches in Caffraria*, part 2, pp. 474–5.
62 B. Shaw, *Memorials*, p. 111; WMMS, *Wesleyan Missionary Notices*, 53 (May 1820), Shaw to WMMS, May 1820, p. 6.
63 Burchell, *Travels*, p. 356.
64 B. Shaw, *Memorials*, p. 111
65 WMMS *Wesleyan Missionary Notices*, 24 (Dec. 1917), B. Shaw, p. 1.
66 WMMS, *Wesleyan Missionary Notices*, 56 (Aug. 1820), B. Shaw to WMMS, Lily Fountain, 19 Dec. 1820, p. 4.
67 *Ibid.*, p. 4.
68 WMMS, *Wesleyan Missionary Notices*, 120 (Dec. 1825), extracts from Shaw's Journal, p. 4.
69 B. Shaw, *Memorials*, p. 111; for another version of the same account, cf. B. Shaw, Journal, section 2, folder 4, p. 109. (KAB.)
70 B. Shaw, *Memorials*, p. 112
71 Bud-M'Belle, *The Kafir Scholar's Companion*, p. 13.
72 Hodgson, 'A Battle for Sacred Power', pp. 71–3; Jeffrey Peires, 'Nxele, Ntsikana and the Origins of the Xhosa Religious Reaction', *Journal of African History*, 20:1 (1979), 51–61.
73 Hodgson, 'Ntsikana's "Great Hymn": A Xhosa Expression of Christianity in the early 19th-Century Eastern Cape', *Communications*, 4 (Cape Town: Centre for African Studies, UCT, 1980), pp. 1, 6–7.
74 Quoted in Janet Hodgson, 'Ntsikana: History and Symbol. Studies in a Process of Religious Change Among Xhosa-speaking People' (Ph.D. thesis, University of Cape Town, 1985).
75 Hodgson, 'A Battle for Sacred Power', p. 71.
76 John Knox Bokwe, *Ntsikana: The Story of an African Hymn* (Lovedale: Lovedale Press, 1914), p. 23.
77 Joseph Williams to G. Marley, 3 Dec. 1827, quoted in Peires, *House of Phalo*, p. 78.
78 KAB, MS A80/2/1, John Ayliff, Journal, Butterworth, 3 June 1832. Emphasis added.
79 *Ibid.*. Cf. Kay, *Researches in Caffraria*, part 2, pp. 271–2, 301.
80 Brigg, *Sunny Fountains*, p. 134.
81 Elbourne, *Blood Ground*, pp: 174–5.

82 W. M. Macmillan, *Bantu, Boer and Briton: The Making of the South African Native Problem* (Oxford: University Press, 1963) (2nd edn), pp. 101n, 150.
83 Brigg, *Sunny Fountains*, pp. 128–9.
84 *Ibid.*, p. 129.
85 B. Shaw, *Memorials*, pp. 271–2.
86 Kay, *Researches in Caffraria*, part 2, pp. 493–4.
87 John Ayliff, Journal, 26 Mar. 1833; Arbousset and Daumas, *Narrative of an Exploratory Tour*, pp. 30–1.
88 W. Shaw, Journal, 26 Feb. 1828.
89 Casalis, *The Basutos*, pp. 260–1.
90 John Ayliff and Joseph Whiteside, *History of the Abambo* (1912) (Cape Town: Struik, 1962), p. 21.
91 John Ayliff, Journal, 3 Sept. 1834.
92 Colin Bundy, *The Rise and Fall of the South African Peasantry* (Berkeley, Calif.: University of California Press, 1979), pp. 32–43.
93 Elbourne, *Blood Ground*, pp. 113–15.
94 Mostert, *Frontiers*, pp. 697–9.
95 Robert Godlonton, *A Narrative of the Irruption of the Kafir Hordes into the Eastern Province of the Cape of Good Hope, 1834–35, Compiled from Official Documents and Other Authentic Sources* (Grahamstown: Neurant & Godlonton, 1836), p. 140; John Ayliff, Journal, 4 Aug. 1836.
96 Lester, 'Humanitarians and White Settlers', p. 64. On settler propaganda on the eastern Cape frontier, see also Lester, *Imperial Networks*, pp. 143–9.
97 *Report from the Select Committee on Aborigines (British Settlements)*,1837, p. 64; *Ibid., Minutes of Evidence*, I, Capt. C. Bradford, p. 171.
98 Godlonton, *A Narrative*, pp. 5–6, 14. According to Peires (*House of Phalo*, pp. 102–3), such killings are not surprising, given Hintsa's apprehension of the threat which white traders posed to Xhosa sovereignty.
99 *Report from the Select Committee on Aborigines (British Settlements)*, 1837, *Minutes of Evidence*, I, W. Shaw, p. 60.
100 Jean Comaroff, 'Missionaries and Mechanical Clocks', pp. 3, 14–16.
101 Moffat, *Missionary Labours*, p. 208; cf. Kay, *Researches in Caffraria*, part 1, pp. 208–9.
102 *Report from the Select Committee on Aborigines (British Settlements)*, 1837, *Minutes of Evidence*, I, W. Shaw, pp. 59–60; W. Shaw, *My Mission*, p. 464. On similar reports concerning the bell, see Robert Moffat (*Missionary Labours*, pp. 216–18), who recorded an episode which took place among the Tswana; and Jean and John Comaroff, *Of Revelation and Revolution, Volume 1: Christianity, Colonialism and Consciousness in South Africa* (Chicago, Ill.: University of Chicago Press, 1991), pp. 211–12, 262.
103 W. Shaw, *My Mission*, p. 465. A very similar account can be found in Kay, *Researches in Caffraria*, part 1, pp. 208–11.
104 Vivian Bickford-Smith, 'Revisiting Anglicisation in the Nineteenth-Century Cape Colony', *Journal of Imperial Commonwealth History*, 31 (May 2003), 82–95, pp. 82, 91.
105 Richard Elphick, 'Writing Religion Into History: The Case of South African Christianity', in Henry Bredekamp and Robert Ross (eds), *Missions and Christianity in South African History* (Johannesburg: Witwatersrand University Press, 1995), p. 21.
106 Elbourne, *Blood Ground*, p. 378.
107 Andrew Porter, 'Religion, Missionary Enthusiasm, and Empire', in Andrew Porter (ed.) *The Oxford History of the British Empire, vol. 3, The Nineteenth Century* (Oxford: Oxford University Press, 1999), p. 239.
108 Mackenzie, *Ten Years North of the Orange River*, p. 473.
109 Elbourne, *Blood Ground*, p. 174.
110 *Native Affairs Commission*, Grahamstown, 1865, Appendix 1, Rev. J. A. Chalmers, p. 183.

CHAPTER SIX

Lovedale: missionary schools and the reform of 'African time'

As bells and Bibles forged inroads into Xhosa cultural territory, the settler frontier advanced eastwards and inexorably in their wake. By the middle of the nineteenth century, the Xhosa had lost vast tracts of land, the eighth frontier war (1850–53) leaving their military strength considerably weakened. It eventually crumbled in the aftermath of the cataclysmic Xhosa Cattle Killings (1856–57), a millenarian response to the pressures of colonisation which resulted in a devastating loss of life, the displacement of some 150,000 people and the breaking up of chiefly authority and Xhosa social structure. Governor George Grey's response was to capitalise on the catastrophe as a solution to the Cape Colony's chronic labour shortage by insisting that food relief be made contingent on work. The effect of this decision, as Jeffrey Peires describes it, was 'the hounding of thousands of famished peoples into slave-like forced labour'. By 1857, nearly 30,000 Xhosa were taken into the Colony as registered workers.[1]

As a result, thousands of formerly independent Xhosa emerged as British subjects, their lands parcelled out to white settlers for whom many of the Xhosa were now forced to work. In the following decades, some began the process of buying back the land and farming it, either in the 'reserves' or as tenants on white-owned land. But the majority remained impoverished and came to depend entirely on a system of indentured and migrant labour.[2] The Xhosa were not defeated: resistance to subjugation took on new forms; some sought empowerment through land-ownership and enfranchisement, others through schooling and education. Most resisted through the 'hidden struggles' of everyday life – by disobeying white timetables and curfews.[3] (Resistance, as Clifton Crais points out, 'involved more than simply avoiding labouring for white settlers'.[4]) Nonetheless, the tens of thousands of Xhosa men and women who took up employment within the colony were thrust into a new temporal matrix of work contracts, apprenticeships, working-hours and calendar months, further reshaping pre-colonial concepts of time, regularity and productivity. Time was encoded in the equation of power that regulated and maintained the flow of African workers entering and exiting the colony. The *Masters and Servants Act* (1856), the *Kaffir Pass Act* and the *Kaffir Employment Act* (1857) prescribed the number of years of service for indentures and apprenticeships, the expiry dates of passes for travel inside the colony, the time limits for residing in the colony after the expiry of a work contract; and even the periods of leave when men and women could leave their jobs to spend holidays with their families. In turn, these temporal limits established the institutional rhythms of life under apartheid in the twentieth century, dominated by the curfew, the bus timetable and by tedious days spent in queues at the employment office. (Under apartheid, as Fanon wrote, '[t]he first thing which the native learns is to stay in his place, and not to go beyond certain limits'.[5])

In this chapter we move from the context of the open frontier, when missionaries worked among the Xhosa beyond the official settler-colonial frontier, to that of the Cape Colony proper. Cast against the backdrop of profound cultural transitions which were in the process of forging the foundations of the South African State, we investigate how the latter came to rely in part on the reform of 'African time'.

Labour, education and time-discipline

Unlike Victoria, where Indigenous labour was valued only seasonally, the Cape Colony was permanently in desperate need of it. By the 1860s, the vast majority of settlers were engaged in farming and, with the boom of the mining industry in 1867 – the year diamonds were discovered in Griqualand – cheap black labour would became even more essential. Heavy reliance on the agricultural and mineral wealth of the South African colonies meant that settler-colonialism had come to depend greatly upon not only the expropriation of land but also the exploitation of African labour. The colony was in need of an African working class which would forsake its traditionally 'irregular' work patterns in favour of a continuous and sustained life of regular work, for 'African time' represented a material threat to profit margins. In the Cape and elsewhere (as Keletso Atkins has documented in the context of colonial Natal, and Frederick Cooper in that of twentieth-century Kenya) the rhythms of pre-colonial life came under attack, with workers being pressured out of systems of casual or day labour and into monthly and yearly indentures and contracts with their employers.[6] To a significant extent, the problem of labour was based on time. 'Time was at the nexus of the "Kafir labor problem"', Atkins writes; 'no sooner was a work agreement made than confusion arose from the disparate notions of the white employer and his African employee regarding the computation of time'.[7]

As colonial regimes attempted to control work rhythms, the language of time itself became the location of conflict. During the 1892 Select Committee on the Labour Question, for instance, a complaint from the Cape's General Manager of Railways reveals that conflicting calendars and understandings of time were at the heart of many labour disputes and misunderstandings:

> Many Kafirs will not stop for longer than a year. Many of them do not understand the difference between a calendar and a lunar month. I know of instances where farmers engaged natives for a year, at the end of which time they were to receive an ox. They made a notch on their stick every day, and they reckoned twenty-eight days as a month; and when they had counted twelve times twenty-eight days they demanded their ox. When they were told that the year was not yet up, they considered they had been swindled, and I have heard of cases where they left and left everything they had worked for nearly a year.[8]

It was not solely white employers who had cause for complaint regarding disparate computations of calendars and time. To many African people, the white man's months also seemed haphazard: some lasted thirty days, others thirty-one; on other occasions there were twenty-nine days in a month. Since African workers counted the days according to a lunar calendar, they expected to be paid at the end of the twenty-eight day period; and when they were told that they would have to wait until the end of the European month, it was not uncommon for many of them to suspect that their employers were attempting to swindle them of two or three days' work in the month. Far from being ignorant of computing exact periods of time, African workers demonstrated that they could be just as resentful of delays in wages being paid on time as their white employers were of 'African time'. This is suggested in an important observation made by a missionary who visited the Cape in 1853 – a statement which also contradicts colonial notions about the innate imprecision of 'African time':

> In their engagements, as to time and place, they are also punctual and regular; and in the case of payment of wages, &c., they look upon *regularity* as a right, and, if not payed systematically at the appointed time, they consider themselves deeply aggrieved, and can never be induced to work again for any person, who has once treated them so. Their punctuality to appointments of time is also the more remarkable, as they seem to experience great difficulty in numerical counting. They reckon by moons, in a very confused way.[9]

If time was to operate as the measure of exchange between black labour and white wages, there had to be a mutual concordance over its definition – a temporal *lingua franca*. The balance of power over time would be determined by which discourse would prevail; and to Europeans, of course, it seemed logical that the Xhosa should be the ones to defer and submit to the temporal vernacular of the dominant society.[10]

Undoubtedly, the calendar of work, time-discipline and regularity was regularly secured simply by way of outright coercion (when the clock's hands wielded a whip) or through indirect compulsion, through the introduction of crippling taxes, vagrancy legislation and pass laws. ('The only object of compelling Natives to have a pass', as a worker would later declare during an official inquiry, 'is really to force them into obtaining employment within four days, at a rate unfavourable to themselves.'[11]) Within the context of an economy ostensibly based on free labour, however, liberal statesmen came to argue that the eradication of 'African time' would be more lastingly achieved through cultural reform, education and industrial training. With this in mind, Sir George Grey – whose previous experience in 'integrating' Maori in New Zealand inspired him to pursue a similar scheme in the Cape – combined his policies of land expropriation and concentrated settlement with the ideals of education and 'civilisation'. Grey's vision was to make the Xhosa 'accustomed to our ways', a project he was able to pursue thanks to a £40,000 grant from the Colonial Office which led to the financing of existing missionary-run schools, such as Lovedale on the western border of British Kaffraria, and the founding of new ones at Healdtown, Salem, Lesseyton, Peddie, Shiloh and elsewhere near the Eastern Frontier.[12] With similar intent, a hospital was established in King William's Town to treat the sick with 'the enlightened methods of English medical practice' and to 'undermine the native practice of witchcraft'.[13] Erected in towns bearing British names, on the verge of the colony's ever-advancing Eastern Frontier, these clock-oriented and bell-governed institutions became symbolic outposts of the Empire, where colonisation and education sometimes converged in truly literal ways. On three occasions, in fact, Lovedale's classrooms were converted into military barracks to fight off Xhosa offensives; and during the Seventh Frontier War (1846–47), lead from the press was melted down into bullets.[14]

When the frontier schools were not converted to forts, they were engaged in a different phase of the war, which entailed manufacturing a new 'brand of native' inured to the workplace and conditioned for docility towards the clock. In a bid to effect an early suppression of 'irregular' and superstitious habits, schools explicitly targeted for reform Indigenous temporalities, seeking to eliminate traces of pre-

6.1 Lovedale: interior of technical building

colonial culture by abolishing its rhythmical qualities and inculcating a new language of hours and minutes, seven-day weeks, Sunday rituals, and the winter/summer division of the European scholastic calendar. Whether in the workplace, the church or during periods of leisure, the 'native school' was intended to be a place where its pupils could be taught to work, rest, play and pray in accordance with the rhythms instituted, and approved of, by colonial society. The colonial school assumed the ideological role which Louis Althusser ascribed to schools in Europe as regards conditioning children to internalise the fundamental rituals of working life from an early age. ('No other ideological State apparatus', Althusser wrote, 'has the obligatory ... audience of the totality of the children in the capitalist social formation, eight hours a day for five or six days out of seven.'[15]) In Europe, the 'nine-to-five' mantra was on its way to becoming one of the fundamental temporal routines of society. Transposed to the colonies, however, this ritual carried added cultural weight, seeking totally to reshape African time-consciousness. And this was precisely the intent of statesmen such as Grey and of missionaries such as James Stewart, who clearly possessed a strong desire to reorient the cultural axis of Africa through the medium of education.

Scottish missionaries in particular viewed education as central to evangelisation, placing as much emphasis on schooling and industrial training as the Methodists did on discipline and accountability. 'The training of the man ought to go along with the training of the tradesman,' declared James Stewart, the celebrated educator and influential principal of Lovedale.[16] The objectives of African education aimed both at practical and ideological outcomes. As historian John MacKenzie writes, missionaries – and the Scots in particular – 'saw themselves as having an obligation both to African and to colonial society to produce black artisans and an educated black proto-bourgeoisie, while supposedly avoiding unnecessary competition with whites'.[17]

Despite this, colonial society was by no means in agreement over the benefits of 'native education'. Settlers – who overtly expressed their aversion towards employing mission-educated workers and evinced a preference for the 'raw Kaffir' – were highly suspicious of imparting literacy and academic knowledge and viewed policies of assimilation to British norms as, at best, misguided and, at worst, dangerous to their security. Nevertheless, missionary-run schools were consistently touted by successive government commissions as the long-term solution to the labour problem.[18] The 1883 Commission on Native Laws and Customs, for instance, praised the missionaries' success in 'remoulding [the natives'] nature and character ... training them in civilized arts and habits and social order of a well-regulated community' and 'recommend[ed] that all the countenance, protection, and support which may be possible should be extended to [missionaries] by the Government.[19] And thus it was that well into the twentieth century educational institutions in southern Africa remained largely under the management of Protestant missionaries.

In their didactic role, missionaries played a crucial role in continuing their predecessors' assault on Indigenous temporalities. However, whilst in the earlier, open frontier phase, they had focused particularly on the dimension of ritual and sacred time, they now also emphasised forms of time-discipline tailored specifically to a working life; thus they preached in a discourse of military-like regimentation and spoke of time as a currency that had to be hoarded and husbanded. Commodified time was proffered as one of the many 'artificial wants' – a term which colonial discourse understood as signifying a 'consumerist' spirit – whose inculcation was viewed by colonial reformers as indispensable for inducing the African to work. Whilst the earlier mission phase had seen an effort to expand frontiers of time across space, the school would see temporal authority directed inwards, both institutionally and ideologically. The fundamental rhythm of the seven-day week, whose foundations had been established during the first evangelical encounters, was further entrenched and intensified in the school environment, which took the regimentation of time to greater lengths by breaking time down into smaller units. An internalisation of clock-oriented timetables (missionaries hoped) would thus habituate pupils to uniform and regimented patterns of behaviour.

Missionaries themselves were changing in character during the second half of the nineteenth century: many of them were better educated than their predecessors and aimed to 'modernise', as well as convert, their followers.[20] In fact, the period of the mission school coincided with a rapid transformation of the landscape through infrastructural and technological development. The growth of the Cape's road system from the 1840s, the establishment of regular postal services and the opening of telegraphic communication between Cape Town and Grahamstown in 1864 all brought events on the colonial peripheries increasingly under the eye of administrative centres. The tide of 'civilisation' and 'modernity' squared the circle of the African hut with the rectangular dwelling and sliced up the countryside with roads and train tracks. 'Railways [now] run where ox races were formerly run,' James Stewart noted with approval as he described the transformed landscape: 'the electric wire stretches one hundred miles where formerly the express messengers of the paramount chiefs ran with the "word" of peace or of war'.[21] Transport and communication sped up the pace of life; and, to maintain it, the colony necessitated not only people working on roads and farms, mines and docks, but also mail couriers, builders, smiths, clerks, railway workers, wagon makers, telegraph operators, and so on. As a Cape solicitor explained, 'there is a continual demand for boys who can read and write, boys who can deliver parcels[;] boys are required at the railway stations, also as clerks and messengers in offices and stores to direct letters, and so on. By educating the Native you are supplying that class of labour.'[22] If the colonial infrastructure was to rely on such a class of semi-skilled workers with basic literacy, teaching Africans punctuality and the virtues of synchronised work was essential. The process of 'educating the Native' for such stations of work entailed the reorientation of African minds around the clock and calendar as the new sources of temporal authority.

In the Cape and across the British Empire, where 'native-education' was pursued, the temporal regime of the school came to reflect that of the modern factory environment. In the schools of British East Africa, as Roland Oliver observes, 'life was regulated almost as severely by the mission bell as it was in England by the factory hooter'.[23] As we have seen, however, the spirit of uniform, centralised time-discipline predates that of the factory. Indeed, whilst missionaries saw themselves as the exporters of modernity, the methods they adopted in order to achieve this fundamental objective belonged to a much older tradition. We can sense clear parallels, in the second half of the nineteenth-century, both in the Cape Colony and in Victoria, between the fortress-like environments of the mission-school and that of the monastery. The legacy of the monastic community permeated the colonial mission-school, its influence most apparent in the bell-regulated timetables which regimented daily life. ('Much of the method of colonization', as Johannes Fabian suggests, 'was the return of monastic "rule" by a detour.'[24]) At Lovedale, pupils were expected to follow a timetable which almost echoes Benedict's own Rule in its veneration of temporal order. Just as in the monastic Rule, we find in Lovedale's 'General Regulations' a section devoted exclusively to the responsibilities of the 'bell-ringer'.

BELL RINGER

I. The Bell-ringer shall ring the bell punctually at the stated hours, and no one shall touch the bell at any other hour.

[...]

III. The bell shall be rung at the following hours:

{As the warning-bell for students and

At 5.30am .... In summer, {pupils for class duties; and the apprentices.

6.30am .... In winter, {to prepare for work.

6.00am .... In summer, {Fort masters and apprentices.

7.00am .... In winter, {to commence work.

8.00am .... Stop for breakfast.

8.05am .... Worship and breakfast.

9.00am .... Work and classes.

1.00pm .... Classes close, and workmen stop work for dinner.

1.15pm .... Dinner.

2.00pm .... Masters and apprentices resume work; native lads commence work in the fields and gardens.

4.00pm .... Native lads stop work.

5.00pm .... Apprentices stop work.

6.00pm .... Warning-bell for worship and supper.

6.05pm .... Worship and supper.

7.00pm .... Evening classes till 8.30.

10.00pm .... Closing bell, and lights out at 10.30pm.[25]

6.2 Lovedale: '9 A.M. Waiting for the bell'

Obedience to the bell was the first and final lesson of the each day.

The Reverend John Ayliff, who was charged with administering the Heald Town Industrial Institution, kept a journal with a very similar account of daily life. By way of a concluding remark concerning the daily schedule (in case the list of times was not clear enough) Ayliff points out: 'It will be perceived that the whole time of each day is fully occupied, it being the understood rule of the institution that *all must be employed in some useful work six days out of seven.*'[26] (The emphasis is Ayliff's.)

Given the monastic discourse pervading the school's institutional environment, missionaries made fitting headmasters, teachers and administrators: they were scrupulous administrators of time and taught by example as well as by precept. But they also encouraged African teachers to take on the role of educators themselves. Thus, as African students progressed through the academic system, the duty of setting an example fell to them. And punctuality, they were told, was one of the most important examples to set for their juniors. 'If the pupils you have under your care are to come to any position', a white teacher instructed a group of African colleagues at the Native Educational Association, 'they must be trained ... to habits of punctuality.' The new class of 'educated native' which emerged through the mission-school thus became an important conduit for dispersing the virtues of time-discipline and punctuality in African society. The

Native Educational Association, for instance, was established by John Tengo Jabavu, one of Lovedale's most influential Xhosa alumni and one of the first Africans to matriculate in the Cape Colony. Jabavu became a preacher, teacher and journalist, as well as founder of *Imvo Zabantsundu* ('Native Opinion'), the first independent newspaper in the Xhosa vernacular. Significantly, it was in *Imvo* that the above lecture on the subject of punctuality was published, presumably for the benefit of a wider audience. Given that it was written specifically for Xhosa teachers and missionaries, it is worth citing in full:

> PUNCTUALITY is said to have been taught to English people by the railways, and no one may live in hope of being more regardful of time in South Africa; but at present the Native people of this Colony are notoriously unpunctual. There was until recently good excuse for this want of a good habit, but now that a really good clock can be purchased in King William's Town for about 5s.; and a good time keeping watch for about 20s. there is no reason why the more intelligent of the people should not mark the hours as they fly. The first person to set the example in a village should be the school-teacher. I know that some will be tempted to reply that a punctual teacher will not find the scholars. But no people learn punctuality by waiting for one another. If the train delayed until all intending passengers found it convenient to take their seats, it would stand in the station all-day. The Missionary who gives his congregation five minutes grace, soon finds that he has to wait ten minutes for the people. The teacher must practice punctuality, and in turn the children will learn to hurry up to school. There must be a keeping of time both ways.[27]

In colonial as well as metropolitan contexts, education was geared around a quasi-monastic culture of veneration for the authority of the clock, ensuring the reproduction of subjects conditioned to uphold the sacrosanct principles of regularity, uniformity and time-thrift. Today, such a culture of time is virtually taken for granted in most schools. But by looking at the manner in which it was extended beyond Europe, we gain a different perspective on the underlying function of time-discipline in the school environment. In places such as the Lovedale Institution, as we will see, obedience to the clock was explicitly presented to so-called 'uncivilised' people as a necessary step on the evolutionary ladder of progress and civilisation.

Lovedale and the reform of time

Situated near the town of Alice, the Lovedale Institution was the most successful of the Cape's educational establishments. Originally founded in 1824 as a mission of the Glasgow Missionary Society beyond the Cape's military frontier, it became, in 1841, an institution for higher education for the children of missionaries and more advanced Xhosa scholars. Under its first principal, the Reverend William Govan, Lovedale became a multi-racial boarding-school which taught Africans side by side with the children of missionaries and other settlers. The first African pupils were drawn mainly from the Mfengu, who had taken eagerly to Christianity and had largely abstained from the cattle-killing, thus becoming prosperous enough to send their children to places such as Lovedale. Gradually, however, the school started to attract large numbers of students from across southern Africa.[28] Male apprentices learned their trades and carried out thirteen hours of manual labour every week for a period of three to six months, after which they were indentured for a period of five years.[29] Female education was another area in which Lovedale led the way, with the opening of a girls' department in the 1860s which saw women bound for three years to the household trades of sewing, tailoring, washing and ironing.[30] In 1870, when Govan was succeeded by James Stewart, the emphasis in education at Lovedale shifted and the advanced academic curriculum gave way to a more practical and industrial bias. Students were inducted into such trades as carpentry, masonry, blacksmithing, printing, wagon-building, tree-planting, beekeeping, shoemaking and bookbinding.

A sense of industry and activity were portrayed as two of the most distinctive characteristics that would first strike a visitor to the school. 'Coming down the hillside and passing two neat little houses,' the Reverend Barbour narrated in his panegyric of the school in 1880, 'the ring of the hammer on the anvil is an audible advertisement to one part of what goes on inside'.[31] On entering the industrial building, a visitor on any given day could observe the 'natives' seated in rows at their appointed tasks, labouring in unison according to the hour of the day: 'This is the bakery,' Barbour wrote; 'passing from that, you find yourself in the kitchen. It is about one o'clock, when everything approaches high pressure'; 'in the workshops you will still find the men busy, until five o'clock'; 'To visit the regular classes of the Institution, you must utilise the forenoon'; 'If you are asked to join in their worship at 6 P.M., you will see a quiet, attentive audience, and hear good singing.' As in the factory and the monastery, uniformity and coordination were everywhere apparent: in the kitchen, Barbour commented, 'the place is filled with people, native servants with dark faces and red turbans; there seems no room for such a number till you see that each has her place'. A similar regime took place outdoors, as men and women were marshalled separately into rank and file, ready to be deployed in their relative tasks: 'So you hear the steady, regular tramp as they go down in

6.3 Lovedale: mustering of afternoon work parties

companies of twelve, under their captains, with spades, picks, or hoes over their shoulders.'[32]

Amid all this, the clock functioned as the paramount source of temporal authority. Thus, according to Stewart, when the bell sounded at noon, all activities regularly came to a collective halt. 'At that hour all work in the place ceases. The blacksmith drops his hammer, the carpenter his saw, and the printer his types, and the classbooks are laid aside, and all adjourn to a meeting.'[33] Time-discipline was a key feature of life for the thousands of students who passed daily through Lovedale's gates and beneath its bell-tower. Pupils were depicted as a disciplined troop, well-acquainted with the clock and the seven-day weekly routine of European society. Accordingly, Barbour described Lovedale's weekly schedule as follows:

> On Monday you may join the different workers as they meet for prayer previous to the weekly board-meeting. Tuesday night is set apart for the sitting of the Native Court, where minor offences among the boys are dealt with and dispatched by the assembled lads themselves ... On Wednesday evening the Christian Association gathers for prayer and conference about its work ... [The] gift of music you will hear in yet greater effect and fullness upon the Sabbath evenings. Then all Lovedale – native and European, master and servant, old and young – gathers together in the native church to worship God.[34]

Lovedale was regarded as a hub of British civilisation and an outpost of modernity. An active postal service plugged Lovedale into colonial information networks, with 10,000 letters outwards and 13,000 inwards reported in 1889, along with 8,000 newspapers and book packets.[35] The school's possession of a telegraph machine attested to its proximity through space and time with the 'civilised' world. 'Lovedale is now within six hours from Edinburgh,' Barbour boasted, 'Telegrams this month, handed in at Edinburgh at 12.30, were received at Lovedale the same evening at 6.' But the strongest testament to Lovedale's modernising influence was the fact that its telegraphists were the 'natives' themselves – proof of the discipline they had acquired under Lovedale's influence. 'The well-known wires that carry the lightnings of intelligence all over the world pass across your head,' Barbour wrote, 'and in at the door opposite you find a native ready to receive your message, while another watches and receives the telegraph instrument.'[36]

The school's methodical organisation also fulfilled that old monastic role of providing a radiating influence beyond the school's walls: on the Sabbath, the Lovedale Christian Association sent small companies of Xhosa evangelists on visits to neighbouring kraals. Here they were seen to bring to the outlying communities the familiar routines of Christian worship. As Barbour reported during one of these visits, 'everything goes on as in a mission service at home'. These idyllic scenes once again echo the mission's sphere of temporal influence which we encountered in the early trans-frontier phase. As Barbour wrote: 'The evidence of the influence of Lovedale outside the walls may be collected in various ways. An hour's ride from here you may stop at the native minister's house, and be received as you would at any country manse in the Highlands of Scotland.'[37]

Lovedale was intent not merely on religious conversion and practical training but also upon a complete remaking of African culture. The 'spiritual and moral change in the individual,' James Stewart declared, '[was] the primary aim of Lovedale'.[38] Stewart did not seek to reshape the African through coercive means – for this was 'a lower kind of result, and subordinate to the one great result which we are always anxious for'. The Institution's aims were overtly hegemonic in nature and intent, as Stewart openly informed his pupils: 'A change of heart, or in other words, conversion, is the one great hope we have, as the power to enable you to turn your education to real use.'[39] Work was at the heart of the curriculum; but the real product of the daily manual labour was calculated in ideological rather than material terms. Once again, the analogy with the monastery is fitting: both institutions aimed at the *internalisation* of a sense of discipline and time-thrift – a new consciousness of time. 'The object is not the value of their labour,' Stewart explained, 'but the principle that Christianity and idleness are not compatible.'[40]

Time propaganda: the Lovedale News

As in the monastery, the outward regimentation of time was accompanied by an internal recoding of time-consciousness. 'The improvement does not appear so much on the surface,' the Reverend William Holden wrote, 'as it affects the body of the people and the status of their habits.'[41] The small Ruthven printing press that Scottish missionary John Ross had brought with him in 1823 accordingly became a key apparatus for the dissemination of Protestant and capitalist values and beliefs. Articles and anecdotes on the topics of morality, sobriety, discipline, rationality and civilisation featured prominently and endlessly in the school's monthly periodicals. The *Kaffir Express*, later renamed as the *Christian Express*, was launched in 1870, while the *Isigidimi sama Xhosa* ('the *Xhosa Messenger*') was inaugurated in 1876 by John Tengo Jabavu. There was also another monthly publication, the *Lovedale News*, which disseminated many of Lovedale's ideological objectives.[42]

Echoing contemporary Victorian tracts aimed at the English masses, the *Lovedale News* functioned as an unabashed conduit for the propagation of bourgeois values and ideas. It advertised time as a commodity and promoted qualities of discipline and time-thrift as models according to which life should be lived. Decidedly lacking in subtlety, one column stressed the convergence between the concepts of time, money and God, asking readers:

> HOW MUCH HAVE YOU IN THE BANK? Not the Savings Bank, though it would be a good thing to have a little there too. This Bank is a better one. Perhaps you have nothing to put in the savings bank, and think you have nothing to put in any other. You are wrong. You may be putting money in every day. Did you ever count up how much or how little you had got there – in the Bank of which God is the manager, and over whose counter pass the well used moments of each day and all the good things a man thinks or says or does. We speak of spending time. Time *spent* does not go into the Bank, any more than money spent. But every moment you use well, for God, you put into the Bank ... I would advise you all to put something in – to put in all you can. For the Bank gives good interest.[43]

Time was certainly an issue which frequently featured in the school magazine; a reminder that moral and temporal reform were parts of the same process. Indeed, the notion that time was a commodity permeated and infused Lovedale's didactic vocabulary. Teachers laboured the fundamental precept of time and money as interchangeable wares – waste of one implying loss of the other. Principal James Stewart himself appeared almost incapable of conversing about time in any-

6.4 Lovedale: inside the printer's shop

thing but monetary terms. Speaking of the school's weekly meeting, for example, he commented that 'pecuniarily, it involves us in a loss, as causing the deduction of 50 hours a week from the different trades' departments. Otherwise it has been a decided gain'.[44]

Under Stewart's direction, education was synonymous with learning the 'proper' use of time and Lovedale sought to act as a powerful agent for encouraging time-thrift, with numerous reminders in assembly speeches and pamphlets condemning the crime of wasting time – both others' and one's own. As Stewart warned his students, 'every boy who comes to Lovedale has a duty to perform towards the Institution ... No one should come here to spend the time in idleness.'[45] Once again, the *Lovedale News* served as a constant reminder of temporal conduct, giving a new meaning to the concept of 'passing time':

> SPENDING TIME. Some people find it difficult to spend their time. They feel it slow in its passing, and are always wishing it would go faster. Others find it quite as difficult to use their time so that it will not pass too quickly, before they get their work done to their own satisfaction. Why is it then that this great difference exists; that one feels time too slow, and another finds it always slipping away too fast? It is nothing about time itself for it goes on at the same rate continually in the case of everyone. It must then be something in people themselves. In most cases it arises from one cause, namely misspending time. The man who misspends all his time or any portion of it, finds it going slowly. While the man who is always busy doing his duty finds time going so swiftly that he cannot do his work as well as he would wish.[46]

Lovedale stressed the distinction between work and recreation – a polarisation of human behaviour that was alien to pre-colonial Xhosa life, where the spheres of labour and leisure had never been as discrete as British middle-class culture demanded. At Lovedale, African pupils were taught about the distinction between work-time and leisure-time, and the moral hierarchy that framed their order. Echoing Samuel Smiles' *Self Help*, parables such as the following were advertised in the *Lovedale News*:

> WORK FIRST PLAY LATER – A man who is very rich now was very poor when he was a boy. When asked how he got his riches, he replied, 'My father taught me never to play till all my work for the day was finished, and never to spend money till I had earned it ... I early formed the habit of doing everything in its time, and it soon became perfectly easy to do so. It is to this habit that I now owe my prosperity.'[47]

'Lazy races die or decay', Stewart wrote in the *Christian Express* as he proselytised the gospel of work: 'The British race, in all its greatest branches, is noted for its restless activity. Its life's motto is WORK! WORK! WORK!'[48] The temporal regime at Lovedale prescribed an official timetable of socially acceptable activities which aimed to condition pupils to the British work calendar. Weekends and extramural hours were marked out as those periods when pupils could indulge in productive amusements; and as always, the *Lovedale News* proffered sober advice to those who were in doubt as to what constituted being productive:

> HOLIDAYS. What are we going to do for the next five weeks? This is a question that many are asking now. When the classes break up we all run away home in great glee, but before long many find the time hang heavily on their heads. Now, in order to avoid this, all of us should set some definite work before ourselves, not work to be undertaken as a task, but as a means of recreation and pleasure.[49]

Replicating concerns about 'rational recreation' in Britain at this time, Lovedale's educators were interested not only in work but also in how the remaining time ought to be spent. Metropolitan anxieties about workers' idleness were paralleled in the colonies by fears of native unproductiveness, reflecting bourgeois unease at seeing the dominant visions of order being jeopardised by displays of unsanctioned pastimes and diversions, which in turn evoked fears of a potential rekindling of subaltern agency and sovereignty. Attempts to shape and control the manner in which 'free-time' was spent manifested themselves in sermons, lectures, denunciatory articles and pamphlets aimed at instilling a pervasive and unremitting sense of temporal diligence and accountability. As such, Lovedale aimed to be a 'total institution, controlling every aspect of student life'.[50] To this end, Lovedale's press dispensed regular columns encouraging the profitable investment of leisure time:

> SPARE TIME. Many are unable to use their spare time. They have no special work to do at certain hours, and these are wasted and lost. There are many ways in which time may be lost ... Now we suspect that there is a great deal of time lost at Lovedale in these ways. We wish to point out a few ways in which spare time may be made useful. ... In half an hour a boy may by reading acquire some fact that he will never forget. This knowledge may be of great use on some occasion in after life ... The Bible cannot be too well known. Time spent in reading it, is time saved in the highest sense ... But boys cannot be always reading. There must be play. This may be made profitable also. A good deal of play in earnest is good for every boy, but no one should spend too much time in play. Games continued long tire boys and unfit them for work for many hours afterwards. Play should be continued only so long as it can be done without fatigue or discomfort.[51]

Other than proselytising, the *Lovedale News* regularly published letters to and from the paper's Editor, as well as students' essays on set topics. The latter shed some light on the Lovedale phenomenon from the perspective of those who experienced it first hand. For example: in the March issue of 1877, the paper invited students to submit their essays on the topic of 'Saturday at Lovedale', asking them to describe their manner of spending their day off. One African student's essay conveys the extent to which Lovedale encouraged an internalisation not only of clock-time and the weekly routines but also of British sports and pastimes. The comments are also particularly interesting in their subtle imputation of the different ways in which black pupils and white pupils were able to spend time on Saturdays.

> SATURDAY AT LOVEDALE. At 9 a.m. the Native boys fall in for work ... The Native boys work in the field from nine to twelve, three hours, instead of two as on other days. The European boys generally have a game of cricket, or something of the kind, during the morning. ... About twelve o'clock the Native boys come back from work; and generally either go to the river or learn their lessons between twelve and two, which is dinner hour. The dinner hour on other days is always one o'clock, but on Saturdays it is two ... Saturday afternoon is the great time for the Lovedale boys to make their purchases.[52]

To the historian, these pages of the newspaper make for interesting reading material; they offer an insight into the tensions between students and authorities which shatter the aura of order, harmony and discipline evoked by Lovedale's panegyrists. To this effect, another student's essay reveals that not all its pupils were indoctrinated with time-thrift ideology: 'Some, I am sorry to say, lie in bed till very nearly breakfast time, and sometimes do not even wake till the breakfast bell rings at eight o'clock.'[53]

These essays were criticised by the paper's Editor in the subsequent issue of the *News*, which reprimanded both authors for shamelessly revealing such unproductive use of their leisure time:

> The extracts given are not satisfactory ... Surely something better could be made of Saturday than to have at night to say, I have done nothing ... The native boys do three hours work, but that is not much. The Europeans often do nothing at all, not even a game at cricket ... We do not like so many going to [the neighbouring town of] Alice, for many reasons ... It also tends to idle habits, and lose their own time as well.[54]

This was not the end of the debacle, however, for the Editor's remarks ended up sparking resentment among *white* parents, who had become angered by the depiction of their children as indolent. The criticism underscores the essential connections between ideas of race, time and identity. The Editor's comments, they claimed, had 'filled every European boy with indignation, as it will surely fill their parents with the same feelings; to think that their sons are at such a place as Lovedale if the statement is true'.[55] (Not surprisingly, a letter such as this, penned by a black parent, never appeared in the *News*.)

The control of pace and space

Lovedale aimed to establish a continuous, year-round, round-the-clock working life. Daily, weekly and annual timetables reconciled apprentices to the idea of a life of continuous labour – as opposed to the irregular bouts of seasonal activity that generally characterised work in pre-colonial society. In this regard, education sought to satisfy the colony's need for African labourers, for both settlers and officials had explicitly declared war on 'task-oriented' attitudes to work, punishing those who reverted to intermittent labour patterns. (In 1892, for example, we read that a group of workers was fined because they had 'refused to do work one day, having done a lot of night-work previously'.[56])

At Lovedale, the Xhosa were provided with new concepts of regularity and compelled to forsake what Europeans perceived as the characteristic 'irregularity' of African work rhythms. James Stewart was adamant in his objective of teaching pupils to work without interruptions: 'They will learn to work,' Stewart argued: 'a better provision can be made for the future, for one's self and one's family, by a *regular* trade, than from *intermittent fits* of work in the cultivation of a little bit of land'.[57] The underlying distinction Stewart made between British and African economies rested upon the timing of work: constancy and regularity were traits of the civilised worker, while intermittent effort pertained to a primitive economy. In Stewart's view, 'native education' ought to impart ideas and training conducive to a class of steady, reliable workers.[58] 'Nothing will lift you to any equality with other nations,' Stewart stated, explicitly addressing the African pupils, 'except that which the majority of your race do not like, and that is hard work, *persevering effort, continuous exertion*, whether of mind or body.' The demand was qualified by a specifically temporal demand; that is, not just hard work, but hard work all the year round. There was no part-time option and that was the only path for the African to climb the ladder of civilisation. As Stewart declared, 'by that road you may arise and by no other'.[59]

At first glance this appears to be another general attempt to impart aspects of a Protestant work-ethic rather than a specific attempt to reform attitudes to time. However, the process of 'moral regeneration' which Stewart prescribed through his reform of the Indigenous work-ethic implicitly involved a fundamental shift in the realm of time-orientation. Subliminally, the objective was one of *temporal* reform; irregularity, inconstancy, lack of punctuality were the perceived defects. 'Educate yourselves in perseverance', Stewart enjoined his pupils; 'that will cure you of your fitfulness and changeableness.'[60] Stewart's reform of the timing of Xhosa activities came to include the very minutiae of the pupils' behaviour. In a set of instructions delivered to Lovedale staff, for instance, Stewart advised that 'an effort should be made to get the pupils out of the old ingrained habit of a long deliberate pause before giving an answer'.[61]

Similarly, Lovedale's quest to stamp out 'vagrancy' was not solely about spatial control. Stewart's administration prescribed a calendar which exercised a temporal control over the movements of students and apprentices. A year-round labour calendar, with scheduled periods dedicated to leave, and a list of penalties for those who disobeyed it, helped enforce the system. A similar strategy was in place at the Wesleyan 'Native Training Institution' in Bensonvale, which allowed scholars to visit their homes for six weeks each year – a relatively long period compared to Lovedale's two weeks of annual leave.[62] Nevertheless, both institutions reserved the right as to when this vacation could be taken. During these times, apprentices were free to travel outside Lovedale so long as they respected the stipulated temporal limitations. And given that these periods of leave were usually scheduled in accordance with the British academic calendar, they effectively imposed the calendar of British society too.

As in Victoria, where colonial authorities sought to limit the movements of Aboriginal people between the missions, anti-vagrancy rules and regulations in the Cape sought to enforce the timing of travel far more strictly than the destination. Indeed, the human subject only became a 'vagrant' in the eyes of the law as a consequence of infringing the temporal curfews imposed by colonial authorities. The unlawfulness of exceeding the amount of time allowed for travel was explicitly emphasised by the *Lovedale News*: 'You know of course, that we are only allowed two weeks' holidays a year,' one passage warns the reader, 'and if we get more than that, it is either through the kindness [of] the authorities, or through taking it upon ourselves to *steal* a few extra days, – sometimes to our cost.'[63] Time could be saved, wasted and spent, and, like money, even stolen, a notion which explicitly classified temporal deviance as a criminal act. As in the monastery, the pilfering of time was punished with substantial penalties – fiscal penalties, since 'stolen' time could not be returned.

> T—s P—u got leave of absence to go to a sister's marriage. He was told that he would have to forfeit a month's wages if he did not return by a certain day. The day came, but not T. Two days after, he arrived. On being called before the Board he wished to deny having agreed to forfeit money for returning late, but on being asked, whether he preferred going to the magistrate, or submitting to the punishment imposed, he thought it was best to keep at a safe distance from the law. We think he was right.[64]

By naming and shaming culprits, such public notices added a moral form of punishment as a further means of deterring any other potential time stealers. Jean and John Comaroff have described the life of African people living on Christian mission stations in South Africa as one 'enveloped in a continuous regime of instruction, veneration, and surveillance'.[65] At Lovedale, the monthly press functioned as a means of enforcing such a regime: readers browsing through the surviving copies of the *Lovedale News* will find, on the back page of each issue, a regular column listing the names of those guilty of 'stealing' time. Although the school never publicised these acts as cases of resistance, the high incidence of such reports testifies to the fact that defiance towards Lovedale's control of space and time was certainly common:

> S—G—went home without leave asked or granted. On his way he, instead of going straight home, spent a night at a kraal on the road. He was away for nearly a week, and on his return did not go to explain his absence, but went direct to his class. He was taken before the Board, and ordered to do a week's work, when his work is done he will not be so ready to undertake a journey of 30 miles on foot. Those who are fond of holidays and walking should also be fond of work.[66]

In some cases, the refusal of Lovedale to grant leave caused open defiance among apprentices who were ready to contravene its temporal sanctions by trading off their wages for an 'illegal' holiday. Given that the fines imposed were quite substantial, such acts suggest that at least some Xhosa valued their freedom of movement over their wages.

> F.—V.—, and J.—S.—, apprentices, went after being refused leave to the Anniversary meeting of the Church at Kat River. On their return they were fined two months wages. They have lost their money, to gain a holiday ... We are sorry for them, and we are also afraid others may laugh at seeing their punishment in the News, but they can keep them from laughing again by staying at their work till they get leave.[67]

Strong parallels might be drawn between Lovedale and Victorian reserves in the way these environments sought to colonise the time of their interns. Both institutions sought to control an enclosed population through a quasi-monastic code of conduct, attempting to dictate not only the time for each and every activity but also the timing of human movements across colonial space. Indeed, the eradication of Indigenous temporalities remained a common objective in both settler-colonies, although the urgent need to reform time-consciousness became a matter of economic necessity only in the Cape. But unlike Victorian missions – where Aboriginal people were contained in view of their supposedly imminent extinction – Lovedale was a place where the students were trained and groomed for a life in the working economy: their future role lay outside the perimeters, in the colonial economy. Thus we may note how the rhetoric of self-improvement was articulated far more strongly at Lovedale than on Aboriginal reserves such as Coranderrk and Lake Tyers, where black labour was valued seasonally, or not at all when compared to the value of the land. At Lovedale, on the other hand, pupils were encouraged to identify as a black proletariat who would work all the year round, every year of their lives, as a means towards an end. This transpires with particular clarity through the nationalist rhetoric of an end-of-year address to Lovedale's students:

> If you should sleep over your every lesson, and dawdle out your precious hours, and days, and months, and years of apprenticeship in merely playing at work, and if then you should all leave Lovedale mere boobies in learning and lazy useless drones at work, we should not lose one penny thereby ... No, no, my lads, it will be yourselves and your nation that will gain or lose by what you do here ... all the habits of industry and sobriety and goodness which you can gain and mature here will only be a mighty lever put into your hands, by which you may do much towards raising the whole body of your brethren out of the dust, and lifting them up into permanent dignity and honour among the best of nations.[68]

Resistance and 'relapse'

> Every native won over, every native who had taken the pledge not only marks a failure for the colonial structure when he decides to lose himself and to go back to his own side, but also stands as a symbol for the uselessness and the shallowness of all the work that has been accomplished. Each native who goes back over the line is a radical condemnation of the methods and of the regime.
>
> Frantz Fanon, *The Wretched of the Earth*

Despite all efforts to transform Xhosa society into an obedient, clock-governed proletariat, and despite the heavily regimented life under the weight of Christian and institutional timetables such as Lovedale's, an acute labour shortage continued to vex settlers in the South African colonies well into the twentieth century. Indeed, by the time the South African Native Affairs Commission (SANAC) sat in 1903, it was generally agreed by colonial employers, in the Cape as well as the Transvaal and Natal, that 'native education' had become more of a hindrance to the free flow of black labour by way of nurturing the growth of an African elite. 'One effect of seminaries such as Lovedale and others is to turn out what you may call the "Native Masher",' a Cape solicitor stated. 'He is a particular class of individual, who goes home and struts around, and is not fond of work.'[69] A magistrate concurred by opining that, 'once educated, he seems to turn from all manual labour as degrading'.[70] Schools and books had made the 'natives' even more selective about their terms of employment: 'This class of Native considers manual labour beneath his dignity, which militates against his general usefulness.'[71]

Missionary education had indeed opened up clerical and non-manual forms of labour to Xhosa-speakers throughout the South African colonies, offering a minority the possibility of avoiding manual labour. Clearly, however, many settlers were not impressed with the benefits provided by education. (Mission schools, Cecil Rhodes observed wryly, 'seemed destined to produce a nation of preachers and editors'.)[72]

Undoubtedly, settlers' criticisms were directed at missionaries and educators as much as towards their pupils and converts, reminding us that missionaries and settlers were themselves often locked in a struggle over competing projects of colonisation. However, the sheer volume of statements from white employers averse to hiring 'educated natives' suggests that this was more than merely a case of anti-missionary propaganda. Keeping in mind Fanon's interpretation of the native's 'relapse' as evidence of resistance rather than failure to assimilate, these criticisms imply that, despite colonialism's coercive and ideological assault on African consciousness and behaviour, many Xhosa chose, and successfully managed, to retain elements of their mores and culture – including certain aspects of 'African time'. Among their criticisms of the 'educated native', settlers regularly complained of the failure of the schools to reform African culture permanently – particularly its sporadic work-ethic and labour rhythms. Once people left the schools, they argued, the 'native' evinced a regular tendency to slip back into 'African time'. As a farmer reported to the Commission on Native Laws and Customs in 1883:

> Many of the natives having been for sometime at Lovedale, preserve, in themselves, and in some instances in their families, houses, furniture ... traces of the life they led at the Institution. But I must say that, except in the matter of dress, there is an absence of pride in acquired accomplishments, and great backwardness in working at the trade learnt ever so well. Thus a good blacksmith, and a fair average wagonmaker are doing nothing but turn a bit of land for Kafir corn, and if pushed to seek work by want, they will prefer to work with the farmers around, and cannot be persuaded to go a little further and earn treble the money a few miles further at their own trade. This is laziness.[73]

Settlers interpreted the Xhosas' 'relapse' into their old, prodigal ways as evidence of their irredeemable nature as savages.

> Who shuts the Native out from the same honest and honourable means of livelihood and improvement? Only his own confirmed and cherished idleness. He plants his mealies and pumpkins just as was done a hundred years ago ... Instead of storing away his corn, as was done of old, that there might be a prolonged supply of food over the season, he carries it in driblets to the nearest shop, to exchange for tobacco, coffee, or some gewgaw. In this respect there has been a positive deterioration of character, rather than improvement.[74]

Missionaries, on the other hand, responded to their critics by accusing settlers of worsening the labour crisis by refusing to pay their black workers decent wages: 'Why do you think that the farmer cannot get labour now – the ordinary European farmer?' asked one of Lovedale's Superintendents during the SANAC inquiry: 'Because he does not pay sufficient wages to his Native servants.'[75] The missionaries' argument was corroborated by their supporters and the educated Xhosa elite: 'The farmers complained of shortage of labour, but it was they themselves who were to blame,' reads an article in *Imvo Zabantsundu*, providing a 'Xhosa Opinion' on the matter: 'They drove labour away. Men were to work for them each and every day, from sunrise to sunset on poor food and a miserable pittance ... The Native was not lazy; he was a willing worker if fairly treated.'[76]

There was some truth in both sides of the story. Not surprisingly, the only real incentive for Africans to sell their labour to whites was the prospect of better wages and work conditions – something which many white farmers seemed unwilling to concede, as Anthony Trollope himself confirmed during his visit to the Cape.[77] Missionaries, however, also tended to play down their own shortcomings in relation to their hegemonic objectives: just as settlers refused to acknowledge truancy and 'regression' as signs of African agency and resistance towards white authority, missionaries concealed their shortcomings in dubious statistics. In 1886, for example, as evidence of its success in remoulding 'natives' for the colonial economy, Lovedale published a book containing the occupations of 2,058 'natives' who had passed through its gates. The 'Native Roll' records thirty-eight occupations, and these included 16 missionaries, 20 evangelists, 251 male teachers, 158 female teachers, 63 carpenters, 37 wagon makers, 6 law agents, 3 journalists and 26 telegraphists.[78] It was an impressive testament to Lovedale's educational philosophy – almost suspiciously impressive, since it claimed that only fifteen natives had 'relapsed into open heathenism'. And yet, as a settler reported during the SANAC inquiry, 'It would be interesting to ascertain what becomes of the Natives who undergo an industrial training at Lovedale. One never meets or hears of them.'[79]

The discrepancy which emerges between the fissures of settler and missionary discourses seems perplexing.

A vital piece of the picture seems to have fallen into one of the intentional blind-spots of colonial discourse and may well lie in the significant number of people who did in fact 'relapse' after leaving the mission-schools – but not because of their irredeemable savagery (as settler polemicists declared) or sin and moral weakness (as missionaries preferred to believe). The narrative of resistance through 'relapse' – which Fanon highlights in this section's opening quote – is difficult to retrieve from colonial discourse precisely because both settlers and missionaries failed or refused to recognise the extent to which natives going 'back over the line' (as Fanon put it), were in fact exercising an active and 'radical condemnation of the methods and of the regime'.

In pointing a finger at one another, farmers and missionaries were seemingly reluctant to consider an alternative explanation; that African workers, and particularly those who had received missionary education, had learned the rules of the capitalist economy all too well; they had imbibed its discourse and, when possible, found ways of deploying it to their own advantage with increasing efficacy. Through the added benefit of missionary education, Xhosa men and women gradually came to assume a capitalist attitude towards time, turning it to their own advantage, in ways that allowed them to negotiate more efficiently over wages, work time, and work terms – in the colonisers' own master language.[80] ('My gentleman Kafir', reads a bitter letter from a farmer to a local newspaper, 'is quite as much, if not more than the European, given to combinations and to strikes.'[81]) In disputes over times of work, holidays and pay – and especially during periods of high demand – workers learned how to request precise work contracts and set hours of work so as to maximise the surplus time for their own leisure- and kinship-time. Thus, '[t]he educated Native', as a settler in Natal complained, 'gets pay, under our pressing needs, entirely out of proportion to the value of his services, he picks and chooses his work, or will not some days work at all, and earning money far ahead of his needs, he returns early to his kraal to spend lengthy periods of idleness'.[82]

Ironically, settler indictments against the inefficacy of missionary influence often seem like unintentional tributes to the resilience of Xhosa culture: 'Christian principle is not a power upon the mass of our Native Tribes,' a piece of settler polemic reads. 'The doctrines of the Christian faith have been assiduously preached among them, and taught in school to their children for over sixty years, yet they are unaffected for good thereby.'[83] In fact, this was quite the opposite; the fundamental precepts of Christian doctrine had provided a discourse which Africans could effectively redeploy – for their *own* good, rather that of the settlers.

As we have seen, missionaries had from the first day taught their followers to keep the Lord's Day holy; it was a lesson which was never forgotten by African converts, who would invoke the Fourth Commandment to secure their right to Sunday rest. Once again, farmers were not impressed.

> We as farmers are against educated Natives.
>
> Why? – Because they are no good, and they do not suit us.
>
> Do you mean that they will not work? – Even if they do go to work they always want their Sundays off, and they want to go to their prayer meetings, and therefore farmers do not hire them.[84]

Not surprisingly, European farmers came to regard with increasing suspicion the practice among educated Christian converts of invoking a frequent desire to respect the religious schedules of the local churches, sensing – perhaps correctly – that Christian time was being adopted and redeployed in ways which gave African workers a means of limiting the power of their employers over working hours:

> At present their instruction seems to tend to increase their national

greed, indolence, and licentiousness ... The Natives are cunning enough to notice that when they ask leave to go to church (which is too often, for them, a social gathering or meeting for general employment), most of their employers do not like to refuse, even if it happens every night.[85]

This was a far-cry from 1818, when the missionary influence had only just begun; back then, according to Barnabas Shaw, farmers in the northern Cape had been able to get away with convincing Khoikhoi servants that the Sabbath actually ended after lunch time on Sunday, after which ploughing and threshing were allowed.[86]

In turn, missionaries responded to their critics by blaming the farmers' unwillingness to provide fairer terms of employment. But in passing the blame from one side to the other both parties failed to consider an alternative possibility: that the cause of the 'problem' lay entirely outside colonial agency and that a new generation of African men and women had started to play an active role in society by appropriating and exploiting the very discourses of their self-styled reformers, asserting their own pace of life, and soon also their political rights. The tensions between colonial agents bring Indigenous agency itself into relief – a reminder that colonisation was 'deeply affected in every dimension', as Cooper and Stoler suggest, 'by the actions of the "colonised"'.[87] ('Colonialism', Fanon observed, 'must accept the fact that things happen without its control, without its direction.'[88]) Such actions did in fact have a deep effect on the colonial economy in the Cape, Natal and elsewhere. By the turn of the century, as the demand for hands on public works, mining, and farms by far exceeded the supply, the labour situation became critical. Even at the beginning of the twentieth century, still less than half of the mining workforce would be composed of African labourers. Frustrated white employers in the Cape and Natal still regarded the African time- and work-ethic as a cause of this. 'It is the *intermittent* working habits of the Native which render him so relatively inefficient as a workman,' a manager on the mines stated in 1903.[89] To the chagrin of white employers, African workers had learnt to converse and negotiate within a capitalist discourse, exploiting the fluctuations of the seasonal labour market only too well. A farmer could still complain in 1892, for example, that the labour supply 'depends entirely upon the season'. In other words, despite legal measures to force the Xhosa into the labour market, their work rhythms were still seasonal and inconstant, oriented around necessity rather than an ethic of yearly work.[90] 'If there is scarcity of food,' the same farmer complained, 'you can obtain any amount of labourers.'

In the urban areas, where the regimentation of time was even greater, Africans found ways of maintaining elements of their temporal identity and independence. Even fines were not always sufficient as disincentives to abandon un-approved seasons and rituals of pre-colonial Xhosa life. As another farmer related: 'For a long time I fined my workboys two days for every day truant, now I fine them ten days for every day truant, and although I only employ young men and boys, that does not deter them during the beer drinking season.'[91] (These were some of the 'hidden battles', in the words of Clifton Crais, 'over the control of the very character of work ... the organisation of space and time'.[92]) Keletso Atkins provides a brilliant analysis of this process in the towns of nineteenth-century Natal. 'Observance of traditional holidays regularly interrupted the flow of labour [in the towns]', Atkins explains: 'The "moon of the new season's fruits' (*umasingana*) was widely celebrated among Natal Zulu ... Therefore, the common practice during the first three or four months of the year was for large numbers of Africans to withdraw to their kraals to help with the harvest and eat green mealies.' Consequently, back in the towns, white employers were forced to reconcile themselves to the idea of doing their own domestic work during these months.[93]

Having failed to achieve hegemony through other means, alternative strategies had to be sought. In Natal it became imperative for cane growers to introduce indentured labourers from India as early as 1860.[94] Likewise, in order to overcome the severe labour shortage in the Cape and the Transvaal following the South African War (1899–1902), Lord Milner decided upon the importation of indentured Chinese workers.[95] After South Africa's Unification in 1910, as the country headed towards the apartheid era, other means – such as labour taxes with remissions to workers, higher hut- and marriage-taxes – would be imposed to squeeze Africans into the workforce. As a clear sign that colonisation was often a case of dominance rather than hegemony, coercion and political exclusion would remain the only means for colonisers to achieve Indigenous compliance with the rhythms, timetables and curfews of an exploitative economy. Such measures were ways of circumventing failure to achieve a straightforward hegemony at the temporal dimension. Despite certain elements of acculturation, 'African time' appeared to have survived through decades of evangelisation, education and coercion – both direct and indirect. Indeed, as African historian, Omari Kokole, feels, 'one of the most resilient aspects of Indigenous African culture is precisely attitudes to time'.[96] This was evidence not of African stubbornness but of resistance to a form of colonisation which failed to offer the 'colonised' a sufficient incentive to alter their own pace of life, their notions of time, work, regularity and productivity. Having failed to enforce and induce the adoption of industrial-capitalist time, colonialism resorted to denying its limits by defining 'irregularity' and compulsive 'lateness' as innate racial defects.

Thus the myth of 'African time' was immortalised in twentieth-century discourse as a stereotype of innate racial inferiority.

—◆◈◆—

Sir George Grey, James Stewart and the many other reformers of Xhosa culture had envisioned education as a tool for Indigenous assimilation; but the way in which it empowered Africans produced unexpected consequences. ('Missionary aims were one thing, as Norman Etherington notes, 'and results were another'.)[97] A minority of Xhosa, who early established the practice of sending at least one child in a family away to boarding school to receive a Western education, in due course gave rise to a new generation of 'respectable', literate and enfranchised African men – such as Jabavu, Bud-M'Belle and S.E.K. Mqhayi. It was from schools such as Lovedale that the cultural and political leaders of black South Africa would emerge. The best-known example is of course that of Nelson Mandela, whose Western education began at the Wesleyan mission-schools of Clarkebury and Healdtown and ended at the University of Fort Hare – an institution which Lovedale itself helped fund and establish, and whose list of alumni includes other key political figures such as Oliver Tambo and Robert Mugabe. Little did George Grey and James Stewart imagine that their schools would nurture a future generation of freedom fighters who would ultimately lead to the democratic overthrow of white-minority rule.

As his memoir will clearly attest, however, Mandela's long walk to freedom began in a Wesleyan mission-school classroom, where he recalls that the daily regime was 'rigorous':

> First bell was at 6 a.m. We were in the dining hall by 6.40 for a breakfast of dry bread and hot sugar water, watched over by the sombre portrait of George VI, the king of England ... At eight we assembled in the courtyard outside our dormitory for 'observation', standing to attention ... We remained in class until 12.45, and then had a lunch of samp, sour milk and beans, seldom meat. We then studied until 5 p.m., followed by an hour's break for exercise and dinner, and then studied again from seven until nine. Lights went out at 9.30.[98]

Throughout the struggle for freedom and equality, time acted as a double-edged sword between empowerment and acculturation, resistance and negotiation. Those who attained Western education were the ones who would lead that struggle into the twentieth century; but they also had to learn to adopt the temporal consciousness, discourses and rituals of the colonisers in order to so.

6.5   Clock-tower at Lovedale (ca 1940)

Notes

1 Jeffrey Peires, *The Dead Will Arise: Nongqawuse and the Great Xhosa Cattle-Killing Movement of 1856–7* (Bloomington: Indiana University Press, 1989), pp. 281, 249; Cf. Mostert, *Frontiers*, pp. 1187–222; Legassick, 'The State, Racism and the Rise of Capitalism', pp. 359–68;
2 Legassick, 'The State, Racism and the Rise of Capitalism', pp. 364–7; Bundy, *Rise and Fall of the South African Peasantry*; Clifton C. Crais, *White Supremacy and Black Resistance in Pre-Industrial South Africa: the Making of the Colonial Order in the Eastern Cape, 1880–1865* (Cambridge: Cambridge University Press, 1992), p. 321;
3 Mostert, *Frontiers*, pp. 1244–59; Crais, *White Supremacy*, pp. 216–20; Legassick, 'The State, Racism and the Rise of Capitalism', p. 366.
4 Crais, *White Supremacy*, p. 64.
5 Fanon, *Wretched of the Earth*, p. 40.
6 Keletso E. Atkins, '"Kafir Time": Preindustrial Temporal Concepts and Labour Discipline in Nineteenth-century Colonial Natal', *Journal of African History*, 29 (1988), 229–44, p. 231; Frederick Cooper, 'Colonizing Time'.
7 Atkins, *'The Moon is Dead, Give us our Money!'*, p. 80, 78–99. Atkins' discussion of the subject of time disputes between whites and Zulu workers in colonial Natal remains one of the best analyses to date.
8 KAB, CCP 2/2/2/27, C2-'92, *Report of the Select Committee on the Labour Question, Printed by Order of the Legislative Council*, 1892 (hereafter: *Report of the Select Committee on the Labour Question*, 1892), *Minutes of Evidence*, C. B. Elliot, pp. 54–5.
9 Francis P. Flemyng, *Kaffraria, and Its Inhabitants* (London: Smith, Elder & Co., 1853), p. 94. Emphasis in the original.
10 According to Atkins, the Zulu year was divided into two separate and distinct seasons which lasted six 'moons': *Unyaka*, the rainy or field work season, and *ubusika*, the dry or winter season. It was 'no accident', Atkins writes, 'that the word denoting the time of greatest activity in the Zulu work schedule [*unyaka*] was redefined to corre-

spond with the Western calendar'. Atkins, *'The Moon is Dead, Give us our Money!'*, pp. 82–3.
11 James B. Mama, *Report of the South African Native Affairs Commission* (1903–5), (hereafter: *SANAC*) (Cape Times Ltd, Government Printer, 1905), vol. 4, *Minutes of Evidence*, p. 645.
12 On Grey's policies see Legassick, 'The State, Racism and the Rise of Capitalism', pp. 359–61; Crais, *White Supremacy*, pp. 200–1; Lester, *Imperial Networks*, pp. 182–3.
13 William C. Holden, *The Past and Future of the Kaffir Races* (1866) (Cape Town: Struik, 1963), p. 447.
14 James Wells, *The Life of James Stewart* (London: Hodder & Stoughton, 1909), p. 103; R. H. W. Shepherd, *Lovedale, South Africa: The Story of a Century, 1841–1941* (Lovedale: Lovedale Press, 1940), p. 400.
15 Louis Althusser, 'Ideology and Ideological State Apparatuses', in L. Althusser, *Lenin and Philosophy and Other Essays*, trans. B. Brewster (London: NLB, 1971), pp. 146–7.
16 Stewart, *Lovedale, South Africa*, p. 27.
17 John M. MacKenzie and Nigel R. Dalziel, *The Scots in South Africa: Ethnicity, Identity, Gender and Race, 1772–1914* (Manchester: Manchester University Press), p. 100.
18 KAB, CCP 4/1/2/1/1, *Report and Proceedings, with Appendices, of the Government Commission on Native Laws and Customs* (Cape of Good Hope, Jan. 1883) (hereafter: *Commission on Native Laws and Customs*, 1883), p. 52; *SANAC*, vol. 1, pp. 80–1; *SANAC*, vol. 5, Appendix D, W. A. Soga, African farmer, Elliotdale, p. 85; *SANAC*, vol. 5, Appendix D, Mr J. Maclaren, Inspector of Schools, p. 56.
19 *Report of Commission on Native Laws and Customs*, 1883, p. 52.
20 MacKenzie and Dalziel, *Scots in South Africa*, p. 100.
21 Stewart, *The Educated Kaffir*, pp. 20, 19.
22 *SANAC*, vol. 2, *Minutes of Evidence*, Mr R.W. Rose Innes, p. 634. The term 'boy' is used here in the racist sense, to describe African men.
23 Roland Oliver, *The Missionary Factor in East Africa* (London: Longmans, Green, 1952), p. 52.
24 Fabian, 'Religious and Secular Colonization', in J. Fabian, *Time and the Work of Anthropology*, pp. 165–6.
25 'Lovedale Missionary Institution Reports' (1872–88), quoted in Graham A. Duncan, *Lovedale: Coercive Agency: Power and Resistance in Mission Education* (Pietermaritzburg: Cluster, 2003), pp. 171–2.
26 KAB, MS A80/4, cf. A80/1, 'Journal of the Heald Town Industrial Institution, 1856–1859'.
27 Mr W. Hay, 'An address to the Native Educational Association', in *Imvo Zabantsundu (Native Opinion)*, King William's Town, 17 (23 Feb. 1885), p. 4 (NLSA Collection: MP 1009). Jabavu also edited the *Isigidimi* newspapers at Lovedale, where he studied (1881–1883) until forced to leave due to his political views.
28 MacKenzie and Dalziel, *Scots in South Africa*, p. 110; Duncan, *Lovedale: Coercive Agency*, p. 19.
29 UCT, MS, BC106, item D1, James Stewart, *Lovedale, South Africa: Its Aims, Principles and Results* (Lovedale: Lovedale Press, 1890), p. 6. This is a published version of a paper originally entitled 'Lovedale, South Africa', which was read at a missionary conference in London in 1878.
30 R. W. Barbour, 'Lovedale, South Africa: "How it Strikes a Stranger"', *African Papers*, 2 (Lovedale: Lovedale Press, 1880), p. 13 (Cory Library Collection: Lovedale Pamphlets); MacKenzie and Dalziel, *Scots in South Africa*, pp. 112–13.
31 Barbour, 'Lovedale', p. 8.
32 *Ibid.*, pp. 8–13.
33 Stewart, *Lovedale, South Africa*, p. 8.
34 Barbour, 'Lovedale', pp. 17–18.
35 Stewart, *Lovedale, South Africa*, p. 13.
36 Barbour, 'Lovedale', p. 8.
37 *Ibid.*, pp. 19–20.
38 *Ibid.*, p. 4.
39 Quoted in John A. Williams, *From the South African Past: Narratives, Documents,*

and Debates (Boston: Houghton Mifflin, 1997), p. 158.
40 Stewart, *Lovedale, South Africa*, p. 6.
41 Holden, *Past and Future of the Kaffir Races*, p. 449.
42 Shepherd, *Lovedale, South Africa*, pp. 62, 175; Stewart, *Lovedale, South Africa*, pp. 13–14.
43 *Lovedale News*, 1:4 (8 Aug. 1876), p. 3. Emphasis in the original.
44 Stewart, *Lovedale, South Africa*, p. 8.
45 *Lovedale News*, 1:4 (8 Aug. 1876), James Stewart, p. 1.
46 *Lovedale News*, 1:5 (23 Aug. 1876), p. 3.
47 *Lovedale News*, 1:19 (15 June 1877), p. 4.
48 Quoted in Wells, *Life of James Stewart*, p. 217.
49 *Lovedale News*, 1:19 (15 June 1877), p. 1.
50 Norman Etherington, 'Education and Medicine', in N. Etherington (ed.), *Missions and Empire* (Oxford: Oxford University Press, 2005), p. 264; Duncan, *Lovedale: Coercive Agency*, pp. 81–7.
51 *Lovedale News*, 1:15 (21 Mar. 1877), p. 1.
52 *Lovedale News*, 1:15 (21 Mar. 1877), p. 2.
53 *Lovedale News*, 1:15 (21 Mar. 1877), p. 2.
54 *Lovedale News*, 1:16 (9 Apr. 1877), p. 1.
55 *Lovedale News*, 1:17 (21 Apr. 1877), p. 2.
56 *Report of the Select Committee on the Labour Question*, 1892, *Minutes of Evidence*, P. H. Faure, Secretary for Native Affairs, 28 June 1892, p. 7.
57 James Stewart, *The Educated Kaffir*, p. 21. Emphasis added.
58 Ibid., p. 27.
59 UCT, BC106, item D29, James Stewart, *The Experiment of Native Education: An Address delivered by James Stewart to the Lovedale Literary Society* (Lovedale: Lovedale Press, 1884), p. 29. Emphasis added.
60 Ibid., p. 29.
61 UCT, MS BC106, item D25, James Stewart, 'Notes for Paper to Lovedale Staff'.
62 Edwin Ward, 'Life at the South African Wesleyan Native Training Institution', in F. W. Macdonald (ed.), *Work and Workers in the Mission Field*, 5 (1896), p. 426.
63 *Lovedale News*, 1:4 (8 Aug. 1876), p. 3. Emphasis in the original.
64 *Lovedale News*, 1:15 (21 Mar. 1877), p.4.
65 Comaroff and Comaroff, *Of Revelation, Vol. 1*, p. 234.
66 *Lovedale News*, 1:2 (23 May 1876), p. 3.
67 *Lovedale News*, 1:2 (23 May 1876), pp. 3–4.
68 UCT, BC106, item D26, James Stewart Papers, address given by Rev. F. Buchanan at the end of the school year, 1877.
69 *SANAC*, vol. 2, *Minutes of Evidence*, Mr R.W. Rose Innes, solicitor, Cape Colony, p. 634.
70 *SANAC*, vol. 5, Appendix D, 'Written Replies to Circular Questions', Mr N. Thompson, Resident Magistrate, Kentani, p. 97.
71 *SANAC*, vol. 5, Appendix D, Mr John Colley, p. 19.
72 Quoted in Etherington, 'Education and Medicine', p. 268.
73 *Report of Commission on Native Laws and Customs*, 1883, Appendix 3, 'Replies to Circular No. 3, to Inspectors and Superintendents of Native Locations', L. Vincent, Esq, Victoria East, p. 336.
74 Cory, PR, doc. 4787, Anon., *A Plea in Vindication of the Colonists* , pp. 11–12.
75 *SANAC*, vol. 2, *Minutes of Evidence*, Dr Alexander Roberts, pp. 805–6.
76 *Imvo Zabantsundu*, ca. 1913, quoted in Thomas Karis and Gail Carter (eds), *From Protest to Challenge: A Documentary History of African Politics in South Africa, 1882–1964*, vol. 1 (Stanford: Hoover Institution Press, 1972), pp. 82–4.
77 Anthony Trollope, *South Africa* (London, 1878), vol. 1, p. 146.
78 *Lovedale Past and Present: A Register of Two Thousand Names, a Record Written in Black and White, but more in White than Black. With a European Roll* (Lovedale: Lovedale Press, 1887).
79 *SANAC*, vol. 5, Appendix D, 'Written Replies to Circular Questions', M. Harison, C. and R. Cradock, p. 42.

80 Jean Comaroff, 'Missionaries and Mechanical Clocks', p. 16.
81 *The Herald* quoted in *Graham's Town Journal*, 11 Jan. 1869, p. 2.
82 *SANAC*, vol. 5, Appendix C, 'Annexures', no. 19, R. Jameson, Chairman Sanitary Committee to Town Council, Durban, p. 35.
83 Anon., *A Plea in Vindication of the Colonists*, p. 13.
84 *SANAC*, vol. 2, *Minutes of Evidence*, G. F. Golding, p. 921.
85 *SANAC*, vol. 5, Appendix D, Mrs S. F. Bournhill, Barberton (Transvaal), p. 192.
86 B. Shaw, Journal, 4 Jan. 1818, section 1, folder 2, p. 43.
87 Cooper and Stoler, *Tensions of Empire*, p. ix.
88 Fanon, *A Dying Colonialism*, p. 48.
89 *SANAC*, vol. 5, Appendix D, Mr. John Colley, General Mining Manager, Indwe, p. 19. Emphasis added.
90 *Report of the Select Committee on the Labour Question*, 1892, *Minutes of Evidence*, W. Hockly, farmer, Somerset, p. 70; see also *Minutes of Evidence*, Mr Frost, JP, pp. 45–6.
91 *Ibid.*, Appendix to the Report, James Bonnar, farmer, p. xxv.
92 Crais, *White Supremacy*, p. 64.
93 Atkins, *'The Moon is Dead, Give us our Money!'*, p. 89.
94 Atkins, '"Kafir Time"', p. 237.
95 Cecil Headlam (ed.), *The Milner Papers: South Africa, 1899–1905* (London: Cassell, 1933), vol. 2, pp. 458, 465.
96 Omari Kokole, 'Time, Language, and the Oral Tradition: An African Perspective', in Joseph K. Adjaye, *Time in the Black Experience* (Westport, Conn.: Greenwood Press, 1994), p. 52.
97 Etherington, 'Education and Medicine', p. 267.
98 Mandela, *Long Walk to Freedom*, p. 44.

CHAPTER SEVEN

Conclusion: from colonisation to globalisation

As the nineteenth century came to a close, the numerous clocks, watches and bells that had been disseminated throughout the British Empire gradually came to be synchronised with one another, marking a gradual shift from the phase of temporal conquest and expansion – explored in this book – towards one of global centralisation and standardisation, which we currently find in full bloom.

The official deployment of GMT in 1884 indeed heralded a new era of global timekeeping – allowing people, towns, cities, ports, railways and colonies to connect with metropolitan centres, and between each other, through a single space-time matrix. As colonies and communities abroad gradually adopted the new standard time, the drop of the time-ball from the Eastern Turret of the Royal Observatory at Greenwich at 1.00 p.m. GMT came to be echoed by colonial time-balls and time signals in the harbours of Madras, Calcutta, Hong Kong, Mauritius, St Helena, Fremantle, Sydney, Melbourne, Wellington and elsewhere. Soon, railway timetables and public clocks in the colonies would also be adjusted to GMT, bringing these outposts in line with the dominant temporal standard of the metropolis.

The Cape Colony adopted GMT in 1892, with the other South African colonies following suit by 1903, when a general notice was issued addressing local authorities and 'all others having control of public clocks':

> It is hereby notified for general information that the Governments of the Cape Colony, Natal, Orange River Colony, Rhodesia ... have all agreed to the adoption of Common Time for Railway, Telegraph and other public purposes in their respective Territories, such time to be that of Meridian of 30 degrees of East Longitude, (that is to say, time two hours fast of Greenwich time) ... on the 28th February, 1903, all clocks on the Cape Railway systems and in all Telegraph Offices will be set forward 30 minutes.[1]

7.1 Firing of noon gun in Cape Town, conveying synergy between time and Empire (*ca* 1911)

7.2 Noon gun (*ca* 1934), showing Cape Town and Table Bay in background

CONCLUSION: FROM COLONISATION TO GLOBALISATION

To a significant extent, the choice of London as the temporal standard by which all other communities should regulate their clocks was a result of the Greenwich Observatory's reputation for possessing the most accurate clocks in the world. But it was above all a matter of practical necessity, for almost three-quarters of the world's shipping tonnage already employed the British *Nautical Almanac*, whose charts computed longitude according to the Greenwich meridian.[2] As far as the non-Western world was concerned, however, GMT was the corollary of temporal imperialism, its unilateral deployment implying the ultimate proclamation of dominance over time and space. As the term 'Prime Meridian' suggests, London effectively became the centre of the world.

This intimate connection between time and Empire was particularly overt in Cape Town, where the blast of an 18-pounder cannon communicated the time signal for ships in Table Bay – an apt symbol of the synergetic relationship between temporal and territorial conquest. From 1864, the 'noon gun' – as it came to be known – was triggered remotely via telegraphic cables connected to the Astronomical Observatory's master clock (see figure 7.1). This ritual dates back to 1806, when Britain took possession of the Cape of Good Hope, and can still be heard in Cape Town today – at 12 noon sharp (two hours ahead of 12.00 GMT), except Sundays and public holidays.

In the same year that the Cape Colony adopted GMT, Melbourne hosted an 'Intercolonial Survey Conference' which campaigned heavily for the adoption of standard time in the local media. As the rhetoric suggests, the shift to the new time system was proffered as a catalyst for ushering the Australian colonies into the age of modernity. Articles in the *Argus* informed readers in Melbourne that the old time system was a relic of 'medieval ages'; standard time would 'bring the reckoning of time into line with the progress of the age'.[3] The reform was advertised as a boon for the public as well as commerce and communication: the ever-increasing flow of people, goods and information along railways, shipping lines and telegraph lines meant that a standard-time system was essential. Without it, a spokesperson of the Conference explained, 'anyone travelling overland from Brisbane to Melbourne or Adelaide would find his watch seriously in error at each of the principal stations'.[4] The proposed new system would resolve such confusion by slicing the continent along the 120th, 135th and 150th parallels east of Greenwich, forming just three time zones: Western, Central and Eastern Standard Time. Thus, in 1895, the Australian colonies made the switch to standard time, which enabled them to assume their place amongst other modern nations on the global temporal map:

THE COLONISATION OF TIME

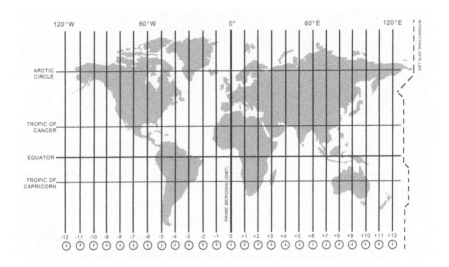

7.3 The GMT space-time matrix, showing lines of longitude and their corresponding local mean times, with Prime Meridian passing through London

7.4 Aerial view of Greenwich Observatory, showing Prime Meridian running through building that houses Airy Transit Circle. Time-ball is visible on east turret of Observatory (*top left*)

CONCLUSION: FROM COLONISATION TO GLOBALISATION

So that at every place on the same meridian as Greenwich, no matter in what part of the world, it will be 1 o'clock when the Greenwich time-ball drops, so at every place on the same meridian as Melbourne it will be 1 o'clock when the Williamstown ball drops, whether that place be in Australia or Kamatchatka. Therefore at all places within the limits of any time zone, from pole to pole, the time will be the same in hour, minute, and second.[5]

Just as 'railway time' had brought an end to the various 'local mean times' of European towns and cities, so did GMT signal the impending demise of local times worldwide. By 1929 almost all major nations in the world had accepted the time-zone system based on GMT coordinates. Following this, time became one of the first units of measurement to go 'global'. And even today it effectively remains unmatched as a worldwide protocol. We are yet to witness a world-currency, a world-government, a world-language or even a world-calendar – and not for want of trying. In a very real sense, however, the world-time system established under GMT was the inauguration of a global language, currency and government, all wrapped into one.

Subsequently, the surface of the globe would be divided into twenty-four time sectors – leading to the establishment of the 'time zones' currently in use. Starting from the Prime Meridian, each zone would measure fifteen degrees of longitude, with all clocks set one full hour ahead or behind adjacent zones.

The turning earth had effectively been re-imagined as a giant, man-made clock.

Under this system, the ability to know *'the'* time made the ownership of a clock or watch indispensable; whilst the sun, stars and constellations which had once oriented human collectives in space and time were gradually rendered increasingly superfluous as timekeepers. Western society became 'civilised and modern' partly by learning to orientate itself according to the constellations on the dial of a clock rather than those in the sky. ('Modern man', as Martin Nilsson observed in 1920, 'is almost entirely without knowledge of the stars; for him they are the ornaments of the night-sky'.[6]) Over the course of the twentieth century – whether by choice or necessity – much of the Western and Westernised world came to be regulated by this idea of time to such an extent that it became difficult to conceive of its marching to the beat of any other drum than that of the clock – as if this were the 'materialisation of some universal time sense'.[7] 'The clock, not the steam engine, is the key machine of the industrial age,' claimed Lewis Mumford in the early 1930s – 'even today no other machine is so ubiquitous.'[8]

As is apparent by now, however, this book does not associate 'time' solely with the rise to power of mechanical clocks; nor has it viewed the latter as devices whose function is exclusively that of keeping time. 'The purpose of timekeepers is said to be that of measuring time,' suggests philosopher of time, Julius Fraser. But 'this function', he argues, 'contrary to popular opinion, is only secondarily a technical virtuosity. Primarily it is a metaphysical enterprise designed to coordinate the earthly organisation of man's life with the temporal order of the universe.'[9] Couched in these broader, philosophical terms, the question of how clock-time was disseminated and imposed throughout so much of the world during the nineteenth century and beyond, reflects a far broader cultural phenomenon – one which suggests an attempt, unprecedented in terms of its global scope and ambition, to impose a centralised, moral and economic order for coordinating the earthly lives and rituals of all men and women with the temporal order of the universe – and more specifically, with the order of the colonisers' universe.

During this process, western Europe's clocks and seven-day weeks came to influence and govern not merely the culture that originally conceived them but also the lives of peoples in other parts of the world. Which brings us back to our original questions: How did 'the rest' of the world come to share the West's culture of time? Who were the first emissaries and agents of the clock to clock-less societies? And by what means did they gain a following? While it is guaranteed that there will always remain much more to be said on a subject like this, this book provides considerable evidence to support its initial claim: that the histories of Western time and European colonisation are inextricably connected.

In revisiting a number of colonial encounters from a temporal perspective, we have explored the manner in which the seeds of today's dominant temporal order were planted beyond European borders and how their growth there was intertwined with the dissemination of Christianity, commerce and civilisation. Focusing on two British settler-colonies – Victoria and the Cape Colony – we have noted various ways in which European understandings of 'Aboriginal time' and 'African time' privileged their advocates by justifying the need to 'civilise the natives' whilst legitimising their dispossession. Both in the Cape Colony and Victoria, the reform of conflicting temporalities, rituals and routines aided settler-colonial and missionary projects – be it with the primary intent of helping to eliminate an Indigenous presence (in Victoria), increasing the productivity of African labour (in the Cape Colony) or helping to justify the dispossession of the natives through Christian and humanitarian intervention (in both settings). In these contexts, the reform of 'alternative' temporalities comple-

CONCLUSION: FROM COLONISATION TO GLOBALISATION

mented the ideals of progress, productivity and civilisation that propelled British imperialism. Thus, the 'wild' and 'erratic' seasons of the hunter-gatherer had to give way to the newcomers' calendars of pastoralism and agriculture. In turn, the introduction of farming calendars and seasons helped convert pastoralists into agriculturalists; while the inculcation of the seven-day week and a capitalist time-consciousness, helped 'elevate' agriculturalists to the level of a proletariat. Each new stage in this apparent rise towards civilisation and redemption helped to bring about a higher degree of acculturation and conformity towards a new consciousness of time – one which was defined, with increasing precision and authority, by western European clocks and calendars.

Effectively, *all* Europeans who travelled to the colonies were emissaries of a Western time-consciousness to the rest of the world, even though they fulfilled this role in different ways and in pursuit of diverging interests and agendas. Missionaries themselves were undoubtedly among its most active and effective propagators. As we have seen, seven-day weeks, clocks and mission bells accompanied the spread of Christianity and were presented to Indigenous populations as sacred rituals for their moral advancement; symbols of modernity and true knowledge; antidotes to superstition, indolence and irregularity. The clock and the bell ultimately became tools, not merely of colonial dominance but also, ostensibly, of salvation and liberation. Thus, on the eve of the formal abolition of slavery in the British Empire in 1834, after experiencing 'the pleasure of tolling the passing bell of Cape slavery', the Reverend Barnabas Shaw announced to his congregation that 'on the clock striking twelve, the monster would expire'.[10] And that same evening, according to another Christian missionary at the opposite end of the world, on the island of St Vincent, 'thousands of poor Negroes upon their bended knees waited for the hour of midnight ... and when the clock struck twelve, which was the death-knell of slavery throughout the British empire ... they then rose to their feet, and sang with one heart and one voice, "Praise God, from whom all blessings flow"'.[11]

Time effectively helped construct a 'trans-imperial discourse of colonialism',[12] as representations of reformed, time-disciplined natives travelled between colonies through imperial and humanitarian networks of information, generating a collective consciousness of Britain as the exporter of the virtues of clock-governed order and Christian regularity amidst the perceived wilderness of the 'irregular world' at large. In the Cape Colony, for instance, the *Lovedale News* published reports from the recently subjugated Fijian islands, where the local Fijians' progress in civilisation was demonstrated by anecdotes such as the following:

THE BELL FOR FAMILY WORSHIP – A visitor to the island of Kandava, one of the Fiji Islands, was taking tea with the missionary, when the bell rang. He was told that this was the signal for family worship, and that of the 10,000 people on the island, the missionary did not know of a house where there would not then be family prayer! And yet Fiji was once a land of cannibalism.[13]

Encoded within such visions of temporal order and uniformity was the belief that Britain and its colonies were connected with one another through a common 'civilised' order of time. The shared temporal discourse which connected Britain and its colonies with one another in turn reflected and reinforced dominant notions of religion, civilisation and modernity, thus helping to construct the colonisers' own identities and civilities. In opposition to the so-called superstitious and irregular rituals of the moon-worshipping savages, missionaries could construct Christianity as a 'true religion', grounded in a biblical chronology with 'regular' rituals and ceremonies. And in contrast to the perceived lack of regard for timekeeping among the 'primitive' peoples, clock-wielding settlers could imagine themselves as a modern, industrialised, efficient and time-aware civilisation – qualities which were reflected in the nation's expansion and synchronisation of its advances in commerce and transport, its bigger cities, faster engines, longer telegraph lines, shorter shipping lines and, of course, a mightier Empire.

This is not to suggest that the colonisation of time was a coherent 'cultural system'. Colonial agendas, discourses and agents were often divided, as Nicholas Thomas suggests, 'by strategic interests and differing visions of the civilising mission'.[14] Time was no exception to this: as we have seen, the temporal discourses which colonisers carried with them to the colonies comprised different vernaculars; settlers and planters spoke about time predominantly in industrial-capitalist terms and sought to reform workers and slaves primarily within those economic parameters. Thus, the seasons of harvest and regular crop husbandry, the organisation of credit, the calendars of industry, and the length of work contracts, indentures and apprenticeships demanded a reformation of time-consciousness oriented around factory rhythms and labour routines. Protestant missionaries, on the other hand, discussed time with their converts in a predominantly Christian, ritualised discourse – exhorting people to observe the Sabbath, attend regular prayer times and accept the notion of a single genesis and destiny at the beginning and end of Christian chronology. These discourses were by no means impermeable to each other, either: both middle-class settlers and missionaries preached the gospel of work, emphasising the distinction between work and rest, public time and private time; both preached about time-discipline, punctuality and productivity, condemning idleness and tardiness. And both sought to establish the dominance of the seasons and calendars of agriculture and industry.

Accordingly, the ways in which colonial agents sought to transform Indigenous temporalities diverged and overlapped at several nodal points. A good example which we have seen is that of the seven-day week. For white farmers, missionaries and planters alike, ensuring the temporal framework of the week's dominance in the colonies was one of the first steps in establishing control over their populations (Crusoe's manner of naming 'Friday' being a symbolic and a practical reminder of this). However, whilst the 'visible' framework of the seven-day ritual was exported universally, its meaning and significance were shaped by local contexts and struggles. Thus, Sundays became one of the locations of conflict, not merely between colonisers and colonised but also amongst settlers, officials and missionaries. Indeed, whilst missionaries preached the benefits of the seven-day ritual in order to fulfil a particular vision of civilisation, settlers were often pursuing another. An unscrupulous farmer and planter, for example, would often fail to appreciate the precept that their workers and slaves were entitled to the weekly respite prescribed by the Fourth Commandment. In response, humanitarians in the metropolis condemned as a 'shameful rebellion against the law of God ... the denial of a Sabbath to our colonial slaves!'[15]

Settler-capitalist and humanitarian projects often came into conflict over the temporal reorientation of Indigenous societies in the colonies. And we have seen in Chapter 6 how these tensions were played out in the colonisers' attempts to reform 'African time'. We also observed how the 'colonised' played a crucial role in shaping the outcome of such reforms, as they pursued their own interests; for example, by appropriating the Sabbath ritual as a means of upholding the right to a day of rest, or for negotiating better pay for work carried out on Sundays. The fact that the seven-day week was exported throughout the Empire is thus a useful reminder that the will to coerce the world into conforming to European modes of order and significance was common to all colonial projects; but the way in which this process unfolded was neither uniform nor coherent, involving (as it inevitably did) frequent tensions within colonial ranks as well as between colonisers and colonised.

As for the question of how the clock gained a following among clock-less societies: we have noted how, despite the enticements associated with acculturation to European temporal values, the triumph of the clock and the seven-day week in the colonies usually relied on threats of physical coercion – no matter how remote the prospect. Whether through consent (as the missionary hoped) or by way of compulsion (as Cape Town's 'noon gun' implicitly reminded any would-be objector), clocks and calendars were ultimately introduced as the dominant authorities of time in the colonies in much the same way as the colonisers' spatial presence was established. The foundation of today's global temporal order is premised, in other words, on the physical interruption of 'other' cultures of time, order and regularity, and its continued dominance is a testament to the ongoing suppression of many such practices and ideas of time.

This, at least, is the way in which Yalmambirra – a contemporary descendant of the Wiradjuri people of southeast Australia – views the impact of the colonisers' clocks on his ancestors. 'Traditional Wiradjuri time began with the Era of Creation,' writes Yalmambirra. 'Traditional Wiradjuri time stopped with invasion.'

> People still move to that tick-tock, tick-tock, rhythm. In light of this, traditional Wiradjuri time you could argue, did not stop. I argue that it did. Traditional Wiradjuri time was stopped ... that space where things continued was taken away by the very act of invasion ... Traditional cultural practices were our clocks; we the people were merely the batteries that kept those clocks going. Invasion took the clocks away from us. The batteries were depleted in numbers, not because of a lack of energy, but because of the genocidal practices that came with invasion.[16]

Australian historian, Mike Donaldson, provides a more positive perspective by looking farther afield from the epicentre of British invasion, citing cases of the continuity of temporal culture in contemporary Aboriginal societies. He goes as far as to argue that time, in fact, was 'fundamental to the contestation which defeated British attempts to crush Aboriginal culture'.[17] One of the cases cited by Donaldson is that of Ernabella, a 'remote' South Australian town located 450 kilometres southwest of Alice Springs, where clock-time has struggled to gain a foothold. Here, in 1977, the local town council had introduced the local Pitjantjatjara peoples to the clock by erecting 'a giant, revolving, electrically operated clock' near the town's centre. Ironically, a white community worker pointed out a decade later that the clock was simply 'a waste of time'. 'The fact is,' the same person explained, 'that nobody looks at [it]. The clock has not been working for months. No one knew that it was not working'.[18]

Both of the above interpretations contain an element of truth. European colonisation was indeed a cataclysmic experience – in Australia, as Yalmambirra reminds us, and elsewhere across the world. Fundamental, material aspects of Indigenous temporal cultures were indeed entirely erased; and to deny this would be to trivialise the impact of colonisation. However, we have also seen that whilst colonisation succeeded in imposing the material and outwardly visible rituals and

CONCLUSION: FROM COLONISATION TO GLOBALISATION

routines of agriculture, capitalism and Christianity, the ideology that accompanied such visions of order was seldom transmitted without being reshaped, appropriated and redeployed in various ways beyond the colonisers' intention and control. This is not a perfunctory gesture towards contemporary Indigenous cultures: the colonisers' idea of 'time' was fundamentally an *idea*. Conversion through consent, rather than dominance through coercion, had in fact always been the ultimate objective of missionaries and reformers, for it was only through internalisation of the colonisers' time-consciousness that the clock exercised its hegemony. In this sense, the survival of alternative temporalities did not depend solely on the continuation of visible rituals and routines – many of which were indeed subsumed by colonisation. It was also about maintaining a sense of continuity with ideas and practices of time associated with a un-colonised identity. The fact that notions of 'African time' and 'blackfella time' are still commonly spoken about in mainstream discourse (even if derogatively) suggests that alternative ideas of time, order and punctuality still continue to exist and defy the colonisers' claim to temporal hegemony. No doubt, if we care to look through the grid of GMT and beyond the clock-governed metropolitan centres, we will find clear evidence of the survival of 'other' cultures and understandings of time.[19]

It would certainly be interesting to know more about what Indigenous peoples themselves made of the colonisers' culture of time; what they thought of their clocks, calendars, rituals and routines. Was it just Europeans who viewed the time of the 'other' as irrational and impractical? Or were such emotions reciprocated from the other side of the looking-glass? The following poem – transcribed in the Northern Territory some time during the 1950s – certainly suggests that at least some Aboriginal peoples had come to regard 'whitefella time' as an oppressive, if not ludicrous, regime.

> White man properly different kind,
> Watch on wrist, then wind ... wind ... wind;
> Pull up sleeve and look all day,
> Look when work and look when play.
>
> Man look time then say, 'Must go.'
> Man look clock and then him know
> Time is boss, all understand
> Must keep eye on face and hand.
>
> 'Tick...tock...tock,' that wrist-watch say,
> 'Me big Boss, you do my way,
> I make you wait and I make you run,
> I make you work when you like fun.

'I send off coach ... I send off train.
My hand start big aeroplane;
Big-fellow boss, he must watch me.
Breakfast, dinner, and supper and tea.'

My man listen and then him say,
'No time sleep,' and 'No time stay,'
Too much hurry down the street,
Terrible place when, 'No time eat.'[20]

Having thoroughly acquainted ourselves with European views and opinions on 'other' cultures of time, texts such as the above provide a refreshing insight into how the clock-wielding colonisers were viewed by their 'timeless other' – a reminder that, on both sides of the colonial encounter, time played a powerful discursive role in constructing notions of difference and identity. Certainly, the images it evokes also invite reflection on the ways in which Western, industrial society came to be governed by the clock's regime more than any other in the world. Taylorism and Fordism had made 'timekeeping' and 'efficiency' watchwords of the early twentieth century – but at what cost? As Georg Lukàcs wrote, when he surveyed the industrial landscape of 1920s Europe and the factories where increasing numbers of the working classes were being employed, '[t]hrough the subordination of man to the machine the situation arises in which ... the pendulum of the clock has become as accurate a measure of the relative activity of two workers as it is of the speed of two locomotives ... Time is everything, man is nothing; he is at the most the incarnation of time.'[21] (It is rather ironic, but darkly appropriate, that Western institutions during this period adopted the practice of rewarding their employees for a lifetime's work with the gift of a watch.)

Over the course of the twentieth century, in spite of its inescapable presence, the clock has become one of the most taken-for-granted aspects of life in the Western world – making its influence even more profound. In the 1970s, Max Horkheimer went so far as to define our era as 'the period of docile masses governed by clocks' – a fitting description of hegemony, given that both the omnipresence and authority of clocks have become an unquestioned and accepted daily reality.[22] Conditioned to identify with the regime of the clock, Western society has indeed all but lost the ability to recognise submission to the clock for what is, let alone resist it. And yet it also continues to harbour pockets of dissent through an unnamed movement that has for centuries defied the clock's claim to hegemony. Protest against the clock and the commodification of time has in fact experienced a revival in the mid-twentieth century and continues to be articulated through the discourses and mediums of art, music and philosophy, forming a sub-

CONCLUSION: FROM COLONISATION TO GLOBALISATION

culture of resistance to the dominant temporal order with a long and important history of its own.[23]

It is particularly fascinating to note how Western representations of 'other' cultures of time have, in turn, also experienced a marked shift, moving away from the self-assuredness and confidence that so brazenly characterised colonial representations of Indigenous societies, such as those explored in this book. Perhaps one of the earliest and most telling instances of this shift in academic discourse came from the eminent English social-anthropologist, Sir Edward Evans-Pritchard, whose investigation of time-reckoning systems among the Nuer people of central-east Africa prompted a famous moment of self-reflection – one which reveals more of his own temporal culture, than the temporal culture of the Nuer. Writers seeking to convey a Western sense of nostalgia for a life free of the clock have frequently quoted this passage from Evans-Pritchard's *The Nuer*:

> I do not think that they ever experience the same feeling of fighting against time or having to coordinate activities with an abstract passage of time, because their points of reference are mainly the activities themselves, which are generally of a leisurely character. Events follow a logical order, but they are not controlled by an abstract system, there being no autonomous points of reference to which activities have to conform with precision. Nuer are fortunate.[24]

This is certainly a far cry from judgments passed on 'African time' and 'Aboriginal time' by nineteenth- and early-twentieth-century anthropologists such as William Willoughby and Martin Nilsson, not to mention the perceptions of earlier colonial observers. Could it be that, after centuries of zealously exporting and enforcing the dominance of the clock throughout the world, Western society has started to question the wisdom of such a temporal regime in terms of its impact on the human quality of life? (and, in more recent times, on the natural environment)? Or has Western society always been gripped by a collective, unspoken and yet familiar aversion towards that sense of 'fighting against time' which Evans-Pritchard describes, ever since its own local, Indigenous temporal cultures were brought under the yoke of the clock's regime?

It often takes an outsider to point out things which have become almost entirely taken for granted within a culture. Noteworthy in this regard is one final piece of literature – this time from Uganda – which provides an idea of how the clock was received in that part of the world, and the tensions sparked within Indigenous societies by its intrusion into daily life. The sentiments of an 'outsider' towards the culture of the clock and the seven-day week are conveyed with great effect by celebrated Ugandan poet, Okot p'Bitek, in the *Song of Lawino*

(1966), a satirical monologue in which the narrator, Lawino – an Acoli woman – voices her protest against the ideas and ways of her Westernised husband, Ocol. The poem is worth citing extensively, since it speaks to many of the issues raised throughout this book.

> Ocol has brought home
> A large clock.
> It goes tock-tock-tock-tock
> And it rings a bell.
> He winds it first
> And then it goes!
> ...
> And Ocol has strange ways
> Of saying what the time is.
> In the morning
> When the sun is sweet to bask in
> He says
> 'It is Eight o'clock!'
> When the cock crows
> For the first time
> He says
> 'It is Five!'
> ...
> My head gets puzzled,
> Things look upside-down
> As if I have been
> Turning round and round
> And I am dizzy.
> ...
> My husband says
> I am useless
> Because I waste time,
> He quarrels
> Because, he says,
> I am never punctual.
> He has no time to waste.
> He tells me
> Time is money.
> ...
> Ocol laughs at me
> Because, he says,
> I do not know
> The names of the moons,
> That I do not know
> How many moons in a year
> And the number of Sabbaths
> In one moon.

CONCLUSION: FROM COLONISATION TO GLOBALISATION

>...
>Time has become my husband's master,
>It is my husband's husband.
>My husband runs from place to place
>Like a small boy,
>He rushes without dignity.
>...
>Listen
>My husband,
>In the wisdom of the Acoli
>Time is not stupidly split up
>Into seconds and minutes,
>It does not flow
>Like beer in a pot
>That is sucked
>Until it is finished.
>
>It does not resemble
>A loaf of millet bread
>Surrounded by hungry youths
>From a hunt;
>It does not get finished
>Like vegetables in the dish.[25]

In the present day

The struggle over time endures. Its significance in terms of the political and cultural ramifications of colonialism can scarcely be overlooked. Time still plays its role in establishing and reinforcing barriers of difference, distance and opposition between the West and 'the Rest', lending itself as an instrument of power and entitlement in economic and political discourse. The cultural imposition of Western time may be latent and silent (as writer Jay Griffiths points out: 'Unless you are a white, male Christian adult, every celebration of the millennium is an act of metaphysical imperialism, to which a thousand, thousand different cultures must submit'[26]); or it can be overtly discriminatory. Indeed, by evoking a perceived lack of knowledge or self-control, discourses of 'time-lessness' and 'irregularity' constitute an ongoing means of perpetuating notions of an inferior Other.

One of the most common illustrations of such prejudices in mainstream discourse occurs when people speak of 'African time' or 'blackfella time', when someone (black) happens to be late. The nature and function of such stereotypes today is of course socially complex and can assume vastly different meanings (such as, for instance, when redeployed ironically by those to whom such terms are supposed to apply). However, associations between time, race and civilisation are a product, as we have seen, of colonial discourse – and evidently also one of its ongoing legacies.

We might consider by way of example the case of a self-help booklet entitled *Whitefella Culture*, first published in 1991 in Darwin. It offers advice to Aboriginal people in the Northern Territory regarding certain aspects of social behaviour that are said to be especially important in white culture: such as 'saving money', 'making promises', 'doing your best' – and, of course, 'being on time'. Echoing the discourse of timelessness which we have encountered so extensively throughout this book, *Whitefella Culture* assumes that punctuality and regularity (like some of the other traits listed) are specific to Western society; that there is only one way to 'be on time' – and that is, to be on clock-time. 'Aboriginal culture is like most other cultures in the world', the book claims, lumping all clock-less cultures into the same time-less category; 'most cultures don't have rules about starting things on time.' 'But in white culture', the book informs its Aboriginal readers, 'many things are supposed to start at a certain time'. Indeed, 'if one thing starts really late, then that makes other things get started late [and] a person who is very late to meetings or who is nearly always late makes some white people a bit angry'.[27] Whilst the purpose of this book might genuinely be to assist so-called 'remote' Aboriginal communities in improving their understanding of 'white culture', it implicitly reinforces the ethnocentric ideology of *terra sine tempore*, which – as well as potentially being offensive to Aboriginal people – continues to shape the ways in which mainstream white society perceives and relates to Aboriginal culture.

Given the repercussions which such views have engendered in the collective consciousness of contemporary society, it would be wise to be aware of the origins of such beliefs; for it is important to remember the ways in which they have been called upon in the past to justify acts of racial disenfranchisement and dispossession. This is still applicable in recent times, when we consider that even academic and official discourses have perpetuated the Western idea of a temporal Other well into the twentieth century – and sometimes even beyond. In the late 1960s, for example, a number of educationalist studies claimed that the time-perspective of Aboriginal peoples was culturally oriented towards the past, geared towards maintaining their past traditions instead of future-planning. This trait, one such study argued, stood in direct contrast to Western cultures, whose forward-looking perspective naturally endowed them with a more highly-developed capacity for deferred gratification.[28] Another time-conscious prejudice which seems to have survived well into recent decades, is the evolutionist belief that 'regularity' and uniformity' are traits pertaining exclusively to more 'developed' societies. In the influential philosophical essay, *Time* (1987), for example, Norbert Elias claimed: 'The property of the self-control patterns of people in simpler societies which is especially striking in comparison to those of people in highly developed industrial societies is their lack of uniformity.'[29]

Grafted onto academic discourse, such ideas cease to be innocuous. In fact, considering that Australian policies regarding Indigenous peoples have consistently been informed by anthropological representations of Aboriginal society, such claims can quickly become potential mechanisms of social disfranchisement. Nineteenth-century colonial constructions of Indigenous temporality have indeed trickled down into government policy, affecting the lives of Aboriginal people in Australia well into the twentieth century. In 1965, for example, during a dispute about rates of pay, the Commonwealth Arbitration Commission of Australia cited the following information regarding Aboriginal society, based on reports from anthropologists:

> Time, in the Western sense, and the significance of time were ... unknown. [Aborigines] had no idea of forward planning, of working out a long term enterprise based on predictions of future planned occurrences. The notions of number, precise distance, and mathematical accuracy were unknown.[30]

From these and other findings, the Commission ruled that, under a slow-workers clause, Aboriginal labourers were not entitled to equal pay with white stockmen.[31]

As we have seen, the belief that Aboriginal people were constitutionally unable (or unwilling) to comply with white demands for discipline and regularity has a long history of its own. The fact that such beliefs have endured in Australian society is evinced by the fact that, in 1984, the periodical *Aboriginal Newsletter* still felt the need to complain about the discrimination faced by Aboriginal people due to a 'commonly-held community belie[f] that Aboriginal workers were unreliable and constantly yearned to go "walkabout"'.[32] Sure enough, even though recent years have seen the exposure of the canards underpinning the doctrine of *terra nullius*, the idea of *terra sine tempore* is often alive and well in contemporary Australian society.

We would like to believe that such beliefs will no longer be held – at least not officially – by those in positions of authority. Yet the reality is that they very much are. As recently as 2001, for example, representatives of USAID shocked the international community with the announcement before the United States Congress that the American government might just as well forgo spending millions of dollars on anti-retroviral drugs for Africa's AIDS pandemic. This was because Africans apparently lacked a pre-requisite concept of *time* for self-administering such complex medications:

> Many people in Africa have never seen a clock or watch their entire lives. And if you say, 'One o'clock in the afternoon' they do not know what you are talking about ... They know morning, they know noon, they know evening, they know the darkness at night.[33]

The derogatory assumptions of the 'First World's' temporal judgment on 'African time' carry implications which highlight with particular clarity one of the many dichotomies with which this study has dealt – the Western world's persistence in its notion that alternative temporal computations and perceptions are in some way inferior to their own. As the USAID spokesperson proceeded to make the above announcement before the Congress, the discourse of a 'time-less other' was officially ushered into the political arena of the twenty-first century – an arena in which such notions continue to influence and determine, even from afar, the supposedly 'clock-less' people of the so-called developing world.

However, the discursive dynamics between 'Western time' and its Others have not remained static; indeed they seem to have switched roles of late. Thus, whilst the Western imagination has come to associate the construct of 'African time' with more positive and exotic connotations of a relaxed, stress-free attitude to life, those who actually live in Africa have come to regard it as a scourge that needs to be eliminated. Ironically, those who now deliver the most scathing invectives against 'African time' are not white, middle-class Europeans, but middle-class black Africans who have themselves come to identify 'African time' as a threat to economic productivity. 'Well, if time is money,' a Ghanian journalist writes in 2010, 'no wonder we're poor ... We need to stop this. We cannot ask to be taken seriously if we lack the basic courtesy to value other people's time as much as we value our own.'[34] The problem of lateness has become so endemic in Ghana that the GMT acronym there has been recoded as 'Ghana Maybe Time'. 'One of the main reasons for the continuing underdevelopment of our country,' the *Ghanian Chronicle* reported in 2004, 'is our nonchalant attitude to time and the need for punctuality in all aspects of life.'[35] Such sentiments are echoed by Victor Dlamini, a black South African journalist, writing in 2010: 'African time continues to give Africans a bad name.'[36]

Not only has the discourse of African time survived into the twentieth century; attempts to reform it have as well. In 2007, an Ivorian

CONCLUSION: FROM COLONISATION TO GLOBALISATION

campaign against 'African time' was backed by President Laurent Gbagbo under the slogan: '"African time" is killing Africa – let's fight it'. In the hope of heightening awareness of the negative effects of unpunctuality and tardiness, the prize of a £30,000 villa was offered to the most consistently punctual employee. The winner of the competition in 2007, an employee who worked as a legal adviser, was so punctual that his colleagues nicknamed him 'Mr. White Man's Time'.[37]

Thus, the discourse of temporal respectability, once vocalised by European colonisers in order to differentiate themselves from their Others, survives in the utterances of those who have adopted it as their own. This too suggests that time will continue to constitute a node of debate well into the future.

Notes

1 KAB, Public Works Department, 1/2/294, Ref. B308, General Notice from the Prime Minister's Office, 'South Africa: Alteration in Standard Time from 1st March 1903', Cape Town, 2 Feb. 1903.
2 Howse, *Greenwich Time*, p. 67.
3 A. M'Dowall, 'The Intercolonial Survey Conference. Proposed Reform in Time-Keeping', *Argus*, 22 October, 1892, p. 7.
4 *Ibid.*, p. 7.
5 *Ibid.*, p. 5.
6 Nilsson, *Primitive Time-Reckoning*, p. 128.
7 Greenhouse, *A Moment's Notice*, p. 47.
8 Mumford, *Technics and Civilization*, p. 14.
9 Julius T. Fraser, *Time as Conflict: A Scientific and Humanistic Study* (Basel: Birkhauser, 1978), p. 131.
10 B. Shaw, *Memorials*, p. 220.
11 Moister, *Memorials of Missionary Labours*, p. 317.
12 Alan Lester, 'British Settler Discourse and the Circuits of Empire', *History Workshop*, 54 (Autumn 2002), p. 25.
13 *Lovedale News*, 1:19 (23 May 1877), p. 4.
14 Nicholas Thomas, *Colonialism's Culture: Anthropology, Travel and Government* (Princeton, NJ: Princeton University Press, 1994), p. 2.
15 Gurney, *Brief Remarks*, p. 110. A typical settler-response to Sabbatarians in the Cape might be found in the records of the *Native Affairs Commission* in 1865. During the proceedings, a Cape settler criticised missionaries for preventing Africans from driving their wagons on Sundays. 'Such must often be the case in a large country like this', was the settler's rebuff to the missionary; 'unless you want to cripple industry'. KAB, CCP 2/2/2/3 G35A – '65Mr, *Proceedings of, and Evidence Taken by the Commission of Native Affairs*, Appendix 1, Alexander Bisset (Special Magistrate in Middle Drift) (Grahamstown, 1865), p. 94.
16 Yalmambirra, 'Black Time…White Time: My Time…Your Time,' *Journal of Occupational Science*, 7:3 (Nov. 2000), 133–37, pp. 133–4.
17 Donaldson, 'The End of Time?', p. 189.
18 Quoted in Mike Donaldson, *Taking Our Time*, p. 151.
19 See, for instance: Robert V. Levine, 'The Pace of Life Across Cultures', in Joseph E. McGrath (ed.), *The Social Psychology of Time* (Newbury Park, Calif.: Sage Publications, 1988), p. 49.
20 W. E. Harney, *Tales From The Aborigines* (Melbourne: Seal Books, 1995; originally published by Rigby, 1959), p. 107. Bill Harney joined the Native Affairs Branch in

1940 as a Protector of Aborigines in the Northern Territory. Over a period of forty years, Harney listened to and recorded many local stories and songs.
21 G. Lukàcs, *History and Class-consciousness* (1922) (Boston: MIT University Press, 1971), pp. 89–90.
22 Max Horkheimer, *Critique of Instrumental Reason* (New York: Seabury, 1974), p. 49.
23 See Roger Neustadter, 'Beat the Clock: The Mid-20th-Century Protest against the Reification of Time', *Time and Society*, 1:3 (1992): 379–98; Thompson, 'Time, Work-Discipline and Industrial Capitalism'; Le Goff, *Time, Work and Culture in the Middle Ages*.
24 Edward E. Evans-Pritchard, *The Nuer: A Description of the Modes of Livelihood and Political Institutions of a Nilotic People* (Oxford: Clarendon Press, 1940), p. 103.
25 Excerpts from Okot p'Bitek, *Song of Lawino and Song of Ocol* (1966) (Nairobi: East African Educational Publishers, 1972), pp. 41–3. Reproduced with permission. Okot p'Bitek (1931–82) was born in Uganda at a time when the country was a still a British Protectorate. Having graduated from Oxford with a degree in social anthropology, p'Bitek returned to Uganda to become one of the most vigorous and original voices in East African twentieth-century poetry. Many of p'Bitek's monologues deal with the conflicts between European and African cultures.
26 Griffiths, *Pip Pip*, p. 274.
27 Susanne Hargrave, *Whitefella Culture* (1991) (Darwin: Summer Institute Linguistics, Australian Aborigines and Islander Branch, 1995), pp. 20-21.
28 J. D. Gallacher, 'Some Problems Facing an Educator in a Programme of Social Change', in S. S. Dunn and C. M. Tatz (eds), *Aborigines and Education* (Melbourne: Sun, 1969); c.f B. H. Watts, 'Achievement Related Values in Two Australian Ethnic Groups', in W. J. Campbell, (ed.), *Scholars in Context* (Sydney: Wiley, 1970); Neil Holm and Keith McConnochie, 'Time Perspectives in Aboriginal Children', in G. E. Kearney and D. W. McElwain (eds), *Aboriginal Cognition: Retrospect and Prospect* (Canberra: Australian Institute of Aboriginal Studies, 1976), pp. 275–87.
29 Norbert Elias, *Time: An Essay*, trans. E. Jephcott (Oxford: Blackwell, 1992), p. 25.
30 Quoted in Charles Fox and Marilyn Lake (eds), *Australians at Work: Commentaries and Sources* (Fitzroy: McPhee Gribble, 1990), p. 81.
31 Perkins, *The Reform of Time*, p. 94.
32 'Beliefs "Insult Aboriginals"', *Aboriginal Newsletter*, 5:4 (June 1984), p. 10.
33 Gumisai Mutume, 'In Fact and Fiction, US Officials Play Games With AIDS in Africa', *Namibian*, 22 June 2001, pp. 7–8.
34 Frances Williams, 'Calling Time on "African Time"', *Afro News*, 4 Jan. 2010 (www.theafronews.eu/commentary-calling_time_on_african_time_1603.html – accessed 25 Feb. 2010).
35 'Progress and Punctuality', *Ghanaian Chronicle* (Asia Africa Intelligence Wire), 17 May 2004.
36 Victor Dlamini, 'What is this thing called African Time?' *Daily Maverick*, South Africa, 22 Jan. 2010 (www.thedailymaverick.co.za/opinionista/2010-01-21-what-is-this-thing-called-african-time – accessed 25 Feb. 2010).
37 Peter Murphy, 'Gives new meaning to getting a house "on time"', Reuters, 8 Oct. 2007 (www.reuters.com/article/idUSL0762200020071008 – accessed 25 Feb. 2010).

SELECT BIBLIOGRAPHY

Unpublished and archival sources

Australia

Australian Archives, Victoria, Melbourne (AAV)
AAV, B313: Mission and reserves 'Correspondence Files' (1869–1957).
AAV, B356: Lake Tyers Correspondence Files (1865–1968).

Public Records Office of Victoria, Melbourne (PROV)
PROV, VPRS 11: Unregistered Inwards Correspondence, Chief Protector of Aborigines.
PROV, VPRS 4467: 'Aboriginal Affairs Records'. Guardian of Aborigines, W. Thomas.

State Library of Victoria, Melbourne (SLV)
SLV, MS 7667, lc. 655: 'Journal of Francis Tuckfield, Missionary to Port Phillip', 1837.
SLV, MS 9556: Mixed papers and newspaper clippings relating to Ramahyuck mission.
SLV, MS 11625, box 16/4: James Dredge, 'Diary: 1 Sept. 1839 – 8 Oct. 1843'.

South Africa

Cory Library for Historical Research, Grahamstown (Cory)
Cory (doc 08); mf 436, box 23/1&2, Rev. Barnabas Shaw, Journal and correspondence, unpublished typescript, 4 sections: 1816–49.

Cape Archives, Cape Town (KAB)
MS A80/1: Rev. John Ayliff Papers: Journal (1821–31).
MS A80/2: Rev. John Ayliff Papers, Journal (1832–50).
MS A80/4: Journal of the Heald Town Industrial Institution, 1865–59.

South African National Library, Cape Town (NLSA)
NLSA, MSB 435, 1/1, typescript, William Shaw, Diary, 'Copy of Rev. William Shaw's Original Diary from February 3rd, 1820 to October 18th, 1829'.

University of Cape Town: Archives (UCT)
UCT, MS BC106: James Stewart Papers, misc.

SELECT BIBLIOGRAPHY

Official government publications

Britain
Report from the Select Committee on Aborigines (British Settlements), with the Minutes of Evidence, Appendix and Index, British Parliamentary Papers, 1837, VII.

Australia
Report of the Board Appointed to Enquire into, and Report upon, the Present Condition and Management of the Coranderrk Aboriginal Station, Together with Minutes of Evidence, PPV, 1882, II, Melbourne: Government Printer.
Report[s] of the Board for the Protection of Aborigines, PPV, 1869 to 1900, Melbourne: Government Printer.
Report[s] of the Central Board Appointed to Watch Over the Interests of the Aborigines in the Colony of Victoria, PPV, 1861 to 1869, Melbourne: Government Printer.
Royal Commission on the Aborigines, Report of the Commissioners Appointed to Inquire into the Present Condition of the Aborigines of this colony, and to Advise as to the Best Means of Caring for, and Dealing with Them, in the Future, Together with Minutes of Evidence and Appendices, PPV, 1877–78, III, Melbourne: Government Printer.
Report of the Select Committee of the Legislative Council on the Aborigines, Together with the Proceedings of Committee, Minutes of Evidence, and Appendices, in *Votes and Proceedings of the Legislative Council of Victoria*, PPV, 1858–59, I, Melbourne: Government Printer.

South Africa
Proceedings of, and Evidence taken by, the Commission on Native Affairs, Appointed by His Excellency the Governor, Grahamstown, 1865 (KAB, CCP 2/2/2/3, G35A–'65).
Report and Proceedings, with Appendices, of the Government Commission on Native Laws and Customs, Cape of Good Hope, January 1883 (KAB, CCP 4/1/2/1/1).
Report of the Select Committee on the Labour Question, Printed by Order of the Legislative Council, August 1892 (KAB, CCP 2/2/2/27, C2–'92).
Report of the South African Native Affairs Commission (1903–5), 5 vols, Cape Times Ltd, Government Printer, 1905.

Published primary sources

Aborigines Protection Society. *Queries Respecting the Human Race, to be Addressed to Travellers and Others.* London: R. & J. E. Taylor, 1841.
Alberti, Ludwig. *Ludwig Alberti's Account of the Tribal Life and Customs of the Xhosa in 1807*, trans. W. Fehr. Cape Town: Balkema, 1968.
Anon. *A Plea in Vindication of the Colonists with Remarks on an Address Lately Published on Behalf of the Kirk-Session of Trinity Church.* Grahams-

SELECT BIBLIOGRAPHY

town: Richards, Slater & Co., 1878 (Cory Collection, PR, doc. 4787).

Arbousset, Thomas, and François Daumas, *Narrative of an Exploratory Tour of the North-East of the Colony of the Cape of Good Hope* (London: Bishop, 1852). Cape Town: C. Struik, 1968.

Barbour, R. W. 'Lovedale, South Africa: How it Strikes a Stranger'. *African Papers*, 2, Lovedale: Lovedale Press, 1880 (Cory Collection: Lovedale Pamphlets).

Bokwe, John Knox. *Ntsikana: The Story of an African Hymn* (London, 189?). Lovedale: Lovedale Press, 1914. Cory Collection.

Brigg, Arthur. *'Sunny Fountains' and 'Golden Sand': Pictures of Missionary Life in the South of the 'Dark Continent'*. London: T. Woolmer, 1888 (Cory Collection).

Broadbent, Samuel. *A Narrative of the First Introduction of Christianity Amongst the Barolong Tribe of Bechuanas, South Africa: With a Brief Summary of the Subsequent History of the Wesleyan Mission to the Same People*. London: Wesleyan Mission House, 1865 (NLSA Collection).

Brough-Smyth, Richard. *The Aborigines of Victoria, with Notes Relating to the Habits of the Natives of Other Parts of Australia and Tasmania*. 2 vols. Melbourne: George Robertson, 1878 (SLV Collection).

Burchell, William, *Travels in the Interior of Southern* Africa, vol. 1. London: Longman, 1822.

Casalis, Eugène. *The Basutos: Or, Twenty-three Years in South Africa* (Paris: Meyrueis, 1859). London: James Nisbet, 1861.

Curr, Edward M. *Recollections of Squatting in Victoria, Then Called the Port Phillip District (from 1841 to 1851)* (1883). H. W. Forster (ed.), Melbourne: Melbourne University Press, 1965.

Dawson, James. *Australian Aborigines: The Languages and Customs of Several Tribes of Aborigines in the Western District of Victoria, Australia*. Melbourne: George Robertson, 1881 (Melbourne University Library, Special Collection).

Edwards, John. *Reminiscences of the Early Life and Missionary Labours of the Rev. John Edwards, Fifty Years a Wesleyan Missionary in South Africa*. W. M. C. Holden (ed.), Grahamstown: T. H. Grocott, 1883 (Cory, Rare Book Collection).

Ferguson, James. *Astronomy Explained Upon Sir Isaac Newton's Principles* (1756). Philadelphia: Mathew Carey, 1809.

Gurney, Joseph J. *Brief Remarks on the History, Authority, and Use of the Sabbath* (London, 1831). 2nd edn, Andover: Flagg, Gould and Newman, 1833.

Holden, William C. *The Past and Future of the Kaffir Races* (London, 1866). Cape Town: Struik, 1963.

Kay, Stephen. *Travels and Researches in Caffraria: Describing the Characters, Customs, and Moral Condition of the Tribes Inhabiting that Portion of Southern Africa: with Historical and Topographical Remarks Illustrative of the State and Prospects of the British Settlement in its Borders, the Introduction of Christianity, and the Progress of Civilization*. London: John Mason, 1833 (Cory Collection).

SELECT BIBLIOGRAPHY

Latrobe, Christian Ignatius. *A Journal of a Visit to South Africa with some Account of the Missionary Settlements of the United Brethren near the Cape of Good Hope* (1818). London: Seeley, 1821.

Lewelyn, William. *A Treatise on the Sabbath.* Leominster: P. Davis, London, 1783.

Lichtenstein, Heinrich. *Travels in Southern Africa in the Years 1803, 1804, 1805 and 1806* (Berlin, 1811–12), trans. A. Plumptre, 2 vols. Cape Town: The Van Riebeeck Society, 1928.

Livingstone, David. *Missionary Travels and Researches in South Africa, Including Sketches of Sixteen Years' Residence in the Interior of Africa.* New York: Harper, 1858.

Mackenzie, John. *Ten Years North of the Orange River: A Story of Everyday Life and Work Among the South African Tribes from 1859–1869* (1871). 2nd edn, London: Frank Cass & Co., 1971.

Moffat, Robert. *Missionary Labours and Scenes in Southern Africa* (1842). 11th edn, New York: Carter & Brothers, 1850.

Moister, William. *Memorials of Missionary Labours in Western Africa, the West Indies, and at the Cape of Good Hope.* 3rd edn, London: W. Nichols, 1866.

Morgan, John. *The Life and Adventures of William Buckley, Thirty-two Years a Wanderer Amongst the Aborigines of the Unexplored Country Around Port Philip, now the Province of Victoria* (1852). C. E. Sayers (ed.), Melbourne: Heinemann, 1967.

Philip, John. *Researches in South Africa; Illustrating the Civil, Moral, and Religious Condition of Native Tribes: Including Journals of the Author's Travels in the Interior; Together with Detailed Accounts of the Christian Missions, Exhibiting the Influence of Christianity in Promoting Civilization.* 2 vols, London: James Duncan, 1828.

Pringle, Thomas. *African Sketches.* London: Edward Moxon, 1834.

Ridsdale, Benjamin. *Scenes and Adventures in Great Namaqualand.* London: T. Woolmer, 1883.

Shaw, Barnabas. *Memorials of Southern Africa.* London: Thomas Riley, 1841.

Shaw, William. *The Story of My Mission in South-Eastern Africa: Comprising Some Accounts of the European Colonists; With Extended Notices of the Kaffir and Other Native Tribes.* London: Hamilton, Adams & Co., 1860.

Smiles, Samuel. *Self Help: With Illustrations of Conduct and Perseverance* (1859). London: IEA Health and Welfare Unit, 1996.

Soga, John H. *The Ama-Xosa: Life and Customs.* Lovedale: Lovedale Press, 1931.

Stewart, James. *Lovedale, South Africa: Its Aims, Principles and Results.* Lovedale: Lovedale Press, 1890 (revision of a paper, *Lovedale, South Africa*, read at a missionary conference in London, Oct. 1878) (UCT Archives, MS BC106, Item D1).

—*Lovedale: South Africa: Illustrated by Fifty Views from Photographs.* Edinburgh: Andrew Elliot, 1894.

—*The Experiment of Native Education: An Address Delivered by James Stewart to the Lovedale Literary Society.* Lovedale: Lovedale Press, 1884

(UCT Archives, MS BC106, item D29).
—'Scepticism and Indifference to Mission Work on the Part of Professing Christians'. Paper read at the Public Meeting, Missionary Conference, King William's Town, Lovedale, 1884 (Cory Collection).
Wesleyan Methodist Missionary Society. *Missionary Papers for the Use of the Weekly and Monthly Contributors to the Church Missionary Society*; also published under the title: *Missionary Notices of the Wesleyan Methodist Missionary Society* and *Papers Relating to the Wesleyan Missions, and to the State of Heathen Countries*. London: WMMS, 1818–45 (NLSA Collection, P4631).
Willoughby, William C. *The Soul of the Bantu, A Sympathetic Study of the Magico-Religious Practices and Beliefs of the Bantu Tribes of Africa*. London: Student Christian Movement, 1928.

Newspapers

Argus (accessed online via 'Australian Newspapers': www.newspapers.nla.gov.au)
Graham's Town Journal (Cory Collection).
Imvo Zabantsundu (NLSA Collection).
Lovedale News (1876–77) (UCT Collection: James Stewart Papers).

Secondary sources

Adam, Barbara. *Time*. Cambridge: Polity Press, 2004.
—*Timewatch: The Social Analysis of Time*. Cambridge: Polity Press, 1995.
Adas, Michael. *Machines as the Measure of Men: Science, Technology, and Ideologies of Western Dominance*. Ithaca, N.Y.: Cornell University Press, 1989.
Adjaye, Joseph K. (ed.). *Time in the Black Experience*. Westport, Conn.: Greenwood Press, 1994.
Anderson, Kay. *Race and the Crisis of Humanism*. New York: UCL Press, 2007.
Atkins, Keletso E. *'The Moon is Dead, Give us our Money!' The Cultural Origins of an African Work Ethic: Natal, South Africa, 1843–1900*. London: Currey, 1993.
—'"Kafir Time": Preindustrial Temporal Concepts and Labour Discipline in Nineteenth-century Colonial Natal'. *Journal of African History*, 29 (1988), 229–44.
Attwood, Bain. *The Making of the Aborigines*. Sydney: Allen & Unwin, 1989.
—'Off the Mission Stations: Aborigines in Gippsland, 1860–1890'. *Aboriginal History*, 10:2 (1986), 131–50.
Aveni, Anthony. *Empires of Time: Calendars, Clocks and Cultures*. New York: Kodansha Globe, 1989.
Barnett, Jo E. *Time's Pendulum: The Quest to Capture Time – From Sundials to Atomic Clocks*. New York: Plenum Trade, 1998.

SELECT BIBLIOGRAPHY

Barwick, Diane E. *Rebellion at Coranderrk*. Canberra: Aboriginal History Inc., 1998.

Bebbington, David W. *Evangelicalism in Modern Britain: A History from the 1730s to the 1980s*. London: Unwin Hyman, 1989.

Bradley, Ian. *The Call to Seriousness: The Evangelical Impact on the Victorians*. London: J. Cape, 1976.

Bredekamp, Henry, and Robert Ross (eds). *Missions and Christianity in South African History*. Johannesburg: Witwatersrand University Press, 1995.

Broome, Richard. *Aboriginal Victorians: A History Since 1800*. Sydney: Allen & Unwin, 2005.

—*Aboriginal Australians: Black Response to White Dominance, 1788–1980*. Sydney: Allen & Unwin, 1982.

Bundy, Colin. *The Rise and Fall of the South African Peasantry*. Berkeley, Calif.: University of California Press, 1979.

Cannon, Michael (ed.). *Historical Records of Victoria*. Melbourne: Victorian Government Printing Office, 1983.

Christie, Michael F. *Aborigines in Colonial Victoria, 1835–86*. Sydney: Sydney University Press, 1979.

Cipolla, Carlo M. *Clocks and Culture: 1300–1700*. London: Collins, 1967.

Comaroff, Jean. 'Missionaries and Mechanical Clocks: an Essay on Religion and History in South Africa'. *Journal of Religion*, 71 (1991), 1–17.

—'Through the Looking Glass: Colonial Encounters of the First Kind'. *Journal of Historical Sociology*, 1:1 (Mar. 1988), 6–32.

—*Body of Power, Spirit of Resistance: the Culture and History of a South African People*. Chicago, Ill.: University of Chicago Press, 1985.

Comaroff, Jean and John. 'Christianity and Colonialism in South Africa'. *American Ethnologist*, 13:1 (Feb. 1986), 1–22.

Comaroff, John L. 'Images of Empire, Contests of Conscience'. In Cooper and Stoler (eds), *Tensions of Empire: Colonial Cultures in a Bourgeois World*. Berkeley, Calif.: University of California Press, 1997.

Comaroff, John and Jean. *Of Revelation and Revolution, Volume 1: Christianity, Colonialism and Consciousness in South Africa*. Chicago, Ill.: University of Chicago Press, 1991.

—*Of Revelation and Revolution, Volume 2: The Dialectics of Modernity on a South African Frontier*. Chicago, Ill.: University of Chicago Press, 1997.

Cooper, Frederick. 'Colonizing Time: Work Rhythms and Labor Conflict in Colonial Mombasa'. In Nicholas B. Dirks (ed.), *Colonialism and Culture*. Ann Arbor, Mich.: The University of Michigan Press, 1992.

Cooper, Frederick, and Ann Laura Stoler (eds). *Tensions of Empire: Colonial Cultures in a Bourgeois World*. Berkeley, Calif.: University of California Press, 1997.

Corbin, Alan. *Village Bells: Sound and Meaning in the 19th-Century French Countryside*, trans. M. Thom. New York: Columbia University Press, 1998.

Crais, Clifton C. *White Supremacy and Black Resistance in Pre-Industrial South Africa: The Making of the Colonial Order in the Eastern Cape, 1880–1865*. Cambridge: Cambridge University Press, 1992.

Cunningham, Hugh. *Leisure in the Industrial Revolution, c.1780–c.1880*.

London: Croom Helm, 1980.
Davison, Graeme. *The Unforgiving Minute: How Australia Learnt to Tell the Time*. Melbourne: Oxford University Press, 1993.
Dohrn-van Rossum, G. *History of the Hour: Clocks and Modern Temporal Orders*, trans. T. Dunlap. Chicago, Ill.: Chicago University Press, 1996.
Donaldson, Mike. *Taking Our Time: Remaking the Temporal Order*. Perth: University of Western Australia Press, 1996.
—'"The End of Time? Aboriginal Temporality and the British Invasion of Australia'. *Time and Society*, 5:2 (1996), 187–207.
Duncan, Graham A. *Lovedale: Coercive Agency: Power and Resistance in Mission Education*. Pietermaritzburg: Cluster, 2003.
Elbourne, Elizabeth. *Blood Ground: Colonialism, Missions, and the Contest for Christianity in the Cape Colony and Britain, 1799–1853*. Montreal: McGill-Queen's University Press, 2002.
—'Early Khoisan Uses of Mission Christianity'. In H. Bredekamp and R. Ross (eds), *Missions and Christianity in South African History*. Johannesburg: Witwatersrand University Press, 1995, pp. 65–96.
Etherington, Norman (ed.). *Missions and Empire*. Oxford: Oxford University Press, 2005.
—'Education and Medicine'. In N. Etherington (ed.), *Missions and Empire*, pp. 261–84.
Evans, Julie, P. Grimshaw, D. Philips and S. Swain. *Equal Subjects, Unequal Rights: Indigenous Peoples in British Settler Colonies, 1830–1910*. Manchester: Manchester University Press, 2003.
Evans-Pritchard, Edward E. *The Nuer: A Description of the Modes of Livelihood and Political Institutions of a Nilotic People*. Oxford: Clarendon Press, 1940.
Fabian, Johannes. *Time and the Work of Anthropology: Critical Essays 1971–1991*. Philadelphia, Pa: Harwood Press, 1991.
—*Time and the Other: How Anthropology Makes Its Object*. New York: Columbia University Press, 1983.
Fanon, Frantz. *A Dying Colonialism*, trans. H. Chevalier. London: Penguin, 1970.
—*The Wretched of the Earth*, trans. C. Farrington. New York: Grove Press, 1963.
Foucault, Michel. *Discipline and Punish: The Birth of the Prison*, trans. A. Sheridan. London: Penguin, 1977.
Gay, Hannah. 'Clock Synchrony, Time Distribution and Electrical Timekeeping in Britain 1880–1925'. *Past and Present*, 181 (Nov. 2003), 107–40.
Glennie, Paul, and Nigel Thrift. 'Reworking E. P. Thompson's "Time, Work-discipline, and Industrial Capitalism"'. *Time and Society*, 5:3 (1996), 275–99.
Greenhouse, Carol. *A Moment's Notice: Time Politics Across Cultures*. Ithaca, N.Y.: Cornell University Press, 1996.
Griffiths, Jay. *Pip Pip: A Sideways Look at Time*. London: Flamingo, 1999.
Grossin, William. 'Technological Evolution, Working Time and Remuneration'. *Time and Society*, 2:2 (1993), 159–77.
Guha, Ranajit. 'Dominance Without Hegemony and Its Historiography'. In

SELECT BIBLIOGRAPHY

R. Guha (ed.), *Subaltern Studies IV: Writings on South Asian History and Society*. Delhi: Oxford University Press, 1994, pp. 210–309.

Hall, Catherine. *Civilising Subjects: Colony and Metropole in the English Imagination, 1830–1867*. Chicago: Chicago University Press, 2002.

Hall, Edward T. *The Dance of Life: The Other Dimension of Time*. New York: Anchor/Doubleday, 1984.

Harrison, Brian. 'Religion and Recreation in Nineteenth-Century England'. *Past and Present*, 38 (1967), 98–125.

Hodgson, Janet, 'A Battle for Sacred Power: Christian Beginnings among the Xhosa'. In R. Elphick and Rodney Davenport (eds), *Christianity in South Africa: A Political, Social, and Cultural History*. Berkeley, Calif.: University of California Press, 1997, pp. 68–88.

Hodson, Sally. 'Nyungars and Work: Aboriginal Experiences in the Rural Economy'. *Aboriginal History*, 17:1 (1993), 73–92.

Hoskins, Janet. *The Play of Time: Kodi Perspectives on Calendars, History and Exchange*. Berkeley: University of California Press, 1993.

Howse, Derek. *Greenwich Time and the Discovery of Longitude*. Oxford: Oxford University Press, 1980.

Keegan, Timothy J. *Colonial South Africa and the Origins of the Racial Order*. Charlottesville, Va.: University Press of Virginia, 1996.

Kern, Stephen. *The Culture of Time and Space, 1880–1918*. Cambridge, Mass.: Harvard University Press, 1983.

Laidlaw, Zoë. 'Aunt Anna's Report: The Buxton Women and the Aborigines Select Committee, 1835–37'. *Journal of Imperial and Commonwealth History*, 32:2 (May 2004), 1–28.

Landes, David S. *Revolution in Time: Clocks and the Making of the Modern World*. Cambridge, Mass.: Harvard University Press, 1983 (and revised 2000 edn).

Le Goff, J. *Time, Work, and Culture in the Middle Ages*, trans. A. Goldhammer. Chicago, Ill.: University of Chicago Press, 1980.

Lester, A. *Imperial Networks: Creating Identities in Nineteenth Century South Africa and Britain*. London: Routledge, 2001.

—'Humanitarians and White Settlers in the Nineteenth Century'. In Norman Etherington (ed.), *Missions and Empire*. Oxford: Oxford University Press, 2005, pp. 64–85.

MacKenzie, John M., and Nigel R. Dalziel, *The Scots in South Africa: Ethnicity, Identity, Gender and Race, 1772–1914*. Manchester: Manchester University Press, 2007.

Malcolmson, Robert W. *Popular Recreations in English Society, 1700–1850*. Cambridge: Cambridge University Press, 1973.

Mandela, Nelson. *Long Walk to Freedom*, London: Abacus, 1994.

Marks, Shula. 'Khoisan Resistance to the Dutch in the Seventeenth and Eighteenth Centuries'. *Journal of African History*, 13:1 (1972), 55–80.

Mazrui, Alamin, and Lupenga Mphande. 'Time and Labor in Colonial Africa: the Case of Kenya and Malawi'. In J. K. Adjaye (ed.), *Time in the Black Experience*. Westport, Conn.: Greenwood Press, 1994, pp. 97–120.

Mbiti, John S. *African Religions and Philosophy*. Garden City, N.Y.: Anchor, 1970.

SELECT BIBLIOGRAPHY

McCann, J. (ed./trans.). *The Rule of Saint Benedict*. London: Sheed & Ward, 1976.

McGrath, Joseph E. *The Social Psychology of Time*. Newbury Park, Calif.: Sage Publications, 1988.

McKenna, Frank. 'Victorian Railway Workers'. *History Workshop*, 1 (Spring 1976), 26–73.

Mostert, Noël. *Frontiers: The Epic of South Africa's Creation and the Tragedy of the Xhosa People*. London: Cape, 1992.

Morus, I. R. '"The Nervous System of Britain": Space, Time and the Electric Telegraph in the Victorian Age'. *British Journal for the History of Science*, 33:4 (Dec 2000), 455–75.

Mumford, L. *The Myth of the Machine: Technics and Human Development*. London: Secker & Warburg, 1967.

—*The Human Prospect*. Boston, Mass.: Beacon Press, 1955.

—*Technics and Civilisation*. London: Routledge, 1934.

Nilsson, Martin P. *Primitive Time-Reckoning: A Study in the Origins and First Development of the Art of Counting Time among the Primitive and Early Culture Peoples*. Lund: Gleerup, 1920.

Nguyen, Dan T. 'The Spatialization of Metric Time: The Conquest of Land and Labour in Europe and the United States'. *Time and Society*, 1:1 (1992), 29–50.

O'Malley, Michael. 'Standard Time, Narrative Film and American Progressive Politics'. *Time and Society*, 1:2 (1992), 193–206.

—'Time, Work and Task Orientation: A Critique of American Historiography'. *Time and Society*, 1:3 (1992), 341–58.

—*Keeping Watch: A History of American Time*. New York: Viking, 1990.

Pagden, Anthony. *European Encounters with the New World: From Renaissance to Romanticism*. New Haven, Conn.: Yale University Press, 1993.

Parry (Abbot, OSB), and Esther de Waal (eds) *The Rule of Saint Benedict*. Leominster: Gracewing, 1990.

Peires, Jeffrey B. *The House of Phalo: A History of the Xhosa People in the Days of Their Independence*, Berkeley, Calif.: University of California Press, 1982.

Perkins, M. *The Reform of Time: Magic and Modernity*. London: Pluto Press, 2001.

—'Timeless Cultures: The "Dreamtime" as Colonial Discourse'. *Time and Society*, 7:2 (1998), 335–51.

—*Visions of the Future: Almanacs, Time and Cultural Change, 1775–1870*, Oxford: Clarendon Press, 1996.

Reynolds, Henry. *The Law of the Land* (1987). Melbourne: Penguin, 2003.

—'Aborigines and European Social Hierarchy'. *Aboriginal History*, 7:2 (1983), 124–33.

Rosman, Doreen M. *Evangelicals and Culture*. London: Croom Helm, 1984.

Sahlins, Marshall D. *Stone Age Economics*. New York: Aldine-Atherton, 1972.

Shepherd, R. H. W. *Lovedale, South Africa: The Story of a Century, 1841–1941*. Lovedale: Lovedale Press, 1940.

Smith, Mark M. *Mastered by the Clock: Time, Slavery, and Freedom in the*

American South. Chapel Hill, N.C.: University of North Carolina Press, 1997.

Storch, Robert D. 'The Problem of Working-Class Leisure: Some Roots of Middle-Class Reform in the Industrial North, 1825–50'. In A. P. Donajgrodzki (ed.), *Social Control in Nineteenth-Century Britain*. London: Croom Helm, 1977, pp. 138–62.

Thomas, Nicholas. *Colonialism's Culture: Anthropology, Travel and Government*. Princeton, N.J.: Princeton University Press, 1994.

Thompson, E. P. 'Time, Work-discipline, and Industrial Capitalism'. *Past and Present*, 38:1 (1967), 56–97.

—*The Making of the English Working Class*, London: Victor Gollancz, 1963.

Thrift, Nigel. 'The Making of a Capitalist Time Consciousness'. In J. Hassard (ed.), *The Sociology of Time*, London: Macmillan, 1990: 105–29.

Weber, Max. *The Protestant Ethic and the Spirit of Capitalism*, trans. T. Parsons. London: Unwin, 1970.

Wiencke, Shirley W. *When the Wattles Bloom Again: The Life and Times of William Barak, Last Chief of the Yarra Yarra Tribe*. Woori Yallock: S. W. Wiencke, 1984.

Wolfe, Patrick. 'Land, Labour and Difference: Elementary Structures of Race'. *American Historical Review*, 106:3 (2001), 866–905.

—*Settler-Colonialism and the Transformation of Anthropology: The Politics and Poetics of an Ethnographic Event*. London: Cassell, 1999.

Zerubavel, Eviatar. 'Private-Time and Public-Time'. In J. Hassard (ed.), *The Sociology of Time*. London: Macmillan, 1990, pp. 168–77.

—*The Seven Day Circle: The History and Meaning of the Week*. New York: The Free Press, 1985.

—'The Standardization of Time: A Sociohistorical Perspective'. *American Journal of Sociology*, 88:1 (1982), 1–23.

Website

'Mission Voices' (ABC and Koorie Heritage Trust):
www.abc.net.au/missionvoices

INDEX

Page numbers in **bold** indicate images. Note: 'n' after a page reference indicates the number of a note on that page.

1820 Settlers 140, 155

Aboriginal people
  agriculture and 14, 60, 79–81, 95, 107–9
  assimilation of 85–6, 102, 116
  belief systems 14, 67, 75–6
  calendar, living 64–6
  culture 67–8, 86, 97, 109–10, 116, 226
  discrimination 233
  education and training 73, 89, 91
  effect of colonisation on 14, 67, 70, 72–3, 78–81, 85–7, 93–7, 149–50, 205, 226–7
  European perception of 11, 59–60, 74–8, 113, 232–3
  'irregularity' of 60, 77–80, 86–7, 89
  labour 13, 77, 94, 97, 107–9, 112–13, 115, 116–17, 205
  land 12, 60, 74, 79–80, 89, 140–1
  meetings 64–5
    see also corroborees
  missionaries and 14, 85, 87, 89–91, 95–115, 149
  resistance of 110–17
  seasons 61, 106–9
  see also under names of specific peoples e.g. Kulin people
Aboriginal Protection Board *see* Board for the Protection of the Aborigines
Aboriginal time 8, 12–14, 59–81, 116, 129–30, 222, 226–7, 231
African time 8, 231–2
  European perception of 12–13, 15, 125–40, 207, 222, 227, 233–5
  reform of 15, 97, 186, 234–5
  survival of 207, 211–12
age: concept of 8, 101, 139–40
agriculture 11, 15, 74, 131, 223, 225–7

Europe 38, 41
  missionaries and 153, 159–60
  see also Aboriginal people; hunter-gatherer economy; Xhosa people
Airy, George 51–3
Alberti, Capt. Ludwig 139
alcohol 79, 150
Algeria 20–1
ancestor-worship 142
anthropology: influence of 10–12, 229, 233
apartheid 186, 211
Arbousset, Thomas 136
Arnhem Land 61
astronomical knowledge 6, 33, 37, 221
  Aboriginal people 63, 71, 76
  Xhosa people 135–6, 138, 140
Australia
  colonisation of 13, 29, 60, 226
    see also Victoria
  time and 219, 221
Ayliff, Rev. John 155, 158, 162, 172–3, 176–7, 193

Babylonian calendar 33, 138
Ballarat 93
Bangerang people 62, 74
  see also Yorta Yorta
Barak, William 117
Barbour, Rev. R.W. 195–7
Basuto people 138, 144, 176
Batman, John 66
Baviaans Kloof *see* Genadendal
bells 37–9, 93, 126
  acoustic range of 40–1, 164–70
  donations of 16–17, 167–70
  Ntsikana's Bell 171–2
  rainmakers and 178–9

[247]

INDEX

resistance to 20, 177
  symbolism of 16–17, 98
  see also mission schools; mission stations; *specific missions* e.g. Ebenezer mission
Benedictine Rule 36–8, 49, 192
Bensonvale Institution 203
Berlin Missionary Society 17, 133
Bethel mission 159–60
Bethelsdorp mission 156
Beveridge, Peter 71–2, 75
Bible 37, 201
  importance of 16, 26, 48, 158, 164, 178
'blackfella time' *see* Aboriginal time
Blackstone, William 46
Board for the Protection of the Aborigines 85, 95–6, 102, 112
Boer culture 133–4
Bonaparte, Napoleon 35
Boon Wurrung people 62
Boorong people 63
Bourke, Sir Richard 89
Brigg, Rev. Arthur 139–40, 161–3, 165, 174
British Kaffraria 161, 164, 180, 188
Broadbent, Rev. Samuel 143, 157
Brough-Smyth, Richard 78, 103
Buckley, William 65–6
Bud-M'Belle, Isaac 148, 149, 212
Bulmer, Rev. John 97, 108
Buntingdale mission 89
Buntingville mission 155
Burchell, William 133–4, 158, 167
Bushmen 30, 131, 150
  European perception of 59, 125, 129, 130–2, 137–8
Butterworth mission 155, 176–7

calendar 3, 6, 31, **32**, 52, 142, 223
  Babylonian 33, 138
  French Revolutionary 7, 35–6
  Gregorian 35
  Jewish 33–4
  Polynesian 182n.20
  see also Aboriginal people; lunar calendar; Xhosa people
Campbell, Rev. John 30, 131
Canada 13, 18
candle-clocks 37
canonical hours 16, 36–7, 55
Canopus 63, 135
Cape Colony 9, 217
  colonisation of 5, 14–15, 129, 150–2, 222
  labour and 13, 15, 97, 186–8, 191, 202, 206, 208–11, 222, 225
  land 13, 186, 222
  missionaries 16, 148–50, 153–6
Cape Town 126–7, 191, **218**, 219, 226

Cape York peninsula 61
Casalis, Rev. Eugène 138, 144, 176
Catholic Church 35–6, 47
children 47–9, 139, 179, 189
  Aboriginal 78, 86, 89, 95, 102, 115
  education *see* Sunday School; *names of schools* e.g. Lovedale; Lily Fountain mission
Chinese people 30, 211
Christian Express 198, 200
Christianity 34–5, 223–4, 227
Christmas Day 14, 92, 108, 111–12, 141–2
clocks and 26–7, 37
chronometer 27–9, **28**, 52, 126
civilisation
  time and 11, 59
  see also clocks
Clarkebury mission 155, 161, **166**, 212
clocks 2–3, 5–6, 39–40, 50, 97, 222, 225–6, 228
  missionaries and 25, 29–30, 122–4, 128
  resistance to 42, 227–31
  symbol of civilisation 25–7, 40, 45, 73–4, 77, 156, 221, 223
  see also Greenwich Mean Time; longitude; watches
cock's crow 37
colonisation 1, 3–4, 13, 19–21, 125
  see also Cape Colony; Victoria
Columbus, Christopher 123
Constantine I 34
Cook, Capt. James 28–9
Coranderrk station 80, 95–6, **98–9**, 99–101, 117
  labour at 103, 105, 107, 113–15, 205
corroborees 36, 62, 75–6, 77, 103, 108, 110–11
craniology *see* phrenology
Crusoe, Robinson 30–1, 101, 225
  calendar 65, **32**
Cummeragunja station 117n.1
curfews 14, 20, 85, 95, 103, 105, 185, 186, 211
Curr, Edward M. 62, 74, 80, 91

Darwin, Charles 69
Daumas, François 136
Daung Wurrung people 62, 64, 110
Davis, Rev. W.J. 127
Dawson, James 63, 109
de Mist, J.A. 134–5
diamonds: discovery of 186
discipline 85, 136, 190, 198
disease 79, 86, 150, 188
Dja Dja Wurrung people 62
Djargurd Wurrung people 62–3
Dredge, James 64, 87, 110, 112

[248]

INDEX

Durkheim, Émile 2
Dutch East India Company 150
Dutch Reformed Church 153
Dutch settlers 133–5, 150–1, 175, 176

Easter 14, 34–5, 141
Eastern Frontier, Cape Colony 14–15, 152, 155, 164, 188
Ebenezer mission 95, 96, 105, 112–13
   bell 16, 98, 100
eclipses 53–4, 122–5
Edgar, James 100
Edgar, Lucy 102
education *see* Lovedale; mission schools; Sunday School
Edwards, Rev. John 127, 133, 143, 157
Eliade, Mircea 34
Elim mission 153
Ernabella 226
Erving, John 170
Europe
   clocks and 39–41, 50–1
   time and 1–3, 11, 52, 221
Evangelicalism 17, 42–3, 48, 87
Evans-Pritchard, Sir Edward 229
evolution
   stadial theory of 11, 129
   time and 10–11
Exeter Hall 66
   see also missionaries

Fabian, Johannes 7, 10, 161, 192
factories 37, 41, 191
family unit 156
Fanon, Frantz 20–1, 101, 113, 186, 206, 208, 210
Fingoes *see* Mfengu people
fire-stick farming 107
First Fleet, arrival of 28–9
Fleming, Sir Sandford 51, 54
Fordism 228
forecasting
   science of 53, 124
   see also eclipses
Fort Hare University 212
Fourth Commandment 33, 162, 209, 225
Framlingham station 95, 105, 118n.28
France 7, 35
Friday 33, 45, 149
   Islam and 6–7, 34, 174
   symbolism of 31, 101, 225
Frisius, Gemma 27
Frontier wars 140, 152, 176–7, 185, 188

Gbagbo, Laurent 235
Gcaleka Xhosa 151, 155, 176–7
Geelong 93
Genadendal mission 133, **152**, 153

Genesis 6, 33, 141–2, 158, 224
geological time 142
'Ghana Maybe Time' 234
Gisborne, Walter 130
Glasgow Missionary Society 153, 194
globalisation
   time and 1–5, 50–4, 217, 219–22
GMT *see* Greenwich Mean Time; 'Ghana Maybe Time'
Godlonton, Robert 177
gold
   discovery of 93, 97, 109
Goodwin, Thomas 115
Govan, Rev. William 195
Gqindiva 178–9
Grahamstown 155, 191
Gramsci, Antonio 24n.36
Green, John 96
Greenwich Mean Time 2–4, 51–2, 54, 93, 217, 219–21
Gregorian calendar 35
Grey, Sir George 185, 188–9, 211
Griqua people 133, 136–7, 143, 155, 157–8, 167
Groenkloof mission 153
Gunai/Kurnai people 62
Gurney, Joseph John 34, 36
gypsies 53, 77

Hagenauer, Rev. Friedrich 98, 100, 103, 106, 112
Harrison, John 28–9
Healdtown Institute 140, 188, 193, 212
Hessequa people 132
Hintsa, Chief 176–7
Hodgson, Rev. Thomas 143
Holden, Rev. William 198
holidays *see* leisure-time
Holyoake, George 49
horology, science of 2, 27
Hottentots *see* Khoikhoi
humanitarianism 17–19, 66–7, 87, 154–5, 177, 225
humanness 9, 12, 59–60, 66, 69, 73–4
hunter-gatherer economy 11–12, 79, 151
   see also Aboriginal people; Bushmen; nature-oriented time

identity, time and 7, 8, 34–5, 40–1, 52–4, 107, 224
Imvo Zabantsundu 194, 207
indentured labour 211
India 13, 30
Indigenous people
   European perception of 2–3, 7–13, 17–19, 30, 53–4, 59, 229
   'irregularity' of 3, 9–13, 42
   missionaries and 36

[249]

INDEX

resistance of 4, 19–21, 150
  see also Aboriginal people; Bushmen; Khoikhoi; Xhosa people
Industrial Revolution 41, 43
insanity: clock-time and 20, 53
International Meridian Conference 54
irregularity 3, 9–13, 41–2, 202–3
  see also Aboriginal people
Isigidimi sama Xhosa 198, 214n.27
Isilimela (Sirius) 135–6, 140
Islam 6, 34

Jabavu, John Tengo 194, 198, 212, 214n.27

Kaffir Employment Act (1857) 186
Kaffir Express 198
Kaffir Pass Act (1857) 186
'Kaffir time' *see* African time
Kaffraria *see* British Kaffraria
Kat River Settlement 17, 134, 149, 167, 175, 177
Kay, Rev. Stephen 136–7, 142, 162–3, 165, 167
  Sabbath and 144, 157, 173, 175
Kendall, Larcum 28–9
Khamiesberg 134
Khoikhoi people
  European perception of 8, 125, 129–30, 132–8, 142
  labour 134–5, 150, 154
  missions to 153, 159–60, 179
  see also Griqua people; Kat River Settlement; Lily Fountain mission; Namaqua people
Khoisan people 132–3, 142, 154–5, 176
  see also Bushmen; Khoikhoi people
Kimberley region, Australia 61
King William's Town 188, 194
Klaarwater 133
Koorie 117n.1
  see also Aboriginal people; Kulin people
Korana people 132
Kramer, Rev. C.W. 113
Kulin people 61–2, 65, 76, 86–7, 89–90, 107
  see also Daung Wurrung people

labour 42, 156
  colonies and 13, 224–5
    see also Cape Colony; Victoria
  legislation 186
  synchronisation of 4, 6, 38, 41–2, 191
    see also 7-day week
  see also Aboriginal people; Xhosa people
Lake Boga mission 91
Lake Condah station 95–6, 105, 107–8
Lake Tyers station 95, 97, 105, 108–9, 205
land: ownership and use 13, 84n.2, 140–1
  see also Aboriginal people; Xhosa people
Langhorne, George 89
language: time and 101, 134–5, 198–9
lateness *see* punctuality
Latrobe, Christian Ignatius 152
laziness 47
  as resistance 20, 113, 206–7
  European perception of 18, 78, 125, 133, 159, 200, 205
leisure-time 47–9, 102–3
  Aboriginal people 103, 105, 114–15
  Lovedale 200–5
Leliefontein mission *see* Lily Fountain mission
Lesseyton school 188
Lévy-Brühl, Lucien 10
Lewelyn, William 36
Lichtenstein, Heinrich 30, 133–5, 138
Lily Fountain mission 153, 156, 159–60, **168–9**, 170, 175
  bell 16–17, 167, 169–70
Links, Jacob 175
Livingstone, David 29, 128, 130–1, 144
London 2, 40–1, 51, 54
  see also Greenwich Mean Time
London Missionary Society 36, 153–6
  see also Philip, Dr John
longitude 2, 26–7, 54, 219
Lord's Day *see* Sabbath
Lord's Day Observance Society 47
Lovedale 15–16, 153, 188, **189**, 192, **193**, 194–205, **196, 199,** 207–8, 212, **213**
Lovedale Christian Association 197
Lovedale News 198–202, 204, 223–4
lunar calendar 12, 36, 138, 144
  Aboriginal people and 64, 71–3, 76, 102
  Khoikhoi people and 133, 135
  Xhosa people and 137–8, 142–4, 187
  Zulu people and 211, 213n.10
lunar eclipse 122–4

Mackenzie, Rev. John 126, 128, 131, 141, 180
Maconochie, Capt. Alexander 90–1
Mandela, Nelson 140, 212
Maori people 18, 188
Maqoma, Chief 174–5
Masters and Servants Act (1856) 186
Matabele people 137
medicine, Western: resistance to 20–1
Melbourne 61, 79–80, 89, 93, 219, 221
mercantilism 39, 41–2, 51
'merchant's time' 39–40, 43–4
Merri Creek mission 91, 102
Methodism 48–9
  missionaries 190
  see also Wesleyan Methodist Mission-

[250]

INDEX

ary Society
Meyfarth, Nikolaus 133
mfecane 140, 176
Mfengu people 138, 151, 163, 176–7, 179, 195
middle classes 8, 26, 43–6, 49, 128
millenarianism 43, 185
Milner, Lord Alfred 211
Mirrar people 61
miscegenation 116
missionaries 7, 8, 15–19, 25–6, 29, 43, 189–90, 223
  relations with settlers 154–5, 175–7, 190, 206–7, 210, 225
  see also under names of missionaries e.g. Rev. J. Stewart
mission schools 188–94, 206–9
  bells in 191–3
  see also Lovedale
mission stations
  bell's importance of 16–17, 37–9, 41, 97–100, 164–72, 223–4
  Cape Colony 150, 153–81
  Victoria 85, 87, 89, 91, 93–117
  see also under specific names e.g. Ebenezer mission; Lily Fountain mission
Mitchell, Thomas 64
modernity 4, 10–12, 26–7, 50–4
  colonies and 128–9, 137, 219, 224
  missionaries and 122–5, 156, 191, 196–7, 223
Moffat, Emily 25, 29, 40
Moffat, Robert 25, 178
Moister, Rev. William 160
monasteries 37–9, 170
  bells in 16, 37, 192–3
  influence of 1, 43, 170, 193–4, 197–8, 204–5
monogenesis/polygenesis debate 69
moon 65, 76, 224
  see also lunar calendar; lunar eclipse
Moravian missionaries 39, 133, 153
  see also under names e.g. Rev. F. Hagenauer
Mordialloc reserve 79
Morley mission 155
Mount Coke mission 155
Mpondo people 151, 155
Mqhayi, S.E.K. 140, 212
Mugabe, Robert 212
Mullett, Uncle Albert 108–9
Mumford, Lewis 221

Namaqua people 122, 132–4, 149
  see also Lily Fountain mission
Narre Narre Warren station 89, 111
Natal 186, 206, 209, 211
'native agents' 163

Native Educational Association 193–4
Native Mounted Police (Victoria) 91
Native Title (Australia) 80
nature-oriented time 9, 11–12, 33, 38, 40, 50, 59–60, 73–4, 131–2
  see also Aboriginal time; African time
Ndebele people 137
Ndlambe Xhosa 151, 155
New South Wales 29, 61, 86
Newton, John 35
New Year's Day 138–9, 231
New Zealand 13, 18, 149, 188
Ngqika, Chief 172
Ngqika Xhosa 151
Nicaea, First Council of 34–5
Nilsson, Martin 59, 221, 229
nomadic peoples 11–12, 53, 77, 80, 84n.82
  see also Aboriginal people; Bushmen; Khoikhoi people
noon gun, Cape Town, **218**, 219, 226
Noongar people 61
Ntsikana 170–2, 179
Nuer people 229

oil-clocks 37
Olney, Justice H.W. 80
Orton, Rev. Joseph 89–90
Other, concept of 7–12, 125, 231
  see also Indigenous people; *names of specific peoples*
Outeniqua people 132
Owenites 49

Palmer, Rev. Francis 162
Parker, Edward Stone 64, 66, 87
pass laws 154, 186, 188
Passover 35
paternalism 47, 113
Pato, Chief 158, 178
p'Bitek, Okot 229–31, 236n.25
Peddie 188
Philip, Rev. Dr John 124, 150
Phillip, Capt. Arthur 28
phrenology 68–70
Pitjantjatjara people 226
Pleiades 63, 76, 135–6, 138, 140
Port Phillip District 61–2
power
  role of time and 1, 3–5, 31
  see also Sabbath
Prichard, James 67
Prime Meridian 27, 54, 219, **220**, 221
Pringle, Thomas 153
prodigality 74, 130, 207
Protectorate (Port Phillip) 87, 89, 91, 94
  see also J. Dredge; E.S. Parker; G.A. Robinson; W. Thomas
Protestantism 8, 18, 35–6, 43–50, 143

[251]

INDEX

missionaries 25, 156, 190, 198, 224;
  see also under specific names and societies
work-ethic 44, 153, 157–8, 203
punctuality 6, 7, 37, 39, 43, 73–4, 113, 234–5
  teaching of 53, 191, 193–4
Puritanism 44, 73

racism 20, 46, 70, 113–14, 133, 212
railway system
  time and 1, 50, 51–3, 60, 127–8, 156, 191, 221
rain-makers 122, 124, 178–9
Ramahyuck mission 95, 99–100, 103, 105, 106, 107
rations 89–90, 95–6, 100, 103, 105, 112, 117
recreation *see* leisure-time
regularity 3, 6, 8, 9–10, 26, 43, 130, 226, 232–3
  Aboriginal people and 74, 77–81, 86, 90–1, 94, 102
  labour and 186–8
  missions and 38, 89, 96, 100, 150, 153, 156
  opposition to 7, 19, 113–15, 116
  railways and 51, 52, 53
  see also 'irregularity'
resistance 4, 19–21, 109–15, 172–80, 206–11
  see also under specific topics e.g. bells; clocks; Sabbath
Rhodes, Cecil John 163, 206
Ridsdale, Rev. Benjamin 122–3, 124, 127, 156
rituals 6–7, 8, 9–10, 12, 75
  see also Sabbath; seven-day week
River Credit Mission 18
Robinson, George Augustus 62, 87
Ross, John 198
Royal Observatory, Greenwich 52, 54, 217, 219, **220**

Sabbath 6–7, 33–6, 76
  importance of 17, 31, 45–7, 49–50
  Indigenous people and 8, 12, 141, 143–4
  legislation 34, 46, 47
  observance 90, 96, 105–6, 148–9, 155–64, 175–6, 179–80, 209
  resistance to 4, 20, 49, 110–12, 126, 172–4
  see also seven-day week
Sadlier, Richard 64
Sahlins, Marshall 132
Said, Edward 10
St Augustine 5
St Benedict 37, 38

St Mary-le-Bow church 40–1
St Monday 49, 113
Salem 188
SANAC *see* South African Native Affairs Commission
sand-glasses 37
Saturday 45, 103, 105, 149, 201–2
  Judaism and 6, 34, 174
Searle, January 48
seasons 61, 86, 106–7, 108–9, 129, 131, 223
settler-colonisation 13, 41, 61, 106
  see also Cape Colony; Victoria
seven-day week 12, 26–7, 33–4, 36, 45–6, 50
  identity and 6–7, 8, 77
  Indigenous people and 8, 143, 149, 223, 225
  missions and 103, 105, 134, 156, 157–8
  see also Friday; Saturday; Sabbath
shadow-tables 37
Shaw, Rev. Barnabas 25, 130, 132–3, 134, 135, 149, 165, 223
  Lily Fountain and 153, 156, 159–60, 167, 170, 210
Shaw, Rev. William 127, 138–9, 142, 143, 155, 158, 163–4, 177–9
Shepstone, Sir Theophilus 137
Shiloh 188
Shoshong mission 180
sin 8, 12, 38, 144
Sirius *see* Isilimela
slaves and slavery 13, 135, 150, 154, 176
  abolition of 17, 18, 140, 223
smallpox 150
Smiles, Samuel 42, 48, 200
Smith, Adam 11
Society for Promoting the Observance of the Sabbath 47
Society for the Protection of Aborigines 67
Society for the Suppression of Vice 47
Soga, John Henderson 136
Sohier, Philemon 68, 69–70
solar time 12, 50, 137, 156
Somerset, Lord Charles 155
Sorrento penal settlement 65
South African Native Affairs Commission 206, 207, 208
South African War 211
Stähle, Rev. J.H. 96, 108
standardisation 1–2, 3, 50, 217
  see also uniformity
standard-time 50–4, 217, 219–21
  see also Greenwich Mean Time
stars, observation of 6, 37, 221
  Indigenous people 63, 71, 76, 135, 136, 138, 140

[252]

INDEX

Stewart, Rev. James 189–90, 191, 195, 198–9, 202–3, 204, 212
Strickland, Rev. F.P. 113–14
Strutt, C.E. 71
Sturt, Capt. Charles 64
Sunday legislation 34, 46, 47
  see also Sabbath
Sunday School 48–9, 160, 163
sundials 5, 37, 39–40, 156
superstition 7–8, 17, 20, 76, 122–4, 125, 142–3
Sydney Cove 29
synchrony *see* standardisation

taboo (Sabbath) 176
Tambo, Oliver 212
Taylorism 228
telegraph, communication by 50, 51–2, 93, 156, 191, 197
Ten Commandments *see* Fourth Commandment
Ten Hours Movement 48
terra nullius 60–1, 233
Thembu 141, 151, 155, 157
theology, indigenous 170–1
Thomas, William, 74, 79–80, 87, 111
  Aboriginal labour 89, 97, 113
  Aboriginal time 62–3, 64, 71, 72
Thompson, E.P. 19, 42–3, 47–8
Thoreau, H.D. 50, 52
Threkeld, Lancelot Edward 182n.20
time *see specific topics e.g.* Aboriginal time; African time; calendar; seven-day week
time-balls 52, 92, **92**, 93, 217
time-consciousness 5, 8, 11, 36, 39–42
  Indigenous peoples and 16, 19, 133–4, 189, 198, 205, 223–4, 227
time-discipline 38, 193, 194–7
timekeepers *see* chronometers; clocks; watches
time-lessness 60, 129–30, 144, 231
timetables 78, 211
  labour and 4, 42, 44, 107
  missionaries and 17, 95, 115, 127, 160, 191–2, 200, 202, 206
  monasteries 16, 37
  railways 51, 217
  resistance to 20, 42, 114, 185
time-thrift 8, 43–4
  missionaries and 26, 48, 126, 128, 194, 197
  propaganda 48, 198–200
  see also leisure-time
total institution 97, 200–1
Trollope, Anthony 208
Tswana people 136, 137, 138, 143
  mission to 155, 157, 165, 170, 180

Tuckfield, Rev. Francis 76, 110, 111
Turner, Isabella 126
Tyumie mission 153

uniformity 5, 9, 19, 50, 52, 53, 163, 224, 233
  labour and 41, 91
  missionaries and 156, 194, 195
United States 13
  standard time 52, 54
University of Fort Hare 212

vagrancy 77, 154, 188, 203–4
  see also gypsies
van der Kemp, Johannes 171
Victoria 93
  colonisation of 5, 14, 61, 86–9, 93, 97, 150, 222
  labour needs 13, 14, 15, 107–9, 186
  land needs 13, 86–7
  missionaries and mission stations in 16, 87, 89–91, 95–117
  see also Aboriginal people

wages 42
  Aboriginal people and 96, 105, 110, 112, 117
  Khoikhoi and 134
  Xhosa people and 187–8, 204–5, 207–9
'walkabout' 77, 87, 89, 108–9, 112–13, 233
Walker, Uncle Colin 85
Wandin, Aunty Joy Murphy 99
Ward, Harriet 138
Warrangesda mission **104**
watches 5, 51, 221
  symbolism of 25–6, 30, 125, 228
water clocks 37
Wathaurong people 62, 65–6
Watts, Isaac 48
Weber, Max 73
week *see* seven-day week
Wesley, John 48, 153, 162
Wesleyan Methodist Missionary Society (WMMS) 153, 155, 162–3
  see also under names of mission stations e.g. Lily Fountain mission; *and names of missionaries e.g.* Rev. B. Shaw
Wesleyan Native Training Institution, Bensonvale 203
Wesleyville mission 178
West Indies 13, 17
Whitaker's Almanac 52
'whitefella time' 227–8, 232
Wilberforce, William 35
Williams, Jan 170
Williams, Rev. Joseph 172
Williamstown lighthouse

[253]

INDEX

time-ball **92**, 93, 221
Willoughby, William 125, 138, 141
Wilmot, Alexander 158
Wiradjuri people 226
witchdoctors 122, 143, 178, 188
WMMS *see* Wesleyan Methodist Missionary Society
Woi Wurrung people 62
Wolff, Christian 84n.82
women 47
  Indigenous 103, 107–8, 115, 136–7, 139, 175–6, 195
work-bell 41
work-clock 41–2
work-ethic 44
  Indigenous people 96, 113, 133, 136, 203
  Protestant 44,153, 157–8, 203
  see also labour; time-thrift
working classes
  time and 8, 20, 26
wristwatch *see* watches
Wurundjeri people 117

Xhosa people
  agriculture 11, 129–30, 135–6, 137
  belief systems 141, 142–3, 172–3
  cattle killing 185, 195
  culture 140, 175, 211–12
  education and training 15–16, 181, 188–91, 206
    see also Lovedale
  European perception of 11, 30, 136
  labour 13, 15, 152, 158, 185–8, 202–3, 205–11
  land and 12, 141, 152, 155, 185, 188
  missions to 15, 142, 148–59, 160–5, 170–81
  resistance to time 172–80, 185
    see also African time; Frontier wars

Yalmambirra 226
Yelta mission 91, 115, 118n.28
Yorta Yorta people 80
  see also Bangerang people

Zoar mission 133
zodiac 33, 63
Zulu people 137, 211, 213n.10

[254]

Lightning Source UK Ltd.
Milton Keynes UK
UKHW021228140720
366519UK00003B/212